IDIOMS ORGANISER

Organised by metaphor, topic and key word

by
Jon Wright

Edited by Jimmie Hill and Morgan Lewis

Illustrated by Bill Stott

LTP
LANGUAGE

Language Teaching Publications

114a Church Road, Hove, BN3 2EB, England
Tel: 00 44 (1) 273 736344
Fax: 00 44 (1) 273 775361

ISBN 1 899396 06 3
© LTP 1999

The Author

Jon Wright is co-founder and Director of Studies of The Language Project, Bristol, a small school with a special focus on developing innovative learner-centred materials. He has many years' experience as a teacher, teacher trainer, materials writer and examiner. His other publications include *Basic Grammar*, with Dave Willis, for Cobuild, and *Dictionaries*, in the OUP Resource Books for Teachers Series.

Author's Acknowledgement

I would like to thank my editors at LTP, Jimmie Hill and Morgan Lewis, for their considerable guidance in shaping this book, as well as acknowledging the many ideas and examples which they gave so generously. The staff and students of The Language Project in Bristol have helped me in many ways both in and outside the classroom. As always, a special thank you to Etsuko.

Acknowledgements

Cover design by Anna Macleod.
Cartoons by Bill Stott.
Printed in England by Commercial Colour Press, London E7.

Idioms are important

Dear Student

Words don't come singly

You have probably spent a long time learning new words. Words, however, do not just come individually, they also come in expressions – in groups. Idioms are among the most common of these expressions. There are thousands of them in English:

> I could **eat a horse.**
> **Money doesn't grow on trees.**
> It's **not up to scratch.**
> I got there **in the nick of time.**

Language is literal and metaphorical

Sometimes when we use language we use it in a very literal way:

> I've been out fishing, but **caught** absolutely nothing!

The same language can be used in a non-literal way – a metaphorical way:

> Yesterday I **caught** the bus. My car wouldn't start.

Here are more examples of this metaphorical use of *catch*:

> He **caught my attention.**
> Wait while I **catch my breath!**
> Look at that tan! You've **caught the sun!**
> I didn't quite **catch what you said.**

The metaphorical uses of a word are often more common than the literal ones.

Idioms have grammar

Some idiomatic expressions are fixed and cannot change:

> **Two heads are better than one.**

Very often you can change the tense and the pronoun:

> I'm/She's/We were **all at sixes and sevens.**

How is *Idioms Organiser* organised?

This book organises the most important idioms in English in four sections:

> 1. **Areas of metaphor**
> 2. **Individual metaphors**
> 3. **Topics**
> 4. **Key Words**

Make sure you study the Introductory Unit of this book before you begin the main units. Plan your study and work regularly through the units on your own or in class.

Jon Wright

CONTENTS

Section 3: Topics

Section 4: Key Words

Section 5: Index of Expressions

Section 6: Answer Key

Introductory Unit

1: What is an idiom?

An idiom is an expression with the following features:

1. It is fixed and is recognised by native speakers. You cannot make up your own!
2. It uses language in a non-literal – metaphorical – way.

The following are examples:

1. I'm **up to my eyes in** work at the moment.
2. At the meeting I felt a bit **out of my depth.**
3. I was **over the moon** when I heard she'd had twins!
4. It **broke my mother's heart** to see her home burn to the ground.

If you are **up to your eyes,** you are very busy. If you are **out of your depth,** you might be in the sea, but you are more likely to be in a situation which you do not understand for some reason. If you are **over the moon,** you are extremely happy about something. If something **breaks your heart,** you are very sad about it.

In these examples it is clear that the idiom is a whole expression. This is the traditional view of idioms. But there is a lot more language which is *idiomatic.* For example, there are lots of individual words with idiomatic uses. On page 3 we saw that *catch* has many more uses than the literal one of *catching a fish.* Here are more examples:

Literal Use	Idiomatic Use
1. The river **flooded** several villages.	The crowd **flooded** on to the pitch.
2. **Piles** of rubbish lay everywhere.	He's got **piles** of money.
3. I love roast **potatoes.**	Euthanasia. Now, that's a very hot **potato!**
4. I've got an uncle **at sea.**	I'm all **at sea.**

Task 1: Identify the idioms

Underline the idioms and idiomatic expressions in the following sentences:

1. I'm feeling a bit under the weather this morning.
2. We arrived in the nick of time.
3. I know London like the back of my hand.
4. Do you think you could pull a few strings for me?
5. I couldn't get a word in edgeways.
6. I'm fed up with the rat race.
7. My father thought I would follow in his footsteps.
8. Hurry up! You're cutting it a bit fine, aren't you?
9. Let's look on the bright side, shall we?
10. Come on, we can't just sweep this under the carpet.

We are familiar with the idea of heavy rain causing a river to overflow and *flood* the surrounding area; crowds are often described as water and the same verb *flood* is used. The literal meaning of *pile* is a heap of something; *piles of money,* however, simply means *lots of money.* A *hot potato* is not for eating; it means a *controversial issue.* An uncle *at sea* works on a boat; if you are *at sea,* it means you are in a situation which you do not understand and where you cannot cope.

Idioms Organiser takes a broad view of idiom. In this book you will practise common idioms such as *the black sheep of the family,* but you will also practise the huge area of idiomatic usage where words are used with non-literal – *metaphorical* – meanings.

"It was a bit of a hot potato."

2: What is a metaphor?

Metaphors exist in all languages. You use them in your own language. A metaphor uses one idea to stand for another idea. Above, we saw the simple idea: **A crowd is water.** When you have that idea in your mind, the *crowd* can *flow, flood,* or *trickle.* Here are some of the common metaphors practised in this book:

1. Time is money.

> We *save* time. We can *spare* 5 minutes. We can *run out of* time.

2. Business is war.

> Advertising is *a minefield* in which you have *targets* and *keep your sights on* what your competitors are doing.

3. Life is a journey.

> You can be *on the road to* recovery. You might be *at a crossroads* in your life because you are in *a dead-end job.*

Task 2: What's the metaphor?

Match the idiomatic expressions on the left with the metaphors on the right:

1. I simply can't afford more than a week off.	a. Moods are weather.
2. You win some, you lose some.	b. A company is a ship.
3. He had a constant stream of visitors.	c. Life is gambling.
4. I think I'm in a rut.	d. People are liquid.
5. Carry on, but keep your head down.	e. Seeing is understanding.
6. We're going to have to weather the storm.	f. Business is war.
7. He was a bit hazy about the amount.	g. Time is money.
8. I just don't see the point.	h. Life is a journey.

3: Why are idioms and metaphors so important?

Firstly, they are important because they are very common. It is impossible to speak, read, or listen to English without meeting idiomatic language. This is not something you can leave until you reach an advanced level. All native speaker English is idiomatic. Every newspaper is full of metaphorical language. You cannot avoid it or leave it till later.

The second reason is that very often the metaphorical use of a word is more common today than its literal use. For example, we know that farmers *plough* their fields, but you can *plough through* a long novel or report; you can *plough on with* your work; you can *plough money into* a business; profits can be *ploughed back into* a company; a lorry can *plough into* a row of parked cars. Using *plough* in its literal farming meaning is now much rarer than all its other non-literal uses. But it is important for you to know the literal meaning. Often the literal meaning creates a picture in your mind and this picture makes the other meanings easier to understand.

"It'll never get off the ground."

Task 3: Literal and non-literal meanings

Look at these pairs of sentences. Decide which contains the literal and which the non-literal use of the words in bold:

1a. I've **lost** my car keys.
1b. I've **lost** my confidence.

2a. I **picked up** a few bargains at the market on Saturday.
2b. I can't **pick up** my suitcase. There's too much in it.

3a. We can't sit here. The **ground** is too wet.
3b. This idea will never get off the **ground.**

4a. So, what's your **side** of the story?
4b. Somebody's put a scratch right down the **side** of my car.

5a. I don't know what I've done to my **back.** It really hurts when I bend.
5b. Have you been talking about me behind my **back**?

6a. She can be a bit aggressive, but her **heart** is in the right place.
6b. Did you hear my father's had a **heart** attack, but he's all right now.

The third reason that this kind of language is important is because it is fun to learn and to use. Because there is so much to learn, anything which helps you to remember things is important and if the language you are learning is more colourful and interesting, there is more chance that you will remember it. You will also sound more natural if your English contains more idioms.

4: Can you translate idioms?

The simplest answer to this question is NO. This is an area where languages can be very different. Sometimes you can translate an idiom from one language to another, but most often this is not possible. For example, there is an English idiom *to let sleeping dogs lie.* The German and Italian equivalents also speak of sleeping dogs, but not the French or Spanish.

It is important that you are very careful if you have to translate idioms. Never translate an idiom word for word. You must translate the whole expression. Sometimes you will be able to translate the English idiom into an idiom in your own language. However, there may be no idiom and you may just have to explain the meaning.

One of the reasons idiomatic language is difficult to translate is because it is the area of language closest to culture. The metaphors of one culture will be different from those of another.

Task 4: Translation

Try translating the expressions in bold into your language:

1. When my father saw what I had done to his car, **he went through the roof.**
   . . . .

2. I should have been a teacher, but I dropped out and became a pop singer. **I was the black sheep of the family.**
   . . . .

3. My car is in a terrible state. **It's on its last legs.**
   . . . .

4. I wish he would shut up. He could **talk the hind legs off a donkey**.
   . . . .

5: Are idioms spoken or written English?

Both! Some people think that idiomatic language is more informal and, therefore, common only in spoken English. This is not true. Idiomatic language is as fundamental to English as tenses or prepositions. If you listen to people speaking, or if you read a novel or a newspaper, you will meet idiomatic English in all these situations.

> "The Liberals are so far in bed with Mr Blair that you can't see them under the duvet."
>
> *Conservative politician on TV news*

SECTION 1

Areas of Metaphor

Some ideas are small and very particular. Other ideas are big. They bring lots of related ideas to mind. For example, we all know what a 'coin' is. It is a small piece of metal which we use to pay for things. It is a part of a much bigger idea – 'money'. When we think of money we think of saving it, earning it, wasting it, spending it, being generous with it, being mean with it. Money is a bigger idea than coins or banknotes. When we use the common metaphor – **time is money** – we know what we mean. Many of the words we use with *money,* we also use with *time:*

> **We have time to *spare.***
> **We *waste* time.**
> **We *spend* time doing something.**
> **We *run out of* time.**
> **We *save* time.**

In this section you will learn about 12 important metaphors which cover major areas of English.

Unit 1 | Time is Money

1: Literal meanings

We spend money. We spend time doing something. We even spend a lot of time spending money! The idea that time is money is very common. Here are 16 sentences – 8 literal and 8 metaphorical. Write the metaphorical sentence under the one with the literal meaning:

a. *Could you spare 5 minutes for a chat?*

b. *40 minutes waiting for a bus! What a waste of time!*

c. *It's worth spending at least two days in Oxford.*

d. *You'll have to finish now. We've run out of time.*

e. *I'm busy today, but I can make time for you tomorrow afternoon.*

f. *Let's get a taxi. It'll save at least 20 minutes.*

g. *Venice is definitely worth a whole week.*

h. *I'm so busy at work. I can't afford more than a week off at a time.*

1. I spent over £100 today.

. . . .

2. I've been trying to save at least £10 a week all year.

. . . .

3. £2000 for a holiday! What a waste of money!

. . . .

4. Can you spare me 50p for a cup of tea?

. . . .

5. I could manage £70 a week, but I simply can't afford £100 for a flat.

. . . .

6. I've run out of cash. Is there a cash machine anywhere near here?

. . . .

7. Buy a second-hand car. New ones just aren't worth the money.

. . . .

8. We made over a thousand pounds at our Christmas Fair.

. . . .

Note: You can say *He spent his life working for the poor.*

> "This government is living on borrowed time."
>
> *News report*

2: Spending time

Fill in one of the following words in each space to complete the idioms:

afford	*waste (verb)*	*plenty*	*make*
save	*ran out of*	*spare*	*waste (noun)*
value	*short of*	*precious*	*spend*

1. I've had to go the doctor about my eyes. I . . . . at least 6 hours a day in front of my computer.
2. If you want to get to college quicker, ... time: don't drive, buy a bike!
3. I don't get home till 10 o'clock every night, so I . . . . the free time I have at weekends.
4. If you're thinking of going to see the new Bond movie, don't bother. It's a . . . . of time.
5. Sorry I wasn't able to get that book for you. I just . . . . time.
6. Can you . . . . a minute or two? I just want to ask you something.
7. I'm sorry I can't . . . . the time right now. I've got a plane to catch.
8. I work long hours so the time I spend with my family is very . . . . to me.
9. I hate airports. You . . . . so much time just queuing!
10. I think we should hurry up. We're . . . . time.
11. There's . . . . of time. Don't worry! The train doesn't leave for an hour.
12. There's no way I can . . . . the time to see you before the end of the week.

"I think I'm running out of time."

3: Revision

Complete these common expressions with words from this unit:

1. I seem to . . . . all my time dealing with other people's mistakes.
2. I'm sorry I just can't . . . . the time at the moment.
3. Could you . . . . me a minute or two?
4. Stop . . . . your time! Get on with your work.
5. Why not ring the helpline? It'll . . . . you hours trying to solve the problem on your own.
6. We'd better get a taxi to the station. We're . . . . of time.

Are you well-organised or do you waste a lot of time?

Unit 2 | Business is War

1: Literal meanings

In business many words are used which come from the area of fighting and war. Use the following words to complete the definitions below:

minefields	*battle*	*captures*	*march*
casualties	*targets*	*flak*	*bombard*
sights	*surrounded*	*reinforcements*	*forces*

1. The worst weapon used against civilians is the mine. The campaign by Princess Diana made the clearing of . . . . an international priority.
2. When one side takes prisoners, it . . . . them.
3. Nelson was killed at the . . . . of Trafalgar.
4. Left, right, left, right. Learning to . . . . properly – in step with others – is one of the first things you have to learn when you train as a soldier.
5. People who are killed or wounded during a battle are . . . .
6. When you learn to shoot, at first you use circular . . . . After a while, you learn to shoot at . . . . in the shape of people.
7. If you shoot from the ground at aircraft, you use shells known as . . . .
8. If you shell a place for a very long time without stopping, you . . . . it.
9. You aim a rifle by looking through the . . . .
10. The Army, Navy, and Air Force are normally called the armed . . . .
11. If you need extra troops, they are called . . . .
12. If you have completely encircled your enemy, you have . . . . him.

2: Gaining ground

Use the following words and expressions to complete these sentences:

reinforce
surrounded
gaining ground on
bombarded
joined forces
give up without a fight

"I don't give up without a fight, you know!"

1. Sales are up! That means we're definitely . . . . our main competitors. They'll soon be trying to take us over!
2. It looks as if we are going to be closed down. We don't want to . . . . so why don't we try to organise a management buy-out?
3. Our image is too old-fashioned. We need to modernise our product range in order to . . . . our market position. Otherwise, we'll lose it!
4. It was obvious that Smiths would close down. They were . . . . by big modern supermarkets with more buying power.
5. In order to expand in the Middle East, we've . . . . with a company who have been working successfully in the region for over 20 years.
6. The new advertising campaign has been a huge success. We've been . . . . with thousands of new enquiries.

3: Keep your head down

Fill in the following words and expressions in the sentences below:

a. *minefield*
b. *capture*
c. *targets*
d. *marching orders*
e. *keep your head down*

f. *taken a lot of flak*
g. *casualties*
h. *own worst enemy*
i. *set our sights on*
j. *battle*

1. I think the boss is in a bad mood. Just get on with your work and . . . .
2. We have . . . . a 10% increase in turnover this year.
3. Promotions and Marketing are having their usual . . . . with the Finance Director over next year's advertising budget.

"Let battle commence!"

4. If you park in the Manager's space, you'll soon get your . . . . !
5. Luke was late again this morning. He's brilliant at his job, but if he's not careful, he'll get the sack. He's his . . . .
6. If you don't set . . . . , you never know if you haven't achieved them!
7. Exporting to some countries can be a . . . . – corrupt customs officials, endless paperwork and red tape, and slow communications.
8. Because we had to lay off 500 people, we've . . . . in the press.
9. We need a more aggressive marketing policy if we want to . . . . a bigger share of the market. Look at Nike. They're everywhere!
10. Small businesses are always the first . . . . in a recession.

4: Revision

Fill in the missing verbs to complete these idioms:

1. . . . . ground
2. . . . . targets
3. . . . . market share
4. . . . . your sights on
5. . . . . up without a fight
6. . . . . your market position
7. . . . . a lot of flak
8. . . . . forces with

Do you know someone who is his/her own worst enemy?

Unit 3 | Seeing is Understanding

1: Literal meanings

We use the verb *see* in English to mean *with our eyes*, but also to mean *understand*. We say *Seeing is believing* and *I see what you mean*. Complete the following definitions with these words:

view	*hindsight*	*mud*	*wide*
blinkers	*short-sighted*	*eye-opener*	*sight*

1. If your eyes are very open they are . . . . open.
2. Something which is very surprising is often called an . . . .
3. . . . . is when you understand something in the past because of new things you have learned.
4. To make horses go in a straight line without looking to either side, they are fitted with . . . . so that they can only see straight ahead.
5. Very wet earth is called . . . .
6. . . . . people cannot see things which are far away.
7. If something disappears along a road, eventually you lose . . . . of it.
8. You usually get a good . . . . of the surrounding countryside from the top of a hill.

2: See the point

Use the following words to complete the sentences below:

    a. *see past the end of his nose*
    b. *made myself perfectly clear*
    c. *opened your eyes*
    d. *saw through*
    e. *through my eyes*
    f. *saw reason*
    g. *eyes wide open*
    h. *see the point*

> "The world will not understand, if you just turn a blind eye to the truth and pretend it is nothing to do with you."
>
> *News report on war in Kosovo*

1. Why do you want me to complain? I can't . . . .
2. I thought I'd . . . . , but I still ended up with the mushroom pizza when I ordered the ham and mushroom!
3. Try to see the situation . . . . I simply can't afford to spend £1,000 on a holiday.
4. Jane and Fred are both in their forties so they're going into marriage with their . . . .
5. It took a long time to persuade Pete, but he finally . . . .
6. My boss is really selfish and small-minded. He can't . . . .
7. Look, you need to change your job. They're paying you peanuts! They make you work all hours. It's time you . . . . and looked for something better.
8. I knew all Justin's stories were exaggerated. I . . . . him the first time I met him.

3: A real eye-opener

Match the two parts of the dialogues below:

1. Why doesn't Steve ever listen to other people's point of view?
2. Did you see the way Simon spoke to his wife?
3. Not you again! What do YOU want?
4. We should never have bought this car. It's been nothing but trouble.
5. Oh, so you didn't know that Jill got the job because her dad knows the Director.
6. These instructions are incomprehensible.

a. > Yes. It was **a real eye-opener**, wasn't it? I never knew he could get so angry!
b. > It's easy to say that **with hindsight**.
c. > Because he's **blinkered**, that's why.
d. > Ah! Now **I get the picture**.
e. > Let me have a look. Yes, **I see what you mean**.
f. > I want to **clear up the misunderstanding** we had earlier.

Note: Another way of saying *with hindsight* is *in retrospect*.

4: As clear as mud

Put the words in italics in the correct order:

1. I can never understand his explanations, can you?
   > No. They're . . . .
   (*as mud as clear*)
2. So I think we should keep the women-only policy.
   > Isn't that a . . . . ?
   (*view short-sighted very*)
3. There are so many possibilities. We could also develop a new —
   > Stop. Slow down. Don't . . . . our aims.
   (*lose of sight*)
4. Don't worry. It's not really a problem.
   > Well, it is . . . .
   (*my from view point of*)
5. Management are giving the smokers their own room.
   > At last. They've . . . .
   (*the seen light*)
6. What exactly does he want us to do?
   > I don't know. Ask him again. . . . .
   (*It's very not clear*)
7. So you add these figures to those and that's how you get this total.
   > Ah, now. . . . .
   (*what I mean you see*)

Have you ever gone into something with your eyes wide open, but regretted it with hindsight?

Unit 4 | Life is a Journey

1: Literal meanings

Many of the words we normally use to talk about going places are used to talk about life – as a journey. Complete the following sentences with these words:

short-cut	*take off*	*rails*	*dead-end*	*crossroads*
tunnel	*ruts*	*track*	*footsteps*	*steam*

1. At Heathrow planes . . . . and land every minute.
2. Do you think there will ever be a . . . . between southern Spain and North Africa?
3. The road up to her house has no surface and in the middle of winter it gets full of . . . .
4. It's really difficult finding the way to her house. She lives in the country, five miles from the nearest town, down a lane off the main road, and then up a little . . . . past an old ruined church.
5. When you get to the . . . . , take the road to the left, heading for Oxford.
6. Before the days of diesel and electric trains, there was only . . . .
7. A train came off the . . . . just outside York station and 3 people were killed.
8. Sh! Listen! Can't you hear the sound of . . . . outside?
9. The police caught the 15-year-old boy who stole my car when he drove up a street which turned out to be a . . . .
10. When we were small, we used to take a . . . . over the fields to school, but now they've built a housing estate on the farm.

2: In a rut

Use the following expressions to complete the sentences below:

a. *in a rut*	**e.** *light at the end of the tunnel*
b. *coming or going*	**f.** *go our separate ways*
c. *short-cut to success*	**g.** *on the road to recovery*
d. *side-tracked*	**h.** *taken off*

1. I've been doing the same job for 15 years. I think I'm . . . . I need a change.
2. I've got so much work on my desk. I'm really confused. I don't know whether I'm . . . .
3. It's been a very difficult year, but I'm happy to say there now seems to be some . . . .
4. Our partnership didn't last. In the end we agreed to . . . .
5. Hard work, long hours, and lots of worry. When you are trying to build up a business, I'm afraid there's no . . . .
6. I'm feeling much better now thanks. I'm well . . . .
7. Sorry it took so long. I got . . . .
8. She's getting frustrated. Her career hasn't really . . . . yet.

3: No turning back

Use the following words to complete the sentences below:

a.	*at a crossroads*	e.	*a dead-end job*
b.	*right off the rails*	f.	*going nowhere fast*
c.	*no turning back*	g.	*running out of steam*
d.	*follow in his father's footsteps*	h.	*arrived*

1. Once you've made your decision, you realise there's . . . . , don't you?
2. I can't make up my mind. It's either stay where I am or apply for a job abroad. I seem to be . . . . in my present job.
3. His father's a doctor and it's obvious Harry's going to . . . .
4. I'm doing my best, but everything I do seems to involve ringing someone who's either on holiday this week or out of the office. I feel as if I'm . . . .
5. Bill's wife died last year. I'm afraid he just hasn't come to terms with it yet. And now he's started drinking. I'm afraid he's just gone . . . .
6. There's no prospect of promotion. I'm in . . . .
7. Now he's been given a company car, he thinks he's really . . . . !
8. I just don't have the enthusiasm I used to have. I'm . . . .

4: Going nowhere fast

> "Death is not the end of the road, but a gateway to a better place."
>
> *Cardinal Hume*

Using idioms from this unit, complete the following dialogues. A key word is given for each.

1. How are you getting on with your assignment?
   > Terrible. I'm . . . . (nowhere)
2. What's Mark going to do after his college course?
   > No doubt . . . . (footsteps)
3. It's a huge decision, you know.
   > I know. And . . . . (turning)
4. Are you and Delia still together?
   > No. We've . . . . (separate)
5. How's your dad?
   > Much better. . . . . (recovery)
6. I'm sorry to hear Katy's still in hospital.
   > Yes. It's been a long time, but there's . . . . (tunnel)
7. The full course takes 5 years, I'm afraid.
   > Oh, I realise that. I know there's . . . . (cut)
8. Are you making much progress?
   > Yes, we're getting there slowly, but we're . . . . (steam)
9. So, you're now European Sales Manager – and not yet 30!
   > Yes, I suppose my career really has . . . . (off)
10. You look a bit harassed. Is everything all right?
    > To tell you the truth, I don't know whether . . . . (going)

Are you in a rut? If so, are you going to do anything about it?

Unit 5 Life is Gambling

1: Literal meanings

Because life is full of uncertainties, we often talk about it in the same way we talk about gambling – horse racing and card games, for example. Complete the following definitions with the words below:

jackpot	toss	sleeve
hand	stake	chips
deals	odds	bluff

1. If you get three aces when you are playing poker, you probably have a winning
   . . . .

2. Before a football match, the captains . . . . a coin to see who will start the game.

3. The . . . . in favour of winning the National Lottery are about 14 million to one.

4. When you are playing cards, one person . . . . the cards to the other players.

5. The top prize you can win in a lottery is the . . . .

6. The money that you gamble on a horse, for example, is a . . . .

7. If you . . . . when playing cards, you pretend to have a better . . . . than you actually have. If you . . . . your way, it means that you pretend to know a lot about something when, in fact, you know very little.

8. In a casino, you don't use money; you use . . . .

2: A lousy hand

Complete the dialogues with the following words and expressions:

a. *a bit of a gamble*	d. *play your cards right*
b. *a lousy hand*	e. *I wouldn't put money on it*
c. *something up your sleeve*	f. *the chips are down*

1. Jim's been made redundant again. He's had no luck at all in the last ten years.
   > You're right. If you ask me, he's been dealt . . . .

2. There's no way we can afford to go on holiday this year.
   > Don't worry. I've got an idea I haven't told you about yet.
   Thank goodness you've always got . . . . !

3. I've decided to give up my job and go self-employed.
   > Well, good luck! Working for yourself can be . . . .

4. I've just got a job at Mexy's.
   > Congratulations. They're a good company to work for. If you . . . .
   . . . . , you'll do very well there.

5. I think the company is having a bad year, from what I've heard.
   > Well, we'll just have to work that bit harder. We usually do when . . . .
   . . . .

6. I hope the weather clears up by the weekend. I've promised I'll take the kids on a picnic.
   > . . . . if I were you! You know what it can be like at this time of year.

3: The luck of the draw

Use the following idiomatic expressions in the sentences below:

a.	*show your hand*	f.	*the luck of the draw*
b.	*at stake*	g.	*against all the odds*
c.	*on the cards*	h.	*a toss-up*
d.	*you win some, you lose some*	i.	*take my chances*
e.	*bluff my way*	j.	*hit the jackpot*

1. So, why do you think I've been chosen to make the speech?
   > Don't ask me! It's just . . . . !
2. When you start negotiating, let the other person make the first offer. Never
   . . . . too early.
3. If you want my opinion, you'll have to change your attitude. Get to work 5
   minutes early, not 5 minutes late. And stop spending all your time talking about
   football. Do you realise your job's . . . . ?
   > Don't worry. I can look after myself. I can always . . . .
   out of trouble.
4. I'm philosophical about failure. My view is: . . . .
5. Thanks for your advice but I don't want to go to university. I'll . . . .
   . . . . in the real world.
6. I don't know how they found that yachtsman in the South Atlantic. But he
   survived . . . .
7. We can't decide where to go on holiday this year. It's . . . .
   between Spain and Italy.
8. I've passed my exam, got the travel grant, and been offered a fantastic job for
   when I get back. I guess I've . . . .
9. I think the Government is going to have to put VAT up. It's been . . . .
   for a while. They can't avoid it any longer.

4: Revision

Put these verbs into the expressions below:

> *put*
> *got*
> *play*
> *show*
> *dealt*
> *take*

1. I've been . . . . a lousy hand.
2. If you . . . . your cards right,
3. I wouldn't . . . . money on it.
4. I've . . . . something up my sleeve.
5. Don't . . . . your hand too early.
6. I'll . . . . my chances.

When was the last time you hit the jackpot in some way?

"Oh Nigel, you've always got
something up your sleeve!"

Unit 6 | A Company is a Ship

1: Literal meanings

The image of a ship is a powerful one in business – the idea that the employees are the crew and the company is the ship. The company is seen as a ship sailing on a sea surrounded by dangers – rocks. Match up the following words with their literal meanings:

1. ropes	a. move from side to side and up and down
2. course	b. to empty water from a boat
3. hands	c. direction
4. deck	d. not yet on a map
5. bail out	e. destroyed on rocks
6. uncharted	f. floor of a boat
7. to rock	g. you use them to secure a sail or a boat
8. wrecked	h. sailors

Note: If you 'weather a storm' in a boat it means that the storm is so serious that you decide not to keep sailing ahead, but just do your best to survive until the storm goes down. This is a rare use of 'weather' as a verb.

2: On course

Fill in the following words and expressions in the sentences below:

      a. *knows the ropes*
      b. *all in the same boat*
      c. *on course*
      d. *wrecked*
      e. *run a tight ship*
      f. *on board*
      g. *it's all hands on deck*
      h. *wait for the storm to pass*

> "For Third World countries to go communist would mean fighting to get on board a sinking ship."
>
> *Confessions of a Philosopher,*
> *Bryan Magee*

1. The half-year figures are looking very good. I'd say we were . . . . for the best year in our company's history.
2. It's not just you that's worried about redundancy. We're . . . .
3. Is this your first day here? Well, don't worry. If you have any questions, ask Di. Nobody . . . . like her. She's been here for over 20 years!
4. I'm afraid we've got four people off sick this morning, so, ...
5. We're in the middle of a world recession. Interest rates are too high and consumer confidence is at an all-time low. Let's just keep calm and
   . . . .
6. Miss Blake and her team of accountants make sure that not one penny is wasted. They . . . .
7. When you get new customers . . . ., keep them!
8. All our planning of the past few months has been . . . . by the new MD, who has decided that nothing will change.

3: Don't rock the boat

Complete these dialogues using the following lines:

> a. *I'm sure the bank will bail us out.*
> b. *We ought to be pulling together.*
> c. *It's like rats leaving a sinking ship.*
> d. *Don't rock the boat.*
> e. *We're just going to have to weather the storm.*
> f. *They're just about on the rocks.*
> g. *There's going to be a mutiny.*
> h. *It's uncharted territory for us.*

1. Look, I'm not going to be treated like this any longer. I've had enough!
   > Now calm down. . . . .

2. Our cash-flow problem is getting serious. In fact, we've reached a crisis.
   > Don't worry. . . . .

3. I think the new range is going to do well in the South American market.
   > Yes but let's take it slowly. . . . .

4. They can't cut our holidays and our overtime rate! It's just ridiculous in this day and age! The whole staff is furious!
   > You're right. . . . .

5. I don't think that Maximedia are going to survive, do you?
   > No, I agree. From what I've heard . . . .

6. Business is still very poor. Everyone is reporting a 15% downturn this year. I don't know what we can do about it.
   > No, I think . . . .

7. There are too many people in this company with different ideas. We really ought to agree about where we're going.
   > Yes, I think . . . .

8. Have you heard the rumours about Maxwell's? Their best staff have gone.
   > Yes, everyone's trying to get out. . . . .

4: Revision

There is one word missing from each of the following idioms:

1. It's . . . . hands on deck.
2. We're all in the . . . . boat.
3. This is . . . . territory.
4. We'd better wait for the storm to . . . .
5. Don't . . . . the boat.
6. You'll get to know the . . . . very quickly.
7. It's good to have you . . . . board.
8. No bank will . . . . out a company with old product and no future.

Are you the sort of person who rocks the boat at work?

Unit 7 | Moods are Weather

1: Literal meanings

Words which describe weather are often used to talk about people and their moods or emotions. Use these words to complete the following definitions:

shower	*storm*	*breeze*	*frosty*
hazy	*gloomy*	*cloud over*	*cool*

1. Another word for a light or moderate wind is a . . . .
2. 10 minutes of light rain is a . . . .
3. When the sun is not clear it is . . . .
4. When the temperature drops to just below zero, it is . . . .
5. A day with lots of dark cloud is . . . .
6. Sometimes even the sunniest skies can . . . . and the day turns dull.
7. When the wind gets very strong, get ready for a . . . .
8. Spring days can be quite warm, but it is usually . . . . in the evening.

2: Storming in

Underline the correct word in the sentences below:

1. It was obvious that Charles was angry. He came *storming/breezing* into the room, threw the contract on the table and demanded to know why he had not been consulted.
2. It was obvious from the way Peter *breezed/stormed* in this morning that Mary had said yes to his proposal.
3. I think I drank too much last night at dinner. I'm afraid I'm feeling a bit under the *sky/weather* this morning.
4. They used to be crazy about each other, but I think the relationship has *cooled/frozen* recently.
5. Meeting Jane's parents for the first time was a bit worrying, but they gave me a very *sunny/warm* welcome. Her mother was lovely.
6. The car broke down on the way to my husband's parents. We were two hours late for Sunday lunch. You can imagine we got a rather *frosty/wet* reception.
7. Ladies and gentlemen, can I start by thanking you for giving me such a *warm/hot* welcome.
8. What's the matter? Cheer up! You look a bit *foggy/gloomy*.
9. I wish Dave was more dynamic. He always seems to be half asleep – he's a bit *damp/wet*, really.
10. My students really annoy me sometimes – particularly when they never do their homework. They really are a *shower/storm*!

3: Matching

Match the following adjectives to their moods:

1. *frosty*	**2. *warm***	**3. *hazy***	**4. *stormy***	**5. *gloomy***
a. angry	b. unfriendly	c. sad	d. confused	e. friendly

4: Under a cloud

Fill in the correct word in the dialogues below:

clouded	*cloud*	*hazy*	*brighten up*
warmed up	*warmed*	*wind*	

1. Did you hear about David?
   > No. Why did he leave so suddenly?
   Well, apparently, he left under a . . . . Someone found out that he had been stealing from the company expense account!

2. How was the office party?
   > A bit slow at first, but it soon
   . . . . when the boss left!

3. So, you met my old friend Larry yesterday. What did you think of him?
   > A great guy! Yes, I . . . .
   to him straightaway.

4. Have you replied to that letter from the bank?
   > Not yet. Can you help me? I'm a bit
   . . . . about what to do, actually.

5. Did you have a good time last night?
   > Not really. Jill had some sad news which
   . . . . the whole evening.

"Richard left under a cloud!"

6. Well, is it going to be a week sightseeing in Belgium or a fortnight in Bali?
   > Let's throw caution to the . . . . Two weeks in the sun! We can worry about paying for it when we come back!

7. Liz seemed a bit depressed this morning.
   > Oh, she'll soon . . . . when I tell her she's being sent to Paris!

5: Revision

Put the following pairs of words into the sentences below:

a. *stormed, room*
b. *feeling, weather*
c. *gave, welcome*
d. *soon, when*
e. *given, frosty*
f. *hazy, do*

1. The party . . . . warmed up . . . . Mark's brother arrived.
2. We were . . . . a very . . . . reception.
3. They . . . . me a very warm . . . .
4. He . . . . into the . . . . and shouted at me!
5. I'm a bit . . . . about what to . . . . next.
6. I'm . . . . a bit under the . . . . this morning.

When was the last time you felt a bit under the weather?

Unit 8 The Office is a Battlefield

1: Literal meanings

Use the following words to complete these definitions:

stab	*command*	*march*	*line*
crossfire	*shots*	*sights*	*ranks*

1. Before taking aim and firing a rifle, you look through the . . . .
2. If you are in . . . . . . of an army, you are its head.
3. When you hear someone shooting a gun, you hear . . . .
4. When soldiers are on parade, they stand in . . . .
5. Private, sergeant, corporal, major are all . . . . . . in the army.
6. Soldiers don't walk. They . . . .
7. If you find yourself between two armies who are shooting at each other, you are caught in the . . . .
8. If someone wounds you with a knife, they . . . . . . you.

2: Marching orders

Complete these short conversations with the following words:

line	*shot*	*marching*	*stick*
fort	*guns*	*gunning*	*stab*

1. Doesn't Ian work here any more?
   > Oh, no. He got his . . . . . . orders when he turned up late three days running.
2. Where's Helen?
   > She's just popped out for something. She asked me to hold the . . . . . . till she got back.
3. I thought Mark was very rude to you in the meeting this morning.
   > Yes, I think he's . . . . for me for some reason. I don't think he likes the fact that our department is so successful.
4. Do you think I should drop my ideas for the new office?
   > No, I think you're right. You should . . . . . . to your guns. Don't give in.
5. What's it like working for your father?
   > Worse than I thought! If I step out of . . . . . . , he's tougher on me than on anyone else in the company.
6. Why are you so angry? You know I disagree with you.
   > But you didn't need to . . . . . . me in the back in front of everyone else!
7. The new product range really has taken off, hasn't it?
   > Yes, it's going great . . . .
8. I know you don't like writing, but I need someone to write a short report of last night's meeting. Do you think you could have a go?
   > OK, I'll have a . . . . . . at it, but I'm not promising anything!

3: Caught in the crossfire

Use the following words to complete the idioms in these sentences:

head	*sights*	*back*	*command*
crossfire	*posts*	*ranks*	*shots*

"Whatever you do, don't get caught in the crossfire!"

1. Ben and Ian were having a heated argument about something. I decided to leave the room as I didn't want to get caught in the . . . .
2. Gill is very ambitious. She's set her . . . . on running her own company by the time she's 30, and I think she'll do it! She's that sort of person.
3. You've met Pete before, haven't you? He's my second in . . . .
4. Sarah and Ewan are business partners, but she's the one who calls the . . . .
5. Mike's in a dreadful mood. Everything's gone wrong. If I were you, I'd keep my . . . . down for a while until things have quietened down.
6. One of the major supermarket chains has broken . . . . with the others and agreed that UK food prices are higher than any other country in Europe.
7. Make sure you put the details on paper and let your head of department have a copy. It's always best to keep your . . . . covered.
8. Lunch can't go on for ever! Come on, everyone, back to our . . . .

4: Revision

What are the expressions?

1. get . . . . . . in the crossfire
2. second . . . . . . command
3. be . . . . for someone
4. get your marching . . . . . .
5. to . . . . . . rank
6. . . . . . . your sights on
7. keep your head . . . . . .
8. . . . . . . the fort
9. have a . . . . . . at something
10. go . . . . . . guns
11. . . . . . . to your guns
12. . . . . . . the shots

> "The sticking point is that extraordinary M&S culture. Those endless corridors still allow far too much shelter for the old guard, and it will probably take office-to-office warfare, against such sniper fire, to winkle them out."

Newspaper article on the management problems at Marks and Spencer's Head Office

Do you always stick to your guns if you think you're right, or are you willing to compromise?

Unit 9 — A Project is a Race

1: Literal meanings

Fill in the following words in the definitions below:

lap	*medal*	*pace*	*record*
straight	*hurdles*	*baton*	

1. If you run round an athletic track once, you have completed one . . . .
2. Every athlete wants to win a gold . . . .
3. The 100 metres world . . . . is just over nine seconds.
4. In relay races, four runners compete. The first runner has to pass a . . . . to the second runner, who passes it to the third, and so on.
5. The final eighty metres of a race is called the home . . . .
6. If you run at the same speed all the time – not too fast and not too slow – you run at a steady . . . .
7. Some races have obstacles which you have to jump over, called . . . .

2: A major hurdle

Complete the dialogues with the following words and expressions:

a. *working at a steady pace*	e. *a major hurdle*
b. *handed the baton*	f. *marathon*
c. *the home straight*	g. *on the last lap*
d. *deserve a medal*	h. *on the starting blocks*

1. Right, what's next?
   > Well, we need to get the Board of Directors to agree to the changes we want to make. That could be . . . .
2. This project is taking ages. We've already been on it for six weeks.
   > Yes, it's become quite a . . . . , hasn't it?
3. We finished our department's annual report in only four days.
   > Four days! That's incredible. You . . . . for that.
4. Have you started the shareholders' report?
   > No. I'm afraid we're still . . . .
5. I think one more week and we should be finished, don't you?
   > Yes, I'd say we're . . . . now.
6. We'll never finish this project in time.
   > Yes, you will if you keep . . . .
7. If Ron's still ill, who's going to be in charge of organising the conference?
   > He's . . . . over to Jeff until he's well enough to return to work.
8. Is there much more to do on this database? I've had enough of it.
   > Don't worry. Only two hundred more addresses. We're on . . . . now.

3: A race against time

Fill in the following words in the sentences below:

finishing
winning
flying
falling
race
hurdle
record
pace

"It's a race against time!"

1. Everything needs to be finished by Friday, so we're in a . . . . against time.
2. Because everyone was so enthusiastic, we got off to a . . . . start and the whole project was finished in two weeks.
3. Everyone's working overtime at the moment to try to get things finished but it's going to be difficult to keep up this . . . .
4. A couple of team members have been ill so we're . . . . behind with the work.
5. The whole project never really got started. It fell at the first . . . .
6. After six months of continuous research, interviews and writing, I'm pleased to say the . . . . line is in sight. The book will be published in the spring.
7. We've had a few problems to overcome but I think we're . . . . now.
8. Everyone worked so well together that the brochure was designed, printed, and in the shops in . . . . time.

4: What would you say?

Use the words in brackets to re-phrase these sentences:

1. We had a very good start. *(got off, flying)* . . . .
2. We've nearly finished. *(home straight)* . . . .
3. It's a big problem. *(hurdle)* . . . .
4. Well done! *(medal)* . . . .
5. We haven't started. *(still, blocks)* . . . .
6. We made a bad start. *(first hurdle)* . . . .
7. We've nearly finished. *(lap)* . . . .

5: Revision

Look back at the idioms in this unit and add the missing prepositions:

1. fell . . . . . . the first hurdle
2. work . . . . . . a steady pace
3. . . . . . . record time
4. still . . . . . . the starting blocks
5. keep . . . . . . this pace
6. hand the baton . . . . . . to
7. . . . . . . the home straight
8. . . . . . . the last lap
9. a race . . . . . . time
10. got . . . . . . to a flying start

Do you know someone who deserves a medal? What for?

Unit 10 | Economics is Flying

1. Literal meanings

Planes and flying provide lots of metaphors for economists and writers on economic matters. It is almost impossible to read a newspaper article without coming across at least one flying metaphor. Make sure you understand all the words used, by completing these sentences:

> *plummets   collision   turbulence   nosedives   free-fall   course*

1. If a plane . . . . , it comes down very quickly and is in danger of crashing.
2. When a plane falls into the sea, we normally say that it . . . . into the sea.
3. If two planes fly into each other, they have a mid-air . . . .
4. We are on . . . . for Athens and expect to land in 45 minutes.
5. Some people take part in . . . . parachuting, which involves jumping out of a plane and not releasing your parachute until you are very close to the ground.
6. If the weather conditions are very poor when flying, you experience
 . . . .

2: Newspaper headlines

Complete the following newspaper headlines:

> *collision   ground   course   nosedive   soar*

1. CITY JOY AS SHARE PRICES . . . .
2. BANK OF ENGLAND ON . . . . COURSE WITH INDUSTRY
3. ECONOMY BACK ON . . . .
4. FLOTATION FAILS TO GET OFF THE . . . .
5. CITY PANIC AS PROFITS . . . .

Now match up the following meanings with each headline:

a. go up very fast
b. go down very fast
c. unsuccessful start
d. going to disagree strongly
e. going in the right direction again

3: A lot of turbulence

The following sentences are taken from newspapers. Complete them with these expressions:

> **a.** *plunging*   **c.** *climb out of*   **e.** *free-fall*
> **b.** *a lot of turbulence*   **d.** *soft landing*   **f.** *taken off*

1. There is . . . . in financial markets at present.
2. We claim the Government's Back-to-Work Plan has never . . . .
3. Several Asian currencies are . . . . to their lowest levels this year.
4. The market is in . . . .
5. Japan has proposed an aid package to help Asian economies . . . . recession.
6. Despite the present difficulties, economists think the British economy will make a . . . . in the autumn.

4: Yesterday's crash

1. Put the following words in the correct place below:

a. *spiral*	c. *stabilise*	e. *back on course*
b. *plummeted*	d. *crash*	f. *regain control*

Financial institutions around the world are panicking after yesterday's . . . .
on Wall Street. Share prices . . . . as banks and lending institutions
struggled to . . . . of the downward . . . .
At the close of trading, the President announced that measures were being taken to
. . . . the situation and get the economy . . . .

2. Do the same with these words:

g. *through the roof*
h. *delayed*
i. *on schedule*
j. *conditions*
k. *steer*
l. *turbulent*

Here in the UK, amid fears that interest
rates will go . . . . ,
the Chancellor gave assurances that the
home economy was still . . . . ,
but that progress might be . . . .
by the adverse . . . . affecting
other major economies. After a . . . .
day's trading he said he was confident that
Britain could . . . . clear of the
US disaster.

"*When interest rates went through the roof, so did Mr Macdonald!*"

5: Revision

Choose the best way to complete these sentences:

1. Good news for investors. Interest rates are *stabilising / going through the roof.*
2. Bad news for borrowers. Interest rates are *plunging / going through the roof.*
3. Good news for industry. Interest rates are *plummeting /soaring.*
4. The rescue plan never really *soared / got off the ground.*
5. We are trying to get the economy *on collision course / back on course.*
6. There is at least one Asian economy which has plummeted *into/out of* control.
7. Industry is finally *climbing into / out of* recession.
8. The latest figures show the economy is *in / on* course to achieve Government
   targets.

Have interest rates in your country soared or plummeted recently?

Unit 11 | Organisations are Gardens

1: Literal meanings

Gardens and plants provide lots of metaphors in English. To make sure you understand the meaning of some gardening words, complete the following sentences using these words:

stem	*dig*	*flourish*	*perennial*	*plough*	*glasshouse*
crops	*weeds*	*branches*	*dead wood*	*root out*	*bear*

1. An older name for a large greenhouse is a . . . .
2. Before farmers can plant a crop, they first have to . . . . the fields.
3. You find a flower at the end of the . . . . of a plant.
4. Children love to build houses in the . . . . of trees.
5. If you want your flowers to grow you must first get rid of the . . . .
6. Potatoes, barley, wheat, and corn are all types of . . . .
7. You use a spade to . . . . the garden.
8. To keep a tree healthy, you must cut away the . . . .
9. Trying to . . . . a large bush or tree is one of the most difficult things to do in a garden.
10. Some fruit trees never . . . . fruit.
11. Some plants . . . . by the sea while others hate it.
12. Flowers which bloom year after year are . . . . plants. Ones which bloom for only one year are called annuals.

2: Dig them out

Fill in the following verbs in the sentences below:

ploughing	*weed*	*cut back*	*dig*
branch	*stem*	*flourish*	*bear*

1. Gary, I can't find last year's sales figures. Have you got a minute? Can you . . . . . . them out for me, please?
2. I'll tell you why we've got problems in this organisation. All our problems . . . . from bad communication. We need to speak to each other far more.
3. We can't go on . . . . more and more money into advertising when people don't want our products. We need new products and we need them fast.
4. Too many people in this organisation have been doing the same thing for too long. We need to . . . . out the weaker ones and re-train our best staff.
5. We are in the middle of a recession. That means we all have to . . . . . . on all unnecessary expense. That way, we may survive till better times.
6. I'm pleased to say the business is starting to . . . . again after a difficult two years. Profits are up, turnover is up, and morale is improving.
7. We've published adult fiction for the past 50 years, but we're planning to . . . . out into a couple of new areas – probably children's books and travel.
8. Two thousand replies this week! Our promotional campaign is beginning to . . . . fruit at last!

3: Dead wood

Put the following words in the sentences below:

off-shoot	*crop*	*spadework*	*cross-fertilisation*
glasshouses	*perennial*	*dead wood*	*up-rooting*

1. If we want to be more efficient, we have to get rid of the . . . . in middle management.
2. Our subsidiary in Papua is an . . . . of our main company in Malaysia.
3. We're planning to re-locate in Scotland but the . . . . process will be difficult for many of the workforce.
4. Our local business college manages to produce an excellent . . . . of keen young potential managers year after year.
5. The . . . . of ideas is essential in any business.
6. We keep losing staff to firms who pay more than we can afford. It's a . . . . problem for a firm of our size.
7. I did all the . . . . setting up the new department, but my boss got all the credit.
8. People who live in . . . . shouldn't throw stones!

4: Matching

Match these eight expressions with their meanings below:

1. **dig out** the sales figures
2. the problems **stem from**
3. **plough** money **into**
4. **weed out** poor staff
5. **cut back on** expenses
6. the business is **flourishing**
7. **branch out into** new markets
8. **bear fruit**

a. invest a lot
b. find and remove
c. successful
d. find something
e. produce results
f. originate from
g. reduce
h. expand and diversify

"Miss Fanshawe was not amused when Mr Weatherspoon asked her to dig out the sales figures."

5: Revision

Which of the following prepositions can go with the verbs below?

back	*out*	*into*	*from*

1. cut . . . . on expenses
2. branch . . . .
3. plough money back . . . . the business
4. stem . . . . . .
5. dig . . . . . . some figures
6. weed . . . . . .

Are you working for a business which is flourishing?

Unit 12 People are Liquid

1: Literal meanings

Fill in the following words in the definitions below:

ripples	streams	pool	flood	splash	tide
surge	overflow	drip	trickles	teeming	pouring

1. If you jump into a swimming . . . . . . you make a big . . . .
2. If it is . . . . with rain, it means the same as the more common word
   . . . . Both mean that the rain is very heavy.
3. Most of us have a tap at home which has a . . . . . . which we are always meaning
   to fix, but never do!
4. Noah built an ark so that he and his family could escape the great . . . .
5. Small . . . . . . eventually flow into big rivers.
6. If a small amount of water escapes slowly from your car engine, it . . . . . . out.
7. Fill your glass too full and it will . . . .
8. It's usually safer to go swimming in the sea when the . . . . . . is coming in rather
   than when it is on its way out.
9. A . . . . . . of water in the sea sends a large wave forward.
10. Drop a stone into a pond on a still day and watch the . . . . move out to the
    edges.

2: Teeming with people

We often think of crowds as moving water. Complete the text with these words:

surge	*trickling*
teeming	*overflowing*
floods	*stream*
pours	*sea*

I go to watch my football team, Manchester United, whenever I can. I love the
atmosphere. Kick-off is usually three o'clock but by half past one, the whole area
around the stadium is . . . . with people. The local pubs are . . . .
with people having their drinks outside on the pavement.

I go into the stadium early and watch people slowly . . . . in. By about two
o'clock, there's a constant . . . . of people coming in and the stadium starts
to fill up. Occasionally, people seem to arrive later than usual and everybody
. . . . in fifteen minutes before the game starts. When it's full, all you can
see is a . . . . of 50,000 faces.

It always amazes me how quickly the stadium empties at the end of a game. Everybody
. . . . out of the exits onto the streets and ten minutes after the game has
finished, the place is almost empty. Occasionally, there's trouble with fans from
opposing teams. You hear shouting and there's a sudden . . . . in the crowd
as the people behind you try to escape the trouble. It can be quite frightening.

Note: You can say *The town has been swamped by refugees escaping the war.*

3: A ripple of laughter

Put the following words into the correct spaces below:

tide	*drip*	*wet*	*splash*
pool	*flow*	*dry up*	*ripple*

1. I started my wedding speech with a joke. It worked. There was a . . . . of laughter across the room and then I started to relax.
2. The government has to find a way to stem the . . . . of refugees, who are now flooding across the border in their thousands.
3. You'll make quite a . . . . if you go to the company party with that dress on. It doesn't leave much to the imagination!

"Joyce certainly knows how to make a splash – and that's before she gets into the water!"

4. You can't expect David to do anything about the problem. He's far too . . . . . . He avoids all sorts of decisions.
5. I'm an easy-going sort of person. I don't usually complain. I just go with the . . . .
6. Our school has twelve permanent teachers and a . . . . of about twenty temporary teachers. We use them in the busy summer months.
7. Come on! Come and dance. It's fun. Don't be such a . . . . !
8. For an unknown reason, fewer people are studying mathematics at university these days. Not surprisingly, the number of new maths teachers applying for jobs is slowly starting to . . . .

4: Revision

Look back at the idioms in this unit and add the missing words to the following collocations:

1. a sudden . . . . .
2. make a . . . . .
3. go with the . . . . .
4. a . . . . . of laughter
5. a . . . . . or . . . . . of people
6. a . . . . . of faces
7. stem the . . . . .
8. . . . . . out of the stadium

Do you know or work with anybody who is "a bit wet"?

1. Time is Money

1. Pay attention! Stop . . . . time.
2. I . . . . two hours on my homework.
3. Hurry or we'll . . . . out of time.
4. Can you . . . . a minute or two?
5. We'll . . . . 10 minutes if we get a taxi.
6. Slow down! We're not . . . . of time.

2. Business is War

1. Never give up without a . . . . .
2. It's time to join . . . . with a bigger firm.
3. Take care or you'll get your . . . . orders.
4. Watch out! This area is a . . . . .
5. . . . . your head down till the boss has left!
6. We're going to be in for a lot of . . . . .

3. Seeing is Understanding

1. Ah, now I . . . . what you mean!
2. It's easy to be right with . . . . .
3. Don't lose . . . . of the details.
4. Let's . . . . up the misunderstanding.
5. I think they've . . . . the light now.
6. Get married with your . . . . wide open!

4. Life is a Journey

1. Change jobs! You're in a . . . . .
2. I think I'm going . . . . – fast!
3. Never follow in your father's . . . . .
4. My career really has . . . . off.
5. There's no turning . . . . now!
6. Is there light at the end of the . . . . ?

5. Life is Gambling

1. I think I've been . . . . a bad hand.
2. You'll be OK if you play your . . . . right.
3. I'll . . . . my chances with everyone else.
4. You . . . . some, you . . . . some.
5. Never show your . . . . too early.
6. Which to choose? It's a . . . . -up!

6. A Company is a Ship

1. We're all in the same . . . . .
2. Keep quiet and don't rock the . . . . .
3. Come on! It's all hands on . . . . .
4. We're in . . . . . territory.
5. It's like . . . . leaving the sinking ship.
6. Mary knows the . . . . . Speak to her.

7. Moods are Weather

1. They gave me a very . . . . reception.
2. Sorry, I feel a bit under the . . . . today.
3. Let's . . . . caution to the wind.
4. I'm a bit . . . . about the details myself.
5. Did you hear that Dave left under a . . . . ?
6. They have a fairly . . . . relationship.

8. The Office is a Battlefield

1. I'm boss and you're my second in . . . . .
2. I've just been given my marching . . . . .
3. If you've any sense, keep your head . . . . .
4. Do you think you could hold the . . . . ?
5. Don't get caught in the . . . . .
6. Keep your . . . . on promotion all the time.

9. A Project is a Race

1. My plan fell at the first . . . . .
2. We finished in . . . . time.
3. We got off to a flying . . . . .
4. Just keep working at a steady . . . . .
5. We're in a . . . . against time.
6. The finishing . . . . is in sight.

10. Economics is Flying

1. At last the economy is taking . . . . .
2. We don't want another Wall Street . . . . .
3. They are slowly . . . . out of recession.
4. The recovery has failed to get off the . . . . .
5. Interest rates have gone through the . . . . .
6. The economy has taken a . . . . .

11. Organisations are Gardens

1. At last my policy is beginning to . . . . fruit.
2. We've already . . . . £2m into the project.
3. Do your best to . . . . back on expenses.
4. We need to . . . . out the weakest staff.
5. Could you . . . . out that address for me?
6. We need to . . . . out the dead . . . . .

12. People are Liquid

1. The crowd . . . . out of the football ground.
2. How do you . . . . the tide of refugees?
3. There's a large . . . . of skilled workers.
4. Applications have suddenly . . . . up.
5. The square was . . . . with people.
6. All I saw was a . . . . of faces I didn't know.

SECTION 2

Individual Metaphors

In this section you will learn about many more *individual* areas of English where metaphors are important. If you look at the areas covered, you will understand that idioms are a very important part of learning English. They are everywhere!

Animals: I smell a rat!
The body: I've put my foot in it, I'm afraid.
Building: You're banging your head against a brick wall.
Cats: That's set the cat among the pigeons.
Clothes: It fits like a glove.
Colours: He went as white as a sheet.
Driving: I'm going to take a back seat from now on.

Unit 14 Animal Idioms

1: Literal meanings

Fill in the following words in the definitions below:

horns	*bonnet*	*chase*	*bull*	*sty*
pants	*swing*	*hind*	*straw*	*bees*

1. A male cow is called a . . . . They usually have . . . .
2. The back legs of horses are called their . . . . . . legs.
3. A . . . . . . is a type of hat with strings which you tie under your chin. Babies sometimes wear them.
4. Trousers are sometimes called . . . .
5. If you run after someone to try to catch them, you . . . . . . them.
6. Honey is made by . . . .
7. . . . . . is dried grass, used for packing things or for animals to sleep on.
8. Farmers keep pigs in a pig- . . . .
9. If you . . . . something, you hold it and wave it around.

2: A bee in his bonnet

Put the following pairs of words into the sentences below:

> *bee – bonnet*
> *sheep – family*
> *bull – horns*
> *ants – pants*
> *fish – water*
> *fish – sea*
> *cat – bag*
> *cows – home*

"I think he's got ants in his pants."

1. He's got a . . . . in his . . . . about only using recycled goods.
2. Pete's girlfriend has just left him. I told him not to worry. There are plenty more . . . . in the . . . .
3. I've arranged a surprise party for my husband's birthday. I just hope nobody lets the . . . . out of the . . . . by accident.
4. I went to a disco for the first time in ten years last night. I looked and felt like a . . . . out of . . . .
5. If you think Jack's not doing his job properly, you're going to have to take the . . . . by the . . . . and tell him.
6. Billy just won't sit still in class. I think he's got . . . . in his . . . .
7. I never liked school. I was always getting into trouble. I suppose I was the black . . . . of the . . . .
8. I love soaps. I could sit and watch them till the . . . . come . . . .

3: Swing a cat

Complete the dialogues with these idioms:

    a. *swing a cat*   **c. *gone to the dogs***
    b. *monkeying around*   **d. *smell a rat***

1. What sort of flat are you looking for?
   > Somewhere with a bit more space. There's not enough room to . . . .
   in my living room.
2. Mick told me he was working late tonight.
   > But there were no lights on when I passed. I . . . .
3. Would you please stop . . . . You'll break something!
   > Oh, come on! We're just having fun.
4. This shopping centre used to be quite good but look at it now.
   > I know. It's really . . . . in the last few years.

Now add these nouns to the following:

    donkey (3)   ***camel***   ***horse***   ***pig***
    chicken   ***goose***   ***wolf***   ***foxed***

5. Did you buy that CD I asked you to?
   > No. You sent me on a wild . . . . . . chase. I must have tried three shops
   before someone told me it doesn't come out till November.
6. Bill! What a surprise!
   > Duncan! How are you? I haven't seen you for . . . .'s years!
7. You can get between twenty and thirty thousand pounds a year as an office
   manager now.
   > That's . . . . . . feed compared to what you can get in the States.
8. Are you sure we're getting a pay rise next month? Who told you?
   > I got it straight from the . . . .'s mouth. The manager himself told me.
9. You get a company pension, don't you?
   > Yes, it's not very much but it helps to keep the . . . . . . from the door.
10. Robert likes the sound of his own voice, doesn't he?
    > Yes. He can talk the hind legs off a . . . .
11. And when they took my company car from me, I just had to resign!
    > That must have been the straw that broke the . . . .'s back.
12. If you do the digging, I'll go and get the seeds.
    > Not likely! I don't see why I should do all the . . . . . . work!
13. I wish you'd tidy your flat up! It's like a . . . . . -sty !
14. I just didn't understand. I didn't know what to do. I was totally . . . . . !

4: Revision

Look back at the idioms in this unit and add the missing verbs:

1. let the . . . . out of the bag
2. take the . . . . by the horns
3. send him on a wild . . . . chase
4. not enough room to swing a . . . .
5. talk the hind legs off a . . . .
6. got a . . . . in his/her bonnet
7. smell a . . . .
8. feel like a . . . . out of water
9. haven't seen you for . . . .'s years
10. keep the . . . . from the door

Have you ever felt like a fish out of water? Where were you?

Unit 15 | Bird Idioms

1: Literal meanings

Fill in the following words in the definitions below:

nest	*boo*	*flap*
wings	*swoop*	*peck*

1. Birds and planes both have . . . .
2. Birds make a . . . . in which to lay their eggs.
3. When birds suddenly fly down to the ground to catch something to eat, they . . . .
4. Birds hop around and . . . . the ground to pick up bits of food.
5. In order to fly, birds have to . . . . their wings.
6. . . . . is the noise you make to surprise or shock someone.

2: What's the idea?

In many languages different birds bring different ideas to mind. Can you match these six birds and the ideas?

1. ostrich   a. thief
2. dodo   b. good eyesight
3. hawk   c. waterproof
4. magpie   d. dead or extinct
5. swan   e. pretends problems don't exist
6. duck   f. head in the air looking superior

3: As the crow flies

Put these birds into the correct space below:

duck	*crow*	*dodo*	*chicken*
hawk	*parrot*	*goose*	*sparrow*

1. It's only forty miles from here to Bristol as the . . . . flies, but it takes an hour by car because the roads are so bad.
2. You have to get used to criticism in this job. It doesn't bother me now. It's like water off a . . . .'s back.
3. I'm supposed to be going on holiday tomorrow. I've been running round like a headless . . . . all day trying to get ready.
4. I made a personal phone call from the office and my boss found out about it. She's watching me like a . . . . now to make sure I don't do it again.
5. Really? I can't believe Carol would say anything to upset you. She wouldn't say boo to a . . . .
6. I'm not surprised Andrea's so thin. She eats like a . . . .
7. Do you know anything about computers? I've just switched mine on and nothing happened. It's as dead as a . . . .
8. I've got tickets for the Cup Final on Saturday. Mark has to work and there's no way he's going to manage to get off. He's as sick as a . . . . about it!

4: In a flap

Fill in the following words and expressions in the sentences below:

a. *in one fell swoop*
b. *flown the nest*
c. *birds of a feather*
d. *in a flap*
e. *their own nest*
f. *under her wing*
g. *parrot fashion*
h. *an early bird*
i. *with one stone*
j. *spring chicken*
k. *the pecking order*
l. *a little bird*
m. *swan around*
n. *nest egg*

1. Calm down. Why are you . . . . ? Everything will be all right.
2. At school, we used to learn French verbs . . . .
3. He's not even a junior manager. He's way down . . . .
4. My new boss has taken a special interest in my career. She's taken me . . . .
5. All my children have grown up and . . . .
6. One stupid comment to the media and your reputation can be destroyed . . . .
7. My husband really is . . . . He gets up at six every morning.
8. I'm saving carefully. I'll have a nice little . . . . by the time I retire.
9. I don't like people who return to their home town and . . . . in expensive clothes and big cars.
10. Let's check the timetable and pick up the tickets at the same time. We might as well kill two birds . . . .
11. . . . . told me you had got engaged. Is it true?
12. I would sack all politicians who feather . . . . – and I would make sure they were banned from public life!
13. I know Sheila looks young, but I can tell you she's no . . . . I should know! I was in her class at school.
14. Did you see Jane having lunch with Mary? Two dreadful gossips! I suppose . . . . flock together!

5: Revision

Look back at the idioms in this unit and complete these phrases:

1. like water off a . . . . . .'s back
2. kill two . . . . . . with one stone
3. watching me like a . . . . . .
4. took me under his . . . . . .
5. running round like a headless . . . . . .
6. in a . . . . . .
7. . . . . . . fashion
8. wouldn't say boo to a . . . . . .
9. as the . . . . . . flies
10. in one fell . . . . . .
11. as dead as a . . . . . .
12. as sick as a . . . . . .
13. flown the . . . . . .
14. . . . . . . around
15. . . . . . . order
16. . . . . . . egg

Are you an early bird or do you get up late?

Unit 16 | Body Idioms

1: Non-literal meanings

Match these five parts of the body with the non-literal ideas on the right:

1. heart   a. confrontation
2. nose   b. skillful
3. hand   c. curiosity
4. face   d. emotions
5. head   e. top

2: On its last legs

Complete the idioms with the following expressions:

a. *an old hand*   **e. *my hands***   **i. *came to a head***
b. *behind my back*   **f. *on its last legs*** **j. *hand it to him***
c. *couldn't face*   **g. *face the fact***   **k. *a good head***
d. *gone to your head*   **h. *a brave face***   **l. *your head***

1. I love my old car, but I'm having more and more problems with it. I think it's
   . . . .
2. My boyfriend and I have always argued quite a lot, but the situation . . . .
   . . . . last week when he accused me of lying.
3. I'm sorry, John, but we have to . . . . that we are not getting on.
4. I can't trust you any more. You've been talking about me . . . .
5. What's the matter with you? You've changed since your promotion. I think
   power's . . . .
6. Bob's an excellent chairman. He's . . . . at controlling difficult
   people.
7. Ask Marianne to help you. She's got . . . . for figures.
8. There's nothing I can do to help, I'm afraid. . . . . are tied.
9. I'm afraid I'm not coming to the concert. You know I'm not keen on classical
   music and I . . . . three hours of it!
10. I know Jane's in a lot of pain, but she puts . . . . on it.
11. Richard's businesses just go from strength to strength. You know, you've got to
    . . . .
12. We'll have to go to the bank and ask for another loan. You just can't go on
    burying . . . . in the sand any longer.

3: Matching

Match these idioms with their definitions:

1. If you *foot the bill,*   a. you really don't feel like doing it.
2. If somebody *got your back up,*   b. you are trying something for the first time.
3. If something *gets on your nerves,* c. it irritates you.
4. If your *heart is not in* something, d. you pay for it.
5. If you *dip your toe in the water,* e. they annoyed you.

4: A pain in the neck

Choose the correct word in the dialogues below:

1. Do you get phone calls from companies trying to sell you things?
   > All the time. They're a pain in the *neck/back*.
2. Did you know that Alan and Moira have stopped seeing each other?
   > Yes, I do now, but I put my *foot/fist* in it yesterday when I asked when they were getting married.
3. I'm really worried about my economics course. I don't know what to do.
   > Do you want to talk about it? It might help to get it off your *back/chest*.
4. Jane's a bit strange, isn't she?
   > Yes, but I'm not sure what it is. I can't quite put my *finger/hand* on it.
5. Jill's not her usual self at the moment. Is there something wrong?
   > I think it's pressure of work. She has to *elbow/shoulder* a lot of responsibility.
6. You need to be more ambitious. You could be a senior manager if you wanted to.
   > No thanks. I don't want to *elbow/shoulder* my way to the top like you did and lose all my friends on the way.
7. Who was that man I saw you with last night?
   Don't be so *nosey/cheeky*! It's none of your business.
8. It was nice to meet your girlfriend last night. She's very nice. Too nice for you!
   > Don't be so *nosey/cheeky*!

> "200 Russian troops occupied the airport in Kosovo's capital Pristina under the noses of Nato forces."
>
> *Newspaper report*

9. Look at that Ferrari!
   > Fantastic! I'd give my right *leg/arm* for a car like that.
10. I've just bought the latest mini-disc walkman.
    > Really? That must have cost you *a leg and an arm/an arm and a leg*.
11. Tony thinks I've got no taste in clothes. He says I'm twenty years out of date.
    Don't take him too seriously. He's only pulling your *arm/leg*.
12. How's your new job going?
    > Not bad, but I've only been there four days so I'm still finding my *feet/hands*.

5: Revision

Put the missing verbs into these expressions:

1. I'd . . . . . . my right arm for it.
2. I . . . . . . my foot in it.
3. I'm only . . . . . . your leg.
4. I can't . . . . . . my finger on it.
5. The situation . . . . . to a head.
6. Power's . . . . . . to his head.
7. It . . . . . . an arm and a leg.
8. I'm still . . . . . . my feet.
9. He just . . . . . . his head in the sand.
10. Come on, ... it off your chest!

What sort of things get on your nerves?

Unit 17 | Breaking Idioms

1: Literal meanings

Fill in the following words in the definitions below:

> *kid*   *fragile*   *crack*   *chip*   *handle*
> *shattered*   *crushed*   *smashed*   *snapped*   *mend*

1. My car windscreen just . . . . when the stone hit it.
2. The crystal glasses I sent to John and Mary arrived in pieces although I had clearly marked the parcel '. . . . .'.
3. I didn't see the lights change and just . . . . straight into the back of a brand new Porsche!
4. A . . . . is a small piece broken off a cup or a piece of china.
5. My key . . . . in two when I tried to open the door.
6. When I opened the box, there was a . . . . in one of the cups.
7. 'Please don't . . . . the goods. All breakages must be paid for.'
8. The driver of the Renault had no hope. His car was . . . . between two huge lorries.
9. I tried to . . . . the plug in the kitchen, and almost got electrocuted.
10. A . . . . is a baby goat.

2: Feeling fragile

Match the following idioms with the meanings below:

1. He's **feeling fragile** this morning. He had a late night.
2. He **went to pieces** when he heard of his mother's death.
3. He's **a smashing person** and a really wonderful friend.
4. He's **at breaking-point**. You should see how much work he has!
5. He **needs careful handling**. He's brilliant, but he's a bit sensitive to criticism.
6. "Do it yourself, if you think you can do it better!" he **snapped** back.
7. After two days of interrogation, his son **cracked** and confessed to the murder.
8. He **comes from a broken home.**

a. He's under too much pressure.
b. You've got to be careful how you treat him.
c. He started to cry.
d. His parents divorced, and he was brought up by his mother.
e. He's not very well.
f. He's very nice.
g. He started to tell the truth.
h. He replied angrily.

3: A chip on his shoulder

Fill in the following words and expressions in the sentences below:

a. *shattered my confidence*
b. *a chip on his shoulder*
c. *put his life back together*
d. *broke up*
e. *handle him with kid gloves*

f. *mend the relationship*
g. *pick up the pieces*
h. *a crushing blow*
i. *knocked me down with a feather*
j. *broke her heart*

1. John's got . . . . about his background.
2. Losing your job can be . . . . to anyone – no matter how strong you are.
3. Be very careful what you say to Richard. You've got to . . . .
   . . . .
4. When Mrs Jones' youngest son was killed in the war, it . . . .
5. Failing my driving test for the second time totally . . . .
   . . . .
6. Diane wants a divorce, but Justin is trying to . . . .
7. When I heard the news, you could have . . . .
8. Didn't you know that Harry and Jane . . . . last year?
9. It was terrible losing Mary, but I'm doing my best to . . . .
10. After Ron's wife died, it took him a long time to . . . . !

4: Revision

Look back at the idioms in this unit and add the missing words:

1. It . . . . . . my heart.
2. He's got a . . . . . . on his shoulder.
3. It . . . . . . my confidence.
4. Please . . . . . . her with . . . . . . gloves!
5. I'm feeling a bit . . . . . . today.
6. He's from a . . . . . . home.
7. I just went to . . . .
8. They . . . . . . up after 20 years!
9. He'll . . . . . . under the pressure.
10. She's trying to pick up the . . . .

Have you got a friend who needs careful handling?

*"When Miss Williams admitted she was a secret naturist,
you could have knocked me down with a feather!"*

Unit 18 Building Idioms

1: Literal meanings

Fill in the following words in the definitions below:

bricks	*doorstep*	*ceiling*
roof	*cement*	*tiles*
foundations	*chimney*	*corridor*

1. Smoke from your fire goes up through the . . . .
2. Before building a house, you have to have good, dry . . . .
3. The . . . . of a house must be watertight.
4. If you are in a room now, look up and you'll see the . . . .
5. . . . . are one of the commonest building materials. They are often red. . . . . is used to hold them together.
6. Your . . . . is just outside your door.
7. Most houses in Mediterranean countries have roofs made of red . . . .
8. A long narrow passage with doors and rooms on either side is a . . . .

2: A foot in the door

Fill in the following idiomatic expressions in the situations below:

a. *against a brick wall*	e. *a foot in the door*
b. *on your doorstep*	f. *hit the roof*
c. *on the tiles*	g. *through the back door*
d. *laid the foundations*	h. *like a ton of bricks*

1. Why are you taking such a low-paid job? I'm sure you could find something better.
   > I know, but it's a good company. I just want to get . . . . and with any luck I can work my way up.
2. I think the business is ready to expand now.
   > I agree, we've . . . . and it's time to build on them.
3. Diana looks cross about something. What's happened?
   > I just asked if I could leave early tonight and she came down on me . . . .
4. I've just told my dad about my exam results. He wasn't very pleased.
   > Neither was mine. He . . . . when I told him I'd failed maths.
5. I don't know how you can live in the middle of town. It must be awful.
   > It's all right once you're used to it. You've got everything right . . . .
6. How did you manage to get a job with the bank?
   > Well, I got in . . . ., really. My dad plays golf with one of the directors.
7. You still haven't got a job, then?
   > No, I'm afraid not. I've applied for maybe thirty and I haven't had one interview. I feel as if I'm banging my head . . . .
8. You look as if you had a late night last night.
   > Yes. It was my brother's birthday so we went out for a night . . . .

3: At death's door

Put these parts of buildings into the sentences below:

brick wall	*chimney*	*corridors*
window	*cement*	*closed doors*
roof	*door*	*wall*

1. I was so ill with flu last week I thought I was at death's . . . .
2. The European Union needs to do more to . . . . its relationship with the old Eastern Bloc countries.
3. They say smoking's bad for you but my grandfather's ninety-seven and he's always smoked like a . . . .
4. After the discovery of the new cancer drug, shares in Bionow Corporation have gone through the . . . .
5. The management and union bosses are having talks behind . . . .
6. Our business is not going too well at the moment. Financially, we've got our backs to the . . . .
7. I'm supposed to be on a diet at the moment. Whenever I have dinner with friends, it just goes out of the . . . .
8. Politicians soon discover that the . . . . of power are not very safe places!
9. You never listen to me. It's like talking to a . . . .

4: Revision

Put these pairs of words into the sentences below:

smokes – chimney
foot – door
bashing – brick
talking – brick
night – tiles
meeting – closed

"You might as well be talking to a brick wall."

1. I'm hoping to get a . . . . in the . . . .
2. I'm . . . . my head against a . . . . wall.
3. She . . . . like a . . . .
4. We're going out for a . . . . on the . . . .
5. They're having a . . . . behind . . . . doors.
6. It's like . . . . to a . . . . wall.

Look back at the idioms in this unit and find the missing words:

7. at death's . . . .
8. like a . . . . of bricks
9. the . . . . of power
10. behind closed . . . .
11. through the back . . . .
12. goes out the . . . .
13. hit the . . . .
14. went through the . . . .
15. on my . . . .
16. . . . . the relationship

What would make you go through the roof?

Unit 19 Cat Idioms

1: Literal meanings

One of the commonest household pets is the cat. It is not surprising that English has lots of idiomatic expressions based on cats and what we believe cats to be like. Fill in the following words in the definitions below:

> *curious*   *fur*   *pussy*   *whiskers*
> *pigeon*   *claws*   *bricks*   *rub*

1. Another name for a kind of dove is . . . .
2. A pet name for a cat is a . . . .
3. Cats have very sharp . . . .
4. Some breeds of cat have long . . . . . . while others have very short . . . .
5. If you . . . . . . a cat's . . . . . . one way, it loves it. If you . . . . . . it the other way, it hates it!
6. If you are . . . . . . about something, you are interested in knowing more about it.
7. . . . . are used for building or paving.
8. Cats have very sensitive . . . .

2: When the cat's away ...

Here are some ideas about cats. Match them with the idioms below:

    a. Cats like to be in charge.   **e. Cats can be cruel.**
    b. Cats are very inquisitive.   **f. Some cats are considered unlucky.**
    c. Stroke cats from front to back. **g. Cats are light on their feet.**
    d. Cats can be aggressive.   **h. Cats can seem sleepy.**

1. When the cat's away, the mice will play.   5. Don't rub him up the wrong way.
2. Curiosity killed the cat!   6. I think I'll just have a catnap.
3. There isn't a cat in hell's chance.   7. That was a very catty thing to say!
4. Stop pussyfooting and say what you mean. 8. They fight like cat and dog.

Note: Some people consider black cats lucky, while others consider them unlucky. They used to be associated with the Devil.

3: By a whisker

Complete these sentences using words from Exercises 1 or 2:

1. We just caught the train by a . . . . – with less than a minute to spare!
2. Mary and her husband get on really well even if sometimes they seem to fight like . . . . . . and dog.
3. Be a bit more careful what you say! Some people might think that was a very . . . . . . remark!
4. You should have been at the meeting yesterday. There was a terrible fight between Jeff and Liz. The . . . . . . was really flying!
5. I suppose now that you've passed your driving test first time you think you're the cat's . . . . . . !
6. Poor Jonathan! At last Miranda has got her . . . . . . into him!

4: Situations

Choose an idiom below which you could say when you want to:

1. Describe a room as very small.
2. Tell someone that there are different ways of doing something.
3. Say that there's going to be trouble because of what someone has said or done.
4. Remind someone to keep something secret.
5. Describe what happens when the boss leaves the office for a day or two.
6. Warn someone not to try to find out private information about others.
7. Tell someone they are being jumpy and nervous.
8. Say that someone you know has an annoying personality.
9. Tell someone to stop being too hesitant and careful in expressing their opinion.
10. Tell someone that they will not succeed at what they are trying to do.

a. When the cat's away, the mice will play.
b. There isn't enough room to swing a cat.
c. You're like a cat on hot bricks.
d. There's more than one way to skin a cat.
e. Stop pussyfooting around.

f. He just rubs me up the wrong way.
g. That's put the cat among the pigeons.
h. Don't let the cat out of the bag.
i. Curiosity killed the cat.
j. You haven't got a cat in hell's chance!

"No, I don't think you've got a cat in hell's chance!"

5: Revision

Look back at the idioms in this unit and add the missing words:

1. fight like cat and . . . . . .
2. stop . . . . . .
3. a cat in . . . . . . chance
4. a . . . . . . remark
5. when the cat's . . . . . .
6. put the cat . . . . . . the pigeons
7. let the cat out of the . . . . . .
8. the cat's . . . . . .

What sort of people rub you up the wrong way?

Unit 20 | Clothes Idioms

1: Literal meanings

Fill in the following words in the definitions below:

belt	sleeves	gloves	tighten
cap	knickers	twist	roll up

1. If you don't want your hands to get cold, wear your . . . .
2. I don't like wearing T-shirts. I prefer shirts with long . . . .
3. A type of flat hat is called a . . . .
4. I always buy jeans which are a bit too long, then I . . . . the bottoms.
5. If I didn't wear a . . . . , my trousers would fall down!
6. I've been on a diet for the past month. I've lost quite a lot of weight. I'm having to . . . . my belt a bit more every week!
7. Lots of beer bottles have got tops you can . . . . off, which is very convenient.
8. Men wear underpants under their trousers, but women wear . . . .

2: It fits like a glove

Fill in the following sentences in the dialogues below:

   a. **Don't get your knickers in a twist.**
   b. **Don't get shirty with me.**
   c. **I've got something up my sleeve.**
   d. **Just speak off the cuff.**
   e. **It fits like a glove.**
   f. **I wouldn't like to be in her shoes.**
   g. **We do everything on a shoestring.**
   h. **I'll collar him.**

> "The weakness of the German economy has started to create doubts about the suitability of the 'one-size fits all' interest rate policy."
>
> *Business news*

1. The colour suits you. How about the size?
   > Perfect. . . . .
2. The dinner's not ready. I still haven't washed my hair. The place is a mess. Jo and Lucy will be here any minute. What am I going to do?
   > Just calm down! . . . .
3. We just can't compete with bigger companies.
   I know. . . . .
4. It's Stuart's birthday tomorrow and we haven't bought or planned anything, Tim.
   > Don't worry. . . . .
5. I've asked Cathy to break the news to the people who are losing their jobs.
   > Poor Cathy. . . . .
6. Where have you been? We've been waiting an hour. You're so inconsiderate!
   > Hey! . . . . The car broke down!
7. I've got to give a short speech tomorrow night at the annual dinner.
   > Oh, don't worry! . . . .
8. I need to speak to John to see if he's free to play golf this Saturday.
   I'll see him tonight. . . . . then and ask him.

3: Hat idioms

Match these meanings with the idioms in bold type in the sentences below:

a. *tell nobody*
b. *admire*
c. *he doesn't know what he's talking about*

d. *old-fashioned, out of date*
e. *do something miraculous*
f. *now, without planning*

1. Don't listen to what Robin is saying. He's talking **through his hat.**
2. I love Italy. If I could get a job there, I'd go **at the drop of a hat.**
3. I'm going to tell you something but you must promise to **keep it under your hat.**
4. Cassettes? Nobody uses them now. They're **old hat.** It's CDs or mini-discs now.
5. Richard's going to replace the heating system in his house all by himself. **I take my hat off to him.** I'd never do it without professional help.
6. So, England are losing 1 – 0 with two minutes to go. They really need to **pull something out of the hat now.**

4: A coat of paint

Put the following words into the sentences below:

| shirt | shoes | sleeves | coat |
| belts | socks | caps | trousers |

1. I've nearly finished decorating the living room. One wall just needs another . . . . of paint and that's it finished.
2. There's a lot of unemployment in this area. People are having to tighten their . . . . just to survive till better times return.
3. I'm sorry you're having a difficult time at work but you can't just quit. You just have to roll up your . . . . and get on with it like everyone else.
4. My boss is going to a new job in New York. We're all going to miss her. It won't be easy to find someone to fill her . . . .
5. Jerry is the most generous man I know. He'd give you the . . . . off his back.
6. Sorry, Sally, I have to say this. You're going to fail this course unless you pull your . . . . up.
7. Don't bother asking Steve about coming for dinner, ask Lydia. She's the one who wears the . . . . in their house.
8. Listen, everybody. We need to decide what to do for Joanne's leaving party and what present to get her. So get your thinking . . . . on!

5: Revision

Look back at the idioms in this unit and add the missing verbs:

1. . . . . your sleeves up
2. . . . . it under your hat
3. . . . . something out of the hat
4. . . . . my hat off to him
5. . . . . you the shirt off his back

6. . . . . your socks up
7. . . . . our belts
8. . . . . like a glove
9. . . . . through your hat
10. . . . . her/his shoes

Do you ever get your knickers in a twist? (Yes, men can answer this, too!)

Unit 21 Colour Idioms: Black / White

1: Literal and non-literal meanings

Match up the ideas on the left with their non-literal meanings on the right:

1. A black look is
2. A white elephant is
3. A black sheep is
4. The black economy is
5. A black picture is
6. A black spot is
7. A white lie is
8. In black and white means

a. not serious and sometimes saves embarrassment.
b. a dangerous road or corner.
c. different from the rest of the family.
d. an angry one.
e. in writing.
f. something useless.
g. a depressing one.
h. unofficial and illegal.

2: Idioms with *white*

Put the following phrases into the dialogues below:

    a. *black or white*
    b. *white lie*
    c. *black and white*
    d. *white elephant*
    e. *white collar*
    f. *as white as a sheet*

"Harold, I know you're very fond of it, but it IS a bit of a white elephant."

1. I thought you didn't like Diane's new flat.
   > I don't, but I didn't want to upset her so I told her a little . . . .
   We all have to now and again, don't we?
2. I'd love a coffee if that's possible.
   > Certainly – . . . . ?
3. I don't feel very well. Have you got an aspirin, Paul?
   > Yes, sit down. You look . . . .
4. Good news, Andy. I've just heard we're finally getting that pay rise we were promised – starting from next month.
   > I'll believe it when I see it in . . . .
5. We should never have bought this table. We never use it. It just takes up space.
   > I know. It's a bit of a . . . . Let's sell it.
6. What exactly are . . . . workers?
   > People who work in offices and administrative positions as opposed to manual workers.

3: Idioms with *black*

Put the following words and expressions in the sentences below:

a. *in the black*
b. *the black market*
c. *a black picture*
d. *black eye*
e. *the black sheep of the family*
f. *a black look*
g. *black spot*
h. *the blackest day of my life*
i. *black economy*
j. *black and white*

1. I said sorry, but he didn't say a word. He just gave me . . . .
2. The official exchange rate is terrible, but if you know the right people, you can get a much better deal on . . . .
3. Be careful driving along here. It's a real . . . . Three people were killed in an accident only last week.
4. My brother and sister were always more successful at school than me. I preferred to have fun. I suppose I was . . . .
5. Things are bad, I'm afraid. We might have to cut 50 jobs this year and another 75 next year. Sorry to paint such . . . . but that's the reality.
6. Have you been in a fight? How did you get that . . . . ?
7. I'm finally in control of my financial situation. For the first time this year, my account is . . . .
8. Every country has a . . . . Some are bigger than others.
9. The day I heard of that plane crash was . . . .
10. The issue isn't as . . . . as the government pretends.

> "WARNING: THINKING IN BLACK AND WHITE MAKES YOU SEE RED
>
> People who think in black and white, convinced of the correctness of their own ideas, are putting their health, jobs and marriages at risk, a psychologist says today."
>
> *Medical news from The Daily Telegraph*

4: Revision

Look back at the idioms in this unit and add the missing nouns:

1. I told her a little white . . . .
2. This is an accident black . . . .
3. She's the black . . . . of the family.
4. Sorry to paint such a black . . . .
5. Concorde has turned out to be a bit of a white . . . .
6. It's cheaper on the black . . . .
7. She gave me a black . . . .
8. The black . . . . means the government loses a lot of tax.

Are you 100% honest or do you sometimes tell white lies?

Unit 22 | Colour Idioms: Red / Blue

1: Literal and non-literal meanings

To help you with some of the idioms in this unit, can you answer the following questions?

1. When a very important person arrives in your country what colour of carpet is brought specially for them to walk on?
2. In your language what colour do you use to describe bruises?
3. What colour does your face go when you are embarrassed?
4. What colour makes bulls angry?
5. What colour do you call pornographic films in your language?
6. If someone punches you in the eye, what colour does the skin around your eye become?

> "The Government has promised a programme to cut bureaucratic red tape."
>
> *Newspaper report*

2: Red or blue?

Choose the colour which completes the idiom – red or blue:

1. The first time I went skiing was great fun but I fell over every five seconds! I was black and *red/blue* all over the next day – bruises everywhere.
2. I got a huge surprise last week. My cousin from Australia just arrived on my doorstep completely out of the *red/blue*.
3. I've just got back from visiting our Swedish factory. They were incredibly welcoming. They gave me the *red/blue* carpet treatment.
4. I used to go the cinema quite a lot but there's not much I want to see these days. I only go once in a *red/blue* moon now.
5. I've never been more embarrassed in my life! Just as the priest asked if anyone knew any reason why we should not be married, in walked my ex-boyfriend. I just went as *red/blue* as a beetroot. He had come with a present for us!
6. Come on, Steve! It's your birthday. We can't stay in tonight. Let's go out and paint the town *red/blue*.
7. What really annoys me about getting a visa these days is all the *red/blue* tape. You know – the documents, the paperwork, the forms to fill in. It's ridiculous!
8. And then she accused me of lying. Can you believe it? I just saw *red/blue* and started shouting at her.
9. I wouldn't use Brian's computer if I were you. He'll scream *red/blue* murder if he finds out you've used it.
10. Look, you've asked me fifty times already and you can keep asking until you're *red/blue* in the face, but the answer is still "No".

3: Caught red-handed

Complete the following dialogues with the word _red_ or _blue_:

1. How can you be sure that it was Rob who's been stealing the CDs?
   > Linda saw him putting them in his bag during his lunch break. He was caught _blue-/red-_ handed.
2. George seems to be the boss's favourite. He's always nice to him.
   > Oh, yes. George can do no wrong. He's the _blue-/red-_ eyed boy.
3. Do you want to try that new late-night cinema? It might be quite good.
   > No thanks. Somebody told me they show _blue/red_ movies. I'm not interested.
4. John gets quite aggressive when you talk about politics, doesn't he?
   > Absolutely. And if you criticise the Labour party it's like a _blue/red_ rag to a bull. He can't resist trying to put you right.
5. Sorry to hear about your father. Had he been ill for some time or ...?
   > No, it was a heart attack. Totally unexpected – a complete bolt out of the _blue/red_.

"Ernest was thinking about the meaning of life when he suddenly had a heart attack. It was like a bolt out of the blue."

6. You look worried. Is everything OK?
   > Not really. I'm in the _blue/red_ again. I'm having real money problems.
7. Why did they spend so long at the meeting talking about the colour of the chairs?
   > It was a complete _blue/red_ herring – just a total waste of time!
8. You can drive, can't you, Helen? Was it difficult to learn?
   > Oh, I found it really hard – especially the test. I failed it three times. The day I passed was a _blue-/red-_ letter day for me. I remember it like it was yesterday.

4: Revision

Look back at the idioms in this unit and add the missing colour:

1. There's too much . . . . . . tape.
2. Let's paint the town . . . .
3. He'll scream . . . . . murder.
4. That's like a . . . . . rag to a bull.
5. Ask till you're . . . . . in the face!
6. I do it once in a . . . . . moon.
7. I was black and . . . . . . all over.
8. He's the . . . . . .-eyed boy.
9. She was caught . . . . . .-handed.
10. It was a . . . . . -letter day.
11. It was a bolt out of the . . . .
12. I got the . . . . . carpet treatment.

What sort of things make you see red?

Unit 23 Driving Idioms

1: Literal meanings

Fill in the following words in the definitions below:

> **lanes**   **crossroads**   **collision**   **gear**   **overtake**
> **bend**   **dead-end**   **backseat**   **steer**   **crash**

1. When you pass another car going in the same direction, you . . . . it.
2. You . . . . the car with the steering-wheel.
3. If you drive down a road and the road stops suddenly, it is a . . . .
4. You change . . . . by first depressing the clutch pedal.
5. Motorways usually have three . . . . , the slow lane for lorries, the middle lane for cars, and the fast lane for overtaking and for breaking the law!
6. A . . . . involves two or more vehicles.
7. A . . . . usually involves more than one vehicle, but not necessarily.
8. Nobody likes a . . . . driver!
9. A curve in a road is called a . . . .
10. When you come to a . . . . , you have to decide which direction to go in.

2: In the driving seat

Match the idioms in bold type with the meanings below:

1. Bill used to be boss, but his nephew is **in the driving seat** now.
2. Italy has **overtaken** France as the number two holiday destination.
3. This new computer is **driving me mad!**
4. Last year was a bit difficult, but I think the company's **turned the corner** now.
5. Come on! **Step on it!** We're going to be late.
6. I wonder if you could help me out. We're **in a bit of a jam.**
7. I wish I could leave. This is a **dead-end job.**
8. I'd **steer clear** of Di today, if I were you. She's in a dreadful mood.
9. The team weren't too bad in the first half, but ten minutes into the second half they seemed to **go up a gear.** Then they won 3 nil!
10. Come on! It's time to **hit the road**, Jack.

    a. *keep away from*
    b. *in control*
    c. *change for the better*
    d. *leave*
    e. *make someone angry*
    f. *have a serious problem*
    g. *replace*
    h. *have no future*
    i. *increase your effort*
    j. *hurry*

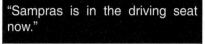

"Sampras is in the driving seat now."

Live television commentary on Wimbledon semi-final

3: Down the road

Fill in the following words and expressions in the sentences below:

a. *at a crossroads* f. *taking a backseat*
b. *on the road* g. *the green light*
c. *in the fast lane* h. *down the road*
d. *driving at* i. *going round in circles*
e. *crashes* j. *put a brake on*

1. Who knows where we will be a couple of years . . . . ?
2. Our reps spend about six months . . . . every year.
3. If the Stock Market . . . . , we're all in serious trouble!
4. I'm afraid we'll have to . . . . our spending for a while.
5. Life . . . . doesn't suit everyone.
6. At last! They've given us . . . . Now we can go ahead!
7. You can decide from now on. I'm . . . .
8. I'm not sure I know what exactly you're . . . .
9. Let's get to the point! For the past hour we've been . . . .
10. I think my career is . . . . I feel like a change of direction.

4: Round the bend

Complete these short dialogues using the following idioms:

a. *We're in the slow lane going nowhere.*
b. *It's driving me round the bend!*
c. *We're on a collision course.*
d. *You won't catch me doing a U-turn.*

1. Have you got to grips with your new software?
   > You must be joking! . . . .
2. Are you going to change your mind?
   > Me? Change my mind? . . . .
3. Do you think you and your head of department are going to agree?
   > No, I don't. . . . .
4. I hear your company's not doing very well.
   > You're dead right. . . . .

5: Revision

Look back at the idioms in this unit and add the missing verbs:

1. . . . . me mad
2. . . . . him round the bend
3. . . . . us the green light
4. . . . . up a gear
5. . . . . the road

6. . . . . a backseat
7. . . . . round in circles
8. . . . . the corner
9. . . . . a brake on
10. . . . . clear

What sort of things drive you mad?

Unit 24 | Eating Idioms

1: Non-literal meanings

Here are some common idioms using 'eating' words. Match them up with their meanings:

1. It's not my taste.
2. I had to eat my words.
3. I've had my fill.
4. That didn't go down well.
5. I bit his head off.
6. I made a meal of it.
7. I could eat a horse.
8. I've got a sweet tooth.

a. I am extremely hungry.
b. I don't like it.
c. It wasn't popular.
d. I was proved to be wrong.
e. I spoke sharply to him.
f. I don't want any more.
g. I love chocolates and other sweets.
h. I took too long to do it.

"How dare you accuse me of biting your head off!"

2: I could eat a horse

Complete these dialogues with the idioms in Exercise 1. You will need to change some of them a little.

1. Are you still hungry?
   > Yes, ...

2. I thought you liked opera.
   > No, ... in music at all.

3. What do you think of the new tax on plane tickets?
   > It won't . . . . with business people or people living in outlying areas.

4. Do you think Jane will have a dessert?
   > I'm sure she will. She's always had . . . .

5. I had said absolutely nothing, so I have no idea why Bill . . . . !
   > I know. I spoke to him and he's sorry he said what he said. He's going to apologise to you personally.

6. My teacher told me I'd fail all my exams. Then I passed with the top grades!
   > I suppose you made him . . . . !
7. I've been working on this essay for weeks. I don't know when I'll get it finished.
   > You'll have to hurry up. You're . . . . !
8. So, Nigel, you're not standing for the committee again this year?
   > No, I've . . . . of committees. I'm stepping down.

3: Swallow your pride

Use the following idiomatic expressions in the situations below:

a. *left a bad taste in my mouth*   e. *swallow your pride*
b. *bit my head off*   f. *something to get my teeth into*
c. *digest*   g. *a second bite at the cherry*
d. *have your cake and eat it*   h. *bite off more than you can chew*

1. I can't afford the rent on my flat. My parents have said I can go back and live
   with them but I'd feel such a failure.
   > I think you'll just have to . . . . and accept their help.
2. Keep away from Christine this morning. She's in a bad mood.
   > I know. She . . . . for no reason when I arrived.
3. So, Tom apologised for what he'd said to you?
   > Yes, but the whole experience has . . . .
4. I thought you liked your job. Why do you want a change?
   > I need a fresh challenge – . . . .
5. I'm going to try to fix the car myself.
   > Well, if it's difficult, don't do it. Don't . . . .
6. So, what do you think about the new budget proposals, then?
   > I haven't really had time to . . . . all the details yet.
7. I feel like a few days off, but I really need the overtime.
   > The problem with you is you always want to . . . .
8. I've failed my university entrance exam. I'm not sure if I can re-take it.
   > I expect you can. You're allowed . . . . , surely?

4: Revision

Choose the correct word in the sentences below:

1. I bit off more than I could *swallow/chew*.
2. You can't have a second *bite/chew* at the cherry.
3. He had to *eat/swallow* his words.
4. *Bite/Swallow* your pride and say you'll accept.
5. I need something to get my *teeth/tooth* into.
6. It left a bad *smell/taste* in my mouth.
7. I said sorry but she just *bit/chewed* my head off.
8. My idea didn't go *up/down* very well.

When was the last time you bit off more than you could chew?

Unit 25 Eye Idioms

1: Literal meanings

Fill in the following words in the definitions below:

blind	*bargain*	*eyelids*
blink	*peel*	*eyebrows*

1. If you buy something at much less than the normal price, it's a . . . .
2. You . . . . thousands of times every day.
3. Before you eat an orange, you have to . . . . . . it.
4. A person who cannot see is . . . .
5. The lines of hair above your eyes are called your . . . .
6. When you close your eyes, they are covered by your . . . .

2: With my eyes closed

Complete the sentences with these expressions containing the word *eye*:

a. *in the public eye*	e. *up to my eyes*
b. *see eye to eye*	f. *more to him than meets the eye*
c. *pull the wool over my eyes*	g. *with my eyes closed*
d. *eyes in the back of your head*	h. *out of the corner of my eye*

1. I spend a lot of time on the road in my job. I've driven from London to Edinburgh so many times now I could do it . . . .
2. I've got three young children. You can't sit down and relax for a minute. You need
   . . . .
3. I wouldn't want to be famous. You live your life . . . .
   You get no privacy whatsoever. It would drive me mad.
4. Sorry, but I'm afraid I have to cancel lunch together. I'm . . . .
   in work at the moment. How about next week?
5. I get on very well with my father. We . . . . on most things.
6. I was lying in bed when I noticed something moving . . . .
   I jumped up and turned the light on to see a massive spider on my pillow.
7. I discovered yesterday that 'Boring Bob' at work is a black belt in karate and has a Japanese wife. There's obviously . . . .
8. Don't try to pretend you've been working late in the office. I rang and they told me you'd left early. You can't . . . .

Now write the idiom with the following meanings:

9. very busy	. . . .
10. agree	. . . .
11. deceive or trick	. . . .
12. be watchful	. . . .

3: Keep your eyes peeled

Match the sentences below to make two-line dialogues:

1. I'm sure this can't be the right way to get on to the motorway.
2. They offered you double your salary? What did you do? Fall off your chair?
3. Malcolm was rather rude to you yesterday, wasn't he? Have you spoken to him?
4. You must spend a lot of money on clothes, Sarah. You always look so smart.
5. Shall we have another bottle? The waiter's just over there.
6. I think Steve rather likes Andrea, don't you? He spent the whole evening talking to her and ignoring everyone else.
7. Are you coming in for a swim? The water looks lovely.
8. What did you think of the best man's speech?
9. I'd like your opinion on this report as soon as you've got a minute.

a. No, I decided to **turn a blind eye** to it. He's under a lot of pressure at work.
b. You can say that again! He **couldn't take his eyes off** her.
c. No. I **didn't bat an eyelid.** I looked straight at them and said it wasn't enough.
d. Good idea. Try and **catch his eye.**
e. Just leave it with me and **I'll run my eye over it**.
f. It **raised a few eyebrows**! I think he should have kept quiet about the baby!
g. No, I'll stay here and **keep an eye on** our things.
h. Well, just **keep your eyes peeled** for a sign. There must be one somewhere.
i. I don't really spend that much. I've just **got an eye for** a bargain.

"There was something strange about Mr Pinkerton that made James think he had eyes in the back of his head."

4: Revision

Look back at the idioms in this unit and add the missing verbs:

1. didn't . . . . . . an eyelid
2. . . . . . . a blind eye to it
3. . . . . . . eyes in the back of your head
4. . . . . . . your eye over something
5. . . . . . . eye to eye
6. . . . . . . your eyes peeled
7. . . . . . . an eye on things
8. more than . . . . . . the eye

Now add the missing prepositions:

9. . . . . . . the public eye
10. . . . . . . to my eyes in work
11. do it . . . . . . my eyes closed
12. turn a blind eye . . . . . . it
13. see eye . . . . . . eye
14. keep an eye . . . . . . my things

Are you up to your eyes at the moment?

61

Face Idioms

1: Literal and non-literal meanings

We all know the literal meaning of *face*. But do you know that a clock or a watch also has a *face*? We can use *face* as a noun. It often has the meaning *appearance*. For example, *put on a brave face*. When we use it as a verb, it often has the meaning *look clearly at* or *confront*. For example, *to face the consequences*.

Face sometimes means the whole person. Someone once said:

I'm not just a pretty face.

Mrs Thatcher was called:

the unacceptable face of capitalism.

Helen of Troy had:

*the face that launched
a thousand ships.*

"I'm glad I'm not Joe. He's facing
the music at the moment!"

2: The grammar of *face*

In these first five examples *face* is used as a verb. Use these words to complete the idioms:

| *the consequences* | *work* | *the music* | *the fact* | *a full meal* |

1. I suppose it's time I faced . . . . that Lydia isn't interested in me because I'm old enough to be her father!
2. Did you hear that Joe didn't back up his computer last night and it crashed this morning? He's with the boss at the moment – no doubt facing . . . . !
3. I couldn't face . . . . A sandwich is enough for me.
4. I just can't face . . . . at the moment – not so soon after the funeral.
5. I'll take the decision. I'm not afraid to face . . . . if things go wrong.

In these examples *face* is used as a noun. Add the following verbs:

| *put* | *got* | *lose* | *keep* | *putting* | *save* |

6. People won't give their opinions during meetings in case they are wrong. They don't want to . . . . face.
7. When Di fell off her chair, it was all I could do to . . . . a straight face.
8. Why have you . . . . such a long face today? Has something happened I don't know about?
9. You've no doubt heard that Frank's mother was in a car accident this morning. I think it's fairly serious, but he seems to be . . . . a brave face on it.
10. It's nice to meet you at last, Mr Lee. It's good to be able to . . . . a face to a name.
11. I think the government is just trying to . . . . face.

3: Expressions with *face*

Fill in the following expressions in the sentences below:

a. *off the face of the earth*
b. *blue in the face*
c. *staring us in the face*
d. *at face value*
e. *all over your face*
f. *face to face*
g. *flat on his face*
h. *to his face*

1. You can keep asking till you're . . . . – I'm not going to change my mind.
2. Maureen always has an ulterior motive. You can never take what she says . . . .
3. Everybody knows that Andy is the wrong person for the new post, but nobody is prepared to say so . . . .
4. Has anyone seen my car keys? I put them down five minutes ago and now they've disappeared . . . . !
5. I've just come back from a holiday in Borneo. It was amazing. I actually came . . . . with a real gorilla!
6. Come on, Pete, somebody's been eating my biscuits. It must've been you. It's written . . . .
7. We've spent ages trying to decide who to send to the conference in Tokyo. The answer's been . . . . Let's ask Ray. He studied Japanese at university!
8. The President was a bit accident-prone. He once fell . . . . as he was getting up to give a major speech.

4: Revision

Put the following pairs of words into the sentences below:

a. *written – face*
b. *blue – face*
c. *face – name*
d. *say – face*
e. *putting – brave*
f. *disappeared – earth*
g. *flat – face*
h. *keeping – straight*

1. . . . . a . . . . face was never one of my talents!
2. You can ask till you're . . . . in the . . . .
3. My pen has . . . . off the face of the . . . .
4. I know what's going on. It's . . . . all over your . . . .
5. I fell . . . . on my. . . . . and hurt my arm.
6. If you want to say something, ... it to my . . . .
7. It's nice to put a . . . . to a . . . .
8. She's very upset, but she's . . . . a . . . . face on it.

Have you been in a situation recently when you found it difficult to keep a straight face?

Unit 27 | Fingers and Thumbs Idioms

1: Literal and non-literal meanings

Match the literal ideas on the left with their non-literal meanings on the right:

1. If you twiddle your thumbs
2. If you never lift a finger
3. If you point the finger
4. If you get your fingers burnt
5. If you get your finger out
6. If you have green fingers
7. If you are all fingers and thumbs
8. If you keep your fingers crossed
9. If you put your finger on something

a. you accuse someone of something.
b. you are good at gardening.
c. you believe in luck.
d. you see the problem.
e. you are lazy.
f. you lose money.
g. you try harder.
h. you are wasting time.
i. you are not good with your hands.

2: *Finger* or *thumb*?

Use *finger(s)* or *thumb(s)* to complete the idioms in these sentences:

1. There's something strange about Graham, but I'm not sure what it is. I can't put my . . . . on it.
2. I was miles from the nearest garage when I ran out of petrol, so I just stood at the side of the road and tried to . . . . a lift.
3. If you want to pass this exam you really need to get your . . . . out and start some serious study.
4. I invested some money in stocks and shares a couple of years ago but I got my . . . . badly burnt. I lost about £10,000. Never again!
5. My dental appointment was supposed to be for four o'clock but I had to sit in the waiting room twiddling my . . . . for an hour.
6. My flatmate is driving me crazy. I have to do all the cleaning. She never lifts a . . . . to help.
7. Robert, you can't wear a suit to Colin's party! Everyone else will be wearing jeans. You'll stick out like a sore . . . .

"Robert's suit wasn't the only thing that stuck out like a sore thumb at Colin's party!"

8. I had a great idea at work that we should have brightly coloured walls, more plants and pictures but it got the . . . . down. They're so conservative.
9. As a rule of . . . . , redheads should never wear bright yellow.
10. It's too easy to point the . . . . at today's parents. There are an awful lot of influences on young people in the modern world.

3: Fingers crossed!

Fill in the following words and expressions in the sentences below:

        a. *under her thumb*
        b. *the fingers of one hand*
        c. *round her little finger*
        d. *at your fingertips*
        e. *green fingers*
        f. *fingers crossed*
        g. *fingers and thumbs*
        h. *finger on the pulse*

> "Mr Portillo claimed that the Prime Minister had his finger on Britain's pulse."
>
> *News report*

1. I've got my final exam tomorrow.
   > Good luck! I'll keep my . . . . for you.
2. Danny and Jane have a strange relationship. She gets her own way all the time.
   > Oh yes. She can twist him . . . .
3. I see. So, you can put all the data onto the computer network.
   > That's right. Then any information you need is . . . . immediately.
4. You've dropped something, Sandra. Here you are.
   > Thanks. I keep dropping things this morning. I'm all . . . .
5. Look at these plants, Viv. They're all dying. I don't know what I'm doing wrong.
   > Speak to Nina. She's the one with . . . .
6. I'm going to ask Tony if he wants to come away with us on the golf weekend.
   > He won't come. His wife won't let him. He's totally . . . .
7. Does anybody know who the new Personnel Manager is going to be?
   > I have no idea. Ask Chris. He's got his . . . .
8. My boyfriend took me out to a lovely Italian restaurant last night.
   > Lucky you. I can count on . . . . the number of times my husband's taken me out for a meal recently.

4: Revision

Look back at the idioms in this unit and add the missing verbs:

1. . . . . out like a sore thumb
2. . . . . him round her little finger
3. . . . . your finger out
4. . . . . my finger on it
5. . . . . on the fingers of one hand
6. . . . . your fingers crossed
7. . . . . it the thumbs down
8. . . . . your thumbs
9. . . . . a lift
10. . . . . my fingers burnt

Are you keeping your fingers crossed about something at the moment?

Unit 28 Fire Idioms

1: Literal meanings

Fire has always been very important in all societies. It is not surprising that the image of fire is used in many situations – particularly human relationships. Fill in the following words in the definitions below:

ambition	*sparks*	*row*	*baptism*
temper	*flames*	*fuel*	*blaze*

1. Gas, coal and oil are all types of . . . .
2. A large, dangerous fire is called a . . . .
3. Another word for a serious argument is a . . . .
4. People who want to improve their lives or achieve something have . . . .
5. The Christian ceremony when a person is dipped in water or is sprinkled with drops of water is called . . . .
6. Fred has a very bad . . . . He gets annoyed about nothing sometimes.
7. When you hit two stones together, you can make . . . . fly.
8. The . . . . were jumping 100 feet into the air and it took the fire brigade over three hours to bring them under control.

2: A burning ambition

Use these nouns to complete the idioms in the sentences below:

burning	*flames*	*sparks*	*blazing*
smoke	*heated*	*fiery*	*fire (3)*

1. I want to be an actor. I've got a . . . . ambition to play Hamlet at the Globe Theatre in London.
2. She's got a lot of potential as a jazz singer, but she's not going to set the world on . . . .
3. I had a . . . . row with my girlfriend last night. I'm beginning to think we don't have that much in common.
4. Be careful what you say to Martin. He's got a . . . . temper.
5. I wouldn't say we had an argument. It was just a . . . . discussion.
6. I met Jackie at a conference and liked her immediately. We got on like a house on . . . .
7. You're playing with . . . . If the company find out what you've done, you'll be looking for a new job.
8. I was planning a quiet weekend, but Sally and Richard invited themselves round on Saturday, so all my plans went up in . . . .
9. Every time I have a new idea you just shoot me down in . . . . without really listening to what I have to say.
10. Have you ever heard Kate and Tina discussing politics? The . . . . really fly when they disagree about something.

3: An old flame

Use the following idiomatic expressions in the sentences below:

> **a.** *an old flame*
> **b.** *no smoke without fire*
> **c.** *adds more fuel to the fire*
> **d.** *a baptism of fire*
> **e.** *a blaze of publicity*
> **f.** *burn my bridges*
> **g.** *fired my imagination*

> "How I survived a baptism of fire."
>
> *Newspaper headline*

1. I didn't know Carol knew Chris.
   > Oh yes. She's . . . . of his from their time at university.
2. Can you remember your first day in the classroom, Pat?
   > Yes, I had to teach maths to a class of 30 very difficult sixteen-year-olds. It was . . . . , I can tell you.
3. Have you seen the new Bond film yet?
   > Yes, but despite . . . . when it came out, it didn't live up to expectations – at least not mine.
4. There's a rumour that the Prime Minister is going to resign, but I can't believe it.
   > Well, you know what they say – there's . . . .
5. So what made you decide to go to Uganda on holiday?
   > Well, I saw this film a couple of years ago and it just . . . .
6. Did I hear you're resigning?
   > Well, I'm looking for a change, but I'm not leaving this job till I've got something fixed up. I don't want to . . . .
7. That's the third government minister who's resigned this week.
   > There's been something funny going on for a long time. This just . . . .

4: Revision

Look back at the idioms in this unit and add the missing verbs:

1. . . . . the world on fire	5. . . . . fuel to the fire
2. . . . . a blazing row	6. . . . . the imagination
3. . . . . with fire	7. . . . . up in smoke
4. . . . . on like a house on fire	8. . . . . your bridges

Have you got a burning ambition to do something?

Unit 29 | Fishing Idioms

1: Literal meanings

It is not surprising that English in particular is a language which is rich in idioms associated with fishing. Underline all the words in this passage to do with fish:

If you fish in the sea you need a fishing line or net. At the end of your line will be a hook or hooks on which you have put bait. To catch fish like cod or haddock you simply lower your line into the water and wait for them to rise to the bait. If you want to catch mackerel you trawl your line behind a slow-moving boat. In some countries fishermen cast nets into the sea from the shore. In the Atlantic fishermen use huge nets from boats called trawlers.

Fresh-water fishing, or angling, is very different. You use a rod and line. You cast your line into a river or lake. Fish such as salmon are caught on their way up or down river. They spawn in ponds. Children often go fishing for tiny fish called 'tiddlers'.

2: Quite a catch!

Use these 10 common idiomatic expressions in the situations below:

a. *There's plenty more fish in the sea.*
b. *He's a big fish in a small pond.*
c. *We've landed a big contract in Japan.*
d. *Are you fishing for compliments?*
e. *They've spawned several new companies.*
f. *I'm hooked!*
g. *He's a cold fish.*
h. *He's quite a catch.*
i. *She's angling for promotion.*
j. *There's something fishy going on.*

> " . . . where tiddlers can swim with the big fish."
>
> *Report on the state of the insurance industry*

1. He's good-looking. He's got a big house. He's powerful.
   > Yes, ... by anybody's standards!
2. Do you play squash every day of the week?
   Yes, I'm afraid . . . .
3. You can never get the tiniest smile out of him. I've never seen him laugh.
   > No, ...
4. Prime Minister of Luxembourg! And he thinks he's important!
   > Well, I suppose . . . . !
5. He just phoned me and told me he didn't want to see me again!
   > Oh, don't worry! . . . .
6. Why are they having all those secret meetings behind closed doors?
   > . . . .
7. What do you think of my hair?
   > . . . . !
8. Why are we thinking of opening an office in Osaka?
   > . . . .
9. This is the third time this week that Lucy has had lunch with the MD!
   > It wouldn't surprise me if . . . .
10. Impex's move to the North has been really successful, hasn't it?
    > Yes, it's been good news for the local economy. . . . .

3: Hook, line and sinker

Fill in the following idiomatic expressions in the sentences below:

a. *trawl through*   d. *rise to the bait*
b. *hook, line, and sinker*   e. *let him off the hook*
c. *slipping through the net*   f. *cast our net wider*

1. We've got the deal and on our terms! They believed our story about not being able to afford the extra 10%. They swallowed it . . . . !
2. We spend a fortune training people, then before we know it, they've moved on to one of our competitors. We must look after them better so that they stay with us. There's too many . . . .
3. This is the first time John's made a mistake. It was a one-off. Trust him. He'll be more careful in future. I think we should . . . . this time.
4. Look, the unions want a strike. If we . . . . , we'll be playing right into their hands.
5. The police are looking for a man in his thirties who has probably been in prison already. They're having to . . . . their computer records.
6. This job is too important to advertise in the local papers. If we want to attract a top sales manager, we need to . . . . and advertise nationally.

4: Different fish

The following idioms mention five different kinds of fish: the flounder, minnow, herring, whale, and shark. Match them with their meanings:

1. They're just floundering about.
2. They're just minnows.
3. That's a red herring.
4. They had a whale of a time.
5. They're sharks.

a. They are unscrupulous and dishonest.
b. It has nothing to do with what we're discussing.
c. They don't know what they're doing.
d. They are very small and unimportant.
e. They had a wonderful time.

5: Revision

Try to remember which idioms these pairs of words come from. Then put them into the spaces below:

whale – time   *landed – contract*
plenty – sea   *let – hook*
rise – bait   *cast – wider*

1. Congratulations! I heard you . . . . the Japanese . . . .
2. You're better off without him. He was totally unreliable. There are . . . . more fish in the . . . .
3. Brian is usually very shy, but if you want to get him talking, start talking about politics. He'll soon . . . . to the . . . .
4. I was late again but my boss . . . . me off the . . . . as long as it doesn't happen again.
5. You'll never find a job if you limit yourself to this area. You really must . . . . your net a bit . . . .
6. What a party! We had a . . . . of a . . . . !

When was the last time you had a whale of a time?

Unit 30 Food Idioms

1: Literal meanings

Fill in the following words in the definitions below:

couch	*pinch*	*sliced*	*variety*
stew	*spices*	*icing*	*pickle*

1. A . . . . is another word for sofa.
2. Some people prefer to buy uncut bread. Some prefer to buy it already . . . .
3. If you . . . . meat, you cook it slowly in liquid in a pan with the lid on.
4. Wedding cakes are usually covered in thick sweet white . . . .
5. Ginger, cinnamon, pepper and cloves are all examples of . . . .
6. My job is not the same every day. There's plenty of . . . .
7. A . . . . of salt is the amount you can pick up between your finger and thumb.
8. If you . . . . onions, you preserve them in vinegar.

2: Not my cup of tea

Complete the idioms in the following sentences with these expressions:

a. *a piece of cake*	f. *in a pickle*
b. *couch potato*	g. *cucumber*
c. *food for thought*	h. *went pear-shaped*
d. *not my cup of tea*	i. *salt of the earth*
e. *hot cakes*	j. *bread and butter*

1. Most of my colleagues go for a drink after work on Fridays but I don't normally go. Going to the pub is . . . .
2. My brother works hard during the week but at the weekends he spends most of his time lying on the sofa watching TV. He can be a real . . . .
3. The whole peace settlement . . . . when the terrorists planted a bomb in the main railway station.
4. I went windsurfing for the first time on Saturday. I thought it was going to be . . . . , but I soon realised it was a lot more difficult than I'd expected.
5. So you write novels and poetry, do you?
   > Yes, but sports journalism's my . . . .
6. Did you see the way Sandra handled that aggressive customer? She was as cool as a . . . .
7. It would only take the cost of a few fighter planes to get rid of leprosy from the world. That's . . . . , isn't it?
8. I really like Janet. She's uncomplicated and honest. What you see is what you get. She's always helping people. She's the . . . .
9. This is the new Nintendo football game. We've only got two left in the shop. They've been selling like . . . .
10. I'm . . . . I've got to be at the dentist's in 10 minutes and I'm expecting an important phone call. Could you answer my phone and say I'll be back in about an hour's time?

3: On the breadline

Fill in the following words and expressions in the dialogues below:

a. *stew in his own juice*   d. *egg on our face*
b. *butter him up*   e. *on the breadline*
c. *cheesed off*   f. *take that with a pinch of salt*

1. It says in the paper that our financial situation has never been better.
   > Try telling that to the people who are living . . . .
2. What's the matter with you? You look totally fed up.
   > I am. I was supposed to have a day off on Friday but I've just been told I can't because there's too much work. I'm really . . . .
3. A few days before we ask our boss for anything, we start being extra nice to her.
   > We do the same with our boss! We just . . . . a bit. It's never failed yet!
4. There's a story going about that we're being sold to the Koreans.
   > I'd . . . . I don't know where nonsense like that starts!
5. I'm going to phone Mike to see if he's ready to say sorry about that argument.
   > No, don't do that. It's his fault, so let him . . . . for a while.
6. We ended up with . . . .
   > How come?
   Well, after we had insisted on everyone else doing things correctly, we discovered that we were the ones who had been breaking the rules!

4: The spice of life

Finish the idioms below with the following phrases:

a. *since sliced bread*   c. *eggs in one basket*
b. *the icing on the cake*   d. *the spice of life*

1. I can't understand people who go on holiday to the same place year after year.
   I go somewhere different every year. For me, variety is . . . .
2. The golden rule with investments is to put your money in a variety of different companies. Don't put all your . . . .
3. My new software is the best thing . . . . It's made my job so much easier.
4. I love my new job – the people, the work, the money. The fact they've given me the car of my dreams is just . . . .

5: Revision

Look back at the idioms in this unit and add the final words:

1. stew in his own . . . .   6. with egg on my . . . .
2. take that with a pinch of . . . . 7. the icing on the . . . .
3. best thing since sliced . . . .   8. salt of the . . . .
4. variety is the spice of . . . .   9. as cool as a . . . .
5. selling like hot . . . .   10. not really my cup of . . . .

Have any of your plans gone pear-shaped recently?

Unit 31 | Foot Idioms

1: Foot or feet?

Use *foot* or *feet* to complete the idiomatic expressions in these sentences:

1. People ask you the most unexpected questions in this job. You really have to think on your *foot/feet*.
2. When I get home from work, the first thing I do is make a cup of tea, put my *foot/feet* up and relax in front of the TV.
3. I'm having my flat decorated at the moment. They're supposed to finish it today but they've been dragging their *foot/feet* so it'll probably be Friday now.
4. You can't live with your parents for ever, Victor. You're twenty-six. It's time you were standing on your own two *foot/feet*.
5. The French goalkeeper played brilliantly. He didn't put a *foot/feet* wrong.
6. I don't mind my son going to discos and clubs but I had to put my *foot/feet* down when he started coming home as late as two or three in the morning.
7. I get on very well with my flatmate now but we got off on the wrong *foot/feet* because she used to play her music so loud. It was fine after we talked about it.

"Now we don't want to get off on the wrong foot, do we, Samantha?"

8. I know you're on holiday, Martin, but you still need to help in the kitchen. I'm not going to wait on you hand and *foot/feet* the whole time.
9. I worked for thirteen hours yesterday. I was dead on my *foot/feet* when I got home.
10. I like the idea of having an office party, but who's going to *foot/feet* the bill?

2: Non-literal meanings

Look back at the exercise and find the idioms with these meanings:

1. think quickly   . . . .
2. work slowly   . . . .
3. be independent   . . . .
4. make no mistakes   . . . .
5. object to something   . . . .
6. pay   . . . .

3: Rushed off our feet

Put the following verbs into the dialogues below:

a. *got cold feet*	**e.** *set foot*
b. *get itchy feet*	**f.** *find my feet*
c. *landed on her feet*	**g.** *put my foot in it*
d. *rushed off our feet*	**h.** *keep your feet on the ground*

1. Have you had a busy day? You look exhausted.
   > Yes, it was the first day of the sale. We were . . . .

2. You've lived in lots of different countries, haven't you, Ian?
   > Yes, I can't stay in one place for too long. After about a year I . . . .
   . . . . and I need to move on somewhere new.

3. Well, Andy, did you go out with Jill over the weekend? Did you ask her?
   > I wanted to phone her but I . . . . at the last minute so I didn't.

4. Has your sister found a job yet?
   > Didn't I tell you? She's got a wonderful job in
   the city – company car, incentives, bonuses –
   she's really . . . .

5. Oh dear, I think I've just . . . . !
   > Why? What have you done?
   I've just asked Jane about her holiday in Africa.
   > Oh, no! And you didn't know that the
   airline had gone bust!

6. So, you had a good time in Paris, then?
   > Yes, but I hope I never . . . .
   in another art gallery! We spent hours walking
   round them because of the rain!

7. How's the new job going, Sam?
   > It's all very new. I think it'll take me a couple of weeks to . . . .

8. It's my first job, and they're giving me a company car! And the salary is twice what
   I expected. What do you think of that, then?
   > Just . . . . , son! That's all I can say!

"I've really landed on my feet!"
said Miss Smiley as she heard
of her promotion.

4: Revision

Choose the correct word to complete the idiom:

1. You have to think . . . . your feet in this job.	*with/on*
2. Somebody has to . . . . the bill.	*foot/feet*
3. You need time to find . . . . feet.	*your/the*
4. I was . . . . on my feet when I got home.	*dead/alive*
5. I was rushed . . . . my feet.	*from/off*
6. Oh dear. I think I've just put my foot . . . . it.	*on/in*
7. I got . . . . feet and changed my mind.	*hot/cold*
8. We got off on the . . . . foot.	*right/wrong*
9. I'll never . . . . foot in that place again.	*set/put*
10. He didn't . . . . a foot wrong.	*put/get*

When was the last time you put your foot in it? What did you do about it?

Unit 32 Hand Idioms

1: Definitions

Read these statements. Each one contains information about an idiom containing *hand.*

1. Shops and houses *change hands* when they are sold.
2. If you *reject* something *out of hand,* you reject it totally, with no discussion.
3. People who *live from hand to mouth* never save for tomorrow.
4. If you *have a big hand* in something, it means that you have had a lot of influence over it.
5. If you've *got your hands full,* you are very busy with lots to do.
6. If *things get out of hand,* they get out of control.
7. If you read everything you can *get your hands on,* you read anything and everything.
8. If you have *time on your hands,* you have time to spare.

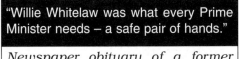

"Willie Whitelaw was what every Prime Minister needs – a safe pair of hands."

Newspaper obituary of a former Deputy Prime Minister

Complete these dialogues using one of the above idioms:

1. Let's go to that Greek restaurant we went to last year. It was nice.
   > It's a Chinese restaurant now. It . . . . last September.
2. Is there any chance you could work on Saturday? Mark's still ill.
   > Normally I would, but . . . . this weekend. I have to look after the children because Mary's visiting her parents.
3. Did you show your ideas to the rest of your department?
   > They didn't even bother to read them. They rejected them . . . . !
4. I hope these drunks aren't going to cause trouble.
   > Don't worry. I'll call the police if . . . .
5. We're decorating the house at the moment. It's taking ages.
   > I could give you a hand. I've got a bit of . . . . at the moment.
6. How do you become a successful writer? Where do you get your ideas from?
   > I read very widely. In fact, I read everything I can . . . .
7. How are you managing since you lost your job?
   > We're just . . . . We aren't able to save anything, but we manage.
8. Thank you for organising such an excellent meeting.
   > Thank you, but don't forget Maria. She . . . . in all the planning as well.

2: Give you a hand

Fill in the following verbs in the sentences below:

turn	*fell*	*count*	*know*
give	*take*	*keep*	*hand*

1. That looks heavy. Let me . . . . you a hand.
2. I love it here. It's so peaceful. You can . . . . the number of cars you see here in a week on the fingers of one hand.
3. Martin's one of those annoying people who can . . . . their hand to almost anything – sport, painting, music – he's good at everything.
4. This report is strictly confidential. If it . . . . into the wrong hands, we would all be in serious trouble.
5. I don't care if you know who did this to your car, you shouldn't deal with it yourself. Call the police. You can't . . . . the law into your own hands.
6. You might not like his style or methods but you've got to . . . . it to him – he's a brilliant salesman.
7. The problem with this company is communication. Half the time the right hand doesn't . . . . what the left hand is doing.
8. I used to play squash three or four times a week, but I just don't have the time now. I still . . . . my hand in by playing occasionally.

"Let me give you a hand."

3: Revision

Complete each idiom with *hand* or *hands*:

1. We're living from . . . . to mouth at the moment.
2. She can turn her . . . . to almost anything.
3. I've got a lot of time on my . . . . at the moment.
4. You can't take the law into your own . . . .
5. I still keep my . . . . in.
6. That shop has changed . . . . again.
7. This information must not fall into the wrong . . . .
8. I've got my . . . . full at the moment.
9. I called the police when things started to get out of . . . .
10. They rejected my idea out of . . . .

Can you turn your hand to painting and decorating? What about cooking?

Unit 33 Head Idioms

1: Literal meanings

Use the following words in the definitions below:

block	*bury*	*examines*
tail	*screw*	*roll*

1. When you are ill, you go to the doctor who . . . . you.
2. Centuries ago, if your head was on the . . . . , it was about to be cut off!
3. Our cat died last week. We decided to . . . . it in the garden.
4. In ten-pin bowling, you have to . . . . the ball down a narrow lane and try to knock over the ten pins.
5. When my dog's happy, he wags his . . . .
6. Make sure you . . . . the top on properly! You don't want the bottle to leak in your luggage.

2: Not off the top of my head

    a. *It's my head that's on the block.*

    b. *A lot of it went right over my head.*

    c. *She's head and shoulders above the rest.*

    d. *I could do it standing on my head.*

    e. *I can't make head nor tail of it.*

    f. *Not off the top of my head.*

    g. *Two heads are better than one.*

    h. *He's got his head in the clouds.*

"He's got his head in the clouds!"

Complete these dialogues using one of the above idioms:

1. Do you know Bill's phone number?
   > . . . . I've got it in my address book.
2. Sorry about the mistakes, but none of them was very serious.
   > That's easy for you to say, but . . . . , not yours!
3. He's a typical teenager. No sense of responsibility. He thinks he'll walk into a job.
   > I know. . . . . most of the time.
4. Is it difficult to make a homepage or a website?
   > Not really. I've done so many now . . . .
5. I've read the instruction booklet, but I couldn't understand it.
   > I've looked at it too, and . . . . either!
6. Could you give me a hand with these month-end figures?
   > Good idea. . . . . !
7. Karen Smith is still top of the class this year, isn't she?
   > Yes. . . . .
8. I see you're reading Stephen King's new book.
   > I've just finished it. It's interesting but . . . .

3: Put our heads together

Complete these sentences using the correct form of these verbs:

put	*bury*	*examine*	*go*
keep	*screw*	*roll*	*laugh*

1. I'm sure we can find a solution to this problem if we all . . . . our heads together.
2. The first two years of running this business were very hard. We just about managed to . . . . our heads above water.
3. This is a problem we have to face. We can't . . . . our heads in the sand and hope it will go away.
4. If you think I'm going to lend you money again, you need your head . . . .
5. The trouble with some politicians is, after a while power . . . . to their heads and they think they can do anything.
6. It's the funniest film I've seen for ages. I . . . . my head off.
7. When I find out who is responsible for this mistake, heads will . . . .
8. You don't need to worry about Marco travelling alone. He's only sixteen but he's got his head . . . . on. He'll be OK.

4: Rewrite

Rewrite these sentences using an idiom from this unit:

1. I can do it very, very easily.

. . . .

2. He's sensible.

. . . .

3. Stop ignoring the problem.

. . . .

4. I couldn't understand it.

. . . .

5. We're surviving.

. . . .

6. You're stupid.

. . . .

5: Revision

Look back at the idioms in this unit and complete these expressions:

1. keep our heads . . . . . . water
2. power has gone . . . . . . her head
3. can't make head nor tail . . . . . . it
4. head and shoulders . . . . . . the rest
5. bury your head . . . . . . the sand
6. went right . . . . . . my head
7. got his head screwed . . . . . .
8. laughed my head . . . . . .
9. . . . . . . the top of my head
10. my head's . . . . . . the block

Have you ever read anything which went right over your head?

Unit 34 | Heart Idioms

1: Literal meanings

The heart has always been seen as one of the most important organs in the body – perhaps the most important.

1. Heart as centre

For centuries the heart was seen as the centre of the body. We can talk about living in *the heart of the city* or going out into *the heart of the countryside.* We even talk about *the heart of the matter* when discussing an issue of some kind.

2. Heart as seat of the emotions

This was a popular idea at one time. We talk about *heart-felt* thanks. We describe a very generous person as having *a heart of gold* while someone who is very unemotional has *a heart of stone.* If we see something very tragic, we say *it would break your heart.* We describe someone who has just lost a husband or child as *heart-broken.*

2: My heart sank

Use these verbs to complete the following:

lose	*set*	*break*
take	*sank*	*have*

1. My heart . . . . when I saw how much washing up there was in the kitchen.
2. My English teacher is awful. She corrects every little mistake I make and she gets very impatient if I don't know the answers. I'm starting to . . . . heart.
3. My sister's only six but she's . . . . her heart on becoming a ballet dancer.
4. I know you're disappointed but you can . . . . heart from the fact that most people in Britain fail their driving test first time.

"I didn't have the heart to say no!"

5. Simon asked if he could play the piano at the wedding. I know he's not very good but I didn't . . . . the heart to say no.
6. My car has finally come to the end of its life. I've had it for 20 years. It'll . . . . my heart to say goodbye to it.

3: Close to my heart

Use the following idiomatic expressions in the sentences below:

a. *in my heart of hearts*
b. *close to my heart*
c. *had a change of heart*
d. *after my own heart*
e. *best interests at heart*

f. *heart's in the right place*
g. *got a heart of gold*
h. *heart's not in it*
i. *learn things by heart*
j. *heart-to-heart*

1. John, you're interested in Third World problems, aren't you?
   > Yes, it's a subject which has always been. . . . .
2. My mother is a great help to us. And she does so much for her neighbours as well.
   > Yes, people are always saying she's . . . .
3. I've decided to give up my piano lessons. I just don't seem to be getting anywhere.
   > Well, there's no point continuing if your. . . . .
4. So, the job in America came to nothing. Are you disappointed?
   > Not really. . . . . , I didn't really want to leave Britain.
5. Why are Tom and Julie going back to Australia? I thought they were going to stay for another six months.
   > That was the plan but they've . . . . They're homesick.
6. I don't know about you, but I find Terry difficult, to say the least!
   > Well, he can be a bit rude, but basically his. . . . .
7. What languages did you study at school?
   > Only French. It was so boring. We just had to . . . . –
   verb tables and stuff like that.
8. I like most sports really – especially rugby.
   > Ah! A man . . . . ! I really love rugby!
9. Where's Lisa? She's not at her desk.
   > No, she's in David's office. They're having a . . . . about her future.
10. I don't know if you realise how demanding you can be.
    > Yes, I know I'm tough, but please believe I have your . . . .

4: Prepositions

Look back at the idioms in this unit and add the missing prepositions:

1. learn something . . . . . heart
2. . . . . . . my heart of hearts
3. a heart . . . . . gold
4. my heart wasn't . . . . . it

5. a man . . . . . my own heart
6. a change . . . . . heart
7. a subject close . . . . . my heart
8. his heart's . . . . . the right place

Do you know someone – a friend or neighbour – who has a heart of gold?

Unit 35 | Horse Idioms

1: Literal meanings

Fill in the following words in the definitions below:

> *reins   saddle   bit   cart   hooves   hurdles*

1. A farm vehicle pulled by a horse is a . . . .
2. Cats and dogs have paws; horses have . . . .
3. You control a horse by using the . . . .
4. A horse's reins are attached to a . . . . – a small metal bar which goes through the horse's mouth and is used to control it.
5. The fences which horses jump over are called . . . .
6. A horse rider sits on a . . . .

2: On the hoof

Use the following idiomatic expressions in the sentences below:

> **a.** *put the cart before the horse*   **e.** *keep a tight rein*
> **b.** *on the hoof*   **f.** *get saddled with*
> **c.** *the bit between my teeth*   **g.** *horses for courses*
> **d.** *straight from the horse's mouth*   **h.** *put it through its paces*

1. What I don't like about this government is the way it makes up policy . . . . There isn't enough planning.
2. I started a new job last month. It was all a bit strange at first but I've got . . . . now and I'm starting to enjoy it.
3. You can buy a computer for as little as £600 or as much as £3000. It depends what you need it for. It's a case of . . . .
4. I hate going to the airport to meet international clients but I always . . . . it because I'm the one who can speak three foreign languages.
5. Listen, Jane, do you really think buying a wedding dress is a good idea? I mean, why not wait till he asks you? Aren't you . . . . ?
6. I've just got my credit card bill. It's enormous. I'm going to have to . . . . on my spending for a while.
7. Believe it or not, we're all getting a pay rise next month. And it's not just a rumour. I got it . . . . Kate told me herself.
8. I hear you've just splashed out on a new car. Have you been out on the motorway yet to . . . . ?

"Mr Harbottle always gets saddled with the job of meeting our international clients."

3: A one-horse race

Put the following words in the sentences below:

dead   **wild**   **one**   **dark**   **high**   **wrong**

1. Manchester United are now nine points clear at the top of the Premier League. It's turning into a . . . .-horse race.
2. There's no point asking the finance department to extend our budget. You're flogging a . . . . . . horse. They'll never change their minds.
3. Just because you've been to university and I haven't, you think you can get on your . . . . . . horse every time we discuss something. Well, you're wrong!
4. Nobody really knows a lot about the Polish team. They are the . . . . . . horse in this World Cup.
5. I don't know why you go to discos. You can't have a conversation and they're full of smoke and sweaty bodies. . . . . horses couldn't drag me into one of those places.
6. If you think Johnson is going to become Director General, you're backing the . . . . . . horse. I reckon it's going to be Robert Newman.

4: Hold your horses!

Complete the dialogues by adding these expressions:

     a. horsing around   **c. hold your horses**   **e. fell at the first hurdle**
     b. eat a horse   **d. hand the reins over**

1. Look at these blank videos. Ten for £5! Let's get twenty of them.
   > . . . . ! They might be useless.
2. So, you've decided to take early retirement, Jim?
   > Yes, I've been manager here for twenty years now. It's time to . . . .
   . . . . to someone younger.
3. Are you hungry?
   > Yes. I could . . . . !
4. Was your idea accepted by the meeting?
   > No, there was a legal objection. I'm afraid it . . . .
5. Jane, put these eggs in the fridge, will you. Here . . . catch!
   > Stop . . . . , Jim. You're going to break something.

5: Revision

Look back at the idioms in this unit and add the missing prepositions:

1. keep a tight rein . . . . costs
2. got the bit . . . . my teeth
3. horses . . . . courses
4. putting the cart . . . . the horse
5. . . . . the hoof
6. straight . . . . the horse's mouth
7. get saddled . . . . a job
8. fall . . . . the first hurdle
9. put it . . . . its paces
10. don't get . . . . your high horse

What kind of jobs do you get saddled with at home?

Unit 36 House and Home Idioms

1: Literal and non-literal meanings

Match the idiomatic expressions on the left with the non-idiomatic equivalents on the right:

1. We got on like a house on fire.
2. She's nothing to write home about.
3. It's as safe as houses.
4. It really brought it home to me.
5. He brought the house down.
6. We did it in-house.
7. They ate us out of house and home.
8. Put your own house in order.

a. Sort out your own problems first.
b. We liked each other a lot.
c. The audience applauded a lot.
d. It made me realise.
e. We had no food left.
f. She's not specially good-looking.
g. It's very safe.
h. We did it ourselves.

2: House or home?

Decide which word – *house* or *home* – correctly completes the idioms below:

1. Hello, Alex. Come in. Make yourself at *house/home*.
2. I met my boyfriend's parents last night for the first time. We spent the evening talking about our love of horses. We got on like a *house/home* on fire.
3. The number one priority of the new Party Leader must be to put his party's *house/home* in order after all the scandals of last year.
4. It wasn't until I got home and sat down that the news about my job really hit *house/home*. Twenty-five years in the same factory and now it's closing.
5. What are we going to do with all these old files? We've got to keep them for legal reasons. Where are we going to find a *house/home* for them in the office?

"Now, Miranda, it's time for a few home truths. If you think I'm your servant, you're mistaken."

6. My flatmate never cleans or does the dishes. I think I'm going to have to tell her a few *house/home* truths.
7. I've just got one more exam to pass on my law course and then I'll be *house/home* and dry. I can't wait!
8. Look, we can't afford to go to an advertising agency. They cost the earth! Can you find someone who can design the adverts *in-house/in-home*?
9. Her performance was superb and really brought the *house/home* down.
10. This might look dangerous, but I can assure you it's as safe as *houses/homes*.

3: Home from home

Fill in the following words and expressions in the dialogues below:

a.	*house and home*	**e.**	*no-one at home*
b.	*write home*	**f.**	*come home*
c.	*home from home*	**g.**	*brought home*
d.	*a good home*	**h.**	*the home straight*

1. You always stay in the same place when you go on holiday, don't you?
   > Yes. The same hotel in Venice every year. It's a real . . . . for us.
2. My brother and his family came to stay with us at Christmas. They nearly ate us out of . . . . We spent a fortune on food.
3. Larry likes to talk, doesn't he? It's sometimes difficult to shut him up.
   > Yes. He'll sit and talk until the cows . . . . if you let him.
4. Pam can be a bit slow sometimes. I often have to explain things three times.
   > I know what you mean. I don't like saying this, but sometimes it seems as if the lights are on but there's . . . .
5. Have you seen Christine's new boyfriend? What's he like?
   > Well, he's OK, I suppose. But nothing to . . . . about.
6. We must've picked enough strawberries by now – surely?
   > Come on. We only need a few more kilos. We're on . . . . now.
7. I wish I knew somebody who would give my old music centre . . . .
8. I didn't use to worry about having a beer or two, but last year a friend of mine had the most terrible car accident. It really . . . . to me the reality of drinking and driving.

4: Revision

Look back at the idioms in this unit and add the final words:

1. We got on like a house on . . . .
2. He'll stay chatting till the cows come . . . .
3. I told him a few home . . . .
4. He needs to put his house in . . . .
5. It took a few days for the news to really hit . . . .
6. He's eating us out of house and . . . .
7. Her last song brought the house . . . .
8. It was nothing to write home . . . .
9. The lights are on but no-one's at . . . .
10. We're on the home . . . .

Is there anywhere you visit which is a real home from home for you?

Unit 37 Life and Death Idioms

1: Literal meanings

Fill in the following words in the definitions below:

lease	*soul*	*warm up*	*kiss*
fate	*dice*	*misery*	

1. In some countries, it is normal to . . . . friends and family members on both cheeks when you meet.
2. If you rent a house or flat, the contract you sign is called a . . . .
3. The spiritual part of a person is sometimes called the . . . .
4. The power which some people believe controls destiny is called . . . .
5. Suffering and discomfort cause . . . .
6. A small wooden or plastic cube with dots, used in games, is called a . . . .
7. You need to . . . . your food, if it goes cold before you have finished it.

2: Bored to death

Choose which word, *life* or *death*, completes the idioms below:

a. *sick to . . . .*
b. *frightened the . . . . out of me*
c. *a new lease of . . . .*
d. *for the . . . . of me*
e. *a fate worse than . . . .*
f. *the . . . . and soul of the party*
g. *dicing with . . . .*
h. *bored to . . . .*
i. *like . . . . warmed up*
j. *to save his . . . .*

"Miss Fotheringham is always the life and soul of the office Christmas party."

Now use the expressions in these sentences:

1. All Mark talked about the whole evening was football! I was . . . .
2. Please be quiet. I'm . . . . of your constant complaining.
3. Taking up golf since I retired has given me . . . .
4. I hope I don't have to sit next to Nigel at the wedding. That would be . . . . He's the most boring person I know.
5. You should get the brakes fixed on your car. You're . . . . every time you go out on the road.
6. I remember his face but . . . . I can't remember his name.
7. Are you ill? You look . . . .
8. Hello? Who's there? Is someone there? Oh, it's you, Joe. You . . . . I thought you were a burglar.
9. My husband? Cook? You must be joking. He can't cook . . . .
10. My sister is normally quite shy but when she has a couple of drinks she's . . . .

3: The kiss of death

Put *life* or *death* into the conversations below:

1. We've decided to have the picnic on Sunday. The weather forecast is good for then.
   > The weather forecast is good? Well, that's the kiss of . . . . The forecast is always wrong.
2. Why did you leave your last job? Did you just want a change?
   > No, it was my boss. For some reason she didn't like me. She made my . . . . a misery.
3. Right, I'm off. See you later.
   > Why aren't you wearing a coat? It's freezing out there. You'll catch your . . . . . . of cold.
4. So, you met my colleague Tony yesterday.
   > Yes, he was a lot of fun. He's a real larger than . . . . character, isn't he?
5. Did you know that Alan collects cigarette packets? He's got hundreds of them.
   > Yes, I know. It's sad, isn't it? He really needs to get a . . . .
6. I'm pleased to hear your father's out of hospital. That's good news.
   > Yes, considering he was at . . . . 's door only last month he's made a remarkable recovery.

4: Rewrite

What expression would you use in the following situations? Use the words in brackets:

1. Your friend looks very ill. *(You, warmed up)*

   . . . .

2. Your friend is taking a dangerous risk. *(You're dicing)*

   . . . .

3. A friend of yours can't sing at all. *(She, save)*

   . . . .

4. A new hobby has made your life better. *(It's, lease)*

   . . . .

5: Revision

Look back at the idioms in this unit and add the missing words:

1. a . . . . . . worse than death
2. like death . . . . up
3. to . . . . . . his life
4. . . . . my life a misery
5. the life and . . . . . . of the party
6. at death's . . . .
7. larger than . . . .
8. the . . . . of death
9. you'll . . . . your death
10. . . . . the life out of me

What sort of things bore you to death? Would your friends call you the life and soul of the party?

Unit 38 | Metal Idioms

1: Gold

When you celebrate your golden wedding, you have been married for 50 years. Because gold is one of the most precious metals, there are quite a few idiomatic expressions containing it. Use the following expressions in the situations below:

a. *a golden handshake*   d. *the golden age*   g. *the golden boy*

b. *worth her weight in gold*   e. *the golden rule*   h. *struck gold*

c. *a golden opportunity*   f. *like gold dust*   i. *as good as gold*

1. I wish I had a secretary like yours, Jeff. She's got everything so well organised.
   > I know. She's . . . .
2. Thanks for looking after the children. It's been such a help. Have they behaved?
   > No problem at all. They were . . . .
3. Do you know if there are any tickets for the England-France match?
   > I doubt it. They're . . . .
4. I sometimes wonder if I have any idea how to run a business!
   > Well, you know . . . . – delegate!
5. For six years he could do no wrong – successful, popular, and in the papers almost every day. He was . . . . of British athletics.
6. I've got a chance to go on a training course in the States.
   > Take it. You won't get the chance again. It's . . . .
7. Did they organise a big party when you retired?
   No party, not even . . . . , nothing! Never work for the state!
8. Hitchcock, the Marx Brothers, Charlie Chaplin, 'Gone with the Wind' – I don't think there's much doubt that . . . . of the cinema was before the days of television.
9. Sandra's been a terrific success. We really . . . . when we recruited her.

Note: When gold is found, the small pieces are called 'nuggets'. We also talk about a *nugget of (valuable) information.*

2: Silver

When you have been married for 25 years, you celebrate your silver wedding anniversary. Choose the explanation which best fits these two idioms:

1. Every cloud has a silver lining.
   a. There's always a good side to a bad situation.
   b. When the weather is bad, there's usually good weather on the way.
2. He was born with a silver spoon in his mouth.
   a. He has a very peculiar accent.
   b. He's always had everything he wanted.

Note: A *'silver-tongued'* person can persuade you to do almost anything. Film stars are sometimes called *'stars of the silver screen'.*

3: Iron, steel, brass, lead

Choose one of the above metals in these expressions:

a. *rule with an . . . . fist*

b. *get down to . . . . tacks*

c. *have nerves of . . . .*

d. *pump . . . .*

e. *rule with a rod of . . . .*

f. *go down like a . . . . balloon*

g. *as bold as . . . .*

h. *had the . . . . neck*

*"When a friend advised Terence to start
pumping iron, he took them literally!"*

Now use the expressions in these sentences:

1. Look at that man working up there on that roof. I can't even bear to look at him!
   > He must . . . . to do a job like that.
2. The thing about Tito was he ruled Yugoslavia with an . . . .
   That's how he kept the country together.
3. What's your boss like? I've heard he's quite tough.
   > Not half! He rules the whole place with a . . . .
4. Let's . . . . ! How much money are
   you offering?
5. I don't know how he . . . . to ask for a rise after
   the mistakes he's made this year.
6. What did your colleagues think of your idea of giving up a day's pay for charity?
   > Not much. It went . . . . , to be honest.
7. I couldn't believe my ears! Sheila just walked straight up to the boss, ...
   . . . . , and said, "OK, I saw you dent my car in the car park. What
   are you going to do about it?"
8. He goes down the gym at least twice a week to . . . .

**Note: The best kind of guarantee you can get is a 'copper-bottomed' guarantee.
A 'tin-pot' dictator thinks he is very important, but isn't.**

4: Revision

Fill in the metal in these phrases:

1. . . . . . . dust
2. the . . . . . . rule
3. a . . . . . . spoon
4. a . . . . . . opportunity
5. a . . . . . . of iron
6. an . . . . . . fist
7. . . . . . . tacks
8. the . . . . . . neck
9. nerves of . . . . . .
10. a . . . . . . handshake

Have you ever been in a situation where you needed nerves of steel?

Unit 39 Mind Idioms

1: I'll bear that in mind

Put the following words and expressions into the dialogues below.

a. *I've got a good mind to*
b. *peace of mind*
c. *springs to mind*
d. *I'll bear that in mind*

e. *something on his mind*
f. *give her a piece of my mind*
g. *take your mind off things*
h. *the thought never crossed my mind*

1. If the Johnsons invite you for dinner, don't take any wine. They're teetotal.
   > Are they? Thanks. . . . .
2. Do you think I really need holiday insurance? It's only a weekend in Brussels.
   > I would get it if I were you. If only for . . . .
3. The service in that shop was terrible. The way that assistant talked to you!
   > Yes, ... write and complain.
4. Jim seems to be very quiet today. He's not his usual self.
   > No, I think he's got . . . .
5. Sorry, Paul, I'm not very good company this evening. I can't stop thinking about that argument I had with Sally at work.
   > Well, why don't we go out? It'll . . . .
6. Did you see that woman hit that little girl?
   > Hang on! I'm going to . . . . !
   Just be careful what you say! You could make things worse.
7. Why didn't you go to university? You had the qualifications, after all.
   > . . . . I just wanted to get a job.
8. Now, who could we get to chair the new committee?
   > Nobody . . . . ,
   I'm sorry to say.

2: Never mind!

Complete these short dialogues using the following lines:

a. *Never mind.*
b. *Are you out of your mind?*
c. *I'm in two minds about it.*
d. *Mind your own business!*

"Nobody's name springs to mind. What about you, Mr Peabody?"

1. I couldn't get your paper. The shops were closed.
   > . . . .
2. Who was that letter from?
   > . . . .
3. I'm fed up with the rat race! I'm giving up my job and going to live in India.
   > . . . .
4. I see they're advertising the Head's job. Are you thinking of applying?
   > . . . .

3: A weight off my mind

Fill in the following idiomatic expressions in the sentences below:

a. *mind over matter*
b. *it's all in his mind*
c. *a weight off my mind*
d. *put your mind at rest*
e. *slipped my mind*

f. *bored out of my mind*
g. *put your mind to it*
h. *with an open mind*
i. *in their right mind*
j. *make up my mind*

1. I've finally finished paying back my car loan. That's . . . .
2. Of course you can get a grade A – if you . . . .
3. Strawberry? No, vanilla! Wait! Oh dear! I can't . . . .
4. Before you read this report, I'm going to tell you there are things in it which you are going to disagree with. All I ask is that you read it . . . .
5. Giving up smoking is just a question of . . . .
6. I'm sure she's arrived safely, but why not phone her to . . . .
7. She talked about nothing but her family all evening. I was . . . .
8. Stuart thinks there's something serious wrong with him, but if you want my opinion, ...
9. I'm sorry, I forgot to give you a message. It completely . . . .
10. Marry Karl? She's mad. Nobody . . . . would marry Karl.

4: Revision

Look back over the exercises in this unit and find 6 idioms with these meanings:

1. *forgot* . . . . . . my . . . . . .
2. *concentrate* put your mind . . . . . . something
3. *not sane* not . . . . . . your . . . . mind
4. *decide* . . . . your . . . . . .
5. *say exactly what you think* . . . . . . someone a . . . . your mind
6. *be worried* have something . . . . . . your mind

Now add the missing prepositions:

7. peace . . . . . . mind
8. take your mind . . . . . . things
9. bored . . . . . . of my mind
10. in two minds . . . . . . something
11. put your mind . . . . . . rest
12. nobody . . . . . . their right mind

13. got a lot . . . . . . my mind
14. give him a piece . . . . . . my mind
15. it's all . . . . . . the mind
16. a weight . . . . . . my mind
17. springs . . . . . . mind
18. can't make . . . . . . my mind

What could you do that would really improve your life if you put your mind to it?

Unit 40 | Number Idioms

1: Numbers

There are some idioms where the numbers are obvious. Can you complete these expressions?

a. Two's company, ... a crowd!
b. Two heads are better than . . . .
c. You've got a . . . . . .-track mind!
d. Might as well kill . . . . . birds with . . . . . . stone.
e. I'm in . . . . . . minds about it.
f. I put two and . . . . . . together.
g. It takes . . . . . . to tango.
h. It's first come, ... served.
i. It was . . . . . . of one and half a dozen of the other.
j. Once bitten, ... shy.

Use the above as responses in the following situations:

1. How did you know I sent the valentine?
   > . . . .
2. I'll pick the dry-cleaning up when I take your mother home.
   Yes, ...
3. Why don't I come with you and Mary?
   No, no, ...
4. So, are you going to buy that flat?
   I'm not sure yet. . . . .
5. I've been trying all morning to find the mistake in the figures.
   Perhaps I can help. . . . .
6. Can members get tickets before the general public?
   No, I'm afraid . . . .
7. I thought you would be desperate to find another boyfriend?
   Not at the moment. . . . .
8. Who was to blame – John or Ken?
   . . . .
9. I'm hungry. Shall we stop for something to eat?
   > Already! It's less than two hours since we finished lunch. . . . .
   . . . .
10. Mary blames John and he blames her, and I must say I think he's right.
    Well, these things are never one person's fault. . . . .

2: Not in a million years!

Complete these four sentences with *million* or *thousand(s)*:

1. I wouldn't have thought he would have behaved so badly – not him – not in a
   . . . . years!
2. I believe you! . . . . wouldn't!
3. Thank you for the flowers. You're one in a . . . . !
4. Now, who is going to replace him? That is the 64- . . . . dollar question!

3: Third time lucky

Use the following idiomatic expressions in the sentences below:

a. *I'm all at sixes and sevens.*
b. *It knocked me for six.*
c. *at the eleventh hour*
d. *I was in seventh heaven!*
e. *He's on cloud nine.*
f. *Third time lucky!*
g. *ten a penny*
h. *It's second to none.*
i. *I'm having second thoughts.*
j. *We're back to square one.*

1. I've failed twice before, but my driving instructor's sure I can do it next time. You know what they say: . . . .
2. Are you ready? The taxi will be here in five minutes.
   > No. I've lost my keys and I can't find my credit card. . . . .
3. I split up with my boyfriend last night. He was so selfish. I hope I never see him again.
   > I never liked him. Men like him, are . . . . , anyway.
4. I'm so sorry to hear about your job. When did they tell you?
   > Only last week. I just wasn't expecting it. It completely. . . . .
5. At first I was sure it was a good idea, but now . . . .
6. I've just phoned some shops and nobody sells that colour of paint any more so we'll have to find another colour. We're . . . .
7. His book's going to be made into a film, so he's on . . . . at the moment.
8. Where's James? We're due to leave in 10 minutes.
   Oh, don't worry. He'll be here at one minute to 9. He always arrives . . . .
9. She's been invited over to Hollywood, so you can imagine she's in . . . .
10. Have you tried this 50-year-old malt? . . . . !

4: Once

All the following phrases contain *once*. Put the words in the correct order:

1. lifetime a in once   . . . .
2. once all and for   . . . .
3. twice or once   . . . .
4. enough is once   . . . .
5. blue once moon a in   . . . .
6. once while a in   . . . .

5: Revision

Look back at the idioms in this unit and add the missing numbers:

1. Back to square . . . .
2. I put . . . . and . . . . together.
3. . . . . 's company, ... 's a crowd.
4. . . . . come, ... served.
5. . . . . bitten, ... shy.
6. I'm all at . . . . and . . . .
7. It knocked me for . . . .
8. They're. . . . . . . a penny.
9. I'm on cloud . . . .
10. It takes . . . . to tango.

Are you always well-prepared or do you leave things till the eleventh hour?

Unit 4 Sports idioms

1: Boxing idioms

There are lots of idioms based on boxing. Use each of these nouns to complete the expressions below:

towel   **bell**   **belt**   **ropes**   **punches**

1. If I take an unfair advantage of you, you could say: That was below the . . . .
2. If I tell you what I think very directly, I won't pull my . . . .
3. If you are in a difficult situation, you can say you're on the . . . .
4. If you are in a difficult situation but you get out of it at the last minute, you can say: Saved by the . . . .
5. If you keep trying to do something but don't succeed and decide it's not worth continuing, you can throw in the . . . .

2: A level playing field

Use the following idiomatic expressions in the situations below:

   a. *keep moving the goalposts*   f. *touch base*
   b. *a level playing field*   g. *neck and neck*
   c. *back the wrong horse*   h. *a major player*
   d. *par for the course*   i. *keep (people) onside*
   e. *horses for courses*   j. *heavyweight*

1. Joining the European Union was supposed to guarantee a . . . . for us. But lower taxes in some continental countries still make it difficult for us to compete.
2. You've been saying Arsenal all season, but United are champions. It looks as if you . . . . , this time.
3. Hello, Dolly. I haven't seen you for a while and I'm going to be in Cambridge on Thursday so I thought I might look in and . . . . Is that convenient?
4. We can't just use one lawyer. It's . . . . We need somebody to do our own contracts of employment and a specialist to deal with the European contracts.
5. The BBC hope to become a . . . . in digital television.
6. Arsenal and Manchester United are still . . . . at the top of the league with only two games to go.
7. Head Office told us we had to achieve an 8% increase. We do what they ask and, guess what, they . . . . Now they want 12%.
8. The British, Americans and the French are all in agreement, but in a situation like this, everyone knows how important it is to keep the Russians . . . .
9. There is strong opposition to the policy from a number of . . . . politicians, including the former Prime Minister.
10. I see Jeff's off ill again.
    > Well, that's . . . . , isn't it? Two Fridays every month on average.

Note: In an informal meeting you can say: *Shall we kick off by looking at this month's figures?* **If Tony wins an argument you can say:** *Game, set and match to Tony!*

3: The ball's in your court

Use these expressions containing the word *ball* **in the situations below:**

    a. *drop the ball*
    b. *on the ball*
    c. *play ball*
    d. *we're in a whole new ball game*
    e. *the ball's in your court*
    f. *run with the ball*

1. I think we should go ahead; I've done everything I promised I would, so now
   . . . .
2. Bob seems to know everything that's going on round here. He's . . . . ,
isn't he?
3. This is a fantastic opportunity. If the sales team . . . . , we'll make a
lot of money.
4. If the Sales Director had dealt with it himself, everything would probably have
been all right but he sent his assistant instead and he . . . .
5. We want to expand the business and take on more staff but we need the help of
the bank and they are refusing to . . . .
6. Since the collapse of communism, there have been major changes in the political
situation. . . . . , in fact.

Note: If someone asks, *"What's the score?"* **they mean,** *What's the present situation?* **It is difficult to play cricket if the pitch** *(wicket)* **is wet** *(sticky)*, **so if someone talks about a** *sticky wicket*, **they mean a difficult situation.**

> "The committee of EU finance ministers has for months been discussing how to create a level playing field for taxation across Europe."
>
> *Newspaper report*

4: Revision

Look back at the idioms in this unit and add the missing words:

1. the ball's in your . . . .
2. keep moving the . . . .
3. throw in the . . . .
4. a . . . . new ball game
5. . . . . for the course

6. touch . . . .
7. neck and . . . .
8. . . . . for courses
9. . . . . your punches
10. saved by the . . . . !

Do you feel on the ball right now?

Unit 42 | Swimming Idioms

1: Literal meanings

Fill in the following words in the definitions below:

sank	*tide*	*deep*	*crest*
drown	*depth*	*tread*	*sorrows*

1. The Titanic . . . . after hitting an iceberg.
2. The . . . . comes in and goes out twice every day.
3. If something is very . . . . , it is of great . . . .
4. The top of a wave is its . . . .
5. If you fall into the sea and you cannot swim, don't panic, just do your best to . . . . water. Otherwise, you might . . . . !
6. Things you feel sad about are your . . . .

> "In an interview yesterday, Tony Blair began to swim with the current of public opposition to the single currency."
>
> *Newspaper leader article*

2: Out of my depth

Put the following expressions into the sentences below:

a. *thrown in at the deep end*
b. *swimming against the tide*
c. *keep our heads above water*
d. *going under*
e. *out of my depth*
f. *in deep water*
g. *on the crest of a wave*
h. *drowned our sorrows*

1. The French class I'm going to is far too difficult for me. I'm completely . . . . I think I need to go down a level.
2. With their new album going straight to number one in the US charts, Oasis have been . . . . for a while now.
3. I didn't get any training when I started work here. I was just . . . . and expected to get on with it.
4. My wife's just lost her job. If we're careful with money, we should just about be able to . . . .
5. You'll have to agree in the end. You can't go on . . . . for much longer.
6. If the recession continues for much longer, a lot of small businesses are in real danger of . . . .
7. When we lost to Brazil, we just found the nearest pub and . . . .
8. I've got some terrible news. Bill's son has just been arrested. He's been involved with some pretty shady business deals. He's . . . . − and he's in right up to his neck.

3: Make a splash

Add the following verbs in the correct form in the sentences below:

throw	*drown out*	*dive*	*sink*
make	*test*	*swim*	*tread*

1. If you really want to . . . . a splash with your new book, you'll have to throw a few parties and give away a few thousand copies to the right people.
2. You said you rang five minutes ago. I'm afraid there's a lot of workmen around the office this morning. The noise they're making must've . . . . the sound of the phone.
3. I wish someone would . . . . me a lifeline! With a loan of a couple of thousand pounds I could just about get myself out of trouble.
4. I think it would be a good idea to . . . . the waters first before we spend any more money on the project.
5. We've been told we've got six months to turn the company around and make a profit. If things haven't improved, the whole thing is being closed down. So, it's a . . . . or . . . . situation.
6. Don't you think too many young people today . . . . straight into relationships without really thinking about what they are doing?
7. I don't think I'm ever going to get promoted here. My job hasn't changed for three years and I'm bored. I feel as if I've been . . . . water.

"Oh, Reginald, how are we going to keep our heads above water?
> It's the other bits I'm worried about, Cynthia!"

4: Revision

Look back at the idioms in this unit and add the missing words:

1. in at the deep . . . .
2. keeping our heads above . . . .
3. throw someone a . . . .
4. . . . . or swim
5. swimming against the . . . .
6. in deep . . . .
7. out of my . . . .
8. . . . . your sorrows
9. . . . . a splash
10. on the crest of a . . . .

Have you ever been thrown in at the deep end in a new job? Did you sink or swim?

Unit 43 Temperature Idioms

1: Cold, cool, and frosty idioms

**Complete these idiomatic expressions
with the words given:**

reception	*cucumber*
water	*feet*
lost	*out*
light	*left*
blood	*cool*

> "Bad language lands canoeist in hot water."
>
> *Newspaper headline*

a. got cold . . . . . .

b. . . . . . . me cold

c. . . . . . . my cool

d. frosty . . . . . .

e. in cold . . . . . .

f. as cool as a . . . . . .

g. in the cold . . . . . . of day

h. poured cold . . . . . . on it

i. . . . . in the cold

j. keep . . . . . .

Now put the above idioms into these dialogues:

1. During the apartheid years South African sportsmen were left . . . . because most countries refused to have anything to do with their teams.
2. Now that you've had time to think about it, what are you going to do?
   Well, I suppose . . . ., I ought to go back home and try and find a job there. There's nothing here for me.
3. I'll murder him! How dare he talk to me like that!
   > . . . . ! Losing your temper won't help. Now tell me what the problem is.
4. You don't look very happy. What's wrong?
   > I just presented my plan for the new office to the rest of the staff, but they all . . . . They didn't like it at all.
5. Did you hear the news? A policeman has been murdered in the town centre.
   > Yes, he was killed . . . . in front of a crowd of shoppers.
6. I see that play you went to see got a marvellous review in the paper.
   > You're joking! I'm amazed. I'm afraid it . . . .
7. Katy's amazing. She always seems calm and in control. The exact opposite of me.
   > I know what you mean. She's always . . . .
8. So, you've met Brian's parents at last! How did you get on?
   > Well, her mother gave me a fairly . . . . at first, but I think she warmed to me. She's just a bit worried that I'm twelve years older than him.
9. Why did you have a fight with Robert?
   > Well, he started saying really stupid things about the Irish. I just got so angry with him. I suppose I . . . .
10. The poor girl was left standing there at the altar! Why didn't you come?
    > I thought about it and decided I just wasn't ready to get married. I . . . .
    . . . .

Note: A liquid which is neither hot nor cold is 'lukewarm' or 'tepid'. If you visit somebody or make a suggestion and other people are not enthusiastic, you can talk about *a lukewarm reception* or *a tepid response*.

2: A hot potato

Fill in the following words and expressions in the sentences below:

  a. *a heated discussion*
  b. *a hot potato*
  c. *hot under the collar*
  d. *into hot water*
  e. *in the hot seat*
  f. *in the heat of the moment*
  g. *warmed to him*
  h. *hot off the press*
  i. *selling like hot cakes*
  j. *a hot-bed*

1. Does anybody know when our contracts are going to be renewed?
   > Nothing's been said. Nobody wants to ask. It's a bit of a . . . .
2. What you said yesterday was unfair and unkind. In fact, it really hurt. I've been very upset about it and couldn't sleep.
   > I'm really sorry. I didn't mean it. I just said it . . . .
3. Were you and Jo having an argument last night? It seemed a bit aggressive!
   > Oh no. We were just having . . . . about politics. That's all.
4. I'm thinking of getting one of the VWs.
   > I hear they're . . . .
5. I've just been made chairman.
   > Well, rather you than me . . . . !
6. I'm glad I don't work at Reception.
   > No, from what I've heard it's . . . . of gossip!
7. Hey Rachel, I hear you met my brother on Friday. He seemed to approve of you!
   > Yes, he's really nice. I . . . . straightaway.
8. That's the third person trying to sell me insurance on the phone this week!
   > That's nothing to get so . . . . about. Just hang up.
9. What I like about Kirsty is she's not afraid to say what she thinks.
   > That's very true. But she gets herself . . . . sometimes!
10. Have our new catalogues arrived yet?
   > Here's the first one . . . .

Note: If your English is 'not all that hot', it is not very good. Someone who is 'hot-tempered' gets angry very easily. Spicy food, for example curry or chilli, is called 'hot' – "This vindaloo is too hot for my taste."

3: Revision

Choose the correct word in the sentences below:

1. He's as *cool/warm* as a cucumber. Nothing upsets him.
2. His speech got a very *lukewarm/tepid* reception.
3. My views occasionally get me into *hot/cold* water but it doesn't bother me.
4. They poured *hot/cold* water on my idea. Naturally I was very disappointed.
5. I got *cold/warm* feet at the last minute. I just wasn't ready to do it.
6. Stop getting so *warm/hot* under the collar. We've got plenty of time.
7. Contracts are a *hot/warm* potato around here at the moment.
8. In the *warm/cold* light of day, I can see it was a mistake. Sorry.

Do you always keep cool or do you sometimes say something in the heat of the moment which you regret later?

Unit 44 Train Idioms

1: Literal meanings

Underline the words in the following which are used to talk about railway trains:

Trains run on railway tracks which are made up of rails. Trains cannot climb hills easily, so in the past tunnels had to be built through hills and mountains. If a train is derailed, it comes off the rails. At the end of a railway line, usually in a station, are buffers. Sometimes, if a train does not stop in time, it hits the buffers. The first trains were steam trains, but today they are more likely to be diesel or electric. Very fast trains are called express trains.

2: Hit the buffers

Use some of the words you have underlined above to complete these idioms:

a. *light at the end of the . . . . . .*
b. *a one-. . . . . . mind*
c. *under my own . . . . . .*
d. *hit the . . . . . .*
e. *ran out of . . . . . .*
f. *right off the . . . . . .*
g. *back on . . . . . .*
h. *let off . . . . . .*
i. *on the right . . . . . .*
j. *like an . . . . . . train*

"I may be on the right track, but I've just run out of steam!"

Now use these idioms in the following situations which show their meaning:

1. The Government's first two years were very successful, but then everything seemed to hit . . . .
2. I don't need a lift, thanks. I'll get there . . . .
3. We want to design an affordable, eco-friendly car. There are one or two serious problems, but basically we're . . . .
4. Our business has had a very difficult two years but things are slowly beginning to improve. There's . . . .
5. The Conservatives lost the election. Their campaign started well enough, but it just ran . . . . a week before the actual election.
6. Since his wife left him, Mark's lost his job and he's drinking heavily. He's really gone . . . .

7. How was your night out with Jerry?
   > Terrible! All he talked about was steam trains. He's got a . . . . mind!
8. Do you fancy a game of squash tonight, Tim?
   > Good idea. I need to do something to . . . . I'm really tense. I've had a very difficult week at work.
9. How are things at work after the fire?
   > It's taken us three months to sort things out, but everything's . . . . now.
10. Did you see the match last night? What about that goal just before half-time?
    > He's incredible. He's . . . . When he gets the ball there's no stopping him!

Note: When two groups are negotiating and something goes badly wrong, we often say that *the talks were derailed.*

3: The end of the line

Line is a common word in several idioms. Use these expressions in the situations below:

> a. *down the line*
> b. *the end of the line*
> c. *somewhere along the line*
> d. *all along the line*

1. So, are we going to give Roger another chance?
   > He's already had 5 warnings about being late. I think we've reached . . . . We'll have to ask him to leave.
2. I'm afraid we've never received your cheque.
   > It's obviously got lost . . . .
3. If you're going to build your own house, make sure you've got the finance organised from the start.
   > Yes, we don't want to have financial problems a couple of months . . . .
4. We've got no alternative but to cancel the new project.
   > I suppose so. We've had so many problems . . . . – since the word go, in fact.

4: Revision

Look back at the idioms in this unit and add the missing words:

1. ran . . . . of steam
2. gone . . . . . . the rails
3. back . . . . . . track
4. the end . . . . . . the line
5. light . . . . . . the end of the tunnel
6. let . . . . . . steam
7. . . . . . . my own steam
8. somewhere . . . . . . the line
9. two months . . . . . . the line
10. . . . . . . the right track

Is your career on the right track? Perhaps you can see problems further down the line?

Unit 45 | Water Idioms

1: Water under the bridge

Match the following idioms containing *water* with the meanings on the right:

1. like a fish out of water	a. get into trouble
2. water under the bridge	b. is not credible
3. keeping our heads above water	c. no effect on me
4. spend money like water	d. just surviving financially
5. land him in hot water	e. feeling strange and out of place
6. like water off a duck's back	f. made less forceful
7. watered down	g. past and forgotten
8. doesn't hold water	h. spend without thinking

Now use these idioms in the following situations:

9. John says the two of you had a serious argument last week.
   > Yes, but that's all . . . . now. We're friends again.
10. Have you found a better job yet, Gary?
   > No, not yet. Money's a bit tight, but we're just about . . . .
11. Why haven't you got a credit card?
   > I know it would just make me . . . .
12. What I like about Philip is he's not afraid to express his opinions.
   > That's all very well, but his opinions often . . . . at work.
13. Were you not upset by all the criticism you got at the meeting?
   > Oh no, I'm used to it. It's just . . . .
14. I thought the Prime Minister's speech was very weak.
   > Yes, I think it had been . . . . to avoid upsetting some people in his party.
15. The only thing which will help the economy is to raise interest rates.
   > But that argument . . . . Higher interest rates are bad for business, not good for it. Listen to the big companies!
16. After the meeting we were taken to one of those big London clubs.
   > I bet you felt . . . . !

2: Sink or swim?

Fill in the following idioms:

sink or swim	*my heart sank*
floating voters	*floated the idea*

1. Right in the middle of the coffee break, Jim . . . . that we should sell the company.
2. Elections aren't decided by people who vote for the same party. It's actually the . . . . who make the difference and elect the Government.
3. When I left school, I got no help from anyone. You just had to . . . . in those days.
4. When I heard about her murder on the evening news, ...

3: All at sea

The following idioms all refer in some way to the sea. Use them in the sentences below:

a. *left high and dry*

b. *a sea change*

c. *make waves*

d. *the tide is turning*

e. *a drop in the ocean*

f. *a wave of protests*

g. *all at sea*

h. *come hell or high water*

"My expenses? Just a drop in the ocean!"

1. The worldwide web. The Internet. Shopping from home. Chat rooms. I'm . . . . with all this new technology!
2. When all the redundancies were announced, there was . . . . in hospitals throughout the country.
3. I can see public opinion is coming round to our way of thinking. At last, ...
4. I don't care if I can't afford to go to the match in Helsinki. I'm going – . . . .
5. No planes, no trains, no buses! When the strike started, we were . . . . in our hotel.
6. There's been . . . . in the way we teach languages during the past 20 years.
7. Spending £10,000 on a trip to the Bahamas is just . . . . for the Government.
8. In private, people are telling you they agree with you, but they won't support you in public! . . . . and you'll regret it!

Note: A container with a small hole is not *watertight*. In the same way, if your argument is weak, it is not *watertight*. Something which is not watertight *leaks*. Politicians try out ideas on the general public by 'leaking' them to the press before they are published officially.

4: Revision

Look back at the idioms in this unit and add the missing prepositions:

1. land . . . . hot water
2. all . . . . sea
3. like water . . . . a duck's back
4. a drop . . . . the ocean
5. water . . . . the bridge
6. keep your head . . . . water
7. like a fish . . . . of water
8. a wave . . . . protests

When did you last feel all at sea?

14. Animal Idioms

1. There isn't enough room to swing a . . . . .
2. He can talk the . . . . legs off a donkey.
3. You've got to take the . . . . by the horns.
4. I got it straight from the horse's . . . . .
5. I haven't seen you for donkey's . . . . .
6. There's plenty more fish in the . . . . .

15. Bird Idioms

1. It's only 20 km as the . . . . flies.
2. They're watching me like a . . . . .
3. All my children have flown the . . . . .
4. We can kill two birds with one . . . . .
5. My boss has taken me under his . . . . .
6. It's like water off a duck's . . . . .

16. Body Idioms

1. I'd give my right . . . . for a car like that.
2. Sorry, I can't help you. My . . . . are tied.
3. My washing machine's on its last . . . . .
4. I can't put my . . . . on the problem.
5. Don't worry. I'm only pulling your . . . . .
6. It was a real stab in the . . . . .

17. Breaking Idioms

1. He went to . . . . when he heard the news.
2. He comes from a broken . . . . .
3. I'm trying to pick . . . . the pieces.
4. We're trying to put our . . . . back together.
5. I'm still feeling a bit . . . . after last night.
6. It's not too late to . . . . the relationship.

18. Building Idioms

1. I got in through the . . . . door.
2. You're banging your head against a . . . wall.
3. Share prices have gone through the . . . . .
4. I want to get my foot in the . . . . .
5. He smokes like a . . . . .
6. It's like talking to a brick . . . . .

19. Cat Idioms

1. You haven't got a cat in . . . . chance.
2. . . . . pussyfooting around!
3. That's set the cat among the . . . . .
4. She rubs me up the . . . . way.
5. Don't let the cat out of the . . . . .
6. Curiosity . . . . the cat.

20. Clothes Idioms

1. Jane wears the . . . . in her house.
2. You need to . . . . your socks up.
3. We'll have to . . . . our belts for a while.
4. I wouldn't like to be in your . . . . .
5. I take my . . . . off to him.
6. I've got something up my . . . . .

21. Colour Idioms: Black/White

1. You can get them on the black . . . . .
2. I told him a little white . . . . .
3. Are you ill? You're as white as a . . . . .
4. How did you get that black . . . . ?
5. It's a very . . . . picture, I'm afraid.
6. White . . . . workers are better educated.

22. Colour Idioms: Red/Blue

1. My account is in the . . . . again.
2. You can ask till you're blue in the . . . . .
3. She arrived completely out of the . . . . .
4. It was a . . . . from the blue.
5. I go there once in a blue . . . . .
6. That's like a red . . . . to a bull.

23. Driving Idioms

1. My boss is driving me round the . . . . .
2. We keep going round in . . . . .
3. My career is at a . . . . .
4. We'll have to put the . . . . on spending.
5. She lives life in the . . . . lane.
6. You'd better steer . . . . of Tim today.

24. Eating Idioms

1. I had to eat my . . . . .
2. I've got a . . . . tooth.
3. You'll have to . . . . your pride.
4. Don't bite off more than you can . . . . .
5. It left a bad . . . . in my mouth.
6. I could eat a . . . . .

25. Eye Idioms

1. We don't always see eye . . . . eye.
2. There's more to him than . . . . the eye.
3. Try and . . . . the waiter's eye.
4. You need eyes in the back of your . . . . .
5. I decided to . . . . a blind eye to it.
6. Can you . . . . an eye on my bag for me?

26. Face Idioms

1. He's sad but he's putting on a . . . . face.
2. I've been face . . . . face with a lion.
3. Don't take everything at face . . . . .
4. I fell . . . . on my face.
5. The answer is . . . . you in the face.
6. You can ask till you're . . . . in the face.

27. Fingers and Thumbs Idioms

1. You need to . . . . your finger out.
2. Keep your fingers . . . . .
3. I sat there twiddling my . . . . .
4. Everything's . . . . your fingertips.
5. He never . . . . a finger to help.
6. My idea got the thumbs . . . . .

28. Fire Idioms

1. My plans went up in . . . . .
2. My first day at work was a . . . . of fire.
3. There's no . . . . without fire.
4. I had a blazing . . . . with my boss.
5. Don't . . . . your bridges.
6. I need something to . . . . my imagination.

29. Fishing Idioms

1. He fell for it hook, ... and sinker.
2. Paul's just landed a great . . . . in London.
3. Cast your . . . . back to last year.
4. Don't let her off the . . . . .
5. I've got to trawl . . . . all this information.
6. There's plenty more fish in the . . . . .

30. Food Idioms

1. It's the best thing since sliced . . . . .
2. Let her stew in her own . . . . .
3. You'll end up with egg on your . . . . .
4. Variety is the . . . . of life.
5. She's the . . . . of the earth.
6. He's as . . . . as a cucumber.

31. Foot Idioms

1. I'm going to . . . . my feet up and watch TV.
2. I'm just starting to . . . . my feet.
3. You've really put your foot . . . . it.
4. Time to stand on your own . . . . feet!
5. I got . . . . feet and changed my mind.
6. I've been . . . . off my feet today.

32. Hand Idioms

1. They rejected my ideas . . . . of hand.
2. He can't take the . . . . into his own hands.
3. Can I . . . . you a hand?
4. Things are getting . . . . of hand.
5. I've got a lot of time . . . . my hands.
6. She can . . . . her hand to anything.

33. Head Idioms

1. Two heads are . . . . than one.
2. I don't know – off the . . . . of my head.
3. My head's on the . . . . .
4. It was so funny. I . . . . my head off.
5. I can't make head nor . . . . of it.
6. He's got his head in the . . . . , as usual.

34. Heart Idioms

1. Her heart's in the . . . . place.
2. I didn't have the heart to . . . . no.
3. I'm not going. I've had a . . . . of heart.
4. In my heart of . . . . , I knew I would fail.
5. My heart's just not . . . . it.
6. My heart . . . . when I saw the price.

35. Horse Idioms

1. I got it . . . . from the horse's mouth.
2. You're putting the . . . . before the horse.
3. I'm keeping a . . . . rein on my spending.
4. I always get . . . . with the washing up.
5. I've got the bit between my . . . . now.
6. You're flogging a . . . . horse.

36. House and Home Idioms

1. Come in. Make yourself . . . . home.
2. I told him a few home . . . . .
3. Nearly finished. We're on the home . . . . .
4. The lights are on but there's . . . at home.
5. We got on like a house on . . . . .
6. My job is as safe as . . . . .

37. Life and Death Idioms

1. It was so dull. I was . . . . to death.
2. You look like death warmed . . . . .
3. That's a . . . . worse than death.
4. It gave me a new . . . . of life.
5. He's the life and . . . . of the party.
6. Don't do that! You're . . . . with death.

38. Metal Idioms

1. Every . . . . has a silver lining.
2. She's got a . . . . of gold.
3. He's worth his . . . . in gold.
4. You need nerves of . . . . in his job.
5. He retired with a golden . . . . .
6. The children were as . . . . as gold.

39. Mind Idioms

1. I'm not sure. I'm in . . . . minds about it.
2. Sorry. It completely . . . . my mind.
3. I'm going to give him a . . . . of my mind.
4. I've got a lot . . . . my mind at the moment.
5. Nobody in their . . . . mind would do that.
6. Mind your own . . . . !

40. Number Idioms

1. I'm all at . . . . and sevens today.
2. . . . . time lucky!
3. We're back to square . . . . , I'm afraid.
4. It takes . . . . to tango.
5. It's six of one and half a . . . . of the other.
6. He's got a one-track . . . . .

41. Sports Idioms

1. They keep moving the . . . . .
2. The . . . . . is in your court.
3. We need to . . . . base soon.
4. It's not a . . . . playing field.
5. You're backing the wrong . . . . .
6. That's par for the . . . . .

42. Swimming Idioms

1. I just got thrown in at the . . . . end.
2. We're just keeping our heads . . . . water.
3. It's a . . . . or swim situation.
4. Pat's company is in danger of going . . . . .
5. I'm completely . . . . of my depth.
6. I'm just treading . . . . till I find a new job.

43. Temperature Idioms

1. I'm sorry I . . . . my cool yesterday.
2. In the cold light of . . . . I see I was wrong.
3. I just said it in the . . . . of the moment.
4. I got cold . . . . at the last minute.
5. I warmed . . . . Katie straightaway.
6. Why are you so hot under the . . . . ?

44. Train Idioms

1. There's light at the end of the . . . . .
2. Can you get there . . . . your own steam?
3. I think we're on the right . . . . .
4. Sam's gone right off the . . . . .
5. I go to the gym to let off a bit of . . . . .
6. The relationship just . . . . out of steam.

45. Water Idioms

1. She spends money . . . . water.
2. I felt like a . . . . out of water.
3. I'm only just keeping my . . . . above water.
4. It's too difficult. I'm out of my . . . . .
5. That's all water under the . . . . .
6. I prefer to just . . . . with the flow.

SECTION 3

Topics

In this section the idioms are organised by topic. It is impossible to speak or write about any subject without using idiomatic English. Here are some examples:

Family: **Debbie and Jill are like two peas in a pod.**
Money: **Go on! Splash out!**
Memory: **I've got a memory like a sieve.**
Reading: **This book is like wading through treacle!**
Work: **I'm afraid I'm tied up at the moment.**
Speed: **You'd better get your skates on.**

This section will be particularly useful to you if you have to write an essay or sit an examination. If your essay is on the topic of holidays or work, study those units in detail. Look at the list of contents and you may find other related topics which will also help you.

Unit 47 Advice

1: Positive advice

Fill in the following verbs in the idiomatic expressions below:

go   *bide*   *take (2)*   *sit*   *make*   *speak*   *tread*   *keep (2)*

      a. . . . . your mind
      b. . . . . the most of it
      c. . . . . your wits about you
      d. . . . . the bull by the horns
      e. . . . . your time
      f. . . . . tight
      g. . . . . carefully
      h. . . . . one day at a time
      i. . . . . a low profile
      j. . . . . for it

Now use the above expressions in these dialogues:

1. Fantastic weather, isn't it? Shall we spend the weekend on the beach?
   > Well, we'd better . . . . It's not going to last. They said it's to be rain again next week!

2. I've never driven in Britain before. Is it hard driving on the left?
   > Not really, but you need to . . . . Especially at roundabouts and coming out of petrol stations.

3. I'd really like to ask Helen out, but I'm not sure she'll say yes.
   > There's only one way to find out, Mark. You've got to . . . . and ask her.

4. I'm never going to earn the kind of salary I want if I stay in this job.
   > Don't ask me who told me, but I heard they're thinking of promoting you to Area Manager. So, I'd . . . . if I were you. Just bide . . . .

5. I don't have the qualifications. I'm probably too young. But I know I can do the job better than anyone. Do you think I should apply or am I wasting my time?
   > If you don't take risks, life passes you by. . . . .!

There are four expressions left. Which one would you use to give advice in these situations?

6. The doctor has told a friend of yours that he only has six months to live:

   . . . .

7. You think your friend Fred is behaving badly towards another friend, Alan. Tell Alan what you think he should do:

   . . . .

8. Your friend is going to visit some old friends from his university days. You know that they have been having some difficulties in their marriage.

   . . . .

9. A friend of yours is a politician. She disagrees with her party's position on education, but has ambitions to lead the party one day:

   . . . .

2: Don't count your chickens

Advice often begins with *Don't* ... .

      a. *Don't count your chickens before they're hatched.*

      b. *Don't lose any sleep over it.*

      c. *Don't let it get you down.*

      d. *Don't throw the baby out with the bath water.*

      e. *Don't overdo it.*

      f. *Don't be silly.*

      g. *Don't beat about the bush.*

      h. *Don't take anything for granted.*

Which of these idioms has the following meaning?

1. Say what you are thinking.
2. Slow down and stop doing so many things.
3. Don't worry about it.
4. Be careful, when you change things, not to lose some of the good old ideas.

Now use the remaining four idioms in these situations:

5. I think all food and drink is included when you go on a cruise.
   > . . . . You don't want to end up with a huge drinks bill on the last day of your holiday!
6. I think we can be fairly sure we're going to win the election. Just look at the polls.
   > Anything can happen in the last few days. . . . .
7. I've had this cold on and off now for three whole months! I just don't know what I can do to get rid of it.
   > It'll go away. Don't worry. Just . . . .
8. I'm sure I failed. I was so nervous. And I know I made lots of mistakes!
   > Now, ... ! You've probably passed with flying colours!

Note: If you pass an exam *with flying colours*, it means you have passed very well. In this idiom 'colours' are, literally, flags.

3: Revision

Which idiom would you use in these situations? The words in brackets will help.

1. Somebody's panicking about the future *(one day)*.
2. Encourage a friend to try something *(go)*.
3. Somebody wants to take some exercise. Tell them to be careful *(overdo)*.
4. Encourage someone to take control of a situation and take action *(bull)*.
5. Tell someone to wait patiently and take no action *(tight)*.
6. Tell someone not to worry about a situation *(sleep)*.
7. Tell someone not to assume that something will happen. *(granted)*
8. Tell someone to be careful. *(wits)*

When was the last time you took the bull by the horns? What happened?

Unit 48 | Agreeing and Disagreeing

1: You must be joking!

Here are six ways to disagree. Use these words to complete the expressions:

question   *joking*   *no*

taken   *contrary*   *dead*

a. You must be . . . . . . !

b. On the . . . . . . !

c. Over my . . . . . . body!

d. . . . . . . way!

e. It's out of the . . . . . . !

f. Point . . . . . . !

Note: You use the last expression when someone says something and you realise they were right and you were wrong.

Now use the expressions in these situations:

1. You said the figures would be ready last week. I told you we needed extra help to get them out. We're only halfway through. We need at least two more people and we need them immediately. Otherwise, you simply won't have the figures when you leave for New York on Monday.

   > . . . . ! I promise you'll have two extra people within the hour.

2. Can I borrow your car for the afternoon?

   > Not this afternoon! Never again! No . . . . ! Not after the state you left it in last time!

"No way! It's out of the question!"

3. I was wondering if I could have tomorrow off to go to my grandfather's funeral?

   > I'm afraid . . . . ! You've already been to two grandfather's funerals in the past year. I wasn't born yesterday, you know!

4. I think we should close the shop in central London. It's not very profitable.

   > . . . . dead . . . . ! It's where the business started in 1895!

5. I thought you believed in capital punishment.

   > . . . . ! I've always been dead against it!

6. What about an ice-cream?

   > . . . . ! It's minus 10 outside!

2: Fair enough!

Here are seven ways to agree with someone. Use these words to complete the expressions:

enough	*again*	*talking*	*tell*
mouth	*me*	*nail*	

a. Fair . . . . !
b. . . . . me about it!
c. Now you're . . . . !
d. You took the words right out of my . . . . !

e. You're telling . . . . !
f. You've just hit the . . . . on the head!
g. You can say that . . . . !

Now use these expressions in the following dialogues:

1. I know I said that our maximum discount was 30%. Well, I've spoken to my head office and we think we can go to 40.
   . . . . ! Well, we can do business after all!

2. You can't go into town without seeing beggars. You can't leave your car anywhere without it being damaged. There's litter all over the place!
   > . . . . ! I don't know what has happened to this town. It used to be totally different.
   I think it's drugs. Most of the crime in this town is drug-related in some way.
   > I think . . . . !

3. Can I finish at four today?
   > No, sorry. That's the third time you've asked this month. It's not fair to the others.
   OK, ... ! I see your point.

4. This weather's incredible, isn't it? It's like the tropics!
   > You're . . . . ! We'll have to start thinking about air conditioning if it goes on any longer.

5. I think Roger is out of his mind if he thinks that Mary is going to change once they're married!
   > . . . . ! She's not going to change at all. If anybody's going to change, it'll have to be him.

6. I've been thinking about this year's holiday. Do we have to go to the Lake District again? This will have been 5 years in a row!
   > You know, ... I think it's time we took the kids abroad, don't you?

3: Revision

Look back at the idioms in this unit and add the missing words:

1. . . . . my dead body
2. you . . . . be joking
3. it's . . . . of the question
4. no . . . .
5. hit the nail on the . . . .

6. fair . . . .
7. you're telling . . . .
8. you can say . . . . again
9. . . . . you're talking
10. . . . . me about it

What would make you say "Over my dead body"?

Unit 49 Annoyance and Frustration

1: Literal meanings

Fill in the following words in the definitions below:

> **tether**   **insult**   **bang**   **patience**   **distractions**
> **straw**   **injury**   **bend**   **tear**   **wits**

1. A comment made to hurt somebody or to make them feel stupid is an . . . .
2. Some people have all the . . . . . . in the world, while others have none.
3. If you are in a difficult situation, you need to use your . . . .
4. A curve in a road is a . . . .
5. You tie a farm animal, for example, a goat, to a post with a . . . .
6. When I'm trying to read a book, I don't like any . . . .
7. If you get an . . . . . . to your back, it can take months to clear up.
8. It really annoys me when people . . . . . . pages out of the telephone book.
9. Be careful. This is a very low doorway. Don't . . . . . . your head.
10. Many farm animals eat and sleep on . . . .

2: At the end of my tether

Put these words into the expressions below:

> **nerves**   **straw**   **nose**   **end**   **insult**   **wits**

a. I'm at the . . . . of my tether.
b. We're at our . . . .' end.
c. It's getting on my . . . .
d. That sort of thing really gets up my . . . .
e. to add . . . . to injury
f. the last . . . .

Now complete these sentences:

1. Do you think you could stop whistling? . . . .
2. Jack's been crying all day. The baby won't go to sleep. I've had a terrible headache since I got up. I can't take any more. I'm . . . .
3. First he told me he wanted to end the relationship, then, ... , he said he hadn't got any money to pay for the meal, and could I lend him enough for a taxi home.
4. The bank have just charged me £25 because I was overdrawn for one day. One day! . . . .
5. I've told my flatmate to find somewhere else. She never tidied the place or cooked. . . . . was when she brought a stray dog home!
6. We don't know what to do with Jane. She's 15. She won't do any homework. She isn't interested in anything. She hardly speaks. . . . . !

3: Tearing your hair out

Here are different ways of expressing frustration:

> *It's driving me round the bend.*
> *It's driving me up the wall.*
> *It's driving me to distraction.*
>
> *I'm running out of patience*
> *I'm going spare.*
> *I'm tearing my hair out.*
>
> *I could have kicked myself.*
>
> *It's like talking to a brick wall.*
> *I'm just banging my head against a brick wall.*

"I'm tearing my hair out!"

Complete these situations using one word from the idioms above:

1. There was a brilliant football match on the TV last night. Six goals!
   > Oh, be quiet! I completely forgot to watch it. I could have kicked . . . .
2. I heard you're having problems getting a visa.
   > Yes, it's so frustrating. I'm tearing my . . . . out trying to find out what the problem is.
3. I see you got another letter from that book club.
   > Yes, it's the third letter this month asking me to pay for books I never ordered. It's driving me round the . . . .
4. You still haven't got your new car then?
   > No, they phoned to say it still hasn't been delivered. I think I'll cancel the order and look somewhere else. I'm . . . . out of patience.
5. When Pete decides he doesn't want to do something, you can't argue with him. It's like talking to a . . . . wall.
6. I'm trying to find a hotel in Barcelona, but there's a big congress on at the same time. I'm going . . . . trying to find somewhere to stay at a price I can afford.
7. We've got some students living in the flat next door. They play really loud music even after midnight. They are driving us to . . . . We've spoken to them several times, but it's like . . . . your head against a brick wall.
8. I wish we could do something about the rats coming from the restaurant next door. They're driving us up the . . . .

4: Revision

Look back at the idioms in this unit and add the missing verbs. Write them in the same form that you find them.

1. . . . . . . me round the bend
2. . . . . . . on my nerves
3. could've . . . . . . myself
4. . . . . . . me to distraction
5. . . . . . . my head against a brick wall
6. . . . . . . spare
7. . . . . . . my hair out
8. . . . . . . to a brick wall
9. . . . . . . up my nose
10. . . . . . . out of patience

What drives you round the bend?

Unit 50 | Being Positive

1: Look on the bright side

Add these words to complete the idiomatic expressions:

life	*world*	*win*	*light*
bright	*fish*	*better*	*another*

a. Look on the . . . . side.
b. There's plenty more . . . . in the sea.
c. It's not the end of the . . . .
d. Tomorrow's . . . . day.
e. You can't . . . . them all.
f. Things can only get . . . .
g. There's . . . . at the end of the tunnel.
h. That's . . . . !

Some of these expressions are used in very similar ways. However, there are three which fit best in these situations:

1. Bad news, Dad. Carol told me last night she didn't want to see me any more.
   > Never mind, son. . . . .
2. I slept in this morning. I missed my bus. I broke the photocopier at work.
   > Never mind! . . . .
3. The business has been going badly for some time, but I'm pleased to say that at last . . . .

Complete the following situations with single words:

4. I travelled all the way to London to see my favourite rock band to discover the concert had been cancelled. I suppose that's . . . . ! I was really looking forward to seeing them. Oh well, you can't win them . . . .
5. When I told Simon there's plenty more . . . . . . in the sea, it didn't really make any difference. He's only sixteen, but he thought Kate leaving him was the . . . . of the world.
6. You've lost everything in the fire. Look on the bright . . . . ! Things can . . . . . . get better!

"Look on the bright side, Nigel. Things can only get better. I mean, now you'll be able to buy a new budgerigar – and this one might talk!"

2: You win some, you lose some

Put these common expressions in the correct order:

> a. *You some lose win you some* . . . .
> b. *You've lose nothing got to* . . . .
> c. *Where a way will a there's there's* . . . .
> d. *His is bite bark worse than his* . . . .

Now put the expressions into the dialogues below:

1. I'm thinking of applying for that manager's position with Plessey's.
   > Yes, good idea. . . . .
2. I haven't met Mr Kramer yet. People tell me he's got a hot temper.
   > Oh, he's OK. . . . .
3. I bought a shirt last month for £25 and now it's in the sale for only £10.
   > Oh well. . . . .
4. I don't know how many jobs I've applied for since I left college.
   > I'm sure you'll find something eventually. . . . . !

3: Third time lucky!

Complete these short dialogues using the following lines:

> a. *Third time lucky!*   d. *You never know!*
> b. *No news is good news!*   e. *It'll be all right on the night!*
> c. *Fingers crossed!*

1. Lynn's failed her driving test again. That's twice now.
   > Oh well. . . . . !
2. We still haven't heard anything from the hospital.
   > Oh, well, I suppose . . . .
3. I bet we don't get a pay rise again this year.
   > . . . . !
4. I'm so nervous about speaking in public at the meeting tomorrow, and I don't
   think I've done anything like the preparation I should have.
   > Don't worry. . . . . !
5. I hope they get home safely. That old car doesn't look as if it could reach the
   bottom of the road, never mind all the way to the south of France!
   Well, ... they make it!

4: Revision

Choose the correct word in italics:

1. There's light at the end of the . . . . .
2. It's not the end of the . . . . .
3. Look on the . . . . side.
4. You never . . . . .
5. Third . . . . lucky!
6. Fingers . . . . !
7. Things can only . . . . better.
8. You . . . . some, you . . . . some.
9. You've got . . . . to lose.
10. His . . . . is worse than his . . . . .
11. . . . . news is good news.
12. You can't . . . . them all.

Do you usually look on the bright side of things?

Unit 51 | Certainty and Doubt

1: Expressions with *it's*

Use the following expressions in the dialogues below:

> a. *It's in the bag.*
> b. *It's on the cards.*
> c. *It's touch and go.*
> d. *It's anyone's guess.*
> e. *It's all up in the air.*
> f. *It's a foregone conclusion.*

1. How's your grandfather? Is he still in hospital?
   > Yes, I'm afraid . . . . at the moment. We'll know within 24 hours whether he's going to pull through or not.
2. What's the news about the German contract? Have we got it?
   > Well, it hasn't actually been signed but I think we can safely say . . . .
   . . . .
3. Are Jim and Anna getting married or not? I hear they're having second thoughts.
   > That's right. They had a big argument about something, so . . . .
   . . . . . . at the moment.
4. Manchester United are going to win. . . . .
5. I wouldn't be at all surprised if Jack and Jill decide to get married, would you?
   > You're right. I'd say a wedding is definitely . . . .
6. We've been waiting five hours and we still don't know when the plane is going to leave. Do you think it'll be tonight?
   > I'm sorry, sir. . . . . We're as much in the dark as you. As soon as we hear anything, we'll make an announcement.

2: The writing's on the wall

Use the following four common expressions in the situations below:

> a. *The writing's on the wall.*
> b. *I can feel it in my bones.*
> c. *Your guess is as good as mine.*
> d. *Without a shadow of a doubt.*

1. 20 red roses! I have no idea who sent them. . . . .
2. It was John. I'm telling you I saw him. It WAS him – . . . .
3. . . . . for David. He'll be looking for a new job pretty soon. He's never in his office and people are starting to complain.
4. There's going to be trouble at the match tonight. . . . .

Note: If you are extremely doubtful that something will happen, you could use the following expressions:

> I'll pay you back the £500 I owe you next week.
> > *That'll be the day!*   or   *Pigs might fly!*

3: The benefit of the doubt

Fill in the following words and expressions in the sentences below:

    a. *just to be on the safe side*
    b. *an educated guess*
    c. *just in case*
    d. *the benefit of the doubt*

1. I'm not sure whether to believe you or not but I'm going to give you . . . .
. . . .
2. The weather should be fine but you can never rule out the possibility of rain in Scotland so take a raincoat, ... you need it.
3. I'm not sure how much my dad earns exactly but . . . . would be about £2,000 a month.
4. If I were you, I'd take out travel insurance . . . .

> "A spokesman for the Prime Minister insisted last night that a deal was still on the cards."
>
> *Newspaper report*

4: Correct the mistake

Find the wrong word and rewrite the idiom correctly in the space provided.

  1. Just to be on the sure side.   . . . .
  2. It's someone's guess.   . . . .
  3. It's all up in the sky.   . . . .
  4. Without a shade of a doubt.   . . . .
  5. And pigs do fly!   . . . .
  6. It's touch or go.   . . . .
  7. I can feel it in my blood.   . . . .
  8. Your guess is as bad as mine.   . . . .
  9. The writing's on the cards.   . . . .
10. I'll give her a benefit of the doubt.   . . . .

When you travel, do you travel light or do you take lots of things with you just to be on the safe side?

Unit 52 Change

1: Literal meanings

Fill in the following words in the definitions below:

tune	horizon	leopard	strength
leaf	spots	recognition	

1. The line in the distance where the land seems to meet the sky is the . . . .
2. The . . . . is a member of the big cat family and is famous for its . . . .
3. The noun from *recognise* is . . . .
4. It grows on trees, but is also used to mean the page of a book. It's a . . . .
5. A . . . . is a series of musical notes.
6. He's been ill for a while, but he's now regaining his . . . .

2: Change your mind

The following nouns are all used in idioms with *change*. Use them below:

subject	tune	plan	heart	recognition
mind	places	ways	hands	direction

1. Are you sure you won't come to the theatre with us? Is there anything I can say to make you change your . . . . ?
2. There's been a change of . . . . We're not going by car. I had an accident yesterday. Nothing serious, but it means we're going to have to get the train.
3. I see that restaurant has changed . . . . again. It's now a Chinese takeaway.
4. Would you mind changing the . . . . ? I'd rather not hear about your operation while we're eating.
5. Jack's very well paid but he's under constant pressure. I wouldn't change . . . . with him.
6. I keep trying to persuade my dad to get a credit card but he prefers cash. He's too old to change his . . . .
7. Robert said he'd always been against cars in town, but he soon changed his . . . . when he passed his driving test!
8. Originally my mother wouldn't allow her sister to come to our wedding, but she's had a change of . . . . At last they've spoken to each other!
9. I've been in the same job for 20 years. I feel as if I need a complete change of . . . .
10. I went back to my home town for the first time for twenty years last month. It wasn't the same place. The town centre had changed out of all . . . .

Note: English has the following two idioms when you want to say that you cannot or will not change. Does your language have similar idioms?

You can't teach an old dog new tricks.
A leopard can't change its spots.

3: Make a clean break

Use the following expressions in the sentences below:

    a. *turn over a new leaf*   **d.** *on the horizon*
    b. *go from strength to strength*   **e.** *make a clean break*
    c. *a breath of fresh air*   **f.** *take shape*

1. So, what are you going to do? Stay here and look for another job?
   > No, I'm going to move up to London and look there. It's time to . . . .
   . . . . Flat, job, girlfriend, the lot!
2. How's your business going, Kathy? Getting plenty of customers?
   > Yes thanks. We're . . . .
3. I really like that new girl in the office. She's so much fun, isn't she?
   > Yes. She's like . . . . in this place.
4. Are you still renovating your house? It's taking a long time, isn't it?
   > Yes, longer than we thought. Still, it's starting to . . . . now.
5. Is Paula still as overweight as she was when we were at university?
   > Goodness no! She . . . . and now she's as thin as a rake!
6. I thought you were going to move flat this month. Have you changed your mind?
   > No, there's a new job . . . . so I've decided to wait a bit.

*"Marjorie wished she could turn over a new
leaf, like Paula – and give up chocolate, too."*

4: Revision

What would you say in these situations? Use the words in brackets to help you.

1. Describe your friend, who is trying to be a better person. *(leaf)*
2. Describe the effect of the new person at work. *(breath)*
3. Say you want to leave and start again somewhere else. *(clean)*
4. Tell your friend how much your home town has changed. *(out of)*
5. Say that people don't basically change character. *(leopard)*
6. Ask your friend to stop talking about something. *(subject)*
7. The newsagent has new owners. *(hands)*
8. Tell your friend that your holiday plans are developing. *(shape)*

**Can you think of somewhere you know which has changed out of all recognition
since you were a child?**

Unit 53 Communicating

1: Literal meanings

Fill in the following words in the definitions below:

> **bricks**   **beat**   **hind**   **gab**
> **bush**   **grapevine**   **wavelength**   **dozen**

1. The back legs of animals are called their . . . . legs.
2. If you want to listen to a particular radio station, you need to know the right
   . . . .
3. A . . . . is smaller than a tree, but larger than a plant.
4. When hunting birds such as grouse or pheasant, people – known as 'beaters' –
   . . . . the ground and bushes to force the birds to fly up so that they can be
   shot.
5. . . . . have been used to build houses for centuries.
6. Another word for 12 is a . . . .
7. Grapes grow on a . . . .
8. An informal and dialect word meaning 'mouth' or 'talk' – . . . .

2: Just between you and me

Use the following expressions in the sentences below:

> a. **talking to a brick wall**
> b. **get it off your chest**
> c. **can't get a word in edgeways**
> d. **talking nineteen to the dozen**
> e. **breathe a word of this**
>
> f. **beating about the bush**
> g. **put in a good word for you**
> h. **just between you and me**
> i. **heard it on the grapevine**
> j. **talk the hind legs off a donkey**

1. This is . . . . , but I think Karen's got a drink
   problem.
2. I wish you would get straight to the point and say what you think. I won't be
   upset. Just stop . . . . !
3. Honestly, I don't know how often I've told you not to leave the door open! It's
   like . . . . !
4. How do you know that the head of the Paris office is leaving the company?
   > Oh, I . . . .
5. If you've got a problem, then it's always best to talk to someone about it.
   . . . . as soon as possible.
6. If Frank disagrees with you about something, he just doesn't stop. Once he starts
   you . . . .
7. If you decide to apply for the job in Hong Kong, let me know. I know one of the
   directors out there, so I can . . . .
8. You know when Fiona's excited about something because she starts . . . .
   . . . . !
9. Whatever you do, don't get into conversation with old Mr Murray. He can
   . . . . !
10. Please don't . . . . , but I've just applied for
    a new job.

3: On the same wavelength

Use the following idiomatic expressions in the situations below:

    a. *on the same wavelength*   **e. *get straight to the point***
    b. *the gift of the gab*   **f. *get the message***
    c. *straight from the horse's mouth*   **g. *have a quick word with you***
    d. *go on a bit*   **h. *keep you posted***

1. You and Sharon seem to get on very well together.
   > Yes, we seem to be . . . .

2. I think Rob likes the sound of his own voice. He just never stops talking.
   > Yes, he does . . . ., doesn't he?

3. Ah, come in, Peter, I've had an idea. I'll . . . .
   I want you to go to Australia and sort out our distribution problems there.

4. Tom is easily the most successful salesman in the company. How does he do it?
   > He's got . . . . He knows how to talk to potential
   customers. He could sell nutcrackers to monkeys!

5. Morning, Pam!
   > Morning, Trevor, can I . . . . in my office?

6. I don't understand why Tom and Mary are ignoring us. Do you . . . .
   . . . . that they don't like us any more?

7. And if there's any change in Tim's condition, you will phone me, won't you?
   > Yes, of course. We'll . . . .

8. I don't believe it! Mark, getting married? Who told you that?
   > I got it . . . . He said he's met someone and
   they're planning to get married in June.

4: Opposites

**Find the idioms which mean the opposite to these sentences. The words in
brackets will help you.**

1. She talks very slowly and calmly. *(nineteen)*
2. We constantly misunderstand each other. *(wavelength)*
3. Keep your feelings to yourself. *(chest)*
4. He listens carefully and then does what I ask. *(brick)*
5. I'm not going to tell you about any changes. *(posted)*
6. He never says a word. *(edgeways)*
7. You can tell as many people as you want. *(between)*
8. A friend of his told me. *(horse's)*

5: Revision

Look back at the idioms in this unit and add the missing word:

1. beat about the . . . . . .   6. talk the hind legs off a . . . .
2. get a word in . . . . . .   7. get it off your . . . .
3. talking to a brick . . . . . .   8. got the . . . . of the gab
4. on the same . . . . . .   9. just between you and . . . . . .
5. straight from the horse's . . . .   10. . . . . it on the grapevine

**Do you know someone who goes on a bit, so sometimes you can't get a word in
edgeways?**

Unit 54 Dishonesty

1: Literal meanings

Fill in the following words in the definitions below:

robbery	*inch*	*snake*	*pretence*
fiddle	*wool*	*stab*	*path*

1. The hair that grows on sheep is called . . . .
2. An . . . . is approximately 2.54 centimetres.
3. If you attack someone with a knife, you . . . . them.
4. Cobras, pythons and vipers are all kinds of . . . .
5. They tried to give the impression of being happily married but it was just a
. . . . They were actually very unhappy together.
6. If someone steals money from a bank, it is called a . . . .
7. In my front garden there's a . . . . leading from the gate to the front door.
8. A . . . . is another word for a violin.

2: Stabbed in the back

Fill in the following idiomatic expressions in the dialogues below:

a. *wouldn't trust him an inch*
b. *leading you up the garden path*
c. *snake in the grass*
d. *stabbed in the back*

e. *take advantage of*
f. *taken for a ride*
g. *pull the wool over my eyes*
h. *under false pretences*

1. I'm sorry to hear you didn't get the promotion you wanted.
   > Yes, well, they told me I would get it and then they gave it to someone else.
   I feel as if I've been . . . .
2. Do you like my new Rolex? I bought it down at the local market for a fraction of
   what they usually cost.
   > I'm afraid it's a fake, Paul. You've been . . . .
3. What about getting a second-hand computer from that shop next to the station?
   > I wouldn't buy anything from that man. I've heard a lot about him. I . . . .
   . . . . !
4. Why has Patricia been sacked? She's only been here a week.
   > We checked her qualifications and found out that she'd never been to university.
   I'm afraid she got the job . . . .
5. After Harry said what he did yesterday, I felt completely betrayed.
   > Yes, I know what you mean. That guy is a real . . . .
   You can't trust him at all.
6. Jim says he loves me and he's promised we'll get engaged later this year. I know
   he means it this time.
   > Come on, Gina! You've heard it all before. He's just . . . . !
7. I told you I didn't want a party for my 50th birthday, but I know you're planning
   something. You can't . . . . !
8. Paul's asked me to work late again this week and I've said yes.
   > The problem with you is you're too nice. People always . . . . you.

3: Daylight robbery

Use the following expressions in the situations below:

a. *behind my back*	**e. *daylight robbery***
b. *two-faced*	**f. *a little white lie***
c. *lying through his teeth*	**g. *on the fiddle***
d. *as far as I could throw him*	**h. *believe a word***

1. I've just looked at a new flat. It was nice but they wanted £500 a week.
   > £500 for a week! That's . . . . !
2. You don't seem very happy, Martin. Is something wrong?
   > Yes, there is, now you come to mention it. I've just been talking to Richard.
   He says you've been talking about me . . . .
3. I've never told a lie in my life.
   > I don't believe you. Everyone has to tell . . . . from time to time!
4. If there's one thing I absolutely hate it's people who are . . . . – you
   know, the kind of person who says one thing to your face and something totally
   different behind your back.
5. After Roger was arrested, it was obvious that he had been . . . .
   . . . . to us for months.
6. How can someone like Bob earn enough to own a Porsche?
   > I don't know, but if you ask me I'd say he's . . . .
7. Michael was telling me how much he earned last year.
   > And exaggerating, no doubt! You can't. . . . . that guy says!
8. So you don't think what he said was true, then?
   > I doubt it very much. I wouldn't trust Michael . . . .

**Note: If you want to talk about someone who is totally dishonest, you could say
that *'he would sell his own grandmother'*. There is a recent idiom in British
English to describe a person who lies: *He is economical with the truth.***

*"Top-of-the-range Porsche, double garage, jacuzzi,
gold-plated taps – he's got to be on the fiddle!"*

4: Revision

Look back at the idioms in this unit and add the missing prepositions:

1. lying . . . . his teeth	6. taken . . . . a ride
2. leading you . . . . the garden path	7. stabbed . . . . the back
3. pull the wool . . . . my eyes	8. take advantage . . . . me
4. . . . . false pretences	9. economical . . . . the truth
5. talking . . . . my back	10. . . . . the fiddle

Do you know anyone who you wouldn't trust as far as you could throw them?

Unit 55 Easy and Difficult

1: Literal meanings

Fill in the following words in the definitions below:

chew	*needle*	*stride*	*crack*	*pie*
bites	*haystack*	*baptism*	*tough*	*nut*

1. A long step is called a . . . .
2. Brazil, almond, and hazel are all kinds of . . . .
3. If meat is . . . . , you have to . . . . it a lot before you can swallow it.
4. The Christian ceremony of . . . . is the ceremony which welcomes new members to the Church.
5. You sew with a . . . .
6. You can make a . . . . with fruit or meat.
7. Farmers used to dry their hay by building . . . .
8. If a snake . . . . you, find a doctor – as fast as possible.
9. If you . . . . something, you break it in some way.

2: A piece of cake

All the idioms in this exercise express the idea that something is easy to do. Use the following expressions:

   a. *it's child's play*
   b. *dead easy*
   c. *all plain sailing*
   d. *take it in your stride*
   e. *it's a piece of cake*
   f. *there was nothing to it*

"Jean-Paul found driving on the left a piece of cake."

1. I'm going to the UK this summer and I've never driven on the left before.
   > Oh, it's a . . . .
   – just keep your wits about you.
2. Congratulations on passing your driving test. Were you very nervous?
   > I was a bit nervous for the first five minutes, but after that it was all . . . . from then on.
3. How's your dad getting on now he's retired? Has he adjusted to being at home?
   > Oh, he's getting on fine. He's taking it all . . . .
4. I haven't used the latest version of this software yet.
   > Oh, don't worry about. There's a tutorial that comes with it. It's . . . . easy.
5. How did your exams go, then?
   > The written exam was really awful, but after that the oral was . . . .
   There . . . .

Note: Another idiom used if the thing you are doing involves using your hands is *I could do it with my eyes closed*.

3: An uphill struggle

All the idioms in this exercise express the idea that something is difficult to do. Complete the idioms with the following words:

chew	*baptism*	*depth*	*deep*	*work*	*uphill*	*boys*
said	*needle*	*blood*	*heavy*	*hard*	*bed*	*nut*

a. it's an . . . . . . struggle
b. easier . . . . . . than done
c. . . . . . . going
d. learned the . . . . . . way
e. sort out the men from the . . . . . .
f. bitten off more than you can . . . . . .
g. got your . . . . . . cut out

h. thrown in at the . . . . . end
i. like looking for a . . . . . . in a haystack
j. out of my . . . . . .
k. not exactly a . . . . . . of roses
l. trying to get . . . . . . out of a stone
m. a tough . . . . . . to crack
n. a . . . . . . of fire

Now use one of these idioms in the following situations:

1. You'll never find Jo's number. There are hundreds of J. Smiths in the phone book.
   > Yes, it's like looking for . . . .
2. Can you believe it? My first day at work and I had to give a presentation on my ideas to the whole department!
   > That's what I call a . . . .
3. So, that's the work rota sorted out. Now we need to look at next year's budget.
   > Yes, that's going to be a tougher . . . .
4. How's life at university? Are you enjoying yourself?
   > Not really. I'm finding it difficult to keep up with the work. To be honest, it's a bit of an uphill . . . . I'm finding all the studying heavy . . . .
5. I can't stop to talk. I've got to get all these documents photocopied, signed and in the post by 5 o'clock.
   > You've certainly got . . . . there. Rather you than me!
6. I'm starting to regret that we ever got involved with CD Rom.
   > Why? Do you think you've bitten . . . . ?

Note: *It's like getting blood out of a stone* means it is difficult to get money, information, or a conversation out of someone.

4: Revision

What would you say in these situations? The words in italics will help you.

1. It's easy because you've done it so many times. *(eyes)*
2. You started something but it became too difficult. *(bitten, chew)*
3. Someone suggests an over-simple solution to a problem. *(said, done)*
4. The work is very straightforward from now on. *(sailing)*
5. Your friend has adjusted to a new situation very well. *(taken, stride)*
6. You find someone very difficult to have a conversation with. *(blood)*

Look back at the idioms in this unit and add the missing nouns:

7. tough . . . . . . to crack
8. baptism of . . . . . .
9. like looking for a . . . . . . in a haystack
10. learned the hard . . . . . .

11. thrown in at the deep . . . . . .
12. not exactly a bed of . . . . . .
13. took it in his . . . . . .
14. an uphill . . . . . .

When something changes in your life, do you worry or just take it in your stride?

Unit 56 The Family

1: Literal meanings

Fill in the following words in the definitions below:

pod   **spitting**   **flesh**   **knot**   **chalk**   **blood**

1. Your heart pumps your . . . . through your body.
2. Peas grow in a . . . .
3. Some teachers still use . . . . to write on blackboards.
4. There's now a taboo about . . . . in public, although it was very common a hundred years ago.
5. The . . . . of an animal is the part we usually eat as meat.
6. When you tie two pieces of string together, you make a . . . .

2: Like father, like son

Use the following idiomatic expressions in the sentences below:

   a. *baby of the family*
   b. *blood is thicker than water*
   c. *fight like cat and dog*
   d. *two peas in a pod*
   e. *the black sheep of the family*
   f. *own flesh and blood*
   g. *like father, like son*
   h. *tie the knot*

1. Jamie's only five but he's mad about football, just like his dad. You know what they say – . . . .
2. I've got two sisters who are older than me and then my younger brother Mark who's twenty-two. He's the . . . .
3. They've got two daughters and they look just the same. They're like . . . .
. . . .

"Ellie and Shelley are just like two peas in a pod."

4. Sam isn't the best person for the job but his father made him head of Marketing in the family business. As you know, ... !
5. My brother and his girlfriend have finally decided to . . . . They're getting married in the spring.
6. I get on very well with my brother now but we used to . . . .
. . . . when we were younger.
7. Everyone expected Susan to go to university like the rest of us, but she got a job in a casino on a ship. She's . . . .
8. My son's in trouble with the police. I normally have no sympathy with people who break the law but it's different when it's your own . . . .

124

3: The spitting image

Put the following words in the sentences below:

cheese	*footsteps*	*homes*	*tree*
relative	*family*	*side*	*image*

1. Look at Marie. She's the spitting . . . . of her mother, isn't she?
2. Pippa's going to medical school. She's following in her father's . . . .
3. A recent survey shows that two out of three convicted criminals come from broken . . . .
4. I've got Scottish blood. My grandparents on my mother's . . . . originally came from Glasgow.
5. George is very interested in his family's history. He can trace his family . . . . back to 1550.
6. Everyone in my family plays a musical instrument. Music runs in the . . . .
7. I got a letter today from a long-lost . . . . in Australia. I didn't even know he existed! He's coming to visit in the summer.
8. My sister and I look alike but when it comes to personality we're like chalk and . . . .

Note: A *long-lost relative* is one whom you have not seen for many years. A *distant relative* is perhaps your cousin's cousin. You can also say you have *a rather distant relationship* with someone. Is there an idiom in your language like this? – Although my sister lives in America, we're *very close*.

4: Definitions

Look back at the idioms used in this unit and find the ones which match the definitions below. The word in brackets will help you.

1. A relative who you have never met or not seen for a long time. *(lost)*
2. The member of the family who seems to get into trouble or has made bad choices. *(sheep)*
3. Brothers or sisters who look just like each other. *(pod)*
4. A situation when the parents are divorced or separated. *(broken)*
5. A situation when loyalty to family is more important that anything else. *(thicker)*
6. When a child looks just like one of the parents. *(image)*

5: Revision

Look back at the idioms in this unit and add the final words:

1. the black sheep of the . . . .
2. the baby of the . . . .
3. it runs in the . . . .
4. like father, like . . . .
5. your own flesh and . . . .
6. fight like cat and . . . .
7. like peas in a . . . .
8. blood is thicker than . . . .
9. like chalk and . . . .
10. follow in his father's . . . .

Are you following in your father's footsteps? What characteristics run in your family?

Unit 57 Good and Bad Quality

1: Literal meanings

Fill in the following words in the definitions below:

scratch   barrel   par   scrape   miles

1. In golf, if a hole should be completed in four strokes, it is a . . . . four.
2. A large, round container for holding beer or oil is called a . . . .
3. An excellent golfer, who no longer has a handicap, is called a . . . . player.
4. Eight kilometres is five . . . .
5. If you burn food onto a pan when you are cooking, you need to . . . . it clean before you wash it.

2: In a league of its own

Put the following nouns into these idioms:

condition   days   legs   league   par
home   gold   head   world   miles

a. It's in a . . . . of its own.
b. It's in mint . . . . .
c. It's . . . . and shoulders above the rest.
d. It's seen better . . . . .
e. It's nothing to write . . . . about.

f. It's . . . . better.
g. It's out of this . . . . .
h. It's on its last . . . . .
i. It's worth its weight in . . . . .
j. It's below . . . . .

Now use these idioms below, changing the grammar to fit the situation:

1. I hear Karen's selling her old Mini for £500. Is it in good condition?
   > Not really. It's on . . . . It's certainly seen . . . .
   . . . .
2. There's no doubt in my mind who should get the job – Mr Sullivan was the best.
   > I agree. He was head . . . . the rest of the candidates, wasn't he? He was in a . . . .
3. Hello, can you help me? I'm looking for a CD player.
   > Well, we've got lots to choose from, sir, but if it's sound quality you want, then this Sony is considered to be . . . . than all the others.
4. Brian, you wanted to see me.
   > Yes, Jeff. Come in and sit down. I'll get straight to the point: your work has been well below . . . . recently and I wondered if you were ill again.
5. What's that new restaurant like in King's Road? You've been there, haven't you?
   > Yes, the food was OK, but it was nothing . . . .
6. Your PA is excellent, Pete. She must make life a lot easier for you.
   > Oh yes, she's worth . . . .
7. Did I see you driving an old Jaguar yesterday?
   > You did! It's over 30 years old, but it's in absolutely . . . .
   It's superb – out . . . . ! Why not come for a drive tonight?

3: Not all it's cracked up to be

Use the following idiomatic expressions in the situations below:

  a. *It's not all it's cracked up to be.*

  b. *You're scraping the bottom of the barrel.*

  c. *It leaves a lot to be desired.*

  d. *It isn't up to scratch.*

  e. *He's over the hill.*

  f. *It's gone downhill.*

"Humphrey, when I married you, my friends said I was scraping the bottom of the barrel."

1. I visited the Tower of London on Saturday. To be honest, I was a bit disappointed.
   > I know what you mean. It's not . . . .
2. Our centre forward is useless. He's only scored three goals this season.
   > Well, he must be about 35 now. If you ask me, ...
3. What do you mean, it's not good enough? I spent all day preparing this report.
   > Well, I'm sorry but it isn't detailed enough. It just . . . .
4. Why have you invited Professor Wolf to give the lecture?
   > Well, everyone else we asked couldn't make that day.
   But he's totally out of date! You really must have been . . . . !
5. What did you think of the National Gallery?
   > It's over 20 years since I was last there and, frankly, I think the place has . . . . .
   . . . .
6. I'm sorry but this report leaves . . . .
   > I am aware that it isn't as good as it could be, but it's not that bad!

Note: An informal expression used to describe any situation where there might be some sort of problem – from milk which might not be fresh to a business deal which might not be very good – is: *It's a bit iffy.*

4: Revision

Look back at the idioms in this unit and add the final word:

1. It's nothing to write home . . . . .
2. They're scraping the bottom of the . . . . .
3. He's head and . . . . above the rest.
4. He's worth his weight in . . . . .
5. It's not all it's . . . . up to be.
6. Your work is not up to . . . . .
7. It's in a league of its . . . . .
8. It leaves a lot to be . . . . .
9. It's on its . . . . legs.
10. It's seen . . . . days.

Rewrite the following using the words in italics:

11. The car has been very well looked after. *(mint)*
12. Their car is very old and falling to bits. *(days)*
13. The new diesel automatic is much better. *(miles)*
14. Your work is not good enough. *(scratch)*

Can you think of a sportsman or woman who is head and shoulders above everyone else at the moment?

127

1: Literal meanings

Fill in the following words in the definitions below:

fiddle   **lease**   **complain**   **split**   **recovery**

1. You . . . . . . to the waiter if you are not happy with your food in a restaurant.
2. When you get better from an illness, you make a . . . .
3. My trousers are too tight. They've just . . . . . . in an embarrassing place!
4. A . . . . . . is another word for a violin.
5. If you rent a house or flat, the contract you sign is called a . . . .

2: Good health

Here are 5 ways of talking about good health. Complete the situations below:

> **a. I'm as fit as a fiddle.**
> **b. I'm as right as rain.**
> **c. I'm fighting fit.**
> **d. I can't complain.**
> **e. She's the picture of health.**

and if you've been ill:

> **f. I'm back on my feet.**
> **g. I've got a new lease of life.**
> **h. I've been given a clean bill of health.**
> **i. I'm well on the way to recovery.**

1. My dad's feeling much better. He's well . . . .
   > Yes, I saw him yesterday. He seems to have got a new . . . .
2. I can't believe your grandfather is 87. He looks fantastic for his age.
   > I know. And he's very active. He's still as . . . .
3. You don't look well. Why don't you go home?
   > It's OK. I've just taken some aspirin. I'll be as . . . . in a minute.
4. How did you get on at the doctor's? Did she give you the test results?
   > Yes, and I'm happy to say there's nothing to worry about. I was given . . . .
   . . . .
5. I've just been to visit my grandmother. She's amazing. She's 84 but she's . . . . . .
   . . . .
6. How are you, Liz?
   > Oh, I can't . . . . I'm back . . . . again. Not exactly
   . . . ., but much better than I was this time last year.

Note: People used to say they were in the pink when they were very well. This expression is now rather old-fashioned.

> "Yeltsin fighting fit again."
>
> *Newspaper headline*

3: Bad health

Complete these idioms expressing bad health with the words given:

killing	*bad*	*colour*	*going*	*out*	
weather	*down*	*run*	*sorts*	*splitting*	

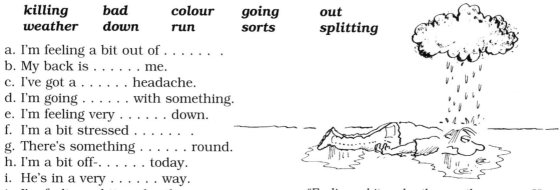

a. I'm feeling a bit out of . . . .
b. My back is . . . . . . me.
c. I've got a . . . . . . headache.
d. I'm going . . . . . . with something.
e. I'm feeling very . . . . . . down.
f. I'm a bit stressed . . . .
g. There's something . . . . . . round.
h. I'm a bit off-. . . . . . today.
i. He's in a very . . . . . . way.
j. I'm feeling a bit under the . . . .

"Feeling a bit under the weather, are we?"

Which of the above expressions would you use in these situations? For number 6 there are two possible answers.

1. You have too much work to do at the moment.
2. You have a friend who is dying.
3. You have just been to a rock concert.
4. You have a sore back.
5. A lot of people seem to be getting colds or flu at the moment.
6. You were partying till the early hours of this morning and don't feel too good.

The other examples mean that you are feeling ill in a general sort of way.

Note: If you know someone who is dying, you can say: *They are living on borrowed time.* If you feel really awful, (but you know it is not actually serious) you can say: *I feel as if I'm at death's door.* And if you look awful, your friend might say: *Are you all right? You look like death warmed up.*

4: Revision

Look back at the idioms and fill in the missing words below:

1. I'm feeling a bit under the . . . .
2. He's as fit as a . . . .
3. He'll soon be back on his . . . .
4. I'm well on the . . . . to recovery.
5. I think I'm going . . . . with the flu.
6. I've got a splitting . . . .
7. I can't . . . .
8. I'm feeling a bit off-. . . . .
9. My grandmother's the . . . . of health.
10. It's given me a new . . . . of life.
11. I'll be as right as . . . . in the morning.
12. I've been given a . . . . bill of health.

What do you do when you are feeling a bit off-colour?

Unit 59 | Holidays

1: A whale of a time

Match these four expressions with their meanings:

1. I had a whale of a time.
2. I recharged my batteries.
3. I like places off the beaten track.
4. It was just what the doctor ordered.

a. It was exactly what I needed.
b. I like going to quiet and unusual places.
c. I had a wonderful time.
d. I'm ready to come back to work.

2: Just what the doctor ordered

Fill in the following expressions in the dialogues below:

> a. *A change is as good as a rest.*
> b. *We had a whale of a time.*
> c. *We've packed everything except the kitchen sink.*
> d. *There's no place like home.*
> e. *It was like home from home.*
> f. *I always travel light.*
> g. *It was just what the doctor ordered.*
> h. *We're going to recharge the batteries.*

1. Welcome back, Chris. You look well. Did you have a good time?
   > Fantastic. Sun, sea and excellent food. . . . .
2. Are you having a holiday this year, Kathy?
   > I'm going to look after my brother's children for a week. It's not exactly a holiday
   but you know what they say – . . . .
3. Are you glad to be back?
   > Very much! We had a wonderful holiday, but you know what they say – . . . . . .
   . . . . !
4. But there's nothing to do in the middle of the forest! How will you fill your days?
   > You don't go to Sweden for a wild time! . . . .
5. Would you like to borrow my suitcase or have you got one of your own?
   > It's OK, thanks. I don't need it. . . . .
6. Are you sure everything's in the cases?
   > Yes, positive. . . . .
7. You've been on a skiing holiday, haven't you? What was it like?
   > Yes, I went with some friends. It was great. . . . .
8. Did you stay in a hotel or an apartment?
   > An apartment. It had everything – fridge, microwave, colour TV, even a washing
   machine. . . . .

**Note: We sometimes forget how many small idioms are used in ordinary everyday
language. We go on a 'package' holiday – perhaps fly on a 'jumbo' jet on a 'long-
haul' flight to 'down-under'! Or you may go to a place which is ideal for
windsurfers – a windsurfers' 'paradise'.**

3: Getting away from it all

Use the following idiomatic expressions in the situations below:

a. *getting away from it all*
b. *in the middle of nowhere*
c. *a short break*
d. *watching the world go by*

e. *the time of our lives*
f. *let your hair down*
g. *make a nice change*
h. *off the beaten track*

1. When are you off on holiday?
   > Tomorrow. I can't wait. I'm really looking forward to . . . .
2. Did I hear you were off on holiday next week?
   > Yes, we're just having . . . . – I'm back in again on Wednesday.
3. The best thing about the town was it was so quiet. We were the only tourists.
   > Yes, I'm like you. I prefer places . . . .
4. Why do you always go to Ibiza?
   > You've never been? It's the best place to really . . . .
5. Have you been to Paris?
   > Yes, I love Paris. I love sitting in a café . . . .
6. How was your holiday, Mike?
   > Fabulous! We had . . . .
7. You normally go to Corfu in the summer, don't you?
   > Yes, but this year we're going cycling in the Alps. It'll . . . .
8. Where's this cottage you're renting in Portugal?
   > Oh, it's miles from anywhere . . . .

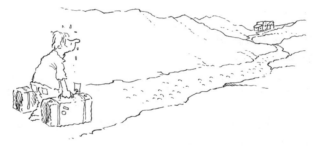

*"Bernard likes places off the beaten track, but this time
he was beginning to think he'd gone too far!"*

4: Revision

Put the following pairs of words into the sentences below:

change, rest	away, all	time, lives
just, doctor	no, home	whale, time

1. A . . . . . . is as good as a . . . .
2. I need to get . . . . . . from it . . . .
3. There's . . . . . place like . . . .
4. We had a . . . . . . of a . . . .
5. It was . . . . . what the . . . . . ordered.
6. We had the . . . . . . of our . . . .

Where do you go to recharge your batteries?

Unit 60 Knowledge and Ability

1: Literal meanings

Fill in the following words in the definitions below:

clues	ropes	rusty	brains
screwed	nature	pick	

1. The typical qualities and characteristics of a person make up their . . . .
2. Police look for . . . . . . when trying to solve crimes.
3. You use . . . . . . to tie a boat to the pier.
4. Two pieces of wood which are . . . . . . together are more secure than if they were nailed together.
5. The wheels on my bike went . . . . . . because I left it out in the rain for a week.
6. You can . . . . . fruit or you can . . . . . your teeth to remove small bits of food stuck between them.
7. In Britain we don't eat the . . . . . of animals, but in some countries they are considered a delicacy.

2: It's second nature

Put the following sentences in the following situations:

a. That's the first I've heard of it.
b. It's second nature.
c. I don't know the first thing about them.
d. I know it like the back of my hand.
e. Can I pick your brains?

1. Can you help me set up a database on my computer?
   > No trouble at all! I've done it so often I don't even need to think about it.
   . . . . to me now.
2. Paul, do you know anything about washing machines? Mine's got a problem.
   > Sorry. I can't help you. . . . .
3. Did you know that Lisa is planning to emigrate to Australia?
   > You're kidding! . . . .
4. Have you been to Oxford before, Kevin?
   > Oxford? I lived there for ten years. . . . .
5. We're off to India next week. . . . . before we go?
   > By all means. What do you want to know?

Now add these expressions:

f. in the dark	i. an old hand
g. a bit rusty	j. a thing or two
h. not very well acquainted with	

6. I'm . . . . Edinburgh. I've only been once.
7. You could tell the tour guide was . . . . He made a fortune in tips!
8. I wish you hadn't kept me . . . . about your plans.
9. Ask Bill. He knows . . . . about old BMWs. He's had half a dozen.
10. I'll have to go on a course. My French is . . . .

132

3: He's got his head screwed on

Add the missing word to these idioms:

a. He's got his . . . . screwed on.
b. He can turn his . . . . to anything.
c. He knows what's . . . . .
d. He hasn't got a . . . . .
e. He's learning the . . . . .
f. He hasn't got the . . . . of it yet.
g. He doesn't know one . . . . of a (car) from the other.
h. It's common . . . . .

end
hang
clue
what
knowledge
ropes
head
hand

Now match them up with these explanations:

1. He knows what is useful and important.
2. He's the sort of person you can ask to do almost any job.
3. He doesn't know.
4. He hasn't mastered it.
5. He's a beginner, but he's improving.
6. He's a bright guy.
7. Everyone knows it.
8. Don't ask him to fix yours!

"I think I've got the hang of it!"

Note: Sometimes you want to talk about a person who is completely incompetent. A common expression is: *He couldn't organise a piss-up (a drunken party) in a brewery!* Some people consider this offensive, so do not use it except with people you know well.

4: Revision

Choose the correct word in these idioms:

1. She knows a thing or *two/three* about cars.
2. You'll soon *get/take* the hang of it.
3. He's an old *arm/hand* at this game.
4. I don't know the first thing *about/from* it.
5. I haven't got *a/the* clue.
6. That's the first I've *known/heard* of it.
7. I know it like the back of *my/the* hand.
8. You'll soon learn the *rope/ropes*.
9. She's got her head screwed *on/in*.
10. It's *first/second* nature to me now.

Is there a place you know like the back of your hand?

Unit 61 Memory

1: Literal meanings

Fill in the following words in the definitions below:

slip	*tip*	*jog*
blank	*sieve*	*dim*

1. The end of your tongue is called the . . . .
2. If a piece of paper is . . . . , there is nothing on it.
3. If a room has very little light, it is . . . .
4. If you . . . . someone's arm when they are holding a drink, they will probably spill it.
5. You use a . . . . in the kitchen to separate solids from liquids and small pieces from big pieces.
6. If you . . . . somewhere, you go quickly and you hope that no-one sees you.

2: Jog your memory

Use the following idiomatic expressions in the situations below:

a. *bear it in mind*	**d.** *refresh my memory*	**g.** *jog your memory*
b. *mind goes blank*	**e.** *escapes me*	**h.** *learned by heart*
c. *slipped my mind*	**f.** *rings a bell*	**i.** *racking my brains*

1. Annabel Giggs? I don't remember anyone in our class called that.
   > Have a look at this photograph. Perhaps it will . . . .
2. I've got a job interview with an insurance company tomorrow.
   > Good luck. I hate interviews. When they start asking difficult questions, my . . . . . . just . . . .
3. Are you sure you know the way to Paris from here? I don't want us to get lost.
   > I've done it before but I'll have a quick look at the map to . . . .
4. Did you remember to buy me a paper?
   > Oh, sorry. It completely . . . .
5. You've heard of Quasimodo, haven't you?
   > Quasimodo? Yes, that name . . . . !
6. Don't forget that Japanese people don't like to talk about business straightaway.
   > Thanks. I'll . . . .
7. Is your speech ready for tomorrow's meeting?
   > Yes, I've written it out and . . . . bits of it . . . .
8. Can you recommend a good Chinese restaurant near the town centre?
   > Oh yes. I know a good one. Let me think. What's it called? It's opposite the Town Hall but sorry, the name . . . .
9. You know that actor we were talking about? It's Morgan Freeman.
   > I knew it was Morgan something! I've been . . . . all day.

Note: If you 'rack' your brains, you make a great effort to remember something. *Rack* is an old word with many meanings which are not used today. One of the meanings is to 'torture' someone by stretching them on a machine called a 'rack'. Another old meaning is to 'exhaust' something.

3: A memory like a sieve

Use the following expressions to complete the situations below:

    a. *a memory like a sieve*   **e.** *ancient history*
    b. *on the tip of my tongue*   **f.** *a photographic memory*
    c. *at the back of my mind*   **g.** *in living memory*
    d. *a good memory for faces*   **h.** *as if it was yesterday*

1. Jane's amazing. She can remember things that happened years ago.
   > I wish I could say the same. I've got . . . .
2. Why aren't you listening? Is anything the matter?
   > Sorry, but . . . . , I know I have to ring Jack before two.
3. If I want to remember anything, I have to write it down.
   > Me too, but my boss is incredible. He's got . . . .

"Mr Pilkington has a photographic memory, but sometimes it puts Miss Lightbody off her work."

4. Who's that actor who played the policeman in *Seventh Heaven*?
   > Oh yes, Bruce someone... Bruce... Oh, wait, it's . . . .
5. Paul, do you remember that time we almost had a crash in the Alps?
   > Yes, ... !
6. Look, John, I'm really sorry about what I said to you last week.
   > You've already apologised. It's all right. I've forgotten about it. It's . . . .
   . . . . Let's just forget it happened, OK?
7. It's terrible, but I can never remember people's names.
   > Nor can I, but I've got . . . .
8. So what kind of weather did you have in Australia?
   > Terrible. It was the coldest winter . . . .

4: Revision

Look back at the idioms in this unit and add the missing nouns:

1. I'll bear it in . . . .
2. Let me refresh my . . . .
3. Learn things by . . . .
4. The name rings a . . . .
5. It completely slipped my . . . .

6. It might jog your . . . .
7. I've got a memory like a . . . .
8. I've been racking my . . . .
9. It's on the tip of my . . . .
10. As if it was . . . .

Have you got a good memory for faces?

Unit 62 | Mistakes

1: Literal meanings

Fill in the following words in the definitions below:

barking   slip   goose   chew   tongue

1. Another word for a small mistake is a . . . .
2. A . . . . is a bird like a duck but with a long neck.
3. Before you swallow food, you should . . . . it well.
4. A dog . . . . can keep you awake all night.
5. It can be very painful if you bite your . . . . !

2: You've missed the boat

Use these idiomatic expressions in the situations below:

a. *get your fingers badly burnt*
b. *fall flat on your face*
c. *miss the boat*
d. *make a real pig's ear of*
e. *put your foot in it*
f. *shoot yourself in the foot*
g. *bark up the wrong tree*
h. *take your eye off the ball*

> "Mika Hakkinen has well and truly shot himself in both feet."
>
> *TV commentator on Grand Prix race*

1. What's this special offer – two cinema tickets for the price of one?
   > It finished last week. You've . . . . , I'm afraid.
2. I've thought about it and I think it must've been Lucy who took my wallet.
   > Hang on a minute! No, you're . . . . there. She was off sick that morning.
3. How was the wedding? Or more importantly, how was your speech?
   > The wedding was fine, but I made . . . . my speech. I was so nervous I kept mixing up people's names.
4. Have you got any stocks or shares?
   > I did have, but I . . . . I lost about £10,000.
5. Why do you think this month's sales figures are so bad?
   > It's quite simple. We've been too busy with other things. We've . . . .
6. I don't know why you've asked Pam AND Tony when they've just split up.
   > Oh no! Have they? I've really . . . . , haven't I?
7. So changing courses hasn't turned out too well, then?
   > No, I should have stuck to architecture. I think I've . . . .
8. If our new office in Japan works, we could make a lot of money.
   > Yes, but if it doesn't, we could . . . .

Note: If you *rock the boat*, it means you cause trouble in an organisation.

3: A slip of the tongue

Fill in the following words and expressions in the sentences below:

    a. *bitten off more than you can chew*   **d.** *made a real mess of it*
    b. *got on the wrong side of*   **e.** *a wild goose chase*
    c. *a slip of the tongue*   **f.** *got the wrong end of the stick*

"Lee has a habit of biting off a lot more than he can chew!"

1. Mary's a psychologist, not a psychiatrist!
   > Did I say psychiatrist? Sorry, it was . . . .
2. Well, did you manage to find some batteries when you were out?
   > No, I've just been on . . . . Nearly all the shops were closed for lunch.
3. How did you get on with Kate? Did you ask her out for a meal?
   > I tried to, but I was so nervous I . . . .
4. I'm surprised Martin hasn't been promoted. He's brilliant at what he does.
   > I think he . . . . one of the directors a few years ago.
5. I thought we were going to Peter's for dinner. He said he's coming to us!
   > Sorry, I think you must've got . . . .
6. I've promised my parents I'll have finished painting the house by the time they get back on Sunday.
   > By Sunday? You must be mad! I think you've . . . .

4: Revision

Which expressions would you use in these situations? The words in brackets will help you.

1. You've upset someone by saying the wrong thing at the wrong time. *(foot)*
2. You've started doing something but it's become too difficult or you don't have enough time to finish. *(bitten, chew)*
3. You've spent a long time looking for something which in fact was impossible to find. *(I've, goose)*
4. You've lost a lot of money in a deal. *(fingers)*

Look back at the idioms in this unit and add the missing verbs:

5. . . . . the boat
6. . . . . fingers badly burnt
7. . . . . off more than I can chew
8. . . . . up the wrong tree
9. . . . . the wrong end of the stick

10. . . . . flat on your face
11. . . . . a pig's ear of it
12. . . . . a real mess of it
13. . . . . my foot in it
14. . . . . your eye off the ball

Have you ever shot yourself in the foot?

Unit 63 Misunderstanding

1: Literal meanings

Fill in the following words in the definitions below:

wires   **purpose**   **head or tail**   **stick**

1. Originally meaning beginning or ending – . . . .
2. When I take my dog for a walk in the park, I try to find a . . . . which I throw for the dog to fetch.
3. Electricity and most telephone signals come to us along . . . .
4. And what is the . . . . of your visit to Britain?

2: At cross purposes

Use these idiomatic expressions in the sentences below:

a. *not on the same wavelength*   d. *get the wrong end of the stick*
b. *twist what someone says*   e. *add up*
c. *go over my head*   f. *at cross purposes*

1. I was talking about my cat and Chris thought I was talking about my mother. It wasn't until I said something about the cat's tail that we realised we'd been talking . . . . for five minutes.
2. I just can't work with Sam. We constantly misunderstand each other. We're just . . . . at all.
3. No, Roger. You must've got . . . . I said we should meet outside the cinema, not at my house.
4. I never said we should cancel the visit. You're . . . .
5. Why should a happily married, successful businessman suddenly decide to kill himself? It just doesn't . . . . , does it?
6. I can't understand anything in my physics class. All the explanations go right . . . .

3: It was all Greek to me

Here are four more idiomatic expressions meaning that something is difficult to understand. Which fit best in the situations below?

a. *It was all Greek to me.*
b. *It was just double Dutch to me.*
c. *The penny still hasn't dropped, has it?*
d. *You're putting words into my mouth.*

1. I read the instructions and looked at the diagram, but they were no help at all.
2. You are renting a house and the contract has just arrived. It is full of legal jargon.
3. I don't believe what you are suggesting I believe.
4. You don't understand or realise what is going on.

4: Out of my depth

Complete these short dialogues using the following lines:

    a. *You've completely missed the point.*
    b. *It beats me!*
    c. *I can't make head nor tail of it.*
    d. *You've lost me.*
    e. *We got our wires crossed.*
    f. *I was completely out of my depth.*

1. How was your first German lesson last night?
   > Terrible. . . . .
2. Push these two buttons, then this one and then these two at the same time.
   > Sorry. . . . . ! Can you show me again?
3. Do you understand this letter from the solicitor – because I don't?
   > Neither do I. I . . . .
4. Why does Denise want to quit her job? I thought she loved it.
   > I don't know. . . . .!
5. So, we're going to waste all this money on advertising on TV?
   > No, ... That's not what
   we've agreed. We're only going to spend it if sales don't improve in the next two
   months.
6. So, you arrived at four o'clock and she arrived at six. How did that happen?
   > Goodness knows! Somehow . . . .!

5: Revision

**Look back at the idioms in this unit
and add the missing words:**

1. We're not on the same . . . .
2. You've got the wrong end of the . . . .
3. We're talking at cross . . . .
4. It went right over my . . . .
5. I can't make head nor . . . . of it.
6. The . . . . still hasn't dropped.
7. It's all . . . . to me.
8. We got our . . . . crossed.
9. I was completely out of my . . . .
10. You've completely missed the . . . .
11. You've . . . . me!
12. It just doesn't . . . . up.

*"Half past four! I wonder if
we've got our wires crossed."*

Were there any subjects at school where you felt out of your depth?

Unit 64 | Money 1

1: Literal meanings

Fill in the following words in the definitions below:

    pick up   *knock off*   *tighten*   *rip off*   *set back*   *splash*

1. If you reduce the price of something you . . . . a few pounds.
2. If something is loose, you need to . . . . it.
3. Children like to . . . . each other with water when they go swimming.
4. When children receive birthday presents, they usually . . . . the paper to see what's inside.
5. If your progress is delayed, for example, doing a project at work, you are . . . . . .
6. If you drop something, you have to . . . . it . . . . .

2: A bit over the top!

Study these idioms, then use them in the correct form in the situations below:

> *You pick up bargains.*
> *Things can cost a bit over the top.*
> *Things can be dirt cheap.*
> *Something which is very expensive can set you back a bit.*
> *You can pay through the nose.*
> *Things can cost an arm and a leg.*
> *You can be ripped off.*
> *A shop can knock money off an item.*

1. I checked the prices in that new restaurant yesterday. Pizzas start at £8!
   > £8! That's . . . ., isn't it?
2. Have you seen John's new car?
   > Yes, lovely, isn't it? I bet it . . . .!
3. What have you been doing this morning?
   > Just shopping. I . . . . a few bargains in the sales.
4. Renting a flat in London is getting more and more expensive. It's ridiculous.
   > I know. You have to . . . . for anything with more than two rooms.
5. Where do you get your blank videos from?
   > A little shop behind the library. They're . . . . there.
6. Hey, I love your new jacket. It IS new, isn't it?
   > Yes, I got it last weekend. It wasn't cheap. It cost me . . . .
7. Sorry I'm late. I had to get a taxi here. He charged me £12. Is that normal?
   > £12? I'm afraid you've just been . . . .
8. £50 for a CD player? How did you manage to get it so cheap?
   > It's an ex-display model so they . . . . £45 . . . . . . the list price.

Note: An informal and amusing way of asking the price of something is 'What's the damage?'

140

3: Tighten our belts

Fill in the following verbs in the dialogues below:

go	*go on*	*tighten*	*put*
break	*splash out*	*save*	*dip into*

1. Bad news, I'm afraid. Our rent is going up £20 per week.
   > Well, we'll just have to be careful what we spend – . . . . our belts a bit!
2. Well, that was delicious. Let's get the bill. I'll pay for this.
   > No, Barry, it's going to be expensive. Let's . . . . halves.
3. Shall we get a bottle of wine for tonight?
   > Come on! It's your birthday. Let's . . . . on a bottle of champagne.
4. You play the National Lottery, don't you? Do you actually make any money?
   > Yes and no. I certainly don't lose money. I reckon I just about . . . . even.
5. My uncle's left me £3000 in his will. I'll probably save it or invest it.
   > Oh, I wouldn't. I'd . . . . a spending spree and buy all the things I've always wanted.
6. I haven't got enough in my bank account to pay for the car to be repaired.
   > OK, we'll just have to . . . . our savings, then.
7. How is it that you can afford to go on holiday somewhere nice every year?
   > Easy! I just . . . . a bit of money aside each month just for my holiday.
8. What are you going to do with the money you got for your birthday? Spend it?
   > No, I'm going to . . . . it for a rainy day.

4: Revision

Complete this review of the idiomatic expressions used in this unit:

1. . . . . halves
2. go on a spending . . . .
3. cost an . . . . and a . . . .
4. . . . . even
5. dirt . . . .
6. splash . . . . on a new watch
7. . . . . up a bargain or two
8. dip . . . . your savings
9. save money for a . . . . day
10. . . . . our belts
11. put £500 . . . . for a holiday
12. pay through the . . . .
13. a . . . . over the top
14. it set us . . . . a bit

"Oh good! A rainy day at last!"

If somebody gave you some extra cash, what would you splash out on?

Unit 65 | Money 2

1: Literal meanings

Fill in the following words in the definitions below:

> *fortune*   *stinks*   *lap*   *loaded*

1. If a gun has bullets in it, it is . . . .
2. My cat often sits on my . . . . when I'm watching TV.
3. If something is extremely smelly, it . . . .
4. A . . . . is a large amount of money.

Note: The informal word for the old British coin known as a shilling (5p) was a bob.

2: A bit hard up

Divide the following expressions into two groups:

> A: Poor:
> B: Not exactly poor, but certainly not rich:

   a. *living on the breadline*   **e.** *my account's in the red*
   b. *enough to get by on*   **f.** *a bit hard up*
   c. *not very well off*   **g.** *can't make ends meet*
   d. *without a penny to his name*   **h.** *living from hand to mouth*

Now complete these situations using the above:

1. We're going up to London for the weekend. Do you want to come?
   > I'd love to but I've just paid out £600 on the car so I'm a . . . . at the moment.
2. What was that letter from the bank about?
   > I'm afraid we're . . . . again.
3. What's the pay like where you work?
   > Not very good, but it's OK. It's . . . .
4. This is a modern, industrialised society but millions of people in this country are still living . . . ., just surviving.
5. I was thinking of inviting Jane and David to come with us to the opera, but I don't think they could afford to. David hasn't got much work at the moment so they're not . . . . at the moment.
6. My sister's husband has just died and she is left alone with 4 children. I don't know how she manages to . . . .
7. He's lost everything – job, house, car. Now he's living on the streets . . . .
8. My job isn't bad but I don't earn enough to save much or buy any nice things. I'm basically . . . .

Note: The 'breadline' is the situation where you are just able to feed yourself and your family. If you had any less, you would go *below the breadline* and not be able to survive.

3: Rolling in it

All these idiomatic expressions mean *very rich* **or** *well off*. **Complete the sentences below using the correct form:**

- a. *He's rolling in it.*
- b. *He's stinking rich.*
- c. *He's got money to burn.*
- d. *He's worth a fortune.*
- e. *He could buy and sell you.*
- f. *He makes a good living.*
- g. *He lives in the lap of luxury.*
- h. *He's very comfortable.*
- i. *He's loaded.*
- j. *He's not short of a bob or two.*

"Money to burn? He could buy and sell the likes of us!"

1. My sister's an accountant and her husband's a merchant banker. They must be . . . . in it!
2. My brother's just got a new job which pays double his old salary. He was well paid before but now he's got money to . . . .
3. People who don't know Mrs Crabtree think she's just a poor old lady, but in actual fact, she's part of a very rich family. She's probably worth a . . . .
4. I wouldn't say I was rich. Let's just say I'm not short of . . . .
5. Look at the car Paul drives and those Armani suits! He must be . . . .
6. My dad was a bank manager so he's got a good private pension. You couldn't describe my parents as rich, but they're very . . . .
7. Bob's just got a teaching job in Brunei – big tax-free salary, all expenses paid. He's living in the . . . .
8. I'm a freelance designer. Work's pretty good at the moment, so I'm lucky to be making quite a . . . .
9. The old man next door looks like a down-and-out, but he's a millionaire. He could . . . .
10. A gold Rolls Royce. A yacht in the Bahamas and a villa in Mustique. I think that's the definition of . . . . !

4: Revision

Look back at the idioms in this unit and fill in the missing words:

1. living . . . . hand . . . . mouth
2. . . . . a penny . . . . his name
3. living . . . . the lap . . . . luxury
4. living . . . . the breadline
5. a bit hard . . . . at the moment
6. enough to get . . . .
7. not very well . . . .
8. rolling . . . . it
9. not short . . . . a few bob
10. . . . . the red

Note: The opposite of *in the red* **is** *in the black*.

Can you think of three well-known people who've got money to burn? Do you know anyone who lives in the lap of luxury?

Unit 66 | Moods

1: Over the moon

Fill in the following words in the sentences below:

cloud	tails	air	world
moon	punch	spirits	bits

1. Our son's just got engaged to a really nice girl. We're over the . . . .
2. I've just passed my driving test. I can't believe it. I'm so pleased. I feel as if I'm walking on . . . .
3. I'm just ringing to thank you for my present. It's exactly what I wanted. I'm thrilled to . . . . with it.
4. Look at Clare. She seems so relaxed and happy these days. She looks as if she hasn't got a care in the . . . .
5. Pete's wife's just had twins. He's going round like a dog with two . . . . !
6. Sorry about all the noise last night. I hope we didn't wake you. We were celebrating our exam results and we were in very high . . . .
7. Mark's just landed his dream job, so he's on . . . . nine at the moment.
8. We've just heard that we've got a big contract which is going to last for five years. We're all as pleased as . . . .

Note: Punch (short for Punchinello) is the main male character in the puppet show Punch and Judy. He is cruel and frightens little children.

2: Blow your top

All the idioms in this exercise are ways of expressing anger or a bad mood. First fill in the correct verbs in the following:

fly	make	spit	give	blow

a. . . . . . . your top
b. . . . . . . off the handle
c. . . . . . . someone a piece of your mind
d. . . . . . . blood
e. . . . . . . your blood boil

Now use the correct form of these expressions:

1. I always try to keep calm, but when the steward spilt the drinks over me, I just blew . . . . and demanded to be upgraded to first class.
2. When I came back and found the dent in my car, I was spitting . . . . !
3. It makes . . . . just to see the pictures of those refugees.
4. I don't often lose my temper, but when I saw that woman hitting her little boy in the street, I flew . . . . and gave her . . . .

3: On the warpath

Add these nouns to complete the expressions:

straw	collar	arms	warpath	rag	tether

a. like a red . . . . . to a bull
b. the last . . . . . .
c. hot under the . . . . . .
d. up in . . . . . .
e. at the end of my . . . . . .
f. on the . . . .

144

Now complete these sentences:

1. Keep away from Felicity today. She's on . . . . about something.
2. If you want to get on with Roger, don't talk about hospitals. It's like . . . .
. . . . He just blows his top.
3. Calm down. There's no need to get so . . . . ! Shouting
won't get you anywhere.
4. It's terrible. They want to build a new road just 20 metres away from our houses.
Everybody's up . . . . about it, as you can imagine.
5. All right. This is it! I've warned you. This is . . . . You said you'd be
home by midnight. It's now twenty past.
6. I've asked you time and time again to keep the flat tidy, not to smoke, and not to
leave things lying about. You just don't listen! I'm at . . . .

**Note: *At the end of your tether* means that you are annoyed. *At your wits' end*
means that you are frustrated.**

> **"We were over the moon when it looked as
> if Bayern were going to clinch it and all I
> can say is that we are as sick as a parrot."**
>
> *Sports report on Manchester United v.
> Bayern Munich*

4: Revision

Look back at the idioms in this unit and put in the missing prepositions:

1. I'm . . . . the end . . . . my tether.
2. Why are you so hot . . . . the collar?
3. I'm . . . . cloud nine.
4. We were . . . . very high spirits.
5. That's like a red rag . . . . a bull.
6. She just flew . . . . the handle.
7. I'm walking . . . . air.
8. I'm thrilled . . . . bits with it.
9. I was . . . . the moon.
10. She's . . . . the warpath.

What would you say in these situations? The words in brackets will help you.

11. A group of people are unhappy about a decision. *(Everyone's, arms)*
12. It's happened one time too many. *(That's, straw)*
13. You want to say that a particular thing makes you angry. *(It, boil)*
14. You are going to tell someone you are angry at their behaviour. *(I, piece, mind)*
15. You are extremely proud of something you've done. *(I, punch)*

5: Literal meanings

Find the words in this unit which complete these definitions:

1. The part of a shirt which goes round your neck is the . . . .
2. An old piece of cloth, used for cleaning things, is a . . . .
3. To make a cup of tea, first . . . . the water.
4. When you are very pleased and excited about something, you are . . . .
5. A . . . . is a rope or chain which ties an animal to stop it running away.
6. You pick up a kettle or a pot by the . . . .

What makes your blood boil? Do you ever fly off the handle?

Unit 67 People

1: Literal Meanings

Fill in the following words in the sentences below:

quantity	*bachelor*	*confirm*	*coach*
blanket	*cannon*	*soul*	*Jekyll and Hyde*

1. Nowadays nearly everyone uses a duvet on their bed but some people still prefer sheets and a . . . .
2. A man who is not married is called a . . . .
3. A . . . . is an amount of something.
4. If you think something is true, but you are not sure, you need to . . . . it.
5. A . . . . is like a bus except they are usually more comfortable and used for longer journeys.
6. A . . . . is a kind of large gun.
7. The spiritual part of a person is sometimes called the . . . .
8. . . . . are two sides of the same person in the novel by Robert Louis Stevenson.

2: An unknown quantity

Use these eight descriptions of people in the sentences below:

        a. *a bit of an old woman*
        b. *a nosey parker*
        c. *a clever dick*
        d. *a down-and-out*
        e. *a confirmed bachelor*
        f. *a backseat driver*
        g. *an unknown quantity*
        h. *a wet blanket*

1. Nobody knows where Jim came from. We don't know if he's got children. He's a bit of . . . .
2. Don't tell Liz anything about yourself or your business. She's a . . . .
3. I don't think Pete will ever get married. He's 45 and very independent. He's . . . .
4. My wife's the worst. She sits there saying "Slow down", "Do you know what speed you're doing?", "Mind that car". She's a classic . . . .
5. James is always worrying about his health, keeping warm, what he eats. He's terrified of burglars. He really is . . . .
6. Richard thinks he knows it all. He's a real . . . .
7. Remember David Brown who was so good at sport when we were at school? Well, I saw him the other day in the centre of town, looking terrible. He'd obviously been drinking and was sitting around with a crowd of . . . .
8. Don't ask Jeff to the party. He'll just sit in the corner looking miserable. He can be such . . . .

3: A slowcoach

Use the following expressions in the correct sentence below:

a. *the salt of the earth*
b. *a loose cannon*
c. *a pain in the neck*
d. *the life and soul of the party*

e. *a Jekyll and Hyde*
f. *a slowcoach*
g. *a trouble-maker*
h. *a show-off*

1. Come on! Hurry up! You're such . . . .
2. I don't know how you can share a car with Simon every morning. All he talks about is motorbikes. I find him a real . . . . !
3. Don't have anything to do with Alan. He's just a . . . .
4. One minute she's happy and friendly, the next she totally ignores you! She's a real . . . . , if you ask me.
5. Mike loves flashing his Rolex around and his latest BMW. He's a . . . .
6. Things are always more interesting when Patricia arrives. She's . . . .
7. The good thing about John is you always know where you are with him. He is totally 100% honest, but the down side is he sometimes says exactly what he's thinking in all the wrong places – a bit of . . . . !
8. I love my grandmother. She's kind, honest, uncomplicated. She's . . . .

4: Who said it?

Look back at the exercises in this unit and decide who said the following:

1. Slow down, there's a cyclist. . . . .
2. No thanks. I don't like parties. . . . .
3. So, how much do you earn? . . . .
4. Are you sure it's safe to eat here? . . . .
5. Do you like my new outfit? It's Armani. . . . .
6. Women just complicate things. . . . .
7. I'll be ready in a minute. . . . .

5: Who are they talking to?

Which type of person is the speaker below talking to?

1. Yes, it's very nice. I expect it cost a fortune. . . . .
2. Look, who's driving – you or me? . . . .
3. Mind your own business! . . . .
4. Come on! You never know, you might enjoy yourself. . . . .
5. I'm so glad you've arrived. It's been really boring. . . . .
6. I didn't know you were married! . . . .
7. Do you think it was wise telling them what our marketing plans are? . . . .
8. I just want you to meet her, that's all. . . . .

Are you a good passenger in a car or are you a backseat driver?

Unit 68 Power and Influence

1: Literal meanings

Here is some information to help you understand some of the idioms in this unit:

1. A puppet is a kind of doll with strings. When you 'pull the strings', the puppet moves.
2. People with a lot of influence are often called the 'movers and shakers'. They are the people who make decisions and have new ideas.
3. 'Beck' is an old word meaning a silent signal. Today we only use it in the expression 'to be at someone's beck and call' – at their command, ready to do anything they wish.

2: Movers and shakers

Fill in the following words and expressions in the dialogues below:

> a. *friends in high places*
> b. *put in a good word for you*
> c. *twist my arm*
> d. *movers and shakers*
> e. *get the upper hand*
> f. *throw his weight around*
> g. *at your beck and call*
> h. *lay down the law*

1. You've met John before, haven't you?
   > Yes, you're one of the . . . . in English teaching, aren't you?
   Well, I'm not so sure about that – more like a big fish in a small pond!
2. There's no way we'll get visas with only four weeks to go before we leave.
   > Don't worry. I'll speak to my friend Jill in the Foreign Office. She's got . . . .
   . . . .
3. Go on, have another chocolate.
   > All right, then, if you . . . .
4. When you've done the washing up, could you go down to the shops. We need milk.
   > "Do this, Do that." I'm not . . . . , you know. I'm not your servant!
5. I see your company are advertising for more staff. I'm thinking of applying.
   > Good idea. If you do, I'll . . . .
6. David's just arrived late again.
   > Has he? That's the third time this week. I'm going to have to . . . .
   . . . . and give him a final warning.
7. What are you watching? Football? Who's winning?
   > Nobody. It's nil – nil but Liverpool are starting to . . . .
   . . . . They nearly scored a minute ago.
8. I wish Bob would stop upsetting people in the office.
   > Yes, I wish he wouldn't . . . . so much.

3: Hold the fort

Complete the following idiomatic expressions with these verbs:

hold	*take (2)*	*eat*	*pass*	*carry*
call	*pull*	*wear*	*twist*	

a. . . . . . . the shots
b. . . . . . . a lot of weight
c. . . . . . . the buck
d. . . . . . . a few strings
e. . . . . . . the trousers

f. . . . . . . the fort
g. . . . . . . out of the palm of my hand
h. . . . . . . a tough line
i. . . . . . . someone around your little finger
j. . . . . . . advantage of someone

Now use these idioms in their correct form in the following sentences:

1. I'm just leaving the office for a couple of hours. Can you . . . . till I get back?
2. Everyone in my office is terrified of the caretaker, Mr Simkins, but I get on with him like a house on fire. I have him . . . . !
3. One piece of advice – arrive on time in the mornings. The company . . . . on people who are late.
4. If you're interested in that job at Plessey's, I know the Managing Director. Maybe I could . . . . and get you an interview.
5. I've just met Robert's wife. Poor man! She never stops talking. It's obvious who . . . . in that house!
6. My daughter's only four but she knows how to get what she wants. She can . . . . me . . . . !
7. I think we should try to get Dr Hodges to support our plan. People respect him and his name would . . . . with the Board.
8. You may not like it, but I'm the boss and I . . . . around here. So, I would like that report on my desk before 5 o'clock today.
9. It's your responsibility. You're in charge, so stop trying to . . . .
10. Once you discover someone's weakness, it's up to you whether you . . . . of them or not.

> **"Tough line taken by police."**
>
> *Newspaper headline*

4: Revision

Complete the following 18 idiomatic expressions from this unit:

1. twist someone's . . . . . .
2. get the . . . . . hand
3. put in a good . . . . . .
4. . . . . . . in high places
5. call the . . . . . .
6. . . . . down the law
7. hold the . . . . . .
8. take . . . . of someone
9. at your . . . . . . and call

10. wear the . . . . . .
11. carry a lot of . . . . . .
12. take a . . . . . line
13. pull a few . . . . . .
14. movers and . . . . . .
15. eating out of the . . . . . . of my hand
16. pass the . . . . . .
17. . . . . your weight around
18. twist you around my little . . . . . .

Are you a mover and shaker?

Unit 69 Problems 1

1: Literal meanings

Fill in the following words in the definitions below:

jam   spanner   hop   limbo   creek   blink   rails

1. If you are in a . . . . . , you are in an awkward or difficult situation.
2. If you are in . . . . . . , you are neither in heaven nor in hell.
3. You tighten nuts and bolts with a . . . .
4. If you jump up and down only on one leg, you . . . .
5. Trains run on . . . . . . and if they crash, they come off the . . . .
6. A small sea inlet is a . . . .
7. To close and then open your eyes very quickly is the most common meaning of
. . . .

Note: An older meaning of *blink* is a 'sudden flash of light'. Today, *on the blink* means 'not working' or 'out of order'.

2: The tip of the iceberg

Five of the following ten statements are True and five are False. Mark the true ones T and the false ones F:

1. If a problem is **only the tip of the iceberg,** it means there are much bigger and more serious problems to emerge.
2. Someone who is **in a tight corner** is too fat to get through a door.
3. If you **go off the rails,** you lose self-respect and, perhaps, start drinking or taking drugs.
4. If you **put the cat among the pigeons,** everyone gets upset.
5. If your TV is **on the blink,** it has stopped working.
6. If two or more people are **in the same boat,** it means they are very similar.
7. A friend who is **in a real state** looks wonderful.
8. If you are **caught on the hop** at work, you are one of the busiest and most energetic employees.
9. If you **threw a spanner in the works**, your boss would probably promote you for your good sense.
10. If you have to resign from your job **under a cloud**, it means you have probably done something you should not have done.

The false statements are . . . . Use them correctly in these sentences:

11. So, we've both lost our jobs! At least we're . . . . !
12. My sister's just had some very bad news about her husband. I'll have to go and see her. She's . . . .
13. You shouldn't have raised the question of holiday pay. That really . . . .
. . . . !
14. The bank is putting pressure on us to bring our overdraft down. We're . . . .
. . . . , but I'm sure it won't last. The market will pick up soon.
15. The biggest order of the year and five staff on holiday! We were really . . . .
. . . .

3: In a bit of a jam

Add *in, on, at, out of,* or *up* to these idiomatic expressions:

  a. . . . . a loss
  b. . . . . the creek
  c. . . . . limbo
  d. . . . . hot water
  e. . . . . my depth
  f. . . . . a bit of a jam
  g. . . . . a standstill
  h. . . . . the wrong foot

"I am not amused, Edward. We are well and truly up the creek and there isn't a paddle in sight!"

Now use the correct expression in the situations below:

1. Sales Department, good morning.
   > John, it's only me – Bob. Listen, I'm . . . . I've got to pick my mother-in-law up from the airport in an hour's time and Helen's got my car. Can I borrow yours? I'll be back by 4.30, so you don't need to worry.
2. Sorry I'm late. The traffic was awful.
   > Tell me about it! I had real problems this morning. There must have been an accident. The traffic was . . . . in the town centre.
3. So, when are you moving house, Jim?
   > I'm not really sure. We've got a buyer for our place, but there's a problem with the people we're buying from. We're . . . . at the moment.
4. So, how was your evening with Kim and Kevin?
   > OK, thanks. The only problem was when the conversation got round to opera. They seem to know so much about it. I was completely . . . .
5. I get the impression you don't like your new neighbours.
   > Well, they had a very noisy party on their first Saturday night and I asked them to keep the noise down. I'm afraid we got off . . . .
6. Miles from anywhere! Blistering sun! And you run out of petrol! We really ARE
   . . . . !
7. I was sorry to hear that Jane isn't speaking to you.
   > Yes, it's a total misunderstanding, but there's nothing I can do about it. I'm . . . . to know what to do.
8. I often use the office phone for personal calls. I don't think it matters.
   > Well, if Helen finds out what you've been doing, you'll be . . . .

Note: You can *be in hot water, land in hot water,* or *get into hot water.*

4: Revision

Look back at the idioms in this unit and add the missing words:

1. We're all in the same . . . .
2. We're in a tight . . . .
3. I was completely out of my . . . .
4. We got off on the wrong . . . .
5. You've caught me on the . . . .
6. She left under a . . . .
7. The traffic was at a . . . .
8. He's gone off the . . . .
9. The TV's on the . . . .
10. You'll be in hot . . . .

Did you ever get into hot water when you were at school?

Unit 70 Problems 2

1: Literal Meanings

Fill in the following words in the definitions below:

bury	*cracks*	*buds*	*flow*	*carpets*
sweep	*nip*	*bull*	*horns*	*doubt*

1. A male cow is called a . . . .
2. Some houses in Britain have wooden floors but most have wall-to-wall . . . .
3. Our cat died last week. We decided to . . . . it in the garden.
4. Spring is here! You can see the . . . . coming out on the trees.
5. The . . . . of water in the river increases in spring when the snow melts.
6. We need a builder. There are . . . . developing in the walls of the kitchen.
7. Don't go in that field! Some of those cows have . . . . !
8. I work in a hairdresser's. I don't cut hair. I just make coffees and . . . . the floor all day!
9. There's no . . . . in my mind that we will soon have holidays in space.
10. If you squeeze something hard between your finger and thumb, you . . . . it.

2: Anything for a quiet life

Use the following idioms, which are about avoiding problems:

        a. *We'll cross that bridge when we come to it.*
        b. *I'll keep a low profile.*
        c. *Let's sleep on it.*
        d. *I'd better give you the benefit of the doubt.*
        e. *We'll have to go with the flow.*
        f. *Anything for a quiet life!*

1. No wonder Bill and Jean are having trouble with their children. They give them everything they ask for.
   > Yes, their philosophy seems to be . . . . !
2. Look, if we discuss this all night, we still won't reach agreement. I just don't know what we should do next.
   > No, I admit it's a difficult problem. We'll start afresh tomorrow morning. In the meantime, ...
3. Have you heard they're looking for someone to open an office in Ulan Bator?
   > Well, I think . . . . I don't fancy a remote place like that.
4. Look, I've told you a dozen times I wasn't even IN the office when the files were erased. It must've been someone after I left.
   > All right, I suppose . . . .
5. Look, if we're going to change the whole company's computer systems, we've got to think about staff training.
   > I've got more urgent problems than that on my mind at the moment. . . . .
6. All the younger staff are keen to go bungee jumping on the staff day out.
   > I know! I don't think we've got any choice! . . . .

3: Bury your head in the sand

Complete the following text by putting the lines in the correct order. The first one has been done for you.

When a problem comes up, people deal with it in different ways. Some people try to ignore it, but you can't just **bury your head**

a. **under the carpet**. Personally, I think that's a mistake. It's better to **face the**
b. **by the horns** and make a decision. When a problem appears they **get to the**
c. **in the sand**, hoping the problem will go away. Or, maybe, you just **sweep it**
d. **buck,** instead of taking responsibility themselves. I like people who **take the bull**
e. **facts**, however difficult that may seem. Another mistake is when people **pass the**
f. **bottom of it** and sort it out. They don't just **paper over**
g. **it in the bud,** if possible, before it gets more serious.
h. **pieces** when facing a difficult situation. When things get too much, they **turn a**
i. **blind eye** and hope things will go away. When there's a problem, **nip**
j. **the cracks** to make things look better. Some people just **go to**

1. *c* **2.** ... **3.** ... **4.** ... **5.** ... **6.** ... **7.** ... **8.** ... **9.** ... **10.** ...

4: Revision

Match the idioms in this unit to the definitions below. The words in brackets will help you.

1. Try to hide a problem. *(carpet)*
2. Deal with a problem in a superficial way. *(cracks)*
3. Deal with a problem if and when it happens. *(bridge)*
4. Deal with a problem as soon as it appears. *(bud)*
5. Take decisive action. *(bull)*
6. Find out the cause of a problem. *(bottom)*
7. Pretend the problem doesn't exist. *(sand)*
8. Ignore somebody's bad behaviour. *(blind)*

Look back at the idioms and find the missing verbs:

9. . . . . . . the buck
10. . . . . . . the problem in the bud
11. . . . . . . to the bottom of it
12. . . . . . . it under the carpet
13. . . . . . . the facts
14. . . . . . . to pieces

Find the missing nouns:

15. turn a blind . . . . . .
16. keep a low . . . . . .
17. go with the . . . . . .
18. cross that . . . . . . when we come to it
19. give her the benefit of the . . . . . .

"No, Mr Higginbottom, you'll never catch me sweeping anything under the carpet. It's more than my job's worth!"

Did your parents sometimes turn a blind eye to things you did when you were a teenager?

Unit 71 Reading

1: Literal Meanings

Fill in the following words in the definitions below:

wade	*jargon*	*cover*	*leaf*	*tripe*
dip	*load*	*twist*	*print*	*grip*

1. Another word for a page in a book is a . . . .
2. Before getting into a bath, to test the temperature, you . . . . your fingers or toes into the water.
3. If you are walking in water which is knee-deep, you . . . . through it.
4. The outside part of a book is called the . . . .
5. I don't like mountain roads. They . . . . and turn very sharply.
6. Something which is written in . . . . uses too many difficult or technical words for no good reason.
7. Another word for a *lot* of is a . . . . of.
8. People with poor eyesight can get special books which use large . . . .
9. When you cook the stomach of a cow, it is called . . . .
10. Hold on to something very tightly and you . . . . it.

2: A load of tripe!

Match the comments with these different kinds of reading material:

a. *a novel*   **c.** *a teenage magazine*
b. *a reference book*   **d.** *a legal document*

1. My boyfriend thinks it's just **a load of tripe**!
2. I had to **wade through** page after page of jargon.
3. I love **dipping into it** from time to time to check dates and that sort of thing.
4. I read her last one **from cover to cover** in one day.
5. There's a brilliant **twist at the end**.
6. It's too **high-brow** – far too intellectual for my taste.
7. It's only **light reading** but some of the articles can be quite informative.
8. Some chapters were fairly **heavy-going**.
9. Make sure you **read the small print** before signing.
10. I read it and re-read it but I **couldn't make head nor tail of it**.
11. I gave up after about fifty pages. I just **couldn't get into it**.
12. You have to be patient at the beginning. **It takes a while to get going**.
13. It's **gripping,** absolutely **riveting,** right to the very end.
14. I just **couldn't put it down** until I'd finished it.
15. It's full of interesting **tit-bits** about history.
16. It's **unputdownable.** I'm sure it's going to be a real **blockbuster**.
17. It's **a good read** every month.
18. **It's a must** for anyone going there.

Note: If a book is very intellectual, you describe it as *high-brow*. If it is full of gossip and trivial information, it is *low-brow*.

3: Very well read

The metaphors of reading and books are important in a number of common idiomatic expressions. Use these expressions in the situations below:

    a. *turn over a new leaf*   d. *reading between the lines*
    b. *an open book*   e. *read too much into it*
    c. *judge a book by its cover*   f. *very well read*

"Ah, Mr Rimmington, after 40 years with the company, it's good to see that at last you're turning over a new leaf!"

1. Karen's very interesting, isn't she? If you want to know anything, ask her.
   > Oh yes. She's . . . .

2. Jim, why can you never find anything on your desk?
   > Because I am naturally untidy! I know. I'm going to . . . .
   . . . . I promise!

3. Brenda completely ignored me this morning. I must have put my foot in it yesterday.
   > She's just not in a good mood at the moment, that's all. I wouldn't . . . .
   . . . .

4. What I like about Susanna is her openness and honesty.
   > Yes, what you see is what you get. She's . . . .

5. Everybody seems to be happy with the idea of Isabel joining our group.
   > Except Jack. He said he wasn't against the idea, but, ...
   . . . . , I think he's got his doubts about her.

6. I was completely wrong about our new Press Officer. When I saw the pigtail, I thought, "What have we got here?"
   > Well, you know what they say: Never . . . .

4: Revision

Look back at the idioms in this unit and fill in the missing nouns:

1. I'm turning over a new . . . .
2. You've got to read between the . . . .
3. It's just a . . . . of tripe.
4. I read it from cover to . . . .
5. I can't make head nor . . . . of this.
6. I didn't read the small . . . .
7. It takes a . . . . to get going.
8. Never judge a book by its . . . .

Are most of the things you read high-brow or low-brow?

Unit 72 Relationships 1

1: Meanings

1. A spot is usually a mark on your skin, but if you *have a soft spot for* someone, you like them. You usually use it for someone who tends to be unpopular with other people.
2. When some animals attack another animal, they often attack the soft area around their throat. In the same way, if two people are arguing you can say that they are *at each other's throats*.
3. If you get on with someone *like a house on fire*, it means you get on very well.
4. If you *don't see eye to eye* it means that you don't agree on something.
5. If *there's no love lost between* two people it is a way of saying they really don't get on at all. They may not even be on speaking terms.

2: A shoulder to cry on

Put the following expressions in the dialogues below:

a.	*at each other's throats*	e.	*ups and downs*
b.	*a shoulder to cry on*	f.	*don't see eye to eye*
c.	*there's no love lost*	g.	*fight like cat and dog*
d.	*through thick and thin*	h.	*clear the air*

1. Thanks for listening, Rachel. I feel better for talking to you.
   > That's OK. You can always come to me if you need . . . .
2. You've had the same flatmate for years, haven't you? You must get on very well.
   > Well, we've had our . . . . over the years but on the whole it's worked very well.
3. Do you get on well with your brother and sisters?
   > Yes, I do, but my brother and older sister . . . .
4. Is it true that Jeff and Laura are having problems?
   > I think so. They seem to be . . . . most of the time these days.
5. How are you getting on with your new business partner?
   > Well, we . . . . on everything, but that's a good thing. It's when we agree on something too quickly that mistakes are made.
6. My parents have been married for 50 years.
   > In those days people stayed together . . . .
7. Why was there such a bad atmosphere in that meeting?
   > You're new here. Didn't you notice that . . . . between George and Andrew?
8. There's a bad atmosphere in our office. Some people aren't talking to each other.
   > Well, it's time you had a meeting to . . . .

Note: Milk *turns sour* if it is not kept in the fridge. It can *go off*. In the same way relationships can *turn sour* if two people *go off* each other.

3: A soft spot

Complete the following statements about good relationships:

1. I think my teacher has a soft . . . . for me.
2. Even if you get married, don't neglect your . . . . friends.
3. It's always fun to meet someone you . . . . it off with.
4. I must say I get on like a . . . . on fire with my mother-in-law.
5. I get on best with people who're on the same . . . . as myself.
6. My children all try to stay in my good . . . .
7. Do someone a good . . . . , and you've made a friend.
8. Do your best not to get off on the wrong . . . .
9. A friend in . . . . is a friend indeed!
10. You can . . . . your friends, but you can't pick your relations!

house
need
books
turn
hit
spot
pick
foot
wavelength
close

Note: A young friend is always young. An *old friend* might be only 35.

"No wonder we never see eye to eye! We're just not on the same wavelength!"

4: Through thick and thin

Look back at Exercises 2 and 3 to find idioms with these meanings:

1. in bad times and good times . . . .
2. don't agree . . . .
3. fight a lot . . . .
4. started with a misunderstanding . . . .
5. help a friend when they have a problem . . . .
6. do someone a favour . . . .

5: Revision

Complete these sentences with the correct preposition:

1. Do you need a shoulder to cry . . . .?
2. We're not . . . . the same wavelength.
3. They stayed together . . . . thick and thin.
4. We got . . . . like a house . . . . fire.
5. We got off . . . . the wrong foot.
6. They're . . . . each other's throats.
7. There's no love lost . . . . them.
8. I'm not . . . . his good books.
9. They don't see eye . . . . eye.
10. I've got a soft spot . . . . her.

Is there a member of your family you don't see eye to eye with?

Unit 73 | Relationships 2

1: Literal Meanings

Fill in the following words in the definitions below:

crush   **rocks**   **knot**   **plunge**   **stand**   **guts**

1. When boats sail too close to the land, ... can be a real danger.
2. If you can't . . . . . . hot water, it means you cannot tolerate it.
3. Everything inside you – your stomach, kidneys, liver etc, are your . . . .
4. If you accidentally sit down on a packet of biscuits, you will . . . . . . them.
5. When you tie two pieces of string together, you make a . . . .
6. The meanings of dive and . . . . . . are very similar. You can . . . . . . or dive into the sea. You can . . . . . . something into water, but you cannot dive something in.

Note: If you _have it in for_ someone, it means that you have some kind of grudge against them. You are annoyed with them for a specific reason.

2: Head over heels in love

Put the following nouns into these expressions:

crush   **heels**   **rocks**   **plunge**   **knot**   **love**

       a. tie the . . . . . .
       b. have a . . . . . . **on someone**
       c. take the . . . . . .
       d. fall in . . . . . .
       e. on the . . . . . .
       f. head over . . . . . . **in love**

Now use the correct form of the idiomatic expressions in these situations:

1. I've never seen Camilla so relaxed and happy. What's happened to her?
   > Didn't you know? She's met Mr Right! She's . . . . with this French chef who works in a restaurant in the town centre.
2. Kate, do you remember our art teacher at school? He was nice, wasn't he?
   > Oh yes, Mr Eastwood. I'll never forget him! I . . . . on him until the day I saw him with his six children and dreadful wife!
3. Tim, you and Sharon have been together now for ten years. Isn't it about time you tied . . . . ?
   > Well, funny you should mention it. Last night we decided to take . . . . so I hope you're free on June 12th! I'm looking for a best man!
4. I hear you've got Tom and Barbara's children staying with you at the moment.
   > Yes. I'm afraid Tom and Barbara's marriage is . . . . They're having a little time and space to talk on their own.
5. If you can . . . . , can you _fall out of_ love?

Note: If you like or admire someone very much you can say that you _think the world of them._

3: Gone their separate ways

All the idiomatic expressions in this exercise deal with relationships going wrong. Match the two parts of each conversation:

1. Are Luke and Louise still together?
2. Has Brian asked you to stay behind late again, Tony?
3. David's told me that he won't come skiing with us if Frank's going to be there. Have you any idea why?
4. What's your honest opinion of our new Head of Marketing?
5. Why won't the three political parties involved get together and cooperate?

a. Well, as far as I can gather, **there's no love lost between them**. They **fell out over something** last year and haven't spoken since.
b. No, I'm afraid not. **They've gone their separate ways**.
c. Yes, it's always me, isn't it? I think he's **got it in for me**.
d. **I can't stand her.** And I can't be more honest than that!
e. It's quite simple. **They hate each other's guts!** They wouldn't even share a taxi!

Note: If you have a disagreement with someone, fall out, then make up, you *patch up your differences* **or, if it was very serious, you** *bury the hatchet.*

> **"Tug of love as couple go their separate ways."**
>
> *Newspaper headline about who gets the children when a couple split up*

4: Revision

Complete the following with one word:

1. We've decided to go our separate . . . .
2. I think I've fallen in . . . . !
3. Have you . . . . it in for me or do you just not like me?
4. We're . . . . the plunge in October.
5. I can't bear to be in the same room as John. I just . . . . stand him.
6. Our 14-year-old daughter has a . . . . on her 23-year-old biology teacher!
7. There's no love . . . . between my brother and his in-laws. He calls them outlaws!
8. I wish people wouldn't fall . . . . so easily over silly little things.
9. So, you're . . . . the knot this Saturday. I hope the weather's nice for you.
10. The trouble with falling head . . . . heels in love with someone is that it's usually totally the wrong person!
11. I wouldn't say I hated Nigel's . . . . , but he's not my favourite person at the moment.
12. Lots of marriages which are on the . . . . could have been saved if the couples had seen a counsellor early on when they were first having trouble.

Do you know someone who's got it in for you? Can you do anything about it?

Unit 74 | Safety and Risks

1: Literal Meanings

1. **Put your head on the block:** Hundreds of years ago, a way of executing people was to cut their heads off. This was done by the criminal putting his head on a *block* of wood.
2. **Skating on thin ice:** If you go skating on a frozen lake, you must be careful not to go near dangerous areas where the ice is thin.
3. **A leap in the dark:** Another word for *jump* is *leap*. If you *leap in the dark*, you do something without thinking about the consequences.
4. **Flying by the seat of your pants:** If you do something *by the seat of your pants*, you do it by instinct and experience rather than with any technical or scientific help. In the early days of flying, before radar, it was said that pilots sometimes *flew by the seat of their pants.*

2: All your eggs in one basket

Use these idiomatic expressions in the situations below:

    a. *play safe*
    b. *put your head on the block*
    c. *sit on the fence*
    d. *put all your eggs in one basket*
    e. *to be on the safe side*
    f. *tread carefully*
    g. *live dangerously*
    h. *stick my neck out*

"*Mervyn was always sticking his neck out.*"

1. What do you think about investing in the Stock Market?
   > Just be careful not to . . . .
   . . . . Otherwise, you run the risk of losing everything.
2. How many bottles do you think we'll need – six?
   > Well, there are fifteen people coming so get eight just . . . .
3. So, who's going to win? England or Brazil?
   > I'll . . . . and say England – two goals to one.
4. I can see both sides of the argument. You're both right, I think.
   > Come on, Bob. You can't . . . . Tell us what you really think.
5. Shall we get the nine o'clock train to the airport?
   > No, that only give us 45 minutes to check in. I'd rather . . . . and get the 8 o'clock.
6. Somebody has to complain about our pay and conditions.
   > Go on, Alan. You're never afraid to . . . .
7. I'm going to go straight round and tell Mary what I think of her.
   > Well, ... She's not very well at the moment.
8. I've never bought a lottery ticket in my life!
   Go on, ... ! You might fall under a bus tomorrow!

3: Flying by the seat of my pants

Use the following idiomatic expressions in the situations below:

a. *at stake*	**e.** *cutting it a bit fine*
b. *skating on thin ice*	**f.** *a leap in the dark*
c. *nothing to lose*	**g.** *safe as houses*
d. *flying by the seat of my pants*	**h.** *sailing close to the wind*

1. I was very impressed by the way you were able to answer all the interviewer's questions so easily.
   > Were you? Well, I had no time to prepare. I was literally . . . .
2. I hope we get the new cleaning contract with British Airways.
   > Yes, there's 200 jobs . . . . if we don't.
3. That Korean deal was a bit dodgy, wasn't it?
   > Yes, it wasn't exactly illegal, but I agree we were . . . . a bit . . . .
4. If we catch the 3.30 train, we'll arrive at the airport half an hour before our flight.
   > That's . . . . What if the train's late?
5. Aren't you worried about your job? Banks seem to be getting rid of people at the moment.
   > No, I'm a merchant banker. My job's as . . . .
6. You're mad! How can you buy a villa in Spain without seeing it first?
   > I know it's . . . . but our friends had no problems with theirs.
7. I really want to ask Diane to go out with me but I don't think she's interested.
   > Go on. Give it a try. You've got . . . .
8. Goodness, when you started talking about divorce in front of Mary, I started to squirm. You know they've just separated?
   > Yes, it wasn't till I started, I suddenly realised that I was . . . .

4: Revision

Put the following pairs of words into the sentences below:

put, block	*stick, neck*
careful, skating	*leap, dark*
sailing, wind	*eggs, basket*
cutting, fine	*just, safe*

1. Four o'clock? That's . . . . it a bit . . . . , isn't it?
2. I'd keep quiet if I were you. You're . . . . a bit close to the . . . .
3. You'd better be . . . . , Tim. You're . . . . on thin ice.
4. I don't want to . . . . my head on the . . . . , so you can do it!
5. Take some extra traveller's cheques . . . . to be on the . . . . side.
6. I don't really know but I'll . . . . my . . . . out and say ...
7. Expanding into Eastern Europe will be a . . . . in the . . . . for us.
8. Don't put all your . . . . in one . . . .

When you travel by air, do you cut it a bit fine or are you there a couple of hours early to be on the safe side?

Unit 75 Similarities and Differences

1: The odd one out

Fill in the following idiomatic expressions in the sentences below:

Meaning similar	Meaning different
a. *in the same boat*	f. *a far cry from*
b. *the spitting image*	g. *the odd one out*
c. *on a par with*	h. *one of a kind*
d. *carbon copy*	i. *poles apart*
e. *six of one and half a dozen of the other*	j. *a world of difference*

1. All my brothers and sisters went to university but I'm . . . .
   I decided to leave school and get a job.
2. I would say that the cost of living in London is . . . . Paris.
3. It's not just you who's worried about losing your job. We're all . . . .
4. There's . . . . between visiting a country and actually living
   there.
5. I love my uncle. He's an eccentric. I don't know anybody quite like him. He's . . . .
   . . . .
6. Nigel and I are good friends but when it comes to politics we're . . . .
7. Don't bother going to see the new Bond film. It's virtually a . . . .
   of the last one.
8. So here you are living in a luxury flat looking out at Buckingham Palace. It's
   . . . . the slums of Liverpool!
9. I've just met David's brother. He's . . . . of that guy who reads
   the 6 o'clock news on TV!
10. Do you want to eat now and work later, or do a bit of work then eat?
    > Oh, I don't care. It's . . . .

2: Join the club!

Fill in the following verbs in the sentences below:

tell	join	stick out
take after	choose	follow

1. I'm absolutely fed-up! I'm over-worked and under-paid.
   > . . . . . . the club! You're not the only one, you know!
2. You can't go to a funeral in a cream suit! You'll . . . . like a sore thumb!
3. I can't . . . . the difference between Coke and Pepsi. Can you?
4. I expect John will . . . . in his father's footsteps and become a lawyer as well.
5. I'm very hot-headed. I lose my temper quite easily. My father's just the same.
   I suppose I . . . . him.
6. I've looked at the Sony system and the Phillips one and there seems to be little to
   . . . . between them. They're both good value for money in my opinion.

3: A different kettle of fish!

Complete the following using these idioms:

> **a. We're in a whole new ball game now.**
> **b. She was a different kettle of fish.**
> **c. As different as chalk and cheese!**

1. I only knew Mary's sister Elizabeth. She led a very quiet life.
   > Oh, you couldn't accuse Mary of that! . . . .
2. Has the change of government made any real difference?
   > Absolutely! . . . .
3. You and your sister are very different characters, aren't you?
   > Completely different. . . . .

4: Literal and non-literal meanings

Look back at the first three exercises and find the idioms which are related to the following information:

1. You cannot get further apart in the world than the North Pole and the South Pole. If you hold very different opinions, we say that your views are . . . .
2. If you hurt your thumb and put a bandage on it, it will look very different from your other fingers. So, if someone is wearing something very different from what is expected, he might . . . .
3. In golf if you take 4 strokes for a hole which is a 'par 4', you take the number of strokes which are expected. If someone is at the same level as you, they are . . . . with you.
4. A dozen means 12. If there is nothing to choose between two options, you can say that the choice is . . . .
5. Many years ago, if you wanted to make two copies of a document, you had to type it using two sheets of paper with a piece of carbon paper between them. If one thing is identical to another it is a . . . .

"Every father wants his son to follow in his footsteps – except Charlie who couldn't get rid of his!"

5: Revision

Look back at the idioms in this unit and add the final word:

1. we're all in the same . . . . . .
2. stick out like a sore . . . . . .
3. a different kettle of . . . . . .
4. as different as chalk and . . . . . .
5. follow in his father's . . . . . .
6. carbon . . . . . .
7. the odd one . . . . . .
8. can't tell the . . . . . .
9. join the . . . . . .
10. poles . . . . . .

Can you think of two people you know who are the spitting image of each other?

Unit 76 Sleep and Dreams

1: Literal Meanings

Fill in the following words in the definitions below:

crash   blink   nightmare   snore   nod   wink   log

1. When you open and close your eyes quickly, you . . . . If you only close one eye, you . . . .
2. When two cars hit each other, they . . . .
3. A very bad dream is a . . . .
4. When you mean "Yes", you . . . . your head.
5. A . . . . is a piece of the trunk or a thick branch of a tree.
6. If you make a loud noise when you sleep, you . . . .

2: Sleep like a log

Choose the word you think completes the idiom:

1. I feel great. I slept like a *log/dog* last night.
2. I was so tired when I got into bed last night that I went out like a *feather/light*.
3. I feel terrible. I didn't sleep a *blink/wink* last night.
4. I wake up at the slightest noise. I'm a very *light/soft* sleeper.
5. I usually go home for lunch but if I'm tired, I sometimes stay in my office and have forty *blinks/winks* at my desk.
6. Don't bother going to see the new Bond film. It was so boring I *fell off/nodded off.*
7. It's time you went to bed. You look dead on your *feet/legs.*
8. When I got in from work last night, I was utterly exhausted. I just *fell out/ crashed out* on the sofa. I didn't wake up till 11 this morning!
9. I was so tired I could hardly keep my eyes *open/apart.*
10. Someone said there was thunder last night, but I didn't hear a thing. I was *asleep/dead* to the world.
11. Wednesday is my day off so I usually *lie in/lie out* till about ten o'clock.
12. Ah! Look at him. Don't babies look lovely when they're *quick/fast* asleep?
13. I think you've had too much to drink. Go home, go to bed and *sleep/snore* it off.
14. I need two alarm clocks to wake me in the morning. I'm a very *heavy/strong* sleeper.

Now complete these expressions using idioms from this exercise:

15. dead on your . . . . . .
16. have forty . . . . . .
17. a . . . . . . or a . . . . . . sleeper
18. sleep like a . . . . . .
19. . . . . . . asleep
20. . . . . . . to the world

"I didn't hear a thing. I was dead to the world."

3: It was a nightmare

We often use words connected with sleep to talk about many different things. Add the following sentences to complete these situations:

a. *Don't lose any sleep over it.*   e. *It was a nightmare.*
b. *Sleep on it.*   f. *You're half asleep.*
c. *It's a dream come true.*   g. *It went like a dream.*
d. *We had him put to sleep.*   h. *I wouldn't dream of it.*

1. How was your holiday?
   > Awful. Everything went wrong. . . . .
2. Sorry to hear about your dog. Was he killed in an accident?
   > No. He was ill and too old to get better. . . . .
3. I'm a bit worried that I upset Amanda. I didn't mean to be rude.
   > I'm sure it was just a misunderstanding. . . . .
4. Sorry? What did you say? I wasn't listening.
   > What's the matter with you this morning? . . . .
5. So, you're off to America at the weekend? Have a good time.
   > I will. I've been wanting to go for years. . . . .
6. How was your date with Richard? Is he Mr Right?
   > Well, it was wonderful. Everything was perfect. . . . .
7. Work in the Madrid office? Well, it sounds good, but it's a big decision to leave home for two years.
   > You don't have to decide now. We can talk again tomorrow. . . . .
8. Do you allow yourself to have a drink when you're driving?
   > No, ... I'd never forgive myself if I had an accident.

> " When I told them it drove like a dream, a number of them swore they would order one as a company car."
>
> *Newspaper review of the launch of a new car*

4: Revision

Look back at the idioms in this unit and add the missing verbs. Put them in the same tense as the examples.

1. I . . . . like a log.
2. I didn't . . . . a wink last night.
3. I just . . . . out on the sofa.
4. I wouldn't . . . . of it.
5. It's a dream . . . . true.
6. Don't . . . . any sleep over it.
7. It . . . . like a dream.
8. I . . . . out like a light.
9. I . . . . in on my day off.
10. I'll . . . . on it and tell you tomorrow.

Do you like to lie in at the weekend?

Unit 77 Speed

1: Literal Meanings

Fill in the following words in the definitions below:

skates	*brake*	*snail*	*flash*	*blink*
drag	*bats*	*shot*	*split*	

1. If something is too heavy or big to carry, you can . . . . it along the ground.
2. You put your foot on the . . . . when you want to slow down or stop your car.
3. When you open and close your eyes quickly, you . . . .
4. If you want to move easily on ice, you need to wear . . . .
5. If you break or cut something from end to end, for example, a piece of wood, you . . . . it.
6. A . . . . is a small, soft animal with a round shell on its back. They are eaten in France.
7. A . . . . is a sudden, brief light – for example a . . . . of lightning during an electric storm.
8. A single bullet fired from a gun is called a . . . .
9. At night you sometimes see animals like mice with wings flying around. These are . . . .

2: Spread like wildfire

Fill in the following idiomatic expressions in the situations below:

a.	*get your skates on*	e.	*as if there was no tomorrow*
b.	*take your time*	f.	*no sooner said than done!*
c.	*spread like wildfire*	g.	*like a bat out of hell*
d.	*put the brakes on*	h.	*made very good time*

1. Everybody seems to know about my engagement!
   > The news . . . . You might have known it would!
2. Rodney, could you photocopy these certificates for me, please?
   > Certainly – . . . . !
3. What's the time?
   > Ten past seven. If you want to catch the quarter past, you'd better . . . .
4. Where's John?
   > Well, I just mentioned that my mother was coming over this evening and he took off . . . . !
5. We've overspent our budget by £15,000.
   > Right, we'd better . . . . our spending for a while.
6. I'm nearly ready. I just want to clean my shoes before we go.
   > There's no rush. . . . .
7. How was your journey? You came by car, didn't you?
   > Yes, it was fine. The roads were clear, so we . . . .
8. Look, just slow down! What's all the rush for? You're eating . . . .

3: At the drop of a hat

Use the following idiomatic expressions in the situations below:

a. *get off to a flying start*　　e. *drag your feet*
b. *in no time at all*　　　　　　f. *like a shot*
c. *in a flash*　　　　　　　　　g. *at a snail's pace*
d. *at the drop of a hat*　　　　h. *for a split second*

1. Kate, is there any chance you could pick up Jane from the airport this afternoon?
   > No, I'm sorry. You can't expect me to stop what I'm doing . . . .
   . . . . I've got too much to do before the conference at the weekend.
2. Have you decided where you're going on holiday yet?
   > No, I want to hurry up and book something but my husband's . . . .
   . . . ., as usual.
3. Your business seems to be doing very well. You only started a year ago, didn't you?
   > Yes, we . . . . and we're still going strong.
4. I was looking forward to seeing the Tour de France, but in the end, it was very
   disappointing. The riders were all past us . . . .
5. Hello, Dad, it's me. I'm at the station. Could you come and get me?
   > Yes, of course. Wait there. I'll be with you . . . . at all.
6. Hello, come in. How was your journey?
   > Awful. The traffic was moving . . . . for the last thirty miles.
7. You know, ... I thought you were your brother!
   > Don't worry, you're not the only person who gets us mixed up.
8. Would you carry on working if you won the lottery? I'd give up work straightaway.
   > So would I. I'd be out of this place . . . .

Note: Did you know that since the introduction of e-mail, the ordinary postal service is known as *snail mail*?

4: Revision

Put the missing words into the idioms below:

1. at the . . . . . . of a hat
2. like a . . . . . . out of hell
3. . . . . . . a shot
4. for a . . . . . . second
5. No sooner . . . . . than done.
6. . . . . . . no time

"*Ethel had to get her skates on or she'd miss the post.*"

Look back at the idioms in this unit and add the missing verbs:

7. . . . . . . the brakes on
8. . . . . . . like wildfire
9. . . . . . . your skates on
10. . . . . . . your time
11. . . . . . . off to a flying start
12. . . . . . . your feet

Which are more dangerous – drivers who drive at a snail's pace or those who drive like a bat out of hell?

Unit 78 | Starting and Stopping

1: Literal Meanings

Floodgates stop water flooding an area of land. If you *open the floodgates*, you start something you cannot stop. Square One is the very beginning of a board game. If you *go back to square one*, you start all over again. At the end of a performance in the theatre, the curtains close. If *it's curtains for you*, that means it is the end. People are buried in coffins. If something is *the final nail in the coffin*, it means it is the very end.

2: Throw in the towel

Fill in the following nouns in the expressions below:

> *curtains*   *bud*   *coffin*   *plug*   *towel*   *life*   *light*   *ice*

a. a new lease of . . . . . .   e. pull the . . . . . . on something
b. give us the green . . . . . .   f. break the . . . . . .
c. it's . . . . . . for you   g. nip something in the . . . . . .
d. throw in the . . . . . .   h. final nail in the . . . . . .

Now use the correct form of these expressions in the situations below:

1. I hear Rachel's finally handed in her resignation.
   > Yes, she's been passed over for promotion so many times now that she decided to . . . . and try somewhere else.
2. I'm worried about this dinner party, Alan. Lots of people won't know each other.
   > Don't worry. Jill's coming. She's a great person to . . . . and get everyone talking to everyone else.
3. When are we going to upgrade our computers? They're useless!
   > Next month. We've been waiting for head office to . . . .
4. You look incredibly well, Barbara. Are you in love or something?
   > No, I've given up smoking and I've been on a new diet for the past six months. It's given me . . . .
5. Why are you looking so depressed, Bill?
   > I've just heard that our American owners have . . . . the project I've spent the last two years of my life on.
6. Listen, everybody! If we don't start making a profit and making it soon, ... for you, for me, and for the whole of this department.
7. There seems to be an awful lot more gossip in the general office than there used to be.
   > We certainly don't want that. We'd better . . . . straightaway.
8. Sacked? Why did they sack you?
   > Well, I'd made a couple of mistakes with orders going to the wrong addresses, but the . . . . was when I lost a cheque for £9,000.

Note: An amusing idiom meaning that the end has not yet come is *It's not over till the fat lady sings.*

3: Back to square one

Use these idiomatic expressions in the sentences below:

> **a. *get cracking***
> **b. *start the ball rolling***
> **c. *back to square one***
> **d. *open the floodgates***
> **e. *the end's in sight***
> **f. *it's still early days***
> **g. *on hold***
> **h. *call it a day***

1. With the breakdown in the peace negotiations in the Middle East, it means we're . . . . all over again!
2. There's enough work here for the next ten years! So, the sooner we get started the better. Let's . . . .
3. I've spent three years trying to make my business work and nothing has gone right for me. I've had enough. It's time to . . . .
4. I'm finding my new job really difficult. There are so many things to remember. But . . . . I'm sure I'll get used to it.
5. I've been working on my course assignment non-stop for two weeks now. I'm pleased to say . . . .
6. Good morning, everyone. Thanks for coming to this meeting to discuss ways of increasing our market share. Now, I don't want to say anything. We want to hear your ideas, so who's going to . . . . ?
7. I'm sorry, Helen, but if we make an exception for your holiday plans, it'll . . . . and everyone will be asking for the same.
8. With all the legal problems we're experiencing in Moscow, we're putting the plans for expansion into Russia . . . . for a time.

Note: If you have to stop something because there are faults in it, you can say you are going *back to the drawing board*. When you start something from the beginning again, you can say that you are *starting from scratch*.

4: Revision

Look back at the idioms in this unit and add the missing verbs:

1. . . . . . . the ice
2. . . . . . . things on hold
3. . . . . . . in the towel
4. . . . . . . us the green light
5. . . . . . . cracking
6. . . . . . . the floodgates
7. . . . . . . it a day
8. . . . . . . it in the bud
9. . . . . . . the plug
10. . . . . . . the ball rolling

"Rachel had had enough. She called it a day, threw in the towel and decided to get a life!"

Are you the sort of person who will start the ball rolling in a meeting or discussion?

169

Unit 79 | Success and Failure

1: Expressions with *ambition*

Most young people have a *burning* ambition which they hope to *achieve*. They might *fulfil* their ambition. It might be *thwarted* or *frustrated*. Not many people *achieve their life's ambition*. Most of us have at least one *unfulfilled* ambition.

2: A burning ambition

Fill in the following expressions in the dialogues below:

- a. *rising stars*
- b. *burning ambition*
- c. *up and coming*
- d. *the sky's the limit*
- e. *the world's your oyster*
- f. *going up in the world*
- g. *hungry for success*
- h. *high flier*

"When Harold was a lad, the world was his oyster."

1. I've always had one . . . .
   > And what's that?
   To climb Mount Everest.
2. What's the pay like in your company?
   > Well, if you work hard and you're good at selling, ...
3. He used to sleep on the floor of a friend's flat and now he owns a chain of hotels.
   > That's what I call . . . .
4. Barbara's only young but I think she's going to do well here.
   > You're right. She's definitely one of the . . . .
5. You play football, don't you? Has your team won anything this season?
   > No but next year will be better. We've got some . . . .
   young players who are . . . .
6. Brian's going to be difficult to replace. I don't know whether we want someone young with lots of fresh ideas or someone a bit older with lots of experience.
   > Well, for what it's worth, I don't think we want a young . . . .
   who leaves in a year's time. We want someone who's still going to be around in 5 years' time.
7. What made you choose to do computing at university?
   > Well, once you've got your degree, you can get a job almost anywhere you want –
   . . . .

Note: Today oysters are expensive and few people eat them, but a hundred years ago, they were eaten by everyone. They were one of the commonest forms of seafood. The idiom – the world's your oyster – is hundreds of years old. A character in a Shakespeare play says: The world's mine oyster, which I, with sword, will open. In other words, he will conquer the world. If you remember what an oyster is, it might help you remember the idiom.

3: Move heaven and earth

Complete the expressions below using these verbs:

leave	*stop*	*move*
get	*pull (2)*	*set (2)*

a. . . . . heaven and earth
b. . . . . your socks up
c. . . . . her heart on
d. . . . . no stone unturned
e. . . . . your sights on something
f. . . . . out all the stops
g. . . . . at nothing
h. . . . . left behind

"You'd better pull your socks up, son, or you'll end up struggling to make ends meet – like me."

Now use the expressions in these sentences:

1. Look, our customer needs the parts in Jakarta by Wednesday this week. I don't care what it costs. We can't afford to lose him. You have my permission to . . . . to get these parts out there.
2. The police said that they were confident of finding the escaped prisoners and would . . . . until every one of them was back under lock and key.
3. If you don't update your computer skills now, you'll . . . .
4. If you want to be successful, aim for the top – . . . . on a gold medal.
5. Jack is ruthless. He stabbed Andrew in the back, and reported Jill for being late. He's determined to become Area Manager. He'll . . . . until he gets the job.
6. My sister doesn't want to go to university. She's . . . . becoming a top actress.
7. Now look, son, if you don't . . . ., you'll end up in a dead-end job, riding a bike when all your friends are in Mercs.

Note: The one remaining idiom is . . . . This idiom means *to make every possible effort* to do something. An organ has 'stops' which the organist can pull out to have a certain effect. If he *pulls out all the stops*, the music will be very loud.

4: Revision

Complete the expressions from this unit:

1. . . . . and coming
2. move . . . . and earth
3. pull your . . . . up
4. a rising . . . .
5. the world's your . . . .
6. the sky's the . . . .
7. leave no . . . . unturned
8. set your . . . . on

9. a high . . . .
10. going up in the . . . .
11. pull out all the . . . .
12. stop at . . . .
13. get . . . . behind
14. . . . . for success
15. a . . . . ambition

Is there anything you would move heaven and earth to achieve?

Unit 80 | Suitability

1: Literal Meanings

Some of the idioms in this unit are very easy to understand with non-literal meanings:

like a fish out of water   fit like a glove   a square peg in a round hole

Some are more difficult. If something is *right up your street,* or is *your cup of tea,* it suits you. The sea is where fish live, the air is where birds fly – that is their element. If you are *in your element,* you are extremely happy where you are at that moment.

2: Fit like a glove

"*I must say I took to scuba diving like a duck to water.*"

Use these expressions in the correct form:

    a. *tailor something to your needs*
    b. *lend itself to something*
    c. *cut out for doing something*
    d. *fit like a glove*
    e. *feel at home*
    f. *fit the bill*
    g. *do the trick*
    h. *take to something like a duck to water*

1. Now, how do these shoes feel?
   > Lovely. They . . . . I'm just not sure about the colour.
2. How's Angela getting on in her new job? Everything OK?
   > Oh yes. She loves it. She has really . . . .
3. I like the computer but I don't really need all the software that's on it. I'd prefer some different software really.
   > That's no problem. We can . . . . the software . . . . exact . . . .
4. Is your son still living in Italy?
   > Yes, he . . . . very much . . . . there.
5. Why did you leave your job so soon? You were only there six months.
   > I just wasn't . . . . selling. I'm not a natural salesman.
6. I've got terrible indigestion. I think we'd better go home.
   > Try a couple of these tablets. They'll do . . . . ! You'll be feeling as right as rain again in a couple of minutes.
7. We're looking for somebody to take over in Scotland.
   > Well, what about Angus? I think he'd . . . ., wouldn't he?
8. How is the new system for claiming unemployment benefit different?
   > Well, the old system . . . . to all kinds of abuse, whereas it's very difficult to cheat the new system.

Note: The difference in meaning between *fit the bill* and *do the trick* is very small. You can use *fit the bill* with a thing or a person, but you cannot use *do the trick* with a person.

3: A fish out of water

Match each sentence on the right with one on the left:

1. I hate wearing a jacket and tie.
2. Everyone else was wearing fancy dress! I was the only one in a suit!
3. I'm an undertaker. Not many people would like my job.
4. I'm worried about Clive. He just doesn't fit in around here.
5. We can't paint the front door red!
6. Thanks for recommending Thailand.
7. Sun, sea, sand, and no phones!
8. I can't stand night clubs!
9. Does this suit me?
10. My sister runs a playgroup. She loves children.

a. It'll stick out like a sore thumb.
b. She's in her element.
c. I'm like a fish out of water at formal occasions.
d. They're just not my cup of tea.
e. It's you! Yes, it's definitely you.
f. Just what the doctor ordered!
g. It was right up my street.
h. He's a square peg in a round hole.
i. I felt completely out of place.
j. But it suits me down to the ground.

"It's at moments like this I feel like a fish out of water."

4: Revision

Put the correct words into these idioms:

1. I was like a fish . . . . of water.
2. I'm not cut out . . . . this.
3. It sticks . . . . like a sore thumb.
4. He's . . . . his element.
5. I felt completely . . . . of place.
6. It fits . . . . a glove.

Find and correct the mistakes in these sentences:

7. He's on his element.
8. She's like a round peg in a square hole.
9. It's not my cup of coffee.
10. It's right up your road.
11. She took to it like a fish to water.
12. It sticks out like a painful thumb.
13. It suits him down to the floor.
14. I felt like a duck out of water.

What kind of music is not your cup of tea?

Unit 81 | Surprises

1: Literal Meanings

Fill in the following words in the definitions below:

feathers	*bump*	*rug*	*disguise*
bargain	*sleeve*	*blessing*	

1. A small carpet is called a . . . .
2. If you negotiate the price of something, you . . . . for it.
3. Something good from God, which brings happiness, is called a . . . .
4. A short, hard knock or impact, for example, when a plane lands on the ground, is called a . . . .
5. If you wear special clothes or a wig so that people will not recognise you, it is called a . . . .
6. Birds have . . . .
7. The part of a shirt, jacket or coat which covers your arms is called the . . . .

2: Knock me down with a feather

Use these idiomatic expressions in the correct form in the situations below:

a. *believe it or not*
b. *pulled the rug from under my feet*
c. *have something up your sleeve*
d. *knock someone for six*
e. *knock me down with a feather*
f. *harder than I had bargained for*
g. *take me by surprise*
h. *came back to earth with a bump*

1. Did you know Tom and Jody are getting married?
   > Yes, you could have . . . . when they told me.
   I didn't even know they were going out together.
2. Congratulations on your promotion, Pat! Were you expecting it?
   > Not at all. It . . . . me completely . . . .
3. How was your exam? Was everything OK?
   > No, it was much . . . .
4. Is your brother back from holiday yet? He went to Thailand, didn't he?
   > Yes, he had a great time. He . . . . though.
   When he got home, he found his flat had been broken into.
5. Peter, it's Mum's birthday on Sunday and we haven't planned anything for her.
   > Don't worry. I've got . . . . Wait and see.
6. Rob's only 45. That's very young to have a heart attack, isn't it?
   > Yes, he's back to normal now, but it really . . . . at the time.
7. So, what about your meeting with the boss? Did you get what you wanted?
   > No, before I could ask him anything, he started to criticise my work, which really . . . .
8. Does anybody know what the weather's going to be like this weekend?
   > . . . . , it's actually going to be warm and sunny!

3: Out of the blue

Use the following idiomatic expressions in the situations below:

a. *out of the blue*
b. *has got another think coming*
c. *a blessing in disguise*
d. *the shock of my life*
e. *a turn-up for the books*
f. *couldn't believe my eyes*
g. *a real eye-opener*
h. *more to her than meets the eye*

1. Is your sister still living in the States?
   > Yes, but actually she's in England at the moment. She arrived last Monday, completely . . . . It was a lovely surprise.
2. Jeff told me you lost your job last month. That was a nasty shock, wasn't it?
   > Well, actually it was . . . . I've found something much better.
3. Did you see Japan beat Spain at football last night?
   > Japan beat Spain? Wow! That's . . . real . . . .
4. That was a brilliant speech Anne gave after dinner, wasn't it?
   > I didn't know she had it in her. It was . . . real . . . .
5. Didn't she phone to say she was coming?
   > No, there was a knock at the door on Monday morning and there she was with her suitcase. I got . . . .
6. Mac says he's taking next Monday off. He wants to go skiing in Scotland.
   > Well, he hasn't asked me about it. If he thinks he can take a day off without checking first, he's got . . . .
7. I didn't know Sarah sings in a professional choir. And she plays the violin, apparently.
   > Oh yes. There's . . . .
8. What did you think of the dress Sandra was wearing last night?
   > Like everyone else, I . . . .! Everyone thought she was so quiet and conservative.

4: Revision

Replace the words in italics with an idiom from this unit. The words given will help you.

1. *I was very surprised* when they told me.   (You, feather)
2. Don't worry. I've got *a secret plan*.   (sleeve)
3. *Nobody thought that would happen.*   (That's, books)
4. *She's got more ability than we realised.*   (There's, eye)
5. *It looked like a bad thing to happen but actually it's been good.*   (blessing)
6. He arrived *unexpectedly*.   (blue)

Look back at the idioms in this unit and add the final word:

7. I couldn't believe my . . . .
8. I got the shock of my . . . .
9. It pulled the rug from under my . . . . . .
10. The news hit me for . . . . . .

Has anything happened to you recently which turned out to be a blessing in disguise?

Unit 82 | Time

1: In the nick of time

Which group of expressions completes the sentences below?

1. The police arrived

    a. for hours on end.
       non-stop.
       into the small hours.

2. Dinner will be ready at six

    b. on the dot.
       or thereabouts.
       sharp.

3. We go to the cinema

    c. in no time.
       in a tick.
       shortly.

4. They argued

    d. in the nick of time.
       just in time.
       not a minute too soon.

5. I'll be with you

    e. from time to time.
       now and again.
       every so often.

> **"Another Chernobyl only a matter of time."**
>
> *Newspaper headline*

2: Long time no see!

Complete the following with a phrase from the right hand column:

1. Long time
2. Tomorrow is
3. It's only
4. We decided
5. There's no time
6. It's very cold

a. a matter of time.
b. on the spur of the moment.
c. like the present.
d. another day.
e. for this time of year.
f. no see.

Which of the above expressions completes these situations?

7. Where've you been for the past six months? . . . . !
8. . . . . before holidays in space will be normal.
9. Here's the number of my dentist. Ring him and make an appointment. Go on,

. . . .
10. What a day! . . . . It's usually much milder.
11. We're off to Bali tomorrow. . . . .
12. Just forget everything that's happened today. . . . .

3: At the crack of dawn

Match the following nine expressions with the meanings below. There are two expressions for numbers 6 and 7.

   a. *at the last minute*
   b. *in due course*
   c. *once in a blue moon*
   d. *at the crack of dawn*
   e. *for donkeys' years*
   f. *at the eleventh hour*
   g. *in this day and age*
   h. *sooner or later*
   i. *not in a month of Sundays*

"I love getting up at the crack of dawn."

1. very early in the morning . . . .
2. not for a very long time . . . .
3. very rarely . . . .
4. never . . . .
5. in modern times . . . .
6. eventually . . . .
7. almost too late . . . .

Now use the expressions in the following situations:

8. We arrived on the platform at the very . . . . , just as they were closing the doors.
9. I can't believe there are so many homeless people . . . . The government should do something about it.
10. When I'm on holiday and the weather's good, I love to get up . . . .
11. I haven't seen my Uncle Roger . . . . He lives in Spain now.
12. I have always found that if you really want something and put your mind to it, you get it . . . .
13. I wouldn't be seen dead in a zoo – . . . . ! I hate the very idea of the places.
14. I'm never early, and I'm never late, but I do admit to doing things . . . .
15. This company has a policy of always replying to complaints. Every single complaint is dealt with carefully and a reply is sent . . . .
16. Although Jill lives on the other side of the road, we only ever see her . . . .

4: Revision

Complete the following idioms by adding the correct preposition:

1. . . . . the dot
2. . . . . . . the nick of time
3. . . . . . . the crack of dawn
4. . . . . . . this day and age
5. . . . . . . donkeys' years
6. . . . . . . time . . . . . . time

If you are invited for dinner at 7 o'clock, would you arrive a little before 7, a little after 7, or on the dot?

Unit 83 | Work 1

1: Literal Meanings

Use these words to complete the following:

rush   candles   loose   fit   thumbs   burn

1. We've got eight fingers and two . . . .
2. I need a new pair of trousers. These are too . . . . round the waist.
3. Don't touch that! It's very hot. You'll . . . . yourself.
4. My car's only small but you can just . . . . five people in it.
5. Sorry, I haven't got time to talk. I'm in a . . . .
6. In Britain, it's traditional to put . . . . on birthday cakes – one for each year.

2: Up to my eyes

Put the following nouns in the idiomatic expressions below:

plate   end   finger   candle   hands   thumbs   feet   eyes

a. lift a . . . .
b. have your . . . . full
c. burn the . . . . at both ends
d. on my . . . .

e. at a loose . . . .
f. twiddle your . . . .
g. up to my . . . .
h. enough on my . . . .

Now use the expressions in these situations:

1. You're late. Did you miss the train?
   > Yes, I didn't leave the office till six. I'm . . . . in work at the moment.
2. How was your first day at work?
   > Really boring. I had nothing to do. I just sat at my desk . . . .
3. Bill wants to know if you can spend some time training the new secretary.
   > I'm afraid I haven't got a minute – I can't. I've already got . . . .
4. You look tired. Are you OK?
   > Yes, I just need to get to bed earlier. I've been . . . . recently – late nights and early starts.
5. Come in. Sit down, make yourself at home.
   > Thanks. I need a rest. I've been . . . . all day.
6. So, I'm going to spend the whole weekend painting the outside of the house.
   > Do you want some help? My boyfriend's away so I'm . . . . this weekend.
7. Do you and Paul share the cooking and cleaning?
   > You must be joking. He never . . . . !
8. My sister's three children are coming to stay with me this weekend.
   > You'll . . . . Rather you than me!

Note: If you have too much to do, you can be either *up to your eyes* or *up to your ears*. If you want to describe a job as low-status and badly-paid, you can say: *If you pay peanuts, you get monkeys.* This expression is completely fixed.

3: One thing after another!

Complete these dialogues using the following idiomatic expressions:

     a. *It's been dead all day.*
     b. *I'm tied up till after lunch.*
     c. *I've been on the go all day.*
     d. *I can fit you in on Thursday.*
     e. *It's been one thing after another.*
     f. *We've been rushed off our feet!*

1. Everything's gone wrong today, hasn't it?
  > Yes. . . . .
2. Shall we go for a drink after work?
  > No thanks. I'm tired. . . . .
3. So, is Wednesday a good day for you?
  > No, but . . . .
4. Have you had many customers today?
  > No, ...
5. You've had a lot of customers in this morning, haven't you?
  > Yes, ...
6. Can I talk to you about a problem that's just come up?
  > Sorry, ...

4: Been

Five of the idioms in this unit are commonly used with *been*. Try to complete them with the key word, then look back to check.

1. I've been   . . . .   *(candle)*
2. I've been   . . . .   *(feet)*
3. It's been   . . . .   *(thing)*
4. I've been   . . . .   *(rushed)*
5. It's been   . . . .   *(dead)*

5: Revision

Put the missing words in the idioms below:

  1. I'm . . . . to my ears in work.
  2. It's been one thing . . . . another.
  3. I've been . . . . my feet all day.
  4. Are you . . . . a loose end this evening?
  5. I'm tied up . . . . after lunch.
  6. I've been . . . . the go all day.
  7. We've been rushed . . . . our feet.
  8. I've already got enough . . . . my plate.
  9. I've been burning the candle . . . . both ends.
10. I can fit you . . . . on Monday.

Have you got a lot on your plate at the moment?

Unit 84 Work 2

1: Literal Meanings

Fill in the following words in the definitions below:

> **pipeline**   **dead-end**   **ropes**   **ladder**   **steady**   **rock**

1. If something is . . . . . . , it doesn't move.
2. Oil, gas and water come to us along a . . . .
3. If you are in a small boat and you make it . . . . . . , it might capsize.
4. A road which goes nowhere is a . . . .
5. On a sailing boat, the sails are controlled by means of . . . .
6. If something is too high and out of your reach, use a . . . .

2: A dead-end job

Use the following expressions in the sentences below:

> **a.** *a steady job*   **c.** *a dead-end job*   **e.** *a new branch*
> **b.** *in the pipeline*   **d.** *the top of the tree* **f.** *a short-list*

1. Imagine just putting letters in envelopes all day. What a . . . . !
2. It's going to be a busy year for us. We've got two major projects to finish and an even bigger one . . . .
3. Marks and Spencers are opening . . . . in town next summer.
4. I just had a really good job interview. I'm on . . . . of five.
5. Where is there to go once you've reached . . . . ?
6. A lot of people are happy with . . . . even if it isn't very interesting. The main thing is the security it offers.

3: Climb the career ladder

Complete these idiomatic expressions with the following verbs:

> **show**   **make**   **rock**   **stand**
> **hold**   **go**   **breathe**   **land**
> **take on**   **climb**   **find**   **stand in**

a. . . . . a name for yourself
b. . . . . the career ladder
c. . . . . staff
d. . . . . the boat
e. . . . . someone the ropes
f. can't . . . . the pace
g. . . . . a job down
h. . . . . down someone's neck
i. . . . . your feet
j. . . . . over someone's head
k. . . . . a job
l. . . . . for somebody

Now use eight of the expressions in the correct form in the following situations:

1. Do you think it's worth me doing a part-time MBA? It's a lot of work.
   > It depends how much you want to . . . .
2. My new job's OK but there are lots of things I'm still not used to.
   > That's normal. It always takes a few months before you really . . . .
   . . . .

3. I suppose your busiest time is around Christmas, isn't it?
> Yes, we always . . . . extra . . . . just for that period.
4. Are you working late again tonight?
> I'm afraid so. Peter's . . . . for last month's sales figures. They've got to be ready for tomorrow morning's meeting.
5. I'm going to have a word with Jack and try to change my holidays.
> Jack's on a course this week and Marie is . . . . , so you'd better wait till he gets back. You know what she's like!
6. You know Frank's not going to put your idea on the agenda for tomorrow's meeting, don't you?
> Isn't he? In that case I'll have to . . . . and talk to his head of department.
7. I bumped into Paul last week. He's just started a new job selling insurance.
> I wonder how long that'll last. He can't . . . . for longer than six months.
8. Where's Andrew working nowadays?
> Haven't you heard? He's just . . . . a great . . . . . with that new American bank in the City.

Note: If you are going to delay, but not cancel, a project, you can say: *Let's put that on the back burner for a while.* If you want to talk about working under pressure, you can say: *If you can't stand the heat, get out of the kitchen.*

"We've got something big in the pipeline."

4: Revision

Look back at the idioms in this unit and add the missing words:

1. climb the career . . . . . .
2. find your . . . . . . in a new job
3. landed a great . . . . . .
4. can't stand the . . . . . .
5. a project in the . . . . . .
6. make a name for . . . . . .
7. breathing down my . . . . . .
8. take on extra . . . . . .
9. go over his . . . . . .
10. hold a job . . . . . .

Have you ever had a dead-end job?

Unit 85 Review Unit

47. Advice

1. You'll have to keep your wits . . . . you.
2. Don't lose any . . . . over it.
3. Make the . . . . of it.
4. Don't let it . . . . you down.
5. Just take one . . . . at a time.
6. Don't count your . . . . before they hatch.

48. Agreeing and Disagreeing

1. That's easier . . . . than done.
2. You can say . . . . again.
3. You're . . . . me!
4. You took the . . . . right out of my mouth.
5. Over my . . . . body!
6. It's . . . of the question.

49. Annoyance and Frustration

1. It's like talking to a . . . . wall.
2. It really gets up my . . . . .
3. To add . . . . to injury.
4. It's driving me round the . . . . .
5. I could've . . . . myself.
6. I'm . . . . spare.

50. Being Positive

1. It's not the . . . . of the world.
2. There's . . . . at the end of the tunnel.
3. You win some, you . . . . some.
4. Third time . . . . .
5. Look on the bright . . . . .
6. Things can . . . . get better.

51. Certainty and Doubt

1. Your guess is as . . . . as mine.
2. What he'll do next is anyone's . . . . .
3. Our holiday plans are up in the . . . . .
4. Buy ten – just to be on the . . . . side.
5. I think a wedding is . . . . the cards.
6. I'll give him the benefit of the . . . . .

52. Change

1. I've turned over a new . . . . .
2. She's changed beyond all . . . . .
3. There's been a change of . . . . .
4. There's trouble . . . . the horizon.
5. My holiday plans are . . . . shape.
6. I'm going to make a . . . . break.

53. Communicating

1. We're on the . . . . wavelength.
2. Stop beating about the . . . . .
3. I'll . . . . you posted.
4. This is just . . . . you and me.
5. He can talk the . . . . legs off a donkey.
6. I got it . . . . from the horse's mouth.

54. Dishonesty

1. I told him a little . . . . lie.
2. You can't pull the . . . . over my eyes.
3. I don't trust him an . . . . .
4. She's lying through her . . . . .
5. He's leading you up the . . . . path.
6. Don't let them . . . . advantage of you.

55. Easy and Difficult

1. It's an uphill . . . . .
2. It's not exactly a . . . . of roses.
3. I took it in my . . . . .
4. You've got your work cut . . . . .
5. It's all . . . . sailing from now on.
6. It'll sort out the . . . . from the . . . . .

56. The Family

1. She's the . . . . sheep of the family.
2. Like father, like . . . . .
3. We've finally decided to . . . . the knot.
4. Blood is thicker than . . . . .
5. We used to fight like . . . . and dog.
6. You're the spitting . . . . of your mother.

57. Good and Bad Quality

1. My car's on its last . . . . .
2. Las Vegas is not . . . . it's cracked up to be.
3. The food is . . . . to write home about.
4. He's worth his . . . . in gold.
5. Sony hi-fi systems take a lot of . . . . .
6. Your suit's seen . . . . days, hasn't it?

58. Health

1. I've been given a clean . . . of health.
2. I'm a bit stressed . . . . .
3. I've got a splitting . . . . .
4. I'm feeling a bit . . . . colour.
5. I'm really . . . . of shape.
6. My grandmother's as fit as a . . . . .

59. Holidays

1. We had the . . . . of our lives.
2. I need to get . . . . from it all.
3. A change is as good as a . . . . .
4. We had a . . . . of a time.
5. I'm . . . . light.
6. I need to . . . . my batteries.

60. Knowledge and Ability

1. I know it like the . . . . of my hand.
2. I don't know the . . . . thing about e-mail.
3. You'll soon . . . . the hang of it.
4. Bob knows a . . . . or two about cars.
5. Sorry, I haven't . . . . a clue.
6. That's news . . . me.

61. Memory

1. I've got a memory like a . . . . .
2. My mind just went . . . . .
3. I've got a good . . . . for faces.
4. I've been racking my . . . . all morning.
5. Sorry. It completely slipped my . . . . .
6. It's on the . . . . of my tongue.

62. Mistakes

1. I really put my . . . . in it, didn't I?
2. You're barking up the . . . . tree.
3. I got my . . . . burned.
4. I think you got the . . . . end of the stick.
5. I bit off more than I could . . . . .
6. You sent me on a . . . . goose chase.

63. Misunderstanding

1. I can't make head nor . . . . of this letter.
2. We got our . . . . crossed somewhere.
3. The explanation went right . . . . my head.
4. You've completely missed the . . . . .
5. I was completely out of my . . . . .
6. We're just not on the . . . . wavelength.

64. Money 1

1. I bet that cost an arm and a . . . . .
2. How much did your new car set you . . . . ?
3. I don't want to . . . . into my savings.
4. I'm going to splash out . . . . a new suit.
5. Please don't go on another spending . . . . .
6. We'll have to tighten our . . . . for a while.

65. Money 2

1. I'm living from hand to . . . . .
2. They're living in the . . . . of luxury.
3. Sam's rolling . . . . it.
4. Sue's got . . . . to burn.
5. I'm a bit hard . . . . at the moment.
6. I earn enough to get . . . . .

66. Moods

1. I'm going to give him a . . . . of my mind.
2. I'm absolutely thrilled to . . . . .
3. He'll blow his . . . . when he sees this.
4. She hasn't got a care in the . . . . .
5. I'm delighted. I'm over the . . . . .
6. We were in very . . . . spirits last night.

67. People

1. I can't stand backseat . . . . .
2. She's the life and . . . . of the party.
3. He's a . . . . in the neck.
4. He's a clever . . . . .
5. She's the salt of the . . . . .
6. Rachel's an . . . . quantity.

68. Power and Influence

1. He's got . . . . in high places.
2. I could pull a few . . . . for you.
3. She . . . . the trousers.
4. He carries a lot of . . . . .
5. I'll put in a good . . . . for you.
6. Can you hold the . . . . till I get back?

69. Problems 1

1. We got off on the . . . . foot.
2. We're in a tight . . . . financially.
3. Mike's gone completely . . . . the rails.
4. We're all in the . . . . boat.
5. I'm afraid you caught me on the . . . . .
6. She left the company . . . . a cloud.

70. Problems 2

1. We'll cross that . . . . when we come to it.
2. I decided to turn a . . . . eye.
3. You can't just paper over the . . . . .
4. I want to get to the . . . . of this problem.
5. I'll give you the benefit of the . . . . .
6. You can't just sweep it under the . . . . .

71. Reading

1. I read it from cover . . . . cover.
2. There's a clever twist at the . . . . .
3. Make sure you read the . . . . print.
4. He's turned over a new . . . . .
5. It takes a while to . . . . going.
6. Don't judge a . . . . by its cover.

72. Relationships 1

1. We got on like a . . . . on fire.
2. We got off on the wrong . . . . .
3. We don't always see eye to . . . . .
4. We need to clear the . . . . .
5. He's not in my . . . . books at the moment.
6. She needs a . . . . to cry on.

73. Relationships 2

1. He's head over . . . . in love.
2. I'm afraid their marriage is on the . . . . .
3. They've gone their separate . . . . .
4. We've finally decided to tie the . . . . .
5. I . . . . his guts.
6. I think he's got it . . . . for me.

74. Safety and Risks

1. Get two extra – just to be the . . . . side.
2. You're skating on thin . . . . .
3. Stop sitting on the . . . . .
4. Three o'clock is cutting it a bit . . . . .
5. Go on. You've got nothing to . . . . .
6. His job is as . . . . as houses.

75. Similarities and Differences

1. You'll stick out like a . . . . thumb.
2. They're like chalk and . . . . .
3. It's six of one and half a . . . . of the other.
4. There's a . . . . of difference between them.
5. We're all in the same . . . . .
6. He's going to follow in his father's . . . . .

76. Sleep and Dreams

1. I didn't sleep a . . . . last night.
2. I crashed . . . . on the sofa before dinner.
3. I was so tired I went out like a . . . . .
4. I wouldn't . . . . of lying to you.
5. My interview went like a . . . . .
6. Don't worry. Don't lose any . . . . over it.

77. Speed

1. No sooner . . . . than done.
2. We'll have to . . . . the brakes on spending.
3. You're late. You'd better get your . . . . on.
4. It'll be ready in no . . . . .
5. The news spread . . . . wildfire.
6. There's no hurry. Take your . . . . .

78. Starting and Stopping

1. I've had enough. Let's . . . . it a day.
2. It's back to square . . . . , I'm afraid.
3. The end is in . . . . .
4. Come on. It's time to get . . . . .
5. I've decided to throw in the . . . . .
6. The wedding plans are . . . . hold.

79. Success and Failure

1. He'll move heaven and . . . . to get it.
2. You've got to set your . . . . on something.
3. She'll stop at . . . . to get what she wants.
4. She's set her . . . . on becoming a dancer.
5. The sky's the . . . . .
6. He's . . . . for success.

80. Suitability

1. I feel like a square peg in a round . . . . .
2. It's not really my cup of . . . . .
3. I felt like a . . . . out of water.
4. Social work suits her down to the . . . . .
5. This novel will be right up your . . . . .
6. I'm just not cut . . . . for university.

81. Surprises

1. I couldn't . . . . my eyes.
2. There's more to him than meets the . . . . .
3. The news knocked me for . . . . .
4. I've got something up my . . . . .
5. She arrived completely out of the . . . . .
6. It took me completely by . . . . .

82. Time

1. It will happen. It's only a matter of . . . . .
2. I decided on the . . . . of the moment.
3. Don't leave everything to the last . . . . .
4. He talks about football for hours on . . . . .
5. There's no . . . . like the present.
6. You'll find out sooner or . . . . .

83. Work 1

1. I'm . . . . to my eyes in work.
2. We've been . . . . off our feet today.
3. I can fit you . . . . on Friday afternoon.
4. Mark never . . . . a finger to help.
5. I've got a lot on my . . . . at the moment.
6. I've been on the . . . . all day.

84. Work 2

1. There's a major new product in the . . . . .
2. He went . . . . my head.
3. It takes a while to really find your . . . . .
4. I need someone to show me the . . . . .
5. We need to take . . . . extra staff.
6. You're always rocking the . . . . , aren't you?

SECTION 4

Key Words

This section organises English idioms by key words. Some of these words are among the most common in English – *thing, way, and, of,* etc. It is interesting that the key words used here are words which, in themselves, have very little meaning. Some of them are important grammatical words – *of, and, to.* They are all very common in different kinds of idiomatic expression. Here are some examples:

all:	**I suspected him all along.**
and:	**It's touch and go.**
end:	**There's been no end of trouble.**
half:	**That's half the battle.**
like:	**I slept like a log.**
line:	**You've got to draw the line somewhere.**
no:	**We got there in no time.**
of:	**That was a stroke of luck.**
point:	**Let's get straight to the point.**
side:	**We'll leave early just to be on the safe side.**
nothing:	**It was nothing to write home about.**
thing:	**It's a thing of the past.**
way:	**We went out of our way to help.**

Unit 86 | All

1: Literal Meanings

All means everything, total, complete. This meaning is clear in expressions such as *It's all over* (It's completely finished); *I'm all for going to the theatre* (I'm totally in favour of going); *I'm all against it* (I'm totally against it).

In other expressions, it is difficult to see the meaning, so it is best not to break the expression down, but to try to remember the whole expression.

2: By all means

Put the expressions with *all* in the dialogues below:

    a. *all yours*
    b. *all for*
    c. *all year round*
    d. *not at all*
    e. *by all means*
    f. *by all accounts*
    g. *25 all told*
    h. *all in all*

"By all accounts, Jim's question and answer session was pretty stormy!"

1. Can I leave my car in this space for 10 minutes?
   > . . . . But you'll have to move it when the manager comes back from lunch – it's her space.
2. Is the castle open to the public 52 weeks a year?
   > Yes, it's open . . . ., except Christmas Day.
3. How many people came to yesterday's meeting?
   > There were . . . ., including our own people.
4. I hope the weather didn't ruin your holiday.
   > Well, it was very disappointing, but everything else was great. . . . ., we had a really good time.
5. I couldn't have fixed the car on my own. Thanks for your help.
   > . . . . Just call me whenever you need help.
6. Have you tried that new Mexican restaurant in Kemp Street?
   > No, I haven't but, ..., it's excellent.
7. People should be allowed to smoke wherever they want. This is a free country, after all.
   > Well, I'm . . . . freedom but you do have to respect other people's health, don't you?
8. Have you finished with the newspaper?
   > Yes, just take it. It's . . . .

Note: 25 *all told* means 25 *in total*.

3: All being well

Fill in the following expressions containing *all* in the sentences below:

    a. *all along*   **e.** *if it's all the same to you*
    b. *all of a sudden*   **f.** *when all's said and done*
    c. *all go*   **g.** *all being well*
    d. *all over*   **h.** *for all I know*

1. I should arrive about six, ... It partly depends on the traffic.
2. Come on, hurry up or the party'll be . . . . by the time we get there.
3. Nobody admitted to damaging my car, but I suspected . . . . that it was my eldest son's wife, Sheila.
4. Sorry I haven't been able to ring you earlier, but my phone hasn't stopped ringing since I got in this morning. It's been . . . . !
5. I haven't spoken to my brother for years. I've got no idea what he's doing these days. He could be in Australia or Timbuctoo . . . .
6. Thanks for offering, but . . . . , I'll walk. I need some fresh air.
7. I was watching TV, having a coffee and . . . . everything went black – the TV, the lights. There was a power cut.
8. I can't say I like my job – there are things I don't like about it, but it pays the bills. . . . . , it's better than having no job at all!

"In this office, it's all go!"

4: Revision

Match the *all* expressions with their meanings:

1. all being well	a. very busy
2. all told	b. in favour of
3. all go	c. people say/apparently
4. all over	d. in total
5. by all accounts	e. suddenly
6. when all's said and done	f. completely finished
7. all for	g. the general conclusion
8. all of a sudden	h. if nothing goes wrong

Look back at the idioms in this unit and add the missing words:

  9. all year . . . .   14. when all's . . . . . . and done
10. not . . . . . . all   15. all . . . . . . well
11. all of a . . . . . .   16. for all I . . . . . .
12. if it's all the . . . . . . to you   17. I knew all . . . .
13. . . . . . . all means   18. . . . . . . all accounts

How many years have you spent in full-time education all told?

Unit 87 | And 1

1: Literal Meanings

Fill in the following words in the definitions below:

bred	**tear**	**leap**	**bound**	**sick**
wears	**pick**	**foremost**	**forth**	

1. If a type of fabric . . . . . . well, it lasts a long time.
2. A word with a similar meaning to 'choose' is . . . .
3. Two words which have a similar meaning to 'jump' are . . . . . . and . . . .
4. The . . . . . . means the most important.
5. An old word which means forward or away is . . . . The Bible says, "Go . . . . . and multiply."
6. Some people breed animals. The past tense of *breed* is . . . .
7. Be careful not to . . . . . your skirt. There's a nail sticking out on that chair.
8. . . . . . . can mean ill, but it can also mean tired. If you are . . . . . . of doing something, you don't want to do it any more.

2: Born and bred

Put these expressions with *and* into the sentences below:

a. *give and take*	f. *wear and tear*
b. *time and again*	g. *peace and quiet*
c. *born and bred*	h. *on and off*
d. *sick and tired*	i. *wait and see*
e. *by and large*	j. *touch and go*

1. I'm not American: I'm Irish – . . . .
2. We don't always come here on holiday, but I suppose we've been coming . . . . now for about 15 years.
3. All successful relationships are a matter of . . . .
4. The main reason I play golf is to have some time on my own. In fact, it's the only time I get any . . . .
5. I need an operation on my knee. It's because of the . . . . of playing football over the past 25 years.
6. The exam didn't go too badly. I think I've passed but it's difficult to say. I'll just have to . . . .
7. My uncle's still in hospital. It's . . . . whether he'll be able to come home for Christmas.
8. I agree with you . . . . , but there are a few points I'm not sure I'd go along with you on.
9. Will you please stop telling me what to do! I'm . . . . of being treated like a child.
10. My neighbour keeps leaving his car in front of my garage. It's driving me mad. I've asked him . . . . not to do it but he still does.

Note: The order in these expressions is fixed. You cannot say *I'm tired and sick of waiting* or *I need a bit of quiet and peace*.

3: Out and about

Now do the same with these:

a. *bright and early*
b. *pick and choose*
c. *up and about*
d. *by leaps and bounds*
e. *out and about*

f. *ups and downs*
g. *odds and ends*
h. *first and foremost*
i. *round and round*
j. *ins and outs*

1. There's no point phoning me at work tomorrow. I'm going to be . . . . all day. Try me at home in the evening.
2. We'll have to leave at 6. See you in the morning . . . . , then.
3. Don't worry, Tim. There's no such thing as the perfect marriage. Every couple have their . . . . It's the same for everyone.
4. This meeting is getting us nowhere. We just keep going . . . . in circles.
5. Tony's in bed with flu but I think he's over the worst. He'll be . . . . in no time. Try phoning again tomorrow.
6. Sorry, but I'll have to go into the office on Saturday. There are a few . . . . I have to clear up before we go on holiday.
7. If you have no qualifications and very little work experience, you're not really in a position to . . . . the kind of job you'd like to do.
8. My sister's Spanish has improved . . . . since she started going out with Miguel.
9. I'm thinking of setting up my own business, but I need to speak to someone who knows the . . . . of how to get started.
10. If you're going to start a business, ... , you need to be sure you've got sound financial advice.

Note: A common idiom is: *You can't have your cake and eat it*. This means that of two courses of action, you can only do one.

4: Revision

Look back at the expressions in this unit and add the missing words:

1. peace and	11. up and . . . .
2. give and	12. wait and . . . .
3. ups and	13. wear and . . . .
4. touch and	14. first and . . . .
5. born and	15. sick and . . . .
6. bright and	16. round and . . . .
7. time and	17. by and . . . .
8. on and	18. out and . . . .
9. pick and	19. leaps and . . . .
10. odds and	20. ins and . . . .

Do you prefer to study in the evenings or do you like to get up bright and early?

Unit 88 And 2

1: Test yourself first

Without looking at the other exercises, try to complete the following expressions. If there are any you do not know, use the exercise as revision when you have finished the unit.

1. cut and . . . .
2. live and . . . .
3. alive and . . . .
4. black and . . . .
5. tried and . . . .
6. few and . . . . between
7. forgive and . . . .
8. pros and . . . .
9. now and . . . .
10. safe and . . . .

11. short and . . . .
12. like chalk and . . . .
13. ham and . . . .
14. in this day and . . . .
15. by trial and . . . .
16. think long and . . . .
17. home and . . . .
18. search high and . . . .
19. left high and . . . .
20. watch your P's and . . . .

2: Live and let live

Put the expressions with *and* into the sentences below:

    a. *alive and kicking*
    b. *now and again*
    c. *pros and cons*
    d. *forgive and forget*
    e. *cut and dried*
    f. *short and sweet*
    g. *live and let live*
    h. *black and white*
    i. *chalk and cheese*
    j. *few and far between*

"They're very few and far between this year!"

1. My philosophy has always been . . . . If more people in the world believed that, there would be no more wars.
2. If I have an argument or fight with someone, I always try to . . . . It's the only way to keep your friends!
3. If you're going to make a speech, my advice to you is keep it . . . .
4. It's so difficult to discuss things with people who always see things in . . . . Life is seldom that simple.
5. I like being self-employed, but obviously there are . . . .
6. I'm completely different from my sister. We're like . . . .
7. I'm not really a smoker but I have a cigarette . . . . if I'm out with friends.
8. The solution to this problem isn't going to be easy. I wish there was a . . . . answer, but there isn't!
9. Last year we picked pounds of mushrooms, but this year they're very . . . .
10. Although it's years since Michael Caine made *The Ipcress File*, he's still . . . . and making successful films.

3: Safe and sound

Now put these expressions with *and* into the sentences below:

a. *high and low*
b. *safe and sound*
c. *long and hard*
d. *home and dry*
e. *trial and error*
f. *day and age*
g. *tried and tested*
h. *high and dry*

1. Fiona's just phoned. She's arrived back home . . . .
2. I can't find my car keys. I've searched . . . . for them, but I can't find them anywhere.
3. When I get a cold I go to bed with whisky and honey. The next day I'm fine. It's a . . . . remedy.
4. Look, Mark, I've thought . . . . about our relationship and it's just not going to work if you continue working till 10 o'clock every night!
5. When I missed the plane back home, I was left . . . . in Calcutta without a penny to my name!
6. I've nearly finished my degree. I just need to finish my final essay, hand it in, and then I'll be . . . .
7. In this country it's not unusual in this . . . . for couples to live together without getting married.
8. I haven't got the patience to read computer manuals. I learned how to use mine by . . . .

4: Ham and eggs

Food and drink is an area of language with a number of important expressions linked by *and*. Match up the following:

1. ham and . . . .
2. bread and . . . .
3. cheese and . . . .
4. steak and . . . .
5. salt and . . . .
6. whisky and . . . .
7. gin and . . . .

a. tonic
b. biscuits
c. eggs
d. butter
e. soda
f. pepper
g. chips

5: Meanings

Remember, the order of these expressions is important: it would seem odd to hear someone offer you *butter and bread*. In Latin *pro* means *for* and *con* means *against*. The *pros and cons* are, therefore, the arguments for and against something. You often begin a speech by saying *Ladies and Gentlemen*, not *Gentlemen and Ladies*. If you find yourself in a rather formal situation, and you want to behave correctly, you need to *mind your P's and Q's*.

Do you tend to see things in black and white terms and prefer cut and dried answers to questions?

Unit 89 | Back

1: Meanings

Your back is often associated with hard work. If you *put your back into something*, you work very hard at it. If you *pat someone on the back*, you are congratulating them. If someone is *on your back* all the time, they may be checking up on you. You want them *to get off your back* and leave you alone.

If you *have your back to the wall*, literally, you are about to be killed by a firing squad. Metaphorically, it means you are in a desperate situation.

2: Get off my back

Use the following idiomatic expressions with *back* in the situations below:

>   a. *deserve a pat on the back*
>   b. *turn your back on something*
>   c. *you scratch my back and I'll scratch yours*
>   d. *put your back into it*
>   e. *break the back of a task*
>   f. *see the back of someone*
>   g. *get someone's back up*
>   h. *get off my back*
>   i. *talk behind my back*

1. Listen Ben, when are you going to get out of the house and start looking for a job?
   > I'm trying my best. Now would you . . . . and give me a break!
2. I rang the police when I saw something strange going on across the road and they caught a couple of burglars red-handed!
   > You certainly . . . . !
3. If you want to criticise me, tell me to my face. If there's one thing I hate it's people who . . . .
4. Could you help me with my essay, Peter? I really need some ideas.
   > Certainly. As long as you check my maths paper for me. You . . . .
5. I admit I was pretty wild in my teens, but I . . . . on all that – clubs, drinking, late nights, and things like that when Daniel was born.
6. I'll never be able to clear the garden by Friday. It's impossible.
   > You will if you . . . . You don't know what hard work is.
7. Did I hear that the headmaster at your school is leaving?
   > Yes, next week, and we won't be sorry to . . . . him! He has not been very popular.
8. How long do you think it'll take to input all these addresses?
   > Oh, we should be able to . . . . of it in a couple of days.
9. People who talk behind my back really . . . . !

3: At the back of my mind

The following expressions use different meanings of the word *back*:

> **a. *backs to the wall***
> **b. *get your own back***
> **c. *at the back of my mind***
> **d. *like the back of my hand***
> **e. *like water off a duck's back***
> **f. *in the back of beyond***
> **g. *fell off the back of a lorry***
> **h. *take a back seat***

1. Although I'm happily married, I've been divorced twice, so . . . . there's always the thought that things could go wrong again.
2. If I want to pass my exams, I think my boyfriend will have to . . . . for a few weeks.
3. Look, Chanel perfume – only £3. It probably . . . . , but it smells just like the real thing.
4. I get criticised a lot at work but it's part of the job. I'm used to it now. It's . . . .
5. A lot of export companies have their . . . . at the moment. Interest rates must come down even further if things are to get any better.
6. My parents moved away from the city when they retired. Now they live . . . . , about two hours drive away.
7. I've been to Dublin lots of times. I know the place . . . .
8. I beat Mike at tennis last week, so now he wants to play me at squash to try to . . . .

Note: If you want to say that someone knows very little about something, you can say: *What James knows about finance could be written on the back of a postage stamp.*

4: Revision

Use the definitions and the words in brackets to write the idioms from this unit in the space provided:

1. it doesn't affect me *(duck)*   like . . . .
2. stolen *(lorry)*   fell . . . .
3. you help me, I'll help you *(scratch)*   you . . . .
4. praise or credit *(pat)*   deserve . . . .
5. know it very well *(hand)*   like . . . .
6. be less important *(seat)*   take . . . .
7. get revenge *(own)*   get . . . .
8. work hard *(put)*   put . . . .
9. miles from anywhere *(beyond)*   in . . . .
10. in a very difficult situation *(wall)*   got . . . .

Was there anything at the back of your mind while you were doing this exercise?

Unit 90 | Cut

1: Meanings

Many of the idiomatic expressions in this unit prove again that it can be difficult to guess the meaning of an idiom from the literal meanings of the individual words which make it up. For example:

1. If you *cut someone dead*, it does not mean that you kill them. It means that you deliberately ignore them and don't speak to them.

2. If you *cut someone down to size*, it means that you tell them that they were acting in a very superior kind of way and they should remember they are no better than everyone else.

3. If an argument *cuts no ice with you*, it does not impress you in any way.

4. If you are not *cut out for* some job or other, it means that it is not suitable for you.

2: To cut a long story short

Use these idiomatic expressions in the sentences below:

      a. *got your work cut out*
      b. *cut him/her down to size*
      c. *a cut above other people*
      d. *to cut a long story short*
      e. *cut your losses*
      f. *cut no ice*
      g. *cut corners*
      h. *cut someone dead*

"Can you believe that when I sacked Roberts, he had the cheek to tell me someone should cut me down to size!"

1. We were at school together, then we went to university. Our relationship was on and off, you know, and then, ... , we got married three years ago.

2. I tried to speak to Frank this morning to apologise for what I said yesterday, but he just . . . .

3. The new secretary thinks she's a . . . . everyone else. She refuses to make coffee for anyone except herself.

4. You're really going to try to decorate the whole flat in two weeks? You've certainly . . . .!

5. I've just bought an old Rolls Royce which I'm going to restore to its original condition. And that means I won't be able to . . . . , so I suppose it'll cost me an arm and a leg!

6. Our Milan branch is losing money every month. I suggest we . . . . and close it down straightaway.

7. My boss is so arrogant. He needs someone to . . . .

8. I told the directors I needed time off because I was suffering from overwork and stress but it . . . . with them. They expect you to work until you drop.

3: It cuts both ways

Fill in the following words and expressions in the sentences below:

> **a.** *a cutting remark*
> **b.** *cut the atmosphere*
> **c.** *cutting it fine*
> **d.** *it cuts both ways*
> **e.** *cut out for it*
> **f.** *cut up about it*
> **g.** *cut-throat business*
> **h.** *half-cut*

1. I'm not a child. When are you going to start treating me like an adult?
   > If you want to be treated like an adult, you need to start behaving like one. It . . . . , you know, Sam.
2. So, his ex-wife turned up at the wedding, did she?
   > Yes, you could have . . . . with a knife.
3. I heard you've given up dentistry. What was wrong?
   > Oh, I just decided I wasn't . . . . I didn't fancy spending the rest of my life looking into other people's mouths!
4. Andy's acting rather strangely. What's the matter with him?
   > He had too much to drink at lunchtime. I think he's . . . . , actually!
5. I must say I was very surprised by what Jane just said to you. She had no right to make such a . . . . about your figure.
   > No, considering her own size, she had no right to say what she said.
6. They'd better get here soon. The train leaves in five minutes.
   > Yes, they're . . . . , aren't they?
7. I hear you're getting out of the restaurant business.
   > Yes, it's too difficult to make a living, and around here it's a . . . .
8. Why's Eric so upset?
   > Someone ran into his new Porsche this morning at the traffic lights and he's really . . . .

4: Revision

Look back at the idioms in this unit and add the missing words:

1. it cuts both . . . .
2. a cut . . . . other people
3. cut the atmosphere with a . . . .
4. you've got your work cut . . . .
5. cut him down to . . . .
6. cut no . . . .
7. a cutting . . . . . .
8. cut up . . . . it
9. to cut a long story . . . .
10. cutting it . . . .

Have you ever done something which didn't turn out too well, so you decided to cut your losses?

Unit 91 End

1: Literal Meanings

Fill in the following words in the definitions below:

bitter   **loose**   **candles**   **deep**   **burn**   **stick**

1. If you can't swim, don't jump in at the . . . . end of the swimming pool.
2. Strawberries taste sweet; lemons taste . . . .
3. Children usually have . . . . on their birthday cakes.
4. I need a belt for these trousers. I've lost weight so they're a bit . . . . around the waist.
5. Don't touch that plate, it's hot; you'll . . . . yourself.
6. People who have difficulty walking sometimes use a . . . .

2: In at the deep end

Use these idiomatic expressions in the sentences below:

a. *not the end of the world*

b. *make ends meet*

c. *at the end of the day*

d. *for hours (days, months) on end*

e. *to the bitter end*

f. *light at the end of the tunnel*

g. *no end of trouble*

h. *in at the deep end*

"In this company we just throw you in at the deep end. It's a carefully considered sink or swim policy."

1. You don't get any training in this job. They just throw you . . . . You either sink or swim!
2. I don't earn much. Just enough to . . . . That's all.
3. The rebel forces have refused to surrender and have said they are ready to fight . . . .
4. The last two years have been financially very hard but things seem to be getting better. There's . . . .
5. I'm worried about my son Peter. He stays in his room playing computer games . . . .
6. Good publicity and customer care are very important, but . . . . , the only way for a business to survive is to make a healthy profit.
7. I'm sorry about your dog, Helen. Come on. You can get another one. It's . . . .
8. Buying a second-hand car is one of the biggest mistakes I've ever made. It's been . . . .

3: The wrong end of the stick

Use the following idiomatic expressions in the situations below:

> a. *to tie up loose ends*
> b. *How are things at your end?*
> c. *on the receiving end*
> d. *End of story!*
> e. *burn the candle at both ends*
> f. *the wrong end of the stick*
> g. *the end is in sight*
> h. *the end of the road*

1. What's the matter with Angela? She's annoyed about something.
   > She heard us talking about political parties and wanted to know why she hadn't been invited. She's just got hold of . . . .
2. I'm so tired. I can't get used to catching the early train.
   > The problem is you go to bed so late. You can't keep . . . .
   . . . . You need to go to bed earlier.
3. Are you leaving soon?
   > I've just got . . . . one or two . . . . , then I'll be on my way.
4. The newspapers are giving the Royal Family a hard time this week.
   > Yes, they've been . . . . of a lot of criticism recently.
5. How many more documents do we have to photocopy? It's taking ages.
   > Don't worry. There's only five more. The . . . .
6. I don't understand why we can't have an office party at Christmas.
   > I've told you before, it's a non-starter. There was too much trouble the last time. If you want to have a party, have it outside this office, but you're not having it here. . . . .! Is that clear?
7. I think maybe it's time we gave up trying to find an agent in Siberia.
   > You're right. There's no point wasting any more time. We've come to . . . .
   . . . .
8. Hello, Mr Lee. I'm fine thanks. We're quite busy here. Sales are up again. How are things . . . .?
   > Terrible. The worst recession for 20 years. I don't know what we're going to do!

Note: If you are *at a loose end*, you have nothing to do.

4: Revision

Look back at the idioms in this unit and add the missing words:

1. it's not the end of the . . . . . .
2. for . . . . . . on end
3. in at the . . . . . . end
4. no end of . . . . . .
5. a few . . . . . . ends to tie up
6. How are . . . . . . at your end?
7. the end is in . . . . . .
8. End of . . . . . .!
9. on the . . . . . . end
10. at the end of the . . . . . .

How much would you need to earn to make ends meet?

Unit 92 | Fall

1: Literal Meanings

Fill in the following words in the definitions below:

lap	*grace*	*seam*	*wayside*
deaf	*heel*	*trap*	*nets*

1. People who can't hear are . . . .
2. The best way to catch mice is to use a . . . .
3. Fishing boats use large . . . . . . to catch fish.
4. When I'm sitting on the sofa, my cat always comes and sits on my . . . .
5. God's mercy and favour towards people is called . . . .
6. The back part of the foot is called the . . . .
7. If you join two pieces of cloth together, you get a . . . . . . where they are joined.
8. An old word for the land at the side of the road is the . . . .

2: Fall into place

Use these idiomatic expressions in the situations below:

a. *fall under the influence*
b. *fall into my lap*
c. *fall on deaf ears*
d. *fall into the wrong hands*
e. *fall into place*

f. *fall about laughing*
g. *fall from grace*
h. *fall apart (at the seams)*
i. *fall head over heels in love*
j. *fall over themselves*

1. For three years after I left university I didn't really know what I wanted to do in life, but then I got a job in New York, made some great friends and everything suddenly seemed to . . . .
2. You do realise that this information is confidential, don't you? If it . . . . , we'd lose our jobs immediately.
3. The government's request that people use public transport more often is . . . . The number of cars on the road is still increasing.
4. My sister's still in Italy. She went there to learn Italian earlier this year and . . . . with her teacher. She's decided to live there.
5. I'm a bit worried about my son at university. He seems to have . . . . of a crowd who are into drugs and alternative life styles.
6. Browning used to be one of the Prime Minister's advisors but he . . . . when he was found guilty of fiddling his expenses.
7. I'm very lucky to have this job. I didn't even apply for it. It just . . . .
8. My marriage began to . . . . when I lost my job.
9. Tim fell backwards off his chair in the office today. I suppose we should have helped him, but we all just . . . .
10. Universities are . . . . to get foreign students onto their courses. They've been forced to do everything they can to make money.

3: Fall into the trap

Use these idiomatic expressions in the sentences below:

a. *fall by the wayside*   e. *fall short of*
b. *(a job) falls to someone*   f. *fall on your feet*
c. *fall into the trap*   g. *fall through the net*
d. *fall foul of*   h. *fall on hard times*

1. There are lots of poor countries which need our help, but we mustn't . . . .
. . . . of thinking they want the same kind of things we want.
2. Diane's just got a job with a company car, pension plan, medical insurance and a really good salary. She's really . . . .
3. The social security system is supposed to protect the elderly and the poor, but the system isn't perfect. There are always some people who . . . .
4. When our head of department left recently, the job of making the speech thanking him for his years here . . . . me.
5. A few years ago I . . . . and life was really difficult. I had to give up my flat and live in a hostel till I got my life back together.
6. My job and family take up so much of my time at the moment that sports and hobbies have just . . . .
7. Whatever you do in business, make sure you've got good people dealing with your VAT returns. The last people you want to . . . . are the VAT inspectors! I speak as one who knows!
8. The language course I went on fell a long way . . . . my expectations.

Note: In business we can say that *the bottom has fallen out of* the market if people have completely stopped buying.

"He fell off his chair and we just fell about laughing!"

4: Revision

Look back at the idioms in this unit and add the final words:

1. fall about . . . . . .
2. fall into the wrong . . . . . .
3. fall head over heels in . . . . . .
4. fall on hard . . . . . .
5. fall into my . . . . . .
6. fall by the . . . . . .
7. fall through the . . . . . .
8. fall on deaf . . . . . .
9. fall apart at the . . . . . .
10. everything fell into . . . . . .
11. fall from . . . . . .
12. don't fall into the . . . . . .

Have you ever fallen on your feet?

Unit 93 Good / Better / Best

1: It did me the world of good

Use the following idiomatic expressions containing *good* in the sentences:

a. *It did me the world of good.*
b. *It took a good hour.*
c. *We're throwing good money after bad.*
d. *What's the good of ...ing?*
e. *It's as good as new.*

f. *He's not in my good books.*
g. *Good for you!*
h. *I paid good money for it.*
i. *It's a good job I didn't ...*
j. *It's for your own good.*

1. I've just come back from a walking holiday in the Alps. You should try it some day. . . . .
2. Harry has been doing some very silly things recently. . . . .
3. Why are we spending so much on advertising when it clearly isn't working? We're just . . . .
4. Look, you're going to have to go on a diet. Believe me, ...
5. I only paid £50 for this camera second-hand, but . . . .
6. I hear you're learning to drive at last! . . . . !
7. I've complained so many times about the smell from the shop next door to our office, but they never do anything about it. I'm absolutely fed up with them. . . . . complaining any more? They just ignore us.
8. I wish you hadn't broken the lock on this cupboard. It . . . . for me to fix it.
9. . . . . get the 7 o'clock train to Glasgow! That's the one that crashed!
10. This umbrella broke the first time I used it. I'm taking it back to the shop. It wasn't cheap. . . . .

2: Better safe than sorry

Match up the following two-line dialogues, each containing *better*:

1. I think we should take an extra £200 on holiday.
2. Hello. Sorry I'm late.
3. When is this meeting going to finish?
4. Excuse me? Can I get a bus from here to the town centre?
5. I hear you've got an old Volkswagen Beetle. What's it like?
6. Frank still hasn't given me back the £20 I lent him.

a. Better late than never. We thought you'd got lost!
b. Well, it's seen better days but it still runs very well.
c. You should know better than to lend him money. That's typical of him.
d. As far as I'm concerned, the sooner the better!
e. You're right. Better safe than sorry.
f. Yes, but you'd be better off walking. It's only a five-minute walk.

Now underline all the expressions which contain *better*.

3: The best of both worlds

Fill in these idiomatic expressions, each using *best*, in the situations below:

    a. *to the best of my knowledge*
    b. *that's your best bet*
    c. *it's probably for the best*
    d. *I wasn't feeling at my best*
    e. *bring out the best in someone*
    f. *at the best of times*
    g. *make the best of a bad job*
    h. *the best of both worlds*

"The morning after the office party Bill wasn't feeling at his best."

1. I live ten minutes from the city centre and ten minutes from the countryside.
   > So, you've got . . . . , haven't you?
2. I think that was the most boring lesson I've ever had. He's so dull.
   > Yes, he's not very interesting . . . . , but I agree that was worse than usual.
3. Do you remember Colin? I wonder what he's doing these days.
   > . . . . , he's still working at the post office.
4. Hello, Jane. Sorry, but I'm afraid I have to cancel our meeting next Monday.
   > Oh, don't worry. . . . . I'm very busy myself.
5. This hotel is awful. If I'd known it was going to be this bad, I'd never have come.
   > Well, there's nothing we can do about it. Let's just . . . .
6. You didn't seem very well yesterday.
   > No, ... I had a bad headache.
7. Angela's doing very well in her new job, isn't she?
   > Yes, the extra responsibility has . . . .
8. Excuse me? Can you tell me how to get to Madame Tussaud's from here?
   > Take the underground to Baker Street. . . . .

4: Revision

Look back at the idioms in this unit and add the missing verbs:

1. It'll . . . . . . out the best in you.
2. Let's . . . . . . the best of a bad job.
3. It's . . . . . . better days.
4. I . . . . . . good money for it.
5. It'll . . . . . . you the world of good.
6. I'm not . . . . . . at my best this morning.
7. It can . . . . . . a good hour.
8. Let's stop . . . . . . good money after bad.

What sort of situations bring out the best in you?

Unit 94 Ground

1: Meanings

The ground is one of the most basic things we know. It is not surprising then if *ground rules* **are basic rules. In a similar way, if you** *have a good grounding* **in a subject, you know the basics.**

Hundreds of years ago, everyone had to hunt animals to stay alive. If you wanted to know if there were any large animals around, you put your ear to the ground and listened. Today if you *keep your ear to the ground* **you are trying to be aware of any ideas or rumours which are around.**

Flying is a more modern idea. A plane literally *gets off the ground.* **This can be applied to a new project in business.**

2: Suit him down to the ground

Complete the idiomatic expressions using these verbs:

get off	*keep (2)*	*cover*	*suit*	*cut*
stand	*hit*	*prepare*	*break*	

a. . . . . you down to the ground

b. . . . . the ground *(eg a project)*

c. . . . . your ear to the ground

d. . . . . your ground

e. . . . . your feet on the ground

f. . . . . the same ground

g. . . . . the ground *(before a meeting)*

h. . . . . the ground from under your feet

i. . . . . the ground running

j. . . . . new ground

Now use the expressions in the sentences below:

1. Paul's good with people; he's patient; he's organised. Personally, I think social work will . . . . him . . . .

2. Another boring meeting! They're a waste of time. We always . . . . the same old . . . .

3. Pauline won't be happy with these sales figures. I suggest you fax them to her before you phone her – just to . . . . before you speak.

4. I like the idea in theory but in practice it'll never . . . .

5. You want to move to the Personnel Department, don't you? I've heard there might be a job there soon so . . . .

6. I was going to tell my boyfriend we were finished but before I could tell him he gave me a present, which completely . . . .

7. I knew I hadn't stolen anything in the shop, so I just . . . . and eventually they believed me. They had mixed me up with someone else!

8. Good morning, everyone. Hope you had a good weekend. There's a huge amount of work to be done so let's . . . .

9. The best advice my grandmother ever gave me was to . . . . even if my head was in the clouds!

10. I've got an idea for a book which I think will . . . . in the field of science fiction.

3: A bit thin on the ground

Use these idiomatic expressions in the situations below:

> a. *ground rules*
> b. *gaining ground*
> c. *on dangerous ground*
> d. *the middle ground*
> e. *a bit thin on the ground*
> f. *working yourself into the ground*
> g. *down to the ground*
> h. *a good grounding*

1. Excuse me, I'm thinking of changing my PC for an Apple Mac. Have you got any second-hand ones?
   > Sorry, we haven't. Second-hand Macs are . . . . at the moment.
2. We've got to do something to reduce our costs.
   > Well, if you start talking about cutting staff, you're . . . .
   We'll have the union reps in here in a flash.
3. What do you mean, I'm a workaholic? I don't work too hard.
   > You do, Peter. Twelve hours a day! You're . . . . !
4. How left-wing are the Social Democrats in your country?
   > They're not really left-wing at all. They certainly see themselves as occupying
   . . . .
5. Thanks for letting me stay with you. You're doing me a big favour.
   > That's OK, but there are one or two . . . . : no smoking, shoes off at the front door and everyone does their own washing up.
6. You're doing a computer course, aren't you?
   > Yes, it's nothing special but it gives you . . . . in the basics.
7. Last time we came here there was a cinema on this corner.
   > There was a fire two years ago. The cinema was burnt . . . .
   . . . .
8. Is there anything interesting in the end-of-year report?
   > Well, apparently, we're . . . . on most of our competitors.

Note: You can have *grounds for complaint* and you can retire *on the grounds of ill-health*.

4: Revision

Look back at the idioms in this unit and add the missing prepositions:

1. working yourself . . . . the ground
2. suits me . . . . to the ground
3. keep your ear close . . . . the ground
4. cut the ground from . . . . my feet
5. thin . . . . the ground
6. get . . . . the ground
7. a good grounding . . . . maths
8. burnt . . . . to the ground

Do you get excited easily or do you always keep your feet on the ground?

Unit 95 | Half

1: Go halves

Use these expressions with *half* in the sentences below:

a. *half the fun*
b. *half a mind to*
c. *my other half*
d. *given half a chance*
e. *half a second*
f. *go halves*

1. Waiter? Can we have the bill please? We'll . . . . , shall we, Tom?
2. I've never been to the Far East but I'd go, ...
3. Trying different kinds of food is . . . . of going on holiday.
4. That shop assistant was so rude. I've got . . . . call the manager and complain.
5. I just need to make a quick phone call. I'll be with you in . . . .
6. Bill, let me introduce you to . . . . Kate, this is Bill from work.

Note: Some people today think that calling your husband/wife 'your other half' is old-fashioned or inappropriate.

2: Half asleep

Now do the same with these:

a. *meet you halfway*
b. *half as good as*
c. *half-hearted*
d. *half the trouble*
e. *half asleep*
f. *half a dozen of the other*

"You've been half asleep all morning. Now pull yourself together!"

1. You're not listening to me. What's the matter with you this morning? You're
. . . .
2. No, I'm sorry. I can't come down to £50. I really want a hundred, but I'll . . . .
. . . . What about £75 – I really can't go any lower than that.
3. The new *Star Wars* isn't . . . . the last one.
4. Jackie says Gary's being unhelpful and rude in the office but if you ask me it's six
of one and . . . . They're as bad as each other. I think we're
going to have to move one of them out of the department.
5. I've just finished reading your homework and it's disappointing. You only made a
. . . . attempt to answer the question.
6. I'm putting on more weight again. I suppose I need more exercise but . . . .
. . . . is my new job. I've just started work in a chocolate factory.

3: That's half the battle

Match the two halves of the dialogues:

1. I can understand English well enough. My problem comes when I've got to speak.
2. Have you finished that book I lent you?
3. I've never seen so much food and drink at a wedding.
4. Let's spend the day sightseeing tomorrow.
5. Listen, I've got a good idea.
6. I don't understand Pam's sense of humour at all.
7. How's your report coming along?
8. Do you like Peter's new girlfriend?

a. Not yet. I'm only **halfway through**.
b. What you need is more confidence. **That's half the battle**.
c. Well, I was **half hoping** to go the beach again, actually.
d. **Not half!** She's great fun!
e. I know what you mean. **Half the time** I don't know whether she's joking or not!
f. Well, we don't believe in **doing things by halves**.
g. I hope it's not as **half-baked** as your others!
h. I think I'm about **halfway there**.

4: Revision

Match the expression with *half* with the definitions on the right:

1. go halves
2. half-baked
3. meet someone halfway
4. I've half a mind to ...
5. given half a chance
6. my other half
7. Not half!
8. half the battle

a. *compromise*
b. *if the opportunity came*
c. *I strongly agree!*
d. *my husband/wife/partner*
e. *share the cost*
f. *not properly thought through*
g. *the most difficult or important step*
h. *I'm thinking about ...*

Look back at the idioms in this unit and add *a* or *the* to the space or leave it blank:

9. go . . . . halves
10. got half . . . . mind to
11. half . . . . trouble
12. half . . . . dozen
13. half . . . . time
14. half . . . . battle
15. given half . . . . chance
16. half . . . . second
17. half . . . . fun
18. meet . . . . halfway

Do you sometimes have half-baked ideas or do you always think things through?

Unit 96 Know

1: Meanings

Know is a very common verb with a simple meaning, but it is also used in many common idiomatic expressions:

I'll let you know.	=	I'll tell you.
I know it inside out.	=	I know it very well.
I know her by sight.	=	I know her, but I've never spoken to her.
I don't actually know him,	=	I don't actually know the person. I've
but I know OF him.		only heard about him.

2: Not that I know of

Use the following idiomatic expressions in the situations below:

> a. *I don't know about you but ...*
> b. *She doesn't know the meaning of the word.*
> c. *Not that I know of.*
> d. *I know her by sight.*
> e. *I don't know whether I'm coming or going.*
> f. *I didn't know which way to look.*
> g. *You know best.*
> h. *How was I to know?*
> i. *I know it like the back of my hand.*
> j. *I don't know the first thing about it/them.*

1. Rick, has there been a fax from Vanessa today?
   > . . . .
2. Let's go by train. It'll be more expensive but much more relaxing than driving.
   > OK. . . . .
3. Brian, do you know anything about electricity? I've got a problem.
   > Sorry. . . . .
4. Ruth asked me to tell you that she was sorry.
   > Sorry? . . . .
5. I didn't like the way Paula criticised Ian in front of us. It just wasn't on, was it?
   > It was extremely embarrassing. . . . .
6. Carol, you've been to Munich, haven't you?
   > Yes. . . . .
7. Do you realise we've been waiting twenty minutes for the menu?
   > . . . . I think we should go. Come on.
8. Sarah, do you know somebody called Rosemary Pinkerton?
   > . . . . but I've never really spoken to her.
9. Mike, you shouldn't have told that joke about cats. You've really upset Cathy.
   > Sorry, but . . . . her cat died last week?
10. New job and new flat in the same week! It's all change for you, isn't it?
    > Yes. . . . . at the moment.

3: You never know

Complete the following idiomatic expressions containing *know*:

> *let*   *out*   *hand*   *of*   *thing*   *far*   *all*   *never*

a. as . . . . . . as I know
b. know a . . . . . . or two about ...
c. I know . . . . . him
d. for . . . . . . I know
e. the right . . . . . . doesn't know what the left is doing
f. you . . . . . . know
g. I'll . . . . . . you know
h. know something inside . . . . . .

Now use the expressions in these sentences:

1. It's probably too late to get a table at that Mexican restaurant but phone them anyway. You . . . . , they might have had a cancellation.
2. I haven't seen my older brother for ten years. He could be on Mars . . . .
3. I'm not sure if I can come on Sunday but . . . . tomorrow.
4. I've had to use the instruction manual so often, I . . . . . . it . . . .
5. Yes, Patrick's married, but . . . . , he hasn't got any children.
6. I don't actually know Rupert Baxter but I . . . .
7. If you're interested in finding out more about the village, ask old Mr Braithwaite. He . . . . the history of the area.
8. The communication in this company is useless. . . . .

"Sorry, I don't know the first thing about electricity."

4: Revision

Complete these idioms from this unit:

1. don't know the . . . . thing about something
2. know someone by . . . .
3. know something . . . . out
4. know a thing or . . . . about something
5. know it like the . . . . of your hand
6. don't know the . . . . of the word
7. You . . . . know!
8. as . . . . as I know
9. for . . . . I know
10. not . . . . I know of
11. You know . . . . !
12. I'll . . . . you know

Can you think of a great book you've read so often that you know it inside out?

Unit 97 Life

1: The story of my life

Underline all the expressions in this passage which contain the word *life:*

When I was young, my parents gave me an excellent start in life and I always played a full part in the life of my school. Later, I enjoyed student life. I have been interested in politics for all of my adult life, and I've always been active in public life. Family life is very important to me and when my son was fighting for his life after his accident, I gave up all political activity for a while. Later, when the scandal hit me, I fought – unsuccessfully – for my political life, so I had to give up for good. If only my private life had stayed private!

2: A double life

Use these collocations in the sentences below:

> *double life*   *public life*   *shelf life*   *everyday life*   *working life*

1. Some men lead a . . . . Even though people think they are happily married, they have another relationship, or even two families.
2. My father spent his whole . . . . in the coal industry.
3. After three weeks in Africa, ... is going to seem pretty dull.
4. This is a policy with a very short . . . . By next month, nobody will be interested in it any more.
5. People in . . . . have to be very careful how they behave.

3: The facts of life

Fill in the following expressions in the sentences below:

> **a.** *way of life*
> **b.** *quality of life*
> **c.** *all walks of life*
> **d.** *spark of life*

> **e.** *the meaning of life*
> **f.** *the kiss of life*
> **g.** *the facts of life*
> **h.** *loss of life*

1. I think I was about ten when my parents told me . . . . A bit too late really. They'd have been shocked to realise how much I already knew.
2. The heavy rains destroyed many homes and resulted in tragic . . . . on a scale not seen for many years.
3. Cocaine is now an extremely common drug. Although it is both dangerous and illegal, people from . . . . use it as a form of recreation.
4. You can improve people's . . . . if you improve their level of education.
5. My sister nearly drowned once. She'd actually stopped breathing and a paramedic had to give her . . . .
6. I sometimes just gaze out of the window and wonder about . . . .
7. I wish Joe had more personality. There's no . . . . in him at all.
8. I'd like to live abroad for a while to experience a completely different . . . .

4: I had the time of my life!

Use these idiomatic expressions in the situations below:

> **a. *I had the time of my life.***   **d. *This is the life!***
> **b. *That's life!***   **e. *Get a life!***
> **c. *Variety is the spice of life.***   **f. *Life must go on.***

1. You've just got back from Hawaii, haven't you? Did you have a good time?
   > Yes, ... !
2. Here we are – golden sand, sea, cold beer and no work for two weeks.
   > Yes, ...
3. I'm sorry to hear about you and Marina splitting up.
   > Yes, it's really sad, but . . . .
4. Typical! The one day we want to go to France and they cancel the ferry.
   > These things happen. . . . .
5. I collect car registration numbers. It's my main hobby, you know.
   > Really? Well, all I can say is – . . . . !
6. When are you going to settle down? You've got a different girlfriend every month and I can't remember the last time you spent a weekend at home.
   > I don't want to settle down. You know what they say – . . . .
   . . . . !

Remember: Today is the first day of the rest of your life.

"You've obviously had the time of your life, Mum!"

5: Revision

Look back at the idioms in this unit and add the missing words:

1. people from all . . . . . . of life
2. active in . . . . . . life
3. they gave her the . . . . . . of life
4. he led a . . . . . . life
5. tragic . . . . . . of life
6. the . . . . . . of my life
7. variety is the . . . . . . of life
8. life must go . . . . . .
9. the . . . . . . of life
10. . . . . . . a life!

How many different jobs do you think you will have during your working life?

Unit 98 Light and Heavy

1: Literal meanings

The literal meanings of *light* and *heavy* are simple – *a light bag, a heavy suitcase*. Both words have many metaphorical uses. We talk about someone being *a light sleeper* or *having a heavy heart*. Often *light* can mean *easy* or *small* while *heavy* can mean *difficult, serious* or *large*. Match the following meanings with the expressions:

1. Clearing the garden was very heavy work.
2. Agatha Christie's books are ideal light reading for taking on holiday.
3. It was the heavy traffic on the ring road that made me late.
4. Anne's got a really heavy cold.
5. Only two a day! That is what I call a light smoker!

a. serious
b. few
c. lots
d. easy
e. tiring

2: A light snack

Sort the following words into three groups:

L	**=**	**only used with light**
H	**=**	**only used with heavy**
L/H	**=**	**can be used with both**

a. snack
b. relief
c. industry
d. going
e. lunch
f. day
g. casualties
h. traffic
i. work
j. rain

k. fighting
l. losses
m. shower
n. reading
o. cold
p. heart
q. sleeper
r. entertainment
s. aircraft
t. meal

3: A heavy meal

Use expressions from Exercise 2 to complete the following:

1. I'm sorry I can't concentrate this afternoon. I had a rather . . . . at lunchtime.
2. In recent years many areas which used to depend on . . . . have suffered from serious unemployment.
3. We got to the airport with two hours to spare. The traffic was very . . . .
4. I'm not feeling well at all. I've got a really . . . .
5. My wife wakes up about six times every night. She's a very . . . .
6. News is just coming in of another earthquake in California. I'm afraid there are reports of very . . . .
7. My favourite television programmes are . . . . such as comedy, soaps, current pop and that kind of thing.
8. Nick seems to have a new joke every day. Thank goodness he brings a spot of . . . . to our dull boring office!
9. Climbing the last couple of hundred metres to the summit was pretty . . . . , I can tell you!
10. On the way home last night I got caught in a very . . . . I got soaked to the skin.
11. Many investors have suffered . . . . in recent days as prices have hit rock bottom.
12. Just let me go and have a bath. I've had a very . . . . at work.
13. You know what they say – many hands make . . . . !
14. We're running late, so we'd better skip lunch and just have a . . . . instead.
15. It was with a very . . . . that Jane left her father in hospital. She had a feeling that she would never see him alive again.
16. If we have a . . . . , we'll be ready for a really lavish meal out this evening.
17. There was almost a disaster over Heathrow yesterday when a jumbo came within 200 metres of a . . . . on a sightseeing flight.
18. If you're going on a long flight, take some . . . . with you.
19. There was no play at Wimbledon yesterday as a result of very . . . . all day.
20. . . . . has been reported on the outskirts of the city as Government forces have tried to regain control of the area.

4: Can you say?

Which of the following are possible? Cross out those which are not possible:

1. a. light relief   b. heavy relief
2. a. a light sleeper   b. a heavy sleeper
3. a. a light shower   b. a heavy shower
4. a. light entertainment   b. heavy entertainment
5. a. a light snack   b. a heavy snack
6. a. a light meal   b. a heavy meal

Do you eat a heavy lunch or do you prefer a light snack at lunchtime?

Unit 99 Like

1: Literal meanings

Fill in the following words in the definitions below:

sieve	*dirt*	*plague*	*clockwork*
bricks	*logs*	*ton*	*maniac*

1. A . . . . is used in the kitchen for separating solids from liquids and small pieces from big pieces.
2. You can cut a tree into . . . . which you then put on your fire.
3. An outbreak of disease which kills thousands of people is called a . . . .
4. A toy or clock which works when wound up by a key works by . . . .
5. My clothes need a wash. They are covered in . . . . because I've been working in the garden.
6. Houses are often built of stone or . . . .
7. Someone who is mad, violent and dangerous is a . . . .
8. A . . . . is a unit of weight – 2240 pounds to be exact.

2: You look like death warmed up

First match these expressions:

1. You look
2. He drinks
3. I've got a memory
4. He smokes
5. He treats her
6. He eats
7. It's
8. She's taken to it

a. like a sieve.
b. like a duck to water.
c. like a horse.
d. like water off a duck's back.
e. like a fish.
f. like a chimney.
g. like dirt.
h. like death warmed up.

Now use the expressions below:

9. I think I'll go home. I feel terrible. I think I need to see a doctor.
   > Yes, go home. . . . .
10. Did you see the way Robert spoke to his wife last night? Disgusting, wasn't it?
   > Yes, but it didn't surprise me. . . . .
11. I don't care if he is the boss; somebody has to tell him he's wrong.
   > You're wasting your time criticising him. . . . .
12. I see Peter's put more weight on.
   > I'm not surprised. . . . .
13. Your sister's just started nursing, hasn't she?
   > Yes and she loves it. . . . .
14. I could smell alcohol on Gerry's breath this morning. Does he drink a lot?
   > Didn't you know? He's got a problem. . . . .
15. Surely you remember Monica. She's the teacher you met at Caroline's house.
   > Sorry. . . . .
16. I suppose I smoke about ten cigarettes a day.
   > That's nothing compared to my brother. . . . .

3: He drives like a maniac

First match up these expressions:

1. He drives	a. like a fish out of water.
2. I felt	b. like a ton of bricks.
3. She spends money	c. like a native.
4. I slept	d. like a maniac.
5. She came down on me	e. like a log.
6. Everything went	f. like there's no tomorrow.
7. He speaks it	g. like the plague.
8. Avoid it	h. like clockwork.

Now add these expressions below:

9. That's the best night's sleep I've had for ages. . . . .

10. My sister's always short of cash. . . . .

11. You should hear Simon's Spanish. . . . .

12. The wedding was perfect. . . . .

13. Never get into a car with Gerry. . . . .

14. I left work early last Friday without asking. When she found out, my boss . . . . .

. . . .

15. I went to a nightclub last night for the first time in ten years. I didn't know what
to do with myself. . . . .

16. Don't go near that new Indian restaurant in Duke Street. . . . .

4: Revision

Say the following in a different way using an idiom suggested by the words in brackets:

1. She speaks English very well. *(native)*
2. He is a bad driver. *(maniac)*
3. Everything went according to plan. *(clockwork)*
4. I often forget things. *(sieve)*
5. I felt out of place at the meeting. *(fish)*
6. You look really ill. *(death)*
7. Criticism doesn't bother me. *(duck's back)*
8. She eats a lot. *(horse)*

Now add the missing verbs:

9. . . . . like a chimney
10. . . . . down on me like a ton of bricks
11. . . . . to it like a duck to water
12. . . . . it like the plague
13. . . . . like a fish
14. . . . . like death warmed up
15. . . . . me like dirt
16. . . . . like a log

Are you a light sleeper or do you usually sleep like a log?

Unit 100 Line

1: Literal meanings

Line is a quite a common word in many idiomatic expressions. It has a range of meanings:

1. If you *drop someone a line*, you write them a letter.
2. The *bottom line* refers to accounts where you see the profit or loss at the bottom.
3. The *dotted line* is the line on which you sign your name for a contract or bill.
4. If you *draw a line under* something on a piece of paper you separate it from what comes before. If you *draw a line under* an experience, it means it is finished and you don't want to hear any more about it. For example: *When John's divorce came through, he drew a line under that episode of his life.*

2: Hold the line

Use the following idiomatic expressions in the situations below:

> **a. *I'll drop you a line.***
>
> **b. *Hold the line, please.***
>
> **c. *We're thinking along similar lines.***
>
> **d. *You've got to draw the line somewhere.***
>
> **e. *You'll have to toe the line.***
>
> **f. *I draw the line at that.***

1. This is Sarah Williams. Can I speak to Amanda Price, please?
   > . . . . I'll just see if she's free.
2. I think security cameras are a good idea in banks and shops but I'm not sure about having them in the streets. What about personal privacy?
   > I agree. . . . . , haven't you?
3. Right. Have a good journey. Good luck with the new job and everything.
   > Thanks. . . . . to let you know how I'm getting on.
4. I agree. Let's move the meeting to the 24th and involve the other departments.
   > Good. I'm pleased . . . .
5. I love almost any sport, but . . . . boxing. I don't think that's really a sport at all.
6. I think it's terrible that we have to work on public holidays.
   > There's no point in complaining about it. . . . . like everyone else.

Note: If you *toe the line*, you conform. In politics you often have to *toe the party line* – support what the party believes. People who rock the boat are said to *step out of line*. If something is different from other similar things, it can be *brought into line* with the others.

3: Sign on the dotted line

Use the following idiomatic expressions in the sentences below:

a. *in line for*
b. *along the line*
c. *on the dotted line*
d. *out of line*

e. *on the line*
f. *the bottom line*
g. *between the lines*
h. *into line with*

1. Make sure you read the contract in detail before you sign . . . .
2. If you step . . . . in this company, they get rid of you. You don't get a second chance.
3. Susan says she's happy with Martin but reading . . . . , something's not quite right. They never seem to go out together.
4. I never received your letter. It must have got lost somewhere . . . .
5. Sales figures are bad again this month. I'm Head of Sales so it's my job that's . . . .
6. Helen's doing very well at work. In fact, I think she's . . . . promotion.
7. The British Government have been under increasing pressure from Brussels to bring interest rates . . . . the rest of Europe.
8. I know you don't want to learn English but . . . . is, if you want to get a better job here, you need to speak a foreign language.

Note: If your job is *on the line*, you are at risk of losing it. If someone is *on the line*, they are on the telephone.

"Right, Mr Smythe, it's gloves off! But I draw the line at pink satin shorts!"

4: Revision

Look back at the idioms in this unit and add the missing verbs:

1. . . . . . . the line, please
2. . . . . . . me a line
3. my job . . . . . . on the line
4. you've got to . . . . . . the line somewhere

5. . . . . . . rates into line with
6. . . . . . . along similar lines
7. . . . . . . between the lines
8. . . . . . . on the dotted line

Are you a bit of a rebel or do you toe the line?

Unit 101 Lose and Lost

1: Meanings

Match the following idiomatic expressions with their meanings:

1. lose heart	a. become lost
2. lose face	b. become angry
3. lose your bearings	c. become disappointed
4. lose touch with someone	d. become confused about something
5. lose your temper	e. become embarrassed
6. lose track of something	f. stop sending letters or ringing

2: Lost for words

Use the following idiomatic expressions in the situations below:

a. *lose heart*	f. *fighting a losing battle*
b. *lost track of the time*	g. *make up for lost time*
c. *losing your touch*	h. *lost count of*
d. *lose face*	i. *lost for words*
e. *lost my way*	j. *no love lost*

1. Was Jackie pleased with her present?
   > Yes, she was delighted. She was so surprised she was . . . .

2. What are you doing this weekend?
   > I'm spending the whole weekend with my sister. I haven't seen her for six months so we want to . . . .

3. Where have you been? You were supposed to be here an hour ago.
   > Sorry. I was walking around town and I just . . . .

4. I haven't been to the cinema for ages.
   > Really? I've . . . . the number of films I've seen this year.

5. I'm finding my university course much more difficult than I expected.
   > A lot of people say that. It's quite normal. Don't . . . .

6. They can't build a road right behind our houses and think we'll just accept it.
   > Well, keep complaining if you want but you're . . . .

7. Why didn't you just tell him he was wrong?
   > Not in front of the others. He'd . . . .

8. I thought Angela would have jumped at the chance of dinner with me, but no – she said she couldn't come out because she was washing her hair!
   > Well, Mike, I think that means only one thing. You're . . . . !

9. I didn't know Bill and Jack didn't get on.
   > No, they've never seen eye to eye. There's . . . . between them.

10. Why has it taken you so long? We were expecting you an hour ago.
    > Well, I'm afraid I . . . . in the one-way system, then I went into the back of a bus! It's just been one thing after another!

3: We've got nothing to lose

Add these responses to the situations below:

> a. *You sound as though you're losing your voice.*
> b. *We must never lose sight of that.*
> c. *I'm sorry I lost my temper.*
> d. *He told me I need to lose some weight.*
> e. *I've completely lost my bearings.*
> f. *Don't lose any sleep over it.*
> g. *Losing touch with all your old school friends.*
> h. *We're losing ground to the competition.*
> i. *We've got nothing to lose.*

1. I know they say there's no tickets left for the final, but why don't we go anyway and see if we can get hold of a couple?
   > Why not? . . . .
2. Am I right in thinking you're ringing to apologise?
   > Yes, ...
3. Look, I made a mistake. I admit it. It was my fault. OK?
   > OK, OK! Everybody makes mistakes. . . . .
4. My throat's quite painful and it's difficult to talk.
   > . . . .
5. What did the doctor say?
   > What do you think? . . . .
6. We're not having a very good year, are we?
   > No, ...
7. Do you know the thing I regret most about leaving school?
   > . . . .
8. Which direction are we going in – east or west?
   > Don't ask me . . . .
9. The whole purpose of this company is to make a profit and . . . .
   . . . .

4: Revision

What would you say in these situations? Use the words in brackets.

1. Somebody surprises you with a wonderful present. *(I'm, words)*
2. Tell someone not to worry about something. *(Don't, sleep)*
3. You didn't realise what time it was. *(I, track)*
4. You're getting fat. *(I, weight)*
5. A friend needs encouraging. *(Don't, heart)*
6. You haven't seen your parents for ages. *(I, make, time)*
7. You're not sure which direction is which. *(I've, bearings)*
8. You want to say you've been to Paris many times. *(I've, count, times)*

Have you lost touch with the people you were at school with?

Unit 102 No

1: It's no wonder!

Put these expressions with *no* into the situations below:

a. *no idea*	**f.** *no chance*
b. *no word*	**g.** *no sign*
c. *no point*	**h.** *no way*
d. *no reason*	**i.** *no joke*
e. *no wonder*	**j.** *no doubt*

1. Did you know David hasn't got a watch? Or if he has, he never wears it.
   > It's . . . . he's always late!
2. Do you know where Valerie is?
   > Sorry, I've got . . . . ! I haven't seen her all day.
3. I'm going to wear this shirt and my new jeans tonight. What do you think?
   > Well, if you wear jeans, there's . . . . they'll let you in. They've got a strict no-jeans policy.
4. Robert phoned me last night. Guess what he wanted.
   > . . . . he was trying to borrow money again.
5. If we miss the last bus we can walk home. No problem.
   > That's easy for you to say. Walking that distance for me is . . . .
6. How are Laura and her friends enjoying their holiday?
   > Goodness knows! There's been . . . . from them since they left.
7. This weather is dreadful, isn't it?
   > Yes, and there's . . . . of it getting any better.
8. Be careful what you're doing!
   > Just calm down! Just because you're in a bad mood, there's . . . . to take it out on me!
9. It's already twenty past six.
   > Well, there's . . . . of us getting the 6.30 train. We may as well forget the idea.
10. Shall we send Geoff a card?
    > There's . . . . He never says thank you and he never sends us one!

2: There's no ...

Here are four common fixed expressions all starting *there's no* ... Which of the following four people is most likely to say each one?

a. a jet-setting businessman on his third trip this month
b. a soldier going into battle
c. a detective investigating the murder of a child
d. a journalist

1. There's no going back.
2. There's no rhyme nor reason to it.
3. There's no place like home.
4. There's no smoke without fire.

3: No hard feelings!

Each response in the following conversations uses an idiomatic expression with *no*. Match them up:

1. Look, I'm really sorry about what I said yesterday.
2. Can I borrow your car?
3. I've just been offered a part in a Hollywood film!
4. Look, we found the hotel in the end, didn't we?
5. Can you get away from work early on Friday?

a. No kidding!
b. No thanks to you!
c. No hard feelings!
d. No such luck!
e. No way!

4: No news is good news

Use the following idiomatic expressions in the situations below:

a. *no bad thing*
b. *a no-go area*
c. *a real no-no*

d. *no news is good news*
e. *no end of problems*
f. *in no time*

1. I haven't heard anything from the hospital but I suppose . . . .
2. I've had . . . . with my new computer.
3. I have to take an exam at the end of the course, which is . . . . because it gives me extra motivation to study.
4. Whatever you do, don't park in Frank's parking space. It's . . . . He gets very annoyed about it.
5. English is actually quite easy. You'll be speaking it like a native . . . .
6. When I was in Naples years ago, the hotel told me not to go near a certain area. They said it was . . . . for tourists.

5: Revision

Rewrite the following idiomatic expressions, correcting the mistake:

1. Parts of Belfast were stop-go areas.

. . . .

2. There's no fire without smoke.

. . . .

3. I'll be with you in any time.

. . . .

4. There's no coming back.

. . . .

5. It's no laugh bringing up children as a single parent.

. . . .

6. There's no house like home.

. . . .

7. It's a real yes-no.

. . . .

8. No news is no news.

. . . .

Is anything a real no-no at the place where you work or study?

Unit 103 Of

1: A flood of enquiries

Complete these expressions with the words given:

1. in the nick of . . . . . .
2. a word of . . . . . .
3. a string of . . . . . .
4. a whole host of . . . . . .
5. a spot of . . . . . .
6. a flood of . . . . . .
7. a mountain of . . . . . .
8. piles of . . . . . .

a. excuses
b. reasons
c. enquiries
d. money
e. work
f. advice
g. time
h. bother

Now use the expressions below:

9. Our advertisement in the local paper worked. We've had . . . . from people interested in renting our villa in the Algarve.
10. OK, you were late. Let's just forget about it. I don't want to listen to . . . . for the next five minutes.
11. If you're going up into the mountains, ... Take warm clothes with you. It might be sunny now but the weather can change without warning.
12. Sorry I'm late. I had . . . . with my car.
13. I decided against taking the job for . . . . , but the main one was it would be too far to travel – two hours on the train every day!
14. We nearly missed the train but we got to the match . . . .
15. Footballers get . . . . for just running around in shorts and complaining to the referee. It's ridiculous!
16. There's no way I can take a day off this week. I'm up to my eyes. I've got . . . .

2: A stroke of luck

Use the following words to complete these idiomatic expressions:

tears   *visitors*   *advice*   *time*   *garlic*   *luck*

a. bags of . . . .
b. a stream of . . . .
c. a hint of . . . .

d. a piece of . . . .
e. floods of . . . .
f. a stroke of . . . .

Now use them in these situations:

1. I've just had an amazing . . . . ! I dropped my keys as I was getting out of the train, didn't realise till I got home, turned round, and there was my neighbour coming up the path with them!
   > Now, that's what I call luck!
2. Congratulations on the new baby! Everything OK at home?
   > Yes, thanks. Sue's very tired. We had . . . . over the weekend – you know – friends and relatives.

3. Has Natalie left the office? I can't find her anywhere.
   > She's in Pam's office. I don't know what's wrong but she's in . . . .
4. It's my job interview tomorrow. I'm nervous already.
   > Well, the best . . . . I can give you is be yourself.
   You'll be fine.
5. What's the unusual flavour I can taste in this bread you've made, Kevin?
   > Do you like it? It's just . . . . I put it in everything.
6. Have we got time for a dessert or do we need to go?
   > We've got . . . . The train doesn't go for another hour.

3: A pack of lies

Now do the same with these:

doubt	*warning*	*lies*
soda	*criticism*	*paint*

"Just having a spot of bother with the car!"

   a. a wave of . . . .
   b. a coat of . . . .
   c. a pack of . . . .
   d. a shadow of a . . . . . .
   e. a dash of . . . .
   f. a word of . . . .

1. What did you think of the statement
   on telly last night by the President?
   > . . . . from start to finish!
2. I think the front door needs a . . . .
   > Yes, so does mine – before the winter.
3. Can I get you a drink? What will you have?
   > Whisky, please. With just . . . .
4. . . . . before you go to India.
   > What's that? Don't drink the water?
   Yes, but just as important, don't buy any drinks from anyone in the street. And
   don't have any drinks with ice in them.
5. The government are planning to cut the benefit paid to single mothers.
   > Well, you can be sure that will provoke a . . . .
6. Do you think the Republicans will win the next election?
   > Without . . . . The Democrats have no chance.

4: Revision

Decide which of the four words in italics does NOT go with the key word:

1. bags of *time/energy/electricity/enthusiasm*
2. a stream of *insults/immigrants/visitors/respect*
3. a flood of *complaints/letters/ideas/enquiries*
4. a hint of *fault/irony/garlic/humour*
5. a pack of *cards/questions/lies/wolves*
6. a trace of *guilt/fear/irony/disaster*

**If you had to give one piece of advice to someone visiting your country, what
would it be?**

Unit 104 Or

1: Believe it or not

Put the following expressions with *or* into the sentences below:

a. *give or take*
b. *take it or leave it*
c. *like it or not*
d. *sooner or later*
e. *rightly or wrongly*

f. *sink or swim*
g. *laugh or cry*
h. *believe it or not*
i. *a thing or two*
j. *make or break*

1. . . . . , I used to be a professional singer.
2. I'll give you £1000 for the car. That's my final offer. . . . . !
3. There's no point complaining about tax. You have to pay it whether you . . . .
. . . .
4. If you're going to buy a second-hand car, speak to Frank. He knows . . . .
. . . . about cars.
5. The business has been going downhill for a while now. The next few months are
. . . . for us.
6. I've just been to the travel agent. Can you believe it costs £700 to fly to South
Africa? I didn't know whether to . . . . when they told me.
7. It'll take three months for your new passport to arrive – . . . . a
week.
8. I believe, ... , that private schools should be abolished.
9. When I started this job, nobody told me how to do anything. I just had to learn
quickly. It was a real . . . . situation.
10. You can't keep being rude to people, Tom. . . . . , somebody's
going to get really angry and hit you.

Note: Make sure you don't mix up the expression *give or take* with *give and take*:
> **It'll be ready in two weeks, *give or take a day or two*. (maybe one or two days longer)**
> **All successful relationships are *a matter of give and take*. (being reasonable with each other)**

2: Nor

Here are two expressions with *nor*. Both of them, like many of the expressions in this book, are absolutely fixed and you need to learn the whole expression.

1. Did you manage to get any tickets for next week's concert, Andy?
> No, they'd sold out. You can't get them *for love nor money*.
2. You can't complain about me being late. Lots of people were late today.
> That's *neither here nor there*. You are always the last to arrive.

For love nor money **is always used in a negative sentence.**
Neither here nor there **means that something is not relevant.**

3: It's now or never

Now fill in the following expressions with *or* in the dialogues below:

      a. *come hell or high water*   **e.** *either or*
      b. *now or never*   **f.** *come rain or shine*
      c. *something or other*   **g.** *all or nothing*
      d. *more or less*   **h.** *for better or worse*

1. I'm thinking of asking Sally to come out for a drink with me.
   > Here she comes now, Steve. Go on! It's . . . . !
2. You play golf, don't you?
   > Occasionally, but my brother plays every Sunday, ...
3. Did Christine leave a message for me before she left?
   > Yes, she said . . . . about meeting outside the theatre at eight.
4. Do you think Jack is up to the job?
   > I hope so. . . . . , he's the man we've appointed.
5. I told you I was going to be at the final in Paris . . . . and I AM going to be there. I don't care what it costs!
6. We're going to have to make a choice – increase wages or give them more holiday.
   > This isn't an . . . . situation. I'm afraid it's 'both and'.
7. What's wrong with John? He either chatters all the time or he won't say a word.
   > You're right. It's . . . . with John. I wish he'd fit in better.
8. Are you ready?
   > . . . . I just need to get my jacket.

Note: As well as *something or other* you can also say: *somebody / somewhere or other*. When you want to estimate how long something might take, you can say *a couple of hours or so*.

"This is a sink or swim situation and I can't swim!"

4: Revision

Look back at the idioms in this unit and add the missing verbs:

1. Two years, ... or take a few months.
2. I once played for England, ... it or not!
3. I didn't know whether to . . . . . . or cry.
4. You either . . . . . . or swim.

Have you ever been in a situation where you didn't know whether to laugh or cry?

Unit 105 | Point

1: Point taken!

Use the following idiomatic expressions in the dialogues below:

a. *refused point blank*   f. *get straight to the point*
b. *the point is*   g. *on the point of*
c. *make a point of*   h. *a case in point*
d. *point the finger*   i. *score points*
e. *point taken*   j. *my point of view*

1. How can you advise other people to cut out the stress in their lives when you are so stressed out yourself?
   > . . . . ! Let's go to the theatre tomorrow night!
2. Come in, Jackie. Sit down. I'll . . . . I'm not happy with your work.
3. I asked Sally if I could borrow her car, but she . . . .
4. Not everybody in Third World countries is on the breadline. Kenya is . . . .
   . . . . There are people there who could buy and sell you and me.
5. My course is getting too difficult for me. I'm . . . . quitting.
6. When I'm in London, I always . . . . getting to see a West End show.
7. My parents keep telling me to stop smoking because it's bad for me. I know it is, but, ... , I don't want to stop. I enjoy it.
8. Instead of trying to . . . . off me all the time, why don't you discuss the real problem?
9. It's not my fault we're lost. Don't . . . . at me. You said you knew the way.
10. From . . . . , I don't care which of the two quotes we accept.

2: What's the point?

Fill in these responses with *point* in the dialogues below:

a. *That's beside the point.*   e. *OK, you've made your point.*
b. *Get to the point.*   f. *Up to a point.*
c. *There's no point in (...ing).* g. *He's got a point.*
d. *I can't see the point.*   h. *What's the point?*

1. Let's go out for a walk.
   > . . . . ? It's raining!
2. You made this mistake last week, you made the same mistake yesterday, and now you've gone and done precisely the same thing again today!
   > . . . . It won't happen again!
3. So what if I was a bit late? You're not always on time yourself.
   > . . . . I specifically asked you to be here at nine today.

4. Jack thinks we would all work much faster if we had separate offices.
   > You know, ... We do waste a lot of time chatting sometimes.
5. Rachel, I was wondering if, maybe, you know, perhaps we could, um... we might ...
   > . . . . ! I haven't got all day.
6. Do you agree with all the money being poured into some countries?
   > . . . . But in some countries money is the last thing they need. They need doctors, nurses, teachers, and people like engineers.
7. Excuse me, can you explain why this train is not moving and, more to the point, why it hasn't moved for the last 20 minutes?
   > There's no . . . . complaining to me, sir. I only work in the buffet car.
8. What do you think of the European Parliament?
   > I'll be perfectly honest with you, ... ! Every country has its own parliament. I think it's all a waste of money – our money!

3: The high point

Complete these sentences using the following:

strong points	*sore point*	*high point*	*low point*
turning point	*whole point*	*talking point*	*vantage point*

1. We had a great time in Kenya. The . . . . was getting so close to the lions on the safari.
2. I never take work with me on holiday. The . . . . of a holiday is to relax.
3. Can you check this letter for me? Spelling is not one of my . . . .
4. The main . . . . at work at the moment is who's going to be the new supervisor.
5. Don't talk to Peter about driving lessons. It's a . . . . That's the third time he's failed his test.
6. The holiday was a disaster, but the really . . . . came when we had to evacuate the hotel in the middle of the night because some idiot set off the fire alarm!
7. When we were in London we were lucky enough to have a good . . . . when the Queen passed and we got some really good photographs.
8. The day I was told I had cancer was a . . . . in my life.

4: Revision

Fill in the missing word in these expressions from this unit:

1. That's . . . . . . the point.
2. She refused . . . . . blank.
3. Don't point the . . . . at me.
4. I agree up . . . . . a point.
5. Stop trying to . . . . . . points.
6. You've . . . . . . a point.
7. Mark is a . . . . . in point.
8. I can't . . . . . . the point.
9. Please . . . . . to the point!
10. Honesty is not his . . . . . . point!

What's been the high point of your life so far?

Unit 106 | Side

1: Literal meanings

Fill in the following words in the definitions below:

$$grass \qquad coins \qquad luck$$

1. I prefer using notes to . . . . They don't make holes in your pockets!
2. It annoys me when you visit a beautiful park and there's a sign which says: Keep Off The . . . .
3. It's my driving test this afternoon. Wish me . . . . . . !

2: Look on the bright side

Put the correct verbs into these expressions:

a.	. . . . . . on the wrong side of someone	*take*
b.	. . . . . . the side down	*hear*
c.	. . . . . . on the bright side	*side*
d.	. . . . . . both sides of the story	*get*
e.	. . . . . . sides	*let*
f.	. . . . . . with someone	*look*

Now use the expressions in their correct form in these sentences:

1. I have to work again this Sunday. I suppose I should . . . .
   – I earn an extra £85 and I need the money at the moment.
2. I'm not going to decide who's right and who's wrong until I've . . . .
   . . . .
3. Everyone played well except me. I feel I've . . . .
4. Janet's got a nasty temper. You don't want to . . . . her.
5. If you've fallen out with your partner, that's strictly between the two of you. I am certainly not going to take . . . .
6. The British are famous for . . . . the underdog in any competition. They are so used to losing themselves!

Note: There is little difference in meaning between *side with* and *take sides*.

3: On the side

Put these expressions into the sentences below:

a. *on the wrong side of*	d. *a bit on the small side*
b. *this side of*	e. *on the side*
c. *to one side*	

1. Maria works for AMEX but she also teaches Spanish . . . .
2. Have you got the same shoes in a 9? These are . . . .
3. Louise looks younger than she is. You'd never guess she's . . . . 50!
4. Sorry I haven't written sooner. After I read your letter, I put it . . . . and then I completely forgot about it.
5. I don't think we'll manage to finish painting the flat . . . . Easter.

4: The other side of the coin

Use the following idiomatic expressions in the situations below:

> a. *Time is not on our side.*
> b. *my mother's side of the family*
> c. *the other side of the coin*
> d. *I'm on your side.*
> e. *He knows which side his bread is buttered.*
> f. *I got out of bed on the wrong side this morning.*
> g. *He'll be laughing on the other side of his face.*
> h. *The grass is always greener on the other side.*

1. Mobile phones are a good idea. You can be contacted any time, any place.
   > Yes, but . . . . is that you never get any privacy.
2. So you say you've got Irish blood in you?
   > Yes, ... are all from Donegal.
3. This coffee's got sugar in it! It's horrible! Get me another one!
   > Temper, temper! I think you . . . . !
4. I wish I had a job like yours. It sounds much more interesting than what I do.
   > Yes, but . . . . , isn't it?
5. You could have given me more support yesterday.
   > Why are you arguing with me? . . . . ! It's all the others you need to persuade.
6. What time does the train leave?
   > Half past. We'd better hurry up. . . . .
7. Sheila still lives at home with her parents, doesn't she?
   > Of course she does! She knows . . . .
8. Mike was so pleased with himself when he left yesterday.
   > Yes, when he comes back . . . . when he discovers that Jane has been made his boss!

5: Revision

Which idiom would you use to talk about these things?

1. You see the advantages and disadvantages. *(coin)*
2. You're in a hurry. *(time)*
3. He's 62 years old. *(wrong)*
4. Your friend is being irritable. *(bed)*
5. You want to be optimistic. *(bright)*
6. I know when I'm lucky. *(bread)*
7. Before December. *(this)*
8. Let's deal with something at a later date. *(put)*

Do you take after your father's or your mother's side of the family?

Unit 107 Something, Anything, Nothing

1: Something of an athlete

Complete these sentences using *something, nothing* or *anything*:

1. When I was younger, I used to be . . . . of an athlete. In fact, I won quite a few trophies. Do you want to see some photos?
2. My car has been . . . . but trouble since the day I bought it! Something goes wrong with it every month.
3. Anyone can use the Internet. It's easy. There's . . . . to it!
4. Have you got . . . . against me, or have you got an attitude problem?
5. Richard? Oh yes, he's a real pain in the neck. It's not for . . . . that nobody wants to share an office with him.
6. Clothes cost next to . . . . in the States compared to England.
7. How old am I? Well, let's just say I'm forty- . . . . !
8. There's always someone looking for something for . . . . !
9. Paul and Sue must have plenty of money. They think . . . . of spending £100 in a restaurant.
10. I don't understand Mike. Why is he working in a supermarket? He could really make . . . . of himself if he wanted to.
11. When I was young, women wore earrings, make-up and had long hair, and men didn't. Nowadays, it seems, ... goes!
12. I'm an interior designer. I sometimes have weeks with no work but when I'm busy, I can earn . . . . up to £1000 a week.
13. Did you see that seven-year-old playing the piano on the TV last night? He's . . . . else, isn't he?
14. Don't believe people when they tell you the weather's awful in England. It's . . . . of the sort. It's just different! Different every day!
15. After spending over a million researching the new engine, the whole thing came to . . . . ! It was scrapped.

Now underline all the expressions which contain *something / anything / nothing*.

2: Nothing doing!

Complete these dialogues using the following lines:

a. *Nothing to write home about!*	c. *Nothing much!*
b. *Nothing ventured, nothing gained!*	d. *Nothing doing!*

1. Any chance of lending me a fiver till tomorrow?
   > Sorry. . . . . ! Once bitten, twice shy!
2. Go on – ask for a reduction. You're paying cash, and it's a lot of money!
   > OK. . . . . !
3. What's on TV tonight?
   > . . . .
4. What was Tony's fiancée like?
   > Nice enough, but . . . . !

3: Nothing to choose between them

Use these idiomatic expressions in the situations below:

   a. *nothing to choose between them*
   b. *to say nothing of*
   c. *nothing in particular*
   d. *nothing short of*
   e. *nothing for it*
   f. *nothing to do with me*

1. So, which one do you recommend? The Sony or the Phillips?
   > To be honest, there's . . . . They're both excellent systems.
2. I heard Josie was in a car accident. Is she all right?
   > Yes, but it was a terrible crash. It's . . . . a miracle that she survived. Two of her friends were killed.
3. What did you do at the weekend?
   > Oh, ... – just a bit of housework, a bit of television, that sort of thing.
4. Your friend Barry must be very well off. He dresses like a film star.
   > I know. Armani suits, Rolex watch – . . . . the Porsche outside.
5. His passport was out of date? So, what did you do?
   > Well, there was . . . . but to go on my own.
6. Who spilt this coffee on my desk? Was it you, Phil?
   > No, it's . . . .! Ask Robert.

*"I don't like the colour. I don't like the style
– to say nothing of the fact they're far too big!"*

4: Revision

Look back at the idioms in this unit and add the missing words:

1. Nothing to . . . . . . home about.
2. It . . . . . . to nothing.
3. It . . . . . . next to nothing.
4. It was nothing . . . . . . of a disgrace.
5. It's nothing of the . . . .
6. There's nothing to . . . . . . between the two.
7. There's nothing . . . . . . it but to complain.
8. My car is nothing but . . . .
9. . . . . . . nothing to it.

Do you always carry your plans through, or do they sometimes come to nothing?

Unit 108 Thing

1: First things first

Use the following idiomatic expressions in the situations below:

> a. *first things first*
> b. *there's only one thing for it*
> c. *it's just one of those things*
> d. *it's been one thing after another*
> e. *first thing in the morning*
> f. *got a thing about*
> g. *a thing of the past*
> h. *know a thing or two about ...*

1. Here's the report you wanted. Do you want to discuss it now?
   > Yes, but . . . . , how was your holiday?
2. I'm afraid the train's gone. The next one's in two hours!
   > Two hours? Right, ... We'll have to get a taxi.
3. You look exhausted!
   > The phone hasn't stopped ringing; we've had more problems in the past hour than we usually have in a week! . . . .
4. Have you seen those new mini-discs? Are they basically the same as CDs?
   > No, they're much better. CDs will soon be . . . .
5. When will all the plans be ready, Fiona?
   > Don't worry, Bill, they'll be with you . . . .
6. I'm meeting the chief executive of Charisma Records tomorrow.
   > Whatever you do, don't be late. He's . . . . punctuality.
7. I'm having a few problems with my car. I think it's the clutch.
   > Talk to Richard. He . . . . cars.
8. We drive all the way here to find the shop has closed early. Typical!
   > Never mind. . . . . We can come back next week.

2: It's not the done thing

Add one of the following fixed expressions to each situation below:

> a. *It's not the done thing.*
> b. *There's no such thing.*
> c. *It's just the thing for (a cold).*
> d. *It amounts to the same thing.*

1. Don't blow your nose in public in Japan. . . . .
2. Drink this. You'll feel much better. . . . .
3. Living together? Married? What's the difference? . . . .
4. Do I believe in ghosts? Of course not. . . . .

Can you think of anything in your culture which is *not the done thing*?

3: All things considered

Use the following idiomatic expressions in the sentences below:

    a. *the first thing*
    b. *make a big thing about it*
    c. *all things considered*
    d. *the thing is*

    e. *a near thing*
    f. *seeing things*
    g. *do your own thing*
    h. *onto a good thing*

1. The weather was a bit disappointing; the journey wasn't easy, but . . . . , we had a good time.
2. Whoops! Be careful. That was . . . . ! Didn't you see that bike coming?
3. I'd love to come to the concert, but . . . . , I'm a bit short of money at the moment.
4. Sorry, I can't help you. I don't know . . . . about cameras.
5. Well, I think really short green hair suits me. I like it and that's the main thing. After all, it's my hair, so stop . . . . such a . . . . !
6. Everyone wants to go camping except me, so I'm just going to . . . .
7. My brother's just got a job in the Middle East with a great salary, all accommodation and three return flights a year.
   > It sounds like he's . . . . there.
8. Is that Martha over there? No, she's in New York. I must be . . . . !

"Richard thinks he knows a thing or two about cars."

4: Revision

Look back at the idioms in this unit and add the missing words:

1. first things . . . .
2. one thing after . . . .
3. onto a . . . . thing
4. first thing in the . . . .
5. just do my . . . . thing

6. all things . . . .
7. it was a . . . . thing
8. just one of . . . . things
9. a thing of the . . . .
10. it's not the . . . . thing

Do you follow the crowd or do your own thing?

Unit 109 To + infinitive

1: To cap it all

Match the two halves of these idiomatic expressions:

1. to cap	. . . .	a. *a long story short*
2. to tell you	. . . .	b. *insult to injury*
3. to set	. . . .	c. *in a nutshell*
4. to add	. . . .	d. *the truth*
5. to cut	. . . .	e. *matters worse*
6. to say	. . . .	f. *the record straight*
7. to make	. . . .	g. *it all*
8. to put it	. . . .	h. *the least*

Now use these these expressions in the following sentences:

9. I found Tim sitting in my office with his feet on my desk, using my phone, and, ... , he'd finished the crossword in my newspaper!

10. I've been very depressed recently. . . . . , it's been so bad I've been thinking of getting professional help.

11. They met, they fell in love and, ... , they got married six months later.

12. I left home late, the traffic was terrible and then, ... , I had a puncture on the motorway. That's why I'm so late.

13. I was involved in an accident last week. My car was a write-off. I only had a small cut on my face and a sprained ankle. I was lucky, ... !

14. Increased sales, profits up, and a full order book – . . . . our best year ever!

15. Before we do anything else, I've read the notes from our last meeting and I want . . . . immediately. I did not, repeat not, criticise the Chairman.

16. They told me I was too old for the job, and then, ... , they offered it to somebody who was less than a year younger than me!

2: Leaves a lot to be desired

Notice these infinitives, which are always passive. Use them below:

        a. *not to be sniffed at*
        b. *leaves a lot to be desired*
        c. *a lot to be said for*
        d. *remains to be seen*

1. The food in this restaurant . . . . I won't be back!

2. I get an extra £75 if I work at weekends and that's . . . .

3. Frank said he'll meet us outside the school no later than seven but whether or not he will, ... He's never on time.

4. There's . . . . working for a year before going to university.

3: To put it mildly

Use the following idiomatic expressions in the situations below:

       a. *to be fair*   **e.** *nothing to write home about*
       b. *to put it mildly*   **f.** *nothing to speak of*
       c. *to be honest*   **g.** *not to mention*
       d. *to sum up*   **h.** *to say nothing of*

1. I'm going to Cannes this summer. You've been there, haven't you?
   > Yes, it's expensive, ... ! But it's a lovely place.
2. Do you like Indian food?
   > I don't want to offend you, but . . . . perfectly . . . . , I don't really.
3. Your journey was OK, I hope – no problems?
   > No. The motorway was a bit busy, but . . . .
4. I don't like Jerry at all. He's loud and he's often rude to other members of staff.
   > I know what you mean, but . . . . , he's one of the best workers here.
5. You can see that Rachel's rich – her clothes, her jewellery, not . . . .
   the brand new Mercedes.
6. So what did you think of your first big London musical?
   > To be honest with you, it was . . . . I've
   seen better on Broadway.
7. I really don't like meetings in the Birmingham office. The place is so enormous.
   > . . . . the dreadful coffee they give you!
8. Now, I've given you all the arguments for and against going into this new market.
   . . . . , and I can't be more honest, I think you would be crazy to go
   ahead.

Note: Another way of saying *to be honest* is *to be frank*.

4: Revision

Look back at the idioms in this unit and add the final words:

1. to cap it . . . .
2. to cut a long story . . . .
3. to set the record . . . .
4. leaves a lot to be . . . .
5. to add insult to . . . .
6. to make matters . . . .
7. nothing to write home . . . .
8. remains to be . . . .
9. there's a lot to be said . . . .
10. to put it in a . . . .

5: Check some literal meanings

Find words from the idioms in this unit to complete the following:

1. I had to stop playing tennis because of a knee . . . .
2. If you . . . . four and eleven, you get fifteen.
3. A . . . . person is honest and direct with opinions.
4. To suggest that only men should be managers is an . . . . to women.
5. We talk about . . . . cheese, weather, punishments, surprise.
6. Some people . . . . when they have a cold.

Have you ever paid a lot of money for a meal which, in the end, left a lot to be desired?

Unit 110 Top and Bottom

1: Literal meanings

Fill in the following words in the definitions below:

blew   **pit**   **list**   **rock**   **bet**   **voice**

1. Before I go shopping, I always make a . . . . in case I forget what I need.
2. I sometimes . . . . on horses. I usually lose more than I win.
3. If you dig deep into the ground, sooner or later you will meet solid . . . .
4. Terrorists . . . . up a government building in the city centre last night.
5. My sister has a wonderful singing . . . .
6. A large, deep hole in the ground – where coal is mined, for example – is called a
   . . . .

2: Top or bottom?

Complete the idiomatic expressions using *top* or *bottom*:

1. When my dad saw what I'd done to the car, he really blew his . . . .
2. Money keeps disappearing from the shop. I don't know who it is but I'm going to
   get to the . . . . of it.
3. Steve needs help. His marriage has broken up and he's drinking heavily again.
   He's hit rock . . . .
4. I can't stand nightclubs. The music's much too loud. You have to shout at the
   . . . . of your voice just to order a drink.
5. When the . . . . fell out of the micro-processor market, lots of small
   companies went bust.
6. I don't actually know how much it costs to fly to Brazil, but off the . . . . of
   my head, I'd say it's at least £500.
7. Every month I have problems paying the bills
   – gas, electricity, phone, rent. I try to be careful
   with money, but the . . . . line is,
   I just don't earn enough to make ends meet.
8. My boyfriend's crazy about football.
   There's a match on TV this evening
   and you can bet your . . . .
   dollar he'll be watching it.

> *"You can bet your bottom
> dollar Simon will be
> watching the match."*

**Note: We talk about someone being *top of the class* in school while someone else
is *bottom of the class*. We talk of *a top-of-the-range Mercedes*, meaning the most
expensive. In business, we talk of the *top end* and *bottom end* of the market,
meaning the most luxurious and the cheapest goods.**

3: On top of the world

Use these idiomatic expressions in the situations below:

a. *from top to bottom*	e. *on top of that*
b. *on top of me*	f. *top of the list*
c. *on top of each other*	g. *on top of the world*
d. *over the top*	h. *thin on top*

1. I hear your daughter's getting married, Rachel.
   > Yes, in November. She's so excited. She's . . . .
2. I hear you want to find somewhere else to live, Joe.
   I'd like to, yes, but I'm not looking too hard at the moment. . . . .
   right now is finding a new job.
3. I can't believe Martin is only 34. He looks at least ten years older than that.
   > I know. It's because he's going . . . .
4. Have you found your purse yet?
   > No, and I've searched the house . . . . I must have lost it.
5. You need a bigger place to live, don't you? Five of you, in that small flat!
   > Yes, we need more space. We're . . . . most of the time.
6. I haven't heard from you for a few weeks, Kate. Is everything all right?
   > Not really. I don't know what's wrong. Everything seems to be getting
   . . . . at the moment. I'm a bit depressed.
7. I think Muriel goes a bit . . . . at times. I mean, turning up
   to work in an Armani suit! Who's she trying to impress?
8. ISP Munich have faxed to say they're going to be a month late with their payment.
   > Yes, I know. And . . . . , they've asked for more discount.

Note: Sometimes people say: *Oh, come on, that's a bit OTT.* **This is short for** *over the top.* **It means you think the person is exaggerating or has gone too far.**

4: Revision

Write the idioms in this unit opposite the meanings below using the words in brackets:

1. absolutely certain *(bet)* . . . .
2. as a guess *(head)* . . . .
3. find the truth *(bottom)* . . . .
4. looked everywhere *(search)* . . . .
5. exaggerated *(top)* . . . .
6. the first priority *(list)* . . . .
7. as emotionally low as possible *(rock)* . . . .
8. not much hair *(thin)* . . . .

Do you like to wear clothes which other people might think are a bit over the top?

Unit 111 'Very'

1: Meanings

In English there are many different words used as intensifiers. They make an adjective stronger. For example, *totally* different, *absolutely* ridiculous, *utterly* stupid. Some adjectives have their own intensifiers which very often go with them. Some are very obvious:

> ***bone dry***   ***razor sharp***   ***paper thin***

Others are less obvious:

> ***stark naked***   ***brand new***

They all have one thing in common. You cannot guess them. You have to learn the words together as a single expression.

2: Brand new

Complete the situations below with these collocations:

> a. *wide awake*
> b. *pitch black*
> c. *brand new*
> d. *fast asleep*
> e. *dirt cheap*
> f. *rock bottom*
> g. *dead easy*
> h. *bone dry*

1. Can I borrow your camera for the weekend?
   > OK, but please be careful with it. It's . . . .
2. I rang you about ten o'clock last night. Where were you?
   > I went to bed early. I was . . . . by ten. Sorry.
3. It's been a long day. You must be very tired.
   > Actually, I feel . . . . Shall we go out?
4. Are those new jeans you're wearing?
   > Yes. I got them in the States. Clothes are . . . . over there.
5. I've never seen the euro so low, have you?
   > No, it's really hit . . . . at the moment.
6. I can't see a thing. Switch the light on.
   > I can't find the light switch. It's . . . . in here.
7. Those clothes are probably still a bit wet, aren't they?
   > No, actually, they're . . . .
8. I'm really worried about my oral.
   > Oh, don't worry. It's . . . . It's the composition you need to worry about!

Note: Instead of *fast asleep*, you can also say *sound asleep*. You can be *dead lucky* or *dead right*.

3: Broad daylight

Put the following expressions in the sentences below:

a. *blind drunk*
b. *crystal clear*
c. *stark naked*
d. *rock hard*
e. *paper thin*
f. *broad daylight*
g. *razor sharp*
h. *bitter end*
i. *stone deaf*
j. *wide open*

"And there I was – stark naked!"

1. My sister was robbed in the street last week in . . . . !
2. And suddenly there was the window cleaner, and I was . . . . !
3. You have to shout at my grandmother. She's . . . .
4. I can't understand people who celebrate things by getting . . . .
5. Who left the door . . . . ? It's freezing in here!
6. I spent most of my holiday in Greece swimming. The sea was . . . .
7. I watched an awful film last night. I should have just switched it off but I watched it until the . . . . to see what happened. I wish I hadn't.
8. The walls of my flat are . . . . You can hear everything.
9. Be careful with that knife. It's . . . .
10. This bread's lovely when it's fresh but next day it goes . . . .

Three of the expressions above can be used in a more metaphorical way. Choose which expressions complete these sentences:

1. This computer manual is brilliant. All the instructions are . . . .
2. He's a brilliant lawyer with a . . . . mind.
3. If you say controversial things like that in public, then you leave yourself . . . . to criticism.

4: Revision

Try to complete these expressions first without looking at the exercises:

1. . . . . open
2. . . . . cheap
3. . . . . drunk
4. the . . . . end
5. . . . . daylight
6. . . . . black
7. . . . . deaf
8. . . . . sharp
9. . . . . dry
10. . . . . clear
11. . . . . awake
12. . . . . asleep
13. . . . . bottom
14. . . . . easy
15. . . . . naked
16. . . . . thin
17. . . . . new
18. . . . . hard

Are you always sound asleep at 3 o'clock in the morning or are you sometimes wide awake?

Unit 112 | Way

1: Different meanings

Way is a very common word in English with many uses and different meanings:

1. You can see the literal meaning in *Could you tell me the way to the bank from here?*

2. *Way* can also mean 'distance': *It's a long way to Tipperary.*

3. It can also mean 'method' or 'style' as in Frank Sinatra's famous song *'I'll do it my way.'*

2: Pave the way

Use these idiomatic expressions in the sentences below:

     a. *work your way to the top*
     b. *have a way with words*
     c. *go out of your way*
     d. *have it both ways*
     e. *meet you halfway*
     f. *pave the way*
     g. *set in your ways*
     h. *keep out of someone's way*
     i. *stand in someone's way*
     j. *way off course*

1. Junior government ministers are in Washington to . . . . for the Prime Minister's visit later this month.
2. My boss is very traditional. It's extremely difficult to get him to make any changes because he's so . . . .
3. It's taken me a long time to get where I am in the company. I started as an office clerk and slowly . . . . It took a lot of hard work.
4. £400 is too much so I'll . . . . Let's say £350.
5. My mother can persuade people to do almost anything. She . . . .
6. I personally think you should go to university. But if you really want to leave school and get a job, I won't . . . .
7. Let's get back to what we're meant to be talking about. We've strayed . . . .
8. I'm never going to help Peter again. I . . . . to make time to help him fix his car yesterday and not a word of thanks! Nothing at all.
9. You'll have to choose between a wage rise or shorter hours. You can't . . . .
10. Martin's in a bad mood so I would . . . . if I were you.

3: The other way round

Fill in the following idiomatic expressions in the situations below:

a. *either way*
b. *to my way of thinking*
c. *the other way round*
d. *on the way*

e. *that way*
f. *by the way*
g. *in a way*
h. *come a long way*

1. So we'll have the finance meeting on Monday and the planning meeting on Wednesday. Is that agreed then?
   > Wouldn't it be better to have them . . . . ?
2. When do you want to talk about your idea? Now or after work?
   > After work would be better – . . . . it wouldn't matter if we needed more time to discuss everything.
3. When do you want to meet? Today after work or tomorrow morning?
   > I don't mind . . . .
4. Have you got any children?
   > Two and one . . . . It's due in three weeks, actually.
5. It only costs £98 on the train to Paris. That's £50 less than going by plane.
   > £98 is still very expensive . . . .
6. I remember the days your company employed only five people, and that included you and your wife! Now it's around two thousand, isn't it?
   > That's right. We've . . . . since those early days.
7. OK Jeff, see you on Monday. Have a good weekend.
   > Thanks. You too. Oh, ... ,
   I'm coming in late on Monday. I've got
   an appointment at the dentist.
8. They've finally got rid of Bruce, and,
   . . . . , I'm not surprised.
   He had a nasty habit of rocking the boat.

4: Revision

Find the wrong word in these idioms and correct it:

1. I gradually worked my way to the bottom.
2. If that's what you want, I won't walk in your way.
3. He's got a way with sentences.
4. She's very solid in her ways.
5. You can't make it both ways.
6. I went out from my way to help her.
7. We've come a short way in the last two years.
8. I don't mind neither way.

Which, to your way of thinking, is more important – good qualifications or a lot of practical experience?

"Oh, by the way, just watch out for Bruce. He's always rocking the boat."

Unit 113 | Word

1: A man of his word

Fill in the following words and expressions in the sentences below:

    a. *trouble from the word go*   **d.** *by word of mouth*
    b. *lost for words*   **e.** *too awful for words*
    c. *a man of his word*   **f.** *word for word*

1. I don't think you need to worry about Stuart changing his mind. He's . . . .
2. Never buy anything second-hand. I bought a second-hand fridge a month ago and it was trouble . . . .
3. My sister should have been a lawyer. She's got an amazing memory for what people say. She can repeat what you said last week . . . .
4. We don't have much of an advertising budget. We don't really need one since most of our customers hear about us . . . . Happy customers are the best advertisements.
5. I told Kevin I was leaving because I'd never worked for anyone as stupid as him. He didn't say anything at all. For once he was . . . .
6. I saw a motorbike accident yesterday. It was terrible. I feel sick when I think about it. It was . . . .

"It's been trouble from the word go."

2: Famous last words!

Complete the dialogues using these expressions:

    a. *In a word,*
    b. *In other words,*
    c. *Famous last words!*
    d. *Actions speak louder than words.*
    e. *You took the words right out of my mouth.*

1. Don't worry, the meeting will be finished no later than four o'clock.
   > . . . . ! We'll be lucky to be out of here by 7!
2. I don't know about you, but I reckon we should stop for lunch.
   > . . . . !
3. So, do you like my ideas or not?
   > . . . . – no! I can't speak plainer than that!
4. These new advertisements are confusing, difficult to read, and too expensive.
   > . . . . , do I take it you don't like them very much?
5. I know we had to have someone new at the top, but Andrew Mitchell seems to be all talk to me. I suppose it's early days.
   > Yes, we'll have to wait and see results. You know what they say: . . . .
   . . . .

3: Don't breathe a word

Put the correct verb in the following idiomatic expressions:

say   have   eat   get   know   take (2)   breathe

a. . . . . someone's word for it
b. . . . . a word in edgeways
c. don't . . . . the meaning of the word
d. . . . . a quick word with someone
e. just . . . . the word
f. don't . . . . a word
g. . . . . someone at their word
h. . . . . your words

Now use the expressions in these situations:

1. Tell me what you know about the changes that are being planned.
   > OK, but don't . . . . of this to anyone. It's confidential.
2. Paul, I might need you to give me a lift to the station a bit later. Is that OK?
   > Sure, no problem. Just . . . .
3. Can I have a break for a coffee? This work is quite tiring.
   > Tiring? You . . . . ! You should try doing my job!
   Then you would know what 'tiring' meant!
4. Yes, Jeff, what can I do for you?
   > Can I just . . . . about what is going to happen over the
   holiday period?
5. Mary was always saying how we could borrow their villa in Portugal if we wanted,
   so I . . . . and asked if we could use it for the last
   two weeks in June. I think she was a bit surprised.
   > I bet she was! It serves her right for always going on about it!
6. I was against Sally when she was appointed. I didn't think she was up to the job
   and I said so, but I've had to . . . . She's been a great
   success.
7. I've never known anyone talk as much as Wendy. She just doesn't stop.
   > I know. You just can't . . . . , can you?
8. You've just got to try these sheep's eyes. They're absolutely delicious!
   > I'll . . . . !

4: Revision

Look back at the idioms in this unit and add the missing words:

1. I'll take your word . . . . . . it
2. . . . . . . word of mouth
3. put . . . . . . a good word for you
4. get a word . . . . . . edgeways
5. . . . . . . a word – no
6. . . . . . . the word go
7. word . . . . . . word
8. a man . . . . . . his word
9. lost . . . . . . words
10. . . . . . . other words

In what sort of situations might you be lost for words?

Unit 114 | Review Unit

86. All

1. When all's said and . . . . , I'm glad I went.
2. I'll arrive at six, all . . . . well.
3. There were ten of us all . . . . .
4. I knew all . . . . you'd pass your exams.
5. The party was all . . . . by ten o'clock.
6. I'm tired. It's been all . . . . today.

87. And 1

1. I just want a bit of peace and . . . . .
2. I'm sick and . . . . of your complaining.
3. You'll just have to wait and . . . . .
4. Every relationship has its ups and . . . . .
5. I'm Scottish – born and . . . . .
6. You're not in a position to pick and . . . . .

88. And 2

1. I've thought . . . . and hard about this.
2. That's unusual in this . . . . and age.
3. I've searched . . . . and low for my keys.
4. There are . . . . and cons to living here.
5. I stay with my parents . . . . and again.
6. It's a long process of . . . . and error.

89. Back

1. I know Paris like the back of my . . . . .
2. You deserve a . . . . on the back.
3. You . . . . my back and I'll . . . . yours.
4. We'll put that idea on the back . . . . .
5. It's like . . . . off a duck's back.
6. Bob talks about you . . . . your back.

90. Cut

1. You could cut the atmosphere with a . . . . .
2. I was never cut . . . . to be an actor.
3. To cut a long . . . . short.
4. Do it properly. Don't cut . . . . .
5. I said hello but he just cut me . . . . .
6. Leave at 3? That's cutting it a bit . . . . .

91. End

1. Don't worry. It's not the end of the . . . . .
2. I've had . . . . end of trouble with my car.
3. I stayed until the . . . . end.
4. I've got a few . . . . ends to tie up at work.
5. You've got the wrong end of the . . . . .
6. No. You can't go. End of . . . . !

92. Fall

1. We all just fell . . . . laughing.
2. My warning fell on . . . . ears.
3. Jo's marriage is falling apart at the . . . . .
4. This job just fell into my . . . . .
5. I fell on my . . . . getting this job.
6. The plans are all falling into . . . . .

93. Good/Better/Best

1. Pete's in Spain, to the best of my . . . . .
2. Better safe than . . . . .
3. A holiday will do you the . . . . of good.
4. My car's seen better . . . . .
5. I paid good . . . . for this.
6. The sooner, the . . . . .

94. Ground

1. We're . . . . ground on our competitors.
2. Maths teachers are . . . . on the ground.
3. We always . . . . the same old ground.
4. Social work suits her . . . . to the ground.
5. You're working yourself . . . . the ground.
6. I've got a good . . . . in the basics.

95. Half

1. I've got half a . . . . to complain.
2. I'd love to visit Venice, given half a . . . . .
3. Here's the bill. Let's . . . . halves.
4. Half the . . . . with you is, you don't think.
5. I don't know if you're joking half the . . . . .
6. I left the cinema halfway . . . . the film.

96. Know

1. I don't know . . . . you but I'm tired.
2. Simon knows a . . . . or two about CDs.
3. As soon as he rings, I'll . . . . you know.
4. I know this book inside . . . . .
5. I don't know whether I'm coming or . . . . .
6. . . . . was I to know you needed a lift?

97. Life

1. I had the time of my . . . . .
2. The war resulted in huge . . . . of life.
3. There were people from all . . . . of life.
4. . . . . is the spice of life.
5. Members of Parliament are all in . . . . life.
6. Even the . . . . of life couldn't save him.

98. Light and Heavy

1. Let's just have a light . . . . for lunch.
2. I'm a light . . . . . I wake up very easily.
3. I'm exhausted. I've had a really heavy . . . .
4. Sorry I'm late. The . . . . was really heavy.
5. There was very heavy . . . . last night.
6. I feel terrible with this heavy . . . . .

99. Like

1. I've got a memory like a . . . . .
2. She spends money like there's no . . . . .
3. I felt like a fish out of . . . . .
4. Are you OK? You look like death . . . . . up.
5. He came down on me like a . . . . of bricks.
6. It's like water off a duck's . . . . .

100. Line

1. We're thinking . . . . the same lines.
2. Reading . . . . the lines, I think he's upset.
3. He still hasn't . . . . on the dotted line.
4. You've got to . . . . the line somewhere.
5. I'll see if she's free. . . . . the line, please.
6. You have to . . . . the line in this company.

101. Lose and Lost

1. Go on. Ask her. You've got . . . . to lose.
2. Don't lose any . . . . over it.
3. There's no . . . . lost between them.
4. Sorry. I just lost track of . . . . .
5. I was shocked. I was lost for . . . . .
6. I need to lose . . . . . I'm getting fat.

102. No

1. There's no place like . . . . .
2. No such . . . . !
3. My car's given me no . . . . of problems.
4. There's no time like the . . . . .
5. There's no . . . . phoning Pam. She's away.
6. It's no . . . . he smells. He goes fishing.

103. Of

1. We had a . . . . of complaints.
2. The whole story was just a . . . . of lies.
3. He came out with a string of . . . . .
4. This room could do with a . . . . of paint.
5. Just a . . . . of warning! Keep away from it.
6. A . . . . of soda?

104. Or

1. Believe it or . . . . , I'm going to Australia.
2. You're coming whether you . . . . it or not.
3. I didn't know whether to laugh or . . . . .
4. Sooner or . . . . you'll have an accident.
5. It's a sink or . . . . situation.
6. It takes an hour, give or . . . . five minutes.

105. Point

1. Spelling is not one of my . . . . points.
2. She refused point . . . . to help.
3. That's a bit of a . . . . point.
4. Please will you get . . . . the point.
5. I agree . . . . to a point.
6. That's completely . . . . the point.

106. Side

1. You got out of . . . . on the wrong side.
2. She lives on the . . . . side of town.
3. Don't get on the . . . . side of Tina.
4. Hurry up! . . . . is not on our side.
5. Cheer up! Look on the . . . . side.
6. Tell me your side of the . . . . .

107. Something, Anything, Nothing

1. That man is . . . . but trouble.
2. Why don't you try to make . . . . of yourself?
3. You're always cross about . . . . or other.
4. Rich? Me? I'm . . . . of the sort.
5. The hotel was . . . . to write home about.
6. The journey takes . . . . up to an hour.

108. Thing

1. I'll ring you . . . . thing tomorrow.
2. I don't know the . . . . thing about rugby.
3. It's been . . . . thing after another today.
4. All things . . . . equal, I'll arrive around 4.
5. Cassette tapes are a thing of the . . . . .
6. It's sad but it's just one of . . . . things.

109. To + infinitive

1. To tell you the . . . . , I don't like blondes.
2. To cut a long story . . . . , I decided to stay.
3. Monaco is expensive, to . . . . it mildly.
4. Your work leaves a lot to be . . . . .
5. To put it in a . . . . .
6. £600 a week is not to be sniffed . . . . .

110. Top and Bottom

1. Off the top of my . . . . , I'd guess it's £35.
2. Things are getting on top . . . . me at work.
3. I'm so happy. I'm on top of the . . . . .
4. My dad's going a bit . . . . on top.
5. The bottom . . . . is, we can't afford to go.
6. She was shouting at the top of her . . . . .

111. 'Very'

1. Clothes are dirt . . . . in the States.
2. The door's wide . . . . again.
3. Karen's got a razor . . . . mind.
4. I was wide . . . . at six o'clock this morning.
5. It's pitch . . . . in here. I can't see a thing.
6. This bread is rock . . . . .

112. Way

1. My mother is very . . . . in her ways.
2. £20 is very expensive, to my way of . . . . .
3. He went . . . . of his way to help me.
4. Fiona's got a way . . . . words.
5. We've come a . . . . way in ten years.
6. You can't have it . . . . ways.

113. Word

1. You took the words right out of my . . . . .
2. I can put in a . . . . word for you.
3. Can I . . . . a quick word with you?
4. David is a man of . . . . word.
5. Please don't . . . . a word of this to anyone.
6. If you need me, just . . . . the word.

SECTION 5

Index of Expressions

The numbers refer to the unit in which the idiom is taught.

arms

They are up in arms about it. 66

around

He's always throwing his weight around. 68

arrive

He thinks he's really arrived. 4

aside

I try to put a bit of money aside each month. 64

asleep

He's fast asleep. 76, 111

Sorry, I was half asleep. 76

The baby's sound asleep. 111

awake

It's late but I'm wide awake. 111

away

I want to get away from it all. 59

When the cat's away, the mice will play. 19

awful

I can't tell you – it's too awful for words. 113

baby

Don't throw the baby out with the bath water. 47

She's the baby of the family. 56

bachelor

Paul's a confirmed bachelor. 67

back (see pages 192 – 193)

At the back of my mind I know there's something I should do. 61

He backed the wrong horse. 41

They decided behind my back, when I was out of the office. 16, 54

He really got my back up. 16

He stabbed me in the back. 8, 54

He'd give you the shirt off his back. 20

I expect that set you back a bit. 64

I got in through the back door. 19

I know London like the back of my hand. 60

I went back to the drawing board. 78

It's back to square one. 40

It's like water off a duck's back. 15, 45

Keep your back covered. 8

Let's put that on the back burner for a while. 84

We came back to earth with a bump. 81

We're back on track now. 44

We've got our backs to the wall. 18

You backed the wrong horse. 35

You need eyes in the back of your head. 25

You'll soon be back on your feet. 58

backseat

He can be a real backseat driver. 67

I'm taking a backseat now. 23

bad

It left a bad taste in my mouth. 24

She's in a bad way. 58

bag

It's in the bag. 51

Who let the cat out of the bag? 14

bail

The bank will bail us out. 6

bait

I won't rise to the bait. 29

ball

Don't drop the ball. 41

Don't take your eye off the ball. 62

He's on the ball. 41

I want to start the ball rolling. 78

It's a whole new ball game. 41, 75

The ball's in their court. 41

They won't play ball. 41

They won't run with the ball. 41

balloon

The joke went down like a lead balloon. 38

bang

You're banging your head against a brick wall. 18, 49

baptism

It was a baptism of fire. 28, 55

bargain

I picked up a bargain yesterday. 64

It was harder than I had bargained for. 81

bark

His bark is worse than his bite. 50

You're barking up the wrong tree. 62

barrel

You're scraping the bottom of the barrel. 57

base

I'm going to touch base for a while. 41

basket

Don't put all your eggs in one basket. 30, 74

bat

He went off like a bat out of hell. 77

I didn't bat an eyelid. 25

bath

Don't throw the baby out with the bath water. 47

baton

He handed me the baton. 9

batteries

I needed to recharge my batteries. 59

battle

We're having a battle with the director. 2

bear

I'll bear that in mind. 39, 61

The campaign bore fruit. 11

beat

Stop beating about the bush. 47, 53

I like places off the beaten track. 59

It beats me why he did it. 63

beck

I'm not at your beck and call. 68

bed

Life's not a bed of roses. 55

bee

He's got a bee in his bonnet. 14

beetroot

I went as red as a beetroot. 22

behind

They decided behind my back. 16, 54

They decided behind closed doors. 18

They got left behind. 79

believe

Believe it or not, I've won! 81

I believe you, millions wouldn't. 40

I couldn't believe my eyes. 81

I don't believe a word of it. 54

bell

His name rings a bell. 61

Saved by the bell. 41

below

It was below par. 57

That was below the belt. 41

belt

That was below the belt. 41

We had to tighten our belts. 20, 64

bend

That noise is driving me round the bend. 23, 49

benefit

I gave him the benefit of the doubt. 51, 70

best

I've got your best interests at heart. 34

They think he's the best thing since sliced bread. 30

bet

You can bet your bottom dollar he's in the bar now. 110

better

It's seen better days. 57

Things can only get better. 50

Two heads are better than one. 40

between

Just between you and me, she's pregnant. 53

You have to read between the lines. 71

bide

You will learn to bide your time. 47

big

He's a big fish in a small pond. 29

They had a big hand in it. 32

bill

I don't think that will fit the bill. 80

The doctor gave me a clean bill of health. 58

Who's going to foot the bill? 16, 31

bird

A little bird told me. 15

He's an early bird. 15

We killed two birds with one stone. 15, 40

Birds of a feather flock together. 15

bit

He does go on a bit. 53

I expect that set you back a bit. 64

It's a bit of a gamble. 5

We've got the bit between our teeth. 35

bite

He bit my head off. 24

He realises now that he's bitten off more than he can chew. 24, 55, 62

His bark is worse than his bite. 50

Once bitten, twice shy. 40

You're very lucky to get a second bite at the cherry. 24

bits

You must be thrilled to bits. 66

bitter

People started leaving at 12, but we stayed until the bitter end. 111

black

It's a black picture. 21

He gave me a black eye. 21

He gave me a black look. 21

I want it in black and white. 21

I was black and blue all over. 22

I'm the black sheep of the family. 14, 21, 56

That sharp bend in the road is a well-known accident black spot. 21

It's pitch black with the light off. 111

My account's in the black. 21

The black economy is growing. 21

blank

My mind went blank. 61

blanket

Don't be such a wet blanket. 67

blaze

There was a blaze of publicity. 28

blazing

We had a blazing row. 28

blessing

It was a blessing in disguise. 81

blind

Everyone at the party was blind drunk. 111

The police turned a blind eye to it. 25, 70

blink

The TV is on the blink again. 69

blinkered

He's too blinkered to see what's staring him in the face. 3

block

My head's on the block. 33, 74

blockbuster

It's this year's blockbuster. 71

blood

Blood is thicker than water. 56

I was spitting blood. 66

It's different when it's your own flesh and blood. 56

It's like getting blood out of a stone. 55

They killed him in cold blood. 43

Things like that make my blood boil. 66

blow

He blew his top when he saw the damage to his new car. 66, 110

It was a crushing blow. 17

blue

He arrived out of the blue. 22, 81

He's our blue-eyed boy. 22

I see him once in a blue moon. 22, 82

I was black and blue all over. 22

Didn't you know it was a blue movie? 22

She screamed blue murder. 22

You can ask until you're blue in the face, but I'm not giving in. 22, 26

bluff

I'll bluff my way in the real world. 5

board

Everyone's on board. 6

I went back to the drawing board. 78

boat

Don't rock the boat. 6, 84

I'm afraid you've missed the boat. 62

We're all in the same boat. 6, 69, 75

bob

She's not short of a bob or two. 65

body

Over my dead body. 48

bold

He's as bold as brass. 38

bombard

We've been bombarded with enquiries. 2

bone

Have you watered this? It's bone dry. 111

bones

I can feel it in my bones. 51

bonnet

He's got a bee in his bonnet. 14

boo

She wouldn't say boo to a goose. 15

book

She's an open book. 71

Try to stay in my good books. 72

You shouldn't judge a book by its cover. 71

It was a turn-up for the books. 81

bored

I was bored out of my mind. 39

We were bored to death. 37

born

He was born with a silver spoon in his mouth. 38

borrow

He's living on borrowed time. 58

both

I've been burning the candle at both ends. 83

You can't have it both ways. 112

bottom

You can bet your bottom dollar he's in the bar now. 110

He promised to get to the bottom of the mystery. 70, 110

I hit rock bottom when I lost my job. 110

Our prices are rock bottom in the summer sale. 111

The bottom fell out of the market about the beginning of December. 110

The bottom line is, if you're not making money, you're not doing your job. 110

The company's got to change from top to bottom. 110

You're scraping the bottom of the barrel. 57

boy

He was the golden boy. 38

He's our blue-eyed boy. 22

That should sort out the men from the boys. 55

brains

I need to pick your brains. 60

I've been racking my brains. 61

brake

He put the brake on spending. 23, 77

branch

They branched out into other things. 11

They're opening a new branch soon. 84

brand

I bought a brand new camera. 111

brass

He had the brass neck to say so. 38

He's as bold as brass. 38

We got down to brass tacks. 38

brave

She put a brave face on it. 16, 26

bread

Teaching's my bread and butter. 30

They think he's the best thing since sliced bread. 30

breadline

They're living on the breadline. 30, 65

break

He comes from a broken home. 17, 56

I had a short break. 59

I normally break even with my betting. 64

I want to make a clean break. 52

It nearly broke my heart. 17, 34

They've broken up. 17

We had a drink to break the ice. 78

breaking-point

He's at breaking-point. 17

breath

He's a breath of fresh air here. 52

breathe

Don't breathe a word of this to anyone. 53, 113

They're breathing down my neck. 84

breeze

He breezed in this morning. 7

brewery

He couldn't organise a piss-up in a brewery. 60

brick

I'm banging my head against a brick wall. 18, 49

It's like talking to a brick wall. 18, 49, 53

She came down on me like a ton of bricks. 18

You're like a cat on hot bricks. 19

bridge

I don't want to burn my bridges. 28

That's water under the bridge now. 45

We'll cross that bridge when we come to it. 70

bright

Look on the bright side. 50

brighten

She'll soon brighten up. 7

bring

It brought the house down. 36

That really brought it home to me. 36

broad

They robbed the bank in broad daylight. 111

buck

You can't pass the buck. 68, 70

bud

You should nip the problem in the bud. 70, 78

buffers

We hit the buffers. 44

bull

It's like a red rag to a bull. 22, 66

We took the bull by the horns. 14, 47, 70

bump

We came back to earth with a bump. 81

burn

He's got money to burn. 65

As a girl, her burning ambition was to be an actress. 28. 79

I don't want to burn my bridges. 28

I've been burning the candle at both ends. 83

We got our fingers badly burnt when the market crashed. 27, 62

burner

Let's put that on the back burner for a while. 84

bury

Don't bury your head in the sand. 16, 33, 70

They buried the hatchet. 73

bush

Don't beat about the bush. 47, 53

business

Mind your own business. 39

butter

Teaching's my bread and butter. 30

You're trying to butter me up. 30

buy

He could buy and sell you. 65

cake

He wants to have his cake and eat it. 24

It's a piece of cake. 30, 55

That's the icing on the cake. 30

They're selling like hot cakes. 30, 43

call

I call the shots around here. 8, 68

I'm not at your beck and call. 68

Let's call it a day. 78

camel

The straw that broke the camel's back. 14

candle

I've been burning the candle at both ends. 83

cannon

He's a loose cannon. 67

cap

Get your thinking cap on. 20

cap

He was drunk, and to cap it, all he'd been drinking my wine. 109

capture

We want to capture a much bigger share of the market. 2

carbon

It's a carbon copy of the last film. 75

cards

If you play your cards right you'll do well. 5

It's been on the cards for a while. 5, 51

care

She hasn't got a care in the world. 66

career

He's climbing the career ladder. 84

carefully

It's a delicate area so tread carefully. 47, 74

carpet

They gave me the red carpet treatment. 22

They wanted to sweep it under the carpet. 70

carry

What he says carries a lot of weight. 68

cart

Don't put the cart before the horse. 35

case

Take an umbrella just in case. 51

cast

We'll have to cast our net wider. 29

casualties

Small businesses are the first casualties. 2

cat

Curiosity killed the cat. 19

He thinks he's the cat's whiskers. 19

That put the cat among the pigeons. 19, 69

There isn't a cat in hell's chance. 19

There isn't enough room to swing a cat. 14, 19

There's more than one way to skin a cat. 19

They fight like cat and dog. 19, 56, 72

When the cat's away, the mice will play. 19

Who let the cat out of the bag? 14

You're like a cat on hot bricks. 19

catch

He's quite a catch. 29

I caught him red-handed. 22

I was caught in the crossfire. 8

Try to catch his eye. 25

We caught them on the hop. 69

You'll catch your death of cold. 37

catnap

I had a catnap. 19

catty

That's a very catty thing to say. 19

caution

Throw caution to the wind. 7

cement

We need to cement our relationship. 18

chalk

They're as different as chalk and cheese. 75

We're like chalk and cheese. 56

chance

I'll take my chances. 5

There isn't a cat in hell's chance. 19

change

A change is as good as a rest. 59

He had a change of heart. 34, 52

He won't change his ways. 52

I changed my mind. 52

I want a change of direction. 52

I wouldn't change places with him. 52

It made a nice change. 59

Let's change the subject. 52

Isn't it time you changed your tune? 52

The place has changed out of all recognition. 52

The restaurant changed hands last year. 32, 52

There was a change of plan. 52

There's been a sea change lately. 45

chase

They sent me on a wild goose chase. 14, 62

cheap

Everything's dirt cheap in Thailand. 64, 111

cheeky

You're so cheeky. 16

cheese

It cheesed me off. 30

They're as different as chalk and cheese. 75

We're like chalk and cheese. 56

cherry

You're very lucky to get a second bite at the cherry. 24

chest

Get it off your chest. 16, 53

chew

He's bitten off more than he can chew. 24, 55, 62

chicken

She's no spring chicken. 15

That's chickenfeed. 14

I've been running around like a headless chicken. 14

Don't count your chickens before they're hatched. 47

child

It's child's play. 55

chimney

She smokes like a chimney. 19

chip

He's got a chip on his shoulder. 17

chips

We work harder when the chips are down. 5

choose

There's little to choose between them. 75

circles

We're going round in circles. 23

claws

She's got her claws into him. 19

clean

I want to make a clean break. 52

The doctor gave me a clean bill of health. 58

clear

I want to clear up the misunderstanding. 3

This contract is as clear as mud. 3

This paragraph is not very clear. 3

I'd steer clear of her. 23

The water was crystal clear. 111

We need to clear the air. 72

clever

He's a clever dick. 67

climb

He's climbing the career ladder. 84

We'll climb out of recession. 10

close

I could do it with my eyes closed. 25, 55

It's a subject close to my heart. 34

They decided behind closed doors. 18

We're close friends. 72

We're sailing close to the wind. 74

cloud

Every cloud has a silver lining. 38

He left under a cloud. 7, 69

I'm on cloud nine at the moment. 40, 66

The news clouded the evening. 7

He's got his head in the clouds. 33

club

Join the club. 75

clue

I haven't got a clue. 60

coat

One more coat of paint. 20

coffin

The bill was the final nail in the coffin. 78

cold

He's a cold fish. 29

I wanted to come to the party with you, but I got cold feet. 31, 43

It left me cold. 43

It looked different in the cold light of day. 43

They killed him in cold blood. 43

They left me out in the cold. 43

They poured cold water on my plans. 43

You'll catch your death of cold. 37

collar

Don't get so hot under the collar. It's not that important. 43, 66

The police collared him. 20

White collar workers earn more. 21

collision

We're on a collision course. 10

colour

I'm a bit off-colour today. 58

colours

She passed with flying colours. 47

come

First come, first served. 40

He could talk until the cows come home. 36

I don't know if I'm coming or going. 4

I'm going, come hell or high water. 45

It's a dream come true. 76

She came down on me like a ton of bricks. 18

Things came to a head. 16

We came back to earth with a bump. 81

We'll cross that bridge when we come to it. 70

You've come a long way since you started the course. 112

You've got another think coming. 81

comfortable

They're not exactly well off, but they're fairly comfortable. 65

coming

She's an up and coming writer. 79

command

When I'm away my second in command takes over. 8

common

It's common sense. 60

company

Two's company, three's a crowd. 40

complain

I can't complain. 58

compliments

She's fishing for compliments. 29

conclusion

It's a foregone conclusion. 51

condition

The car's in mint condition. 57

We were affected by adverse conditions. 10

confirm

Paul's a confirmed bachelor. 67

consequence

I'll have to face the consequences. 26

contrary

On the contrary, I'm in favour of what you're suggesting! 48

control

They regained control of the market. 10

cool

Keep cool – don't lose your temper. 43

She's as cool as a cucumber. 43

cooled

Their relationship has cooled. 7

copy

It's a carbon copy of the last film. 75

corner

I saw him out of the corner of my eye. 25

They've turned the corner now. 23

We're in a tight corner. 69

corridors

Some people just love being in the corridors of power. 18

cost

Private medicine can cost an arm and a leg if you're not insured. 16, 64

couch

He's a couch potato. 30

could

I could eat a horse. 24

count

Don't count your chickens before they're hatched. 47

You can count the invitations I've had on the fingers of one hand. 27, 32

course

I was way off course with my guess. 112

I'll be with you in due course. 82

It's horses for courses. 35, 41

That's par for the course. 41

We're back on course to meet our sales targets. 6, 10

We're on a collision course, unless we change our ideas. 10

court

The ball's in their court. 41

cover

I read it from cover to cover. 71

Keep your back covered. 8

You shouldn't judge a book by its cover. 71

cows

He could talk until the cows come home. 36

crack

I got up at the crack of dawn today. 82

It wasn't all it's cracked up to be. 57

It's a tough nut to crack. 55

cracking

We have to get cracking now. 78

cracks

They're just papering over the cracks. 70

crash

The Wall Street crash. 10

I crashed out on the sofa. 76

The market is going to crash again. 23

creek

Now we're up the creek. 69

crest

She's on the crest of a wave. 42

crop

This year's crop of graduates. 11

cross

Fingers crossed! 50

I'm keeping my fingers crossed. 27

The thought never crossed my mind. 39

We got our wires crossed. 63

We were talking at cross purposes. 63

We'll cross that bridge when we come to it. 70

cross-fertilisation

We rely on the cross-fertilisation of ideas. 11

crossfire

I was caught in the crossfire. 8

crossroads

My career is at a crossroads. 4, 23

crow

It's a mile as the crow flies. 15

crowd

Two's company, three's a crowd. 40

crush (noun)

I had a crush on my teacher when I was at school. 73

crushing (adjective)

It was a crushing blow. 17

cry

I need a shoulder to cry on. 72

It's a far cry from what I'm used to. 75

crystal

The water was crystal clear. 111

cucumber

He's as cool as a cucumber. 30, 43

cuff

Just speak off the cuff. 20

cup

Lying on a beach just isn't my cup of tea. 30, 80

curiosity

Curiosity killed the cat. 19

curtains

It's curtains for you. 78

cut back

We cut back on advertising. 11

cut (see pages 194–195)

I'm not cut out for this job. 80

I've got my work cut out with this job. 55

That's cutting it a bit fine. 74

To cut a long story short, we decided to move house. 109

damage

What's the damage? 64

dangerously

I enjoy living dangerously. 74

dark

He's a dark horse. 35

I was in the dark about it. 60

It was a leap in the dark for us. 74

dawn

I got up at the crack of dawn today. 82

day

Don't worry, it's still early days. 78

He's taking one day at a time. 47

I'm saving for a rainy day. 64

It looked different in the cold light of day. 43

It was the blackest day of my life. 21

It's seen better days. 57

It's unusual in this day and age. 82

Let's call it a day. 78

That'll be the day. 51

Tomorrow's another day. 50, 82

daylight

They robbed the bank in broad daylight. 111

£50 – that's daylight robbery. 54

dead

We must cut out all the dead wood. 11

He's in a dead-end job. 4, 23, 84

I was dead lucky to be there. 111

I was dead on my feet. 31, 76

I was dead to the world. 76

It's as dead as a dodo. 15

The shop's been dead all day. 83

It's dead easy. 55

Over my dead body. 48

This exercise is dead easy. 111

You're flogging a dead horse. 35

deaf

He can't hear anything – he's stone deaf. 111

deal

He's been dealt a lousy hand. 5

death

He was at death's door. 18, 37

I'm sick to death of him. 37

It's a fate worse than death. 37

It's the kiss of death. 37

We were bored to death. 37

You look like death warmed up. 37

You'll catch your death of cold. 37

You're dicing with death. 37

deck

It's all hands on deck. 6

deep

I was thrown in at the deep end. 42, 55

Now we're in deep water. 42

delayed

Progress might be delayed. 10

depth

He's out of his depth. 42, 55, 63, 69

deserve

You deserve a medal. 9

desired

Your work leaves a lot to be desired. 57, 109

dice

You're dicing with death. 37

dick

He's a clever dick. 67

difference

I can't tell the difference between them. 75

There's a world of difference between them. 75

They patched up their differences. 73

different

That's a different kettle of fish. 75

They're as different as chalk and cheese. 75

dig

Could you dig out that report? 11

digest

We digested the news. 24

dip

It's a good book to dip into. 71

We dipped our toes in the water. 16

We had to dip into our savings. 64

direction

I need a change of direction. 52

dirt

Everything's dirt cheap in Thailand. 64, 111

disappear

It's disappeared off the face of the earth. 26

disguise

It was a blessing in disguise. 81

distraction

It drove me to distraction. 49

dive

She just dived into that relationship. 42

do

A glass of water should do the trick. 80

He did me a good turn. 72

I could do it with my eyes closed. 55

It's easier said than done. 55

No sooner said than done. 77

Of course you don't have to do what we do. Do your own thing. 108

We did it on a shoestring. 20

doctor

This is just what the doctor ordered. 59, 80

dodo

It's as dead as a dodo. 15

dog

He's like a dog with two tails. 66

They fight like cat and dog. 19, 56, 72

This place has gone to the dogs. 14

dollar

It's the sixty-four thousand dollar question. 40

You can bet your bottom dollar he's in the bar now. 110

don't

Don't be silly. 47

Don't beat about the bush. 47

Don't count your chickens before they're hatched. 47

Don't let it get you down. 47

Don't lose any sleep over it. 47, 76

Don't overdo it. 47

Don't take anything for granted. 47

Don't throw the baby out with the bath water. 47

donkey

He can talk the hind legs off a donkey. 14, 53

I haven't been to the theatre in London for donkey's years. 14, 82

I did all the donkey work. 14

door

He was at death's door. 18, 37

I got in through the back door. 19

I need to get a foot in the door. 18

That kept the wolf from the door. 14

They decided behind closed doors. 18

doorstep

The station is right on our doorstep. 18

dot

I'll be there at four on the dot. 82

double

It's just double Dutch to me. 63

doubt

I gave him the benefit of the doubt. 51, 70

Without a shadow of a doubt. 51

down

Don't let it get you down. 47

He can never hold a job down for long. 84

I couldn't put it down. 71

I don't want any problems one year down the line. 44

I had to lay down the law. 68

I put my foot down at that. 31

I'm going down with something. 58

It brought the house down. 36

It didn't go down very well. 24

It got the thumbs down. 27

It suited me down to the ground. 80

Look at all the down-and-outs. 67

We've had our ups and downs. 72

What'll happen a year down the road? 23

I was so shocked you could have knocked me down with a feather. 17, 81

downhill

It's gone downhill. 57

dozen

I didn't know which to choose. It was six of one and half a dozen of the other. 40, 75

She talks nineteen to the dozen. 53

drag

Stop dragging your feet. 31, 77

Wild horses couldn't drag me in there. 35

draw

I went back to the drawing board. 78

That's the luck of the draw. 5

dream

Everything went like a dream. 76

I wouldn't dream of hurting you. 76

It's a dream come true. 76

drip

Don't be a drip. 12

drive

He drives me mad. 23

He drives me round the bend. 23, 49

It drove me to distraction. 49

It's driving me up the wall. 49

driver

He can be a real backseat driver. 67

driving seat

He's in the driving seat now. 23

drop

Don't drop the ball. 41

I'd do it at the drop of a hat. 20, 77

The penny finally dropped. 63

£1000 is a drop in the ocean. 45

drown

He's drowning his sorrows. 42

The noise drowned the sound of the phone. 42

drunk

Everyone at the party was blind drunk. 111

dry up

The money dried up. 12

dry

Have you watered this? It's bone dry. 111

He left me high and dry. 45

We're home and dry. 36

duck

He took to it like a duck to water. 80

It's like water off a duck's back. 15, 45

due

I'll be with you in due course. 82

dust

Tickets are like gold dust. 38

Dutch

It's just double Dutch to me. 63

each

They're at each other's throats. 72

ear

We made a real pig's ear of it. 62

early

Don't worry, it's still early days. 78

He's an early bird. 15

earth

I moved heaven and earth to help him. 79

It's disappeared off the face of the earth. 26

She's the salt of the earth. 30, 67

We came back to earth with a bump. 81

easy

It's dead easy. 55

It's easier said than done. 55

This exercise is dead easy. 111

eat

He wants to have his cake and eat it. 24

I'm so hungry! I could eat a horse. 24, 35

I had to eat my words. 24, 113

At last! I've got him eating out of the palm of my hand. 68

She eats like a sparrow. 15

They ate us out of house and home. 36

economical

He was a bit economical with the truth! 54

economy

The black economy is growing. 21

edgeways

You can't get a word in edgeways when she's talking. 113

egg

I've got a nice nest egg. 15

They got egg on their face. 30

Don't put all your eggs in one basket. 30, 74

either

We can start late or finish early, it's fine by me either way. 112

elbow

He elbowed his way to the top. 16

element

She's in her element here. 80

elephant

It's of no use to anyone! It's just a white elephant. 21

eleventh

They agreed at the eleventh hour. 82

end (see pages 196–197)

At last – the end's in sight. 78

He can't see past the end of his own nose. 3

It's a dead-end job. 4, 84

I don't know one end of a car from the other. 60

I was thrown in at the deep end. 42, 55

I'm at a loose end. 83

I'm at my wits' end. 49

I'm at the end of my tether. 49, 66

I've been burning the candle at both ends. 83

People started leaving at 12, but we stayed until the bitter end. 111

That was the end of the line for him. 44

There's light at the end of the tunnel. 4, 44, 50

They played for hours on end. 82

We just can't make ends meet. 65

You've got the wrong end of the stick. 62, 63

enemy

John's his own worst enemy. 2

enough

I don't have enough to get by on. 65

Once is enough! 40

That's fair enough. 48

escape

His name escapes me. 61

even

I normally break even with my betting. 64

every

Every cloud has a silver lining. 38

I go out every so often. 82

examined

You need your head examined. 33

express

He's like an express train. 44

eye

Don't take your eye off the ball. 62

He couldn't take his eyes off her. 25

He gave me a black eye. 21

He ran his eye over it. 25

He's got an eye for bargains. 25

He's our blue-eyed boy. 22

I could do it with my eyes closed. 25

I saw him out of the corner of my eye. 25

I'm up to my eyes in work. 83

It's a job in the public eye. 25

Keep an eye on things. 25

The police turned a blind eye. 70

There's more to her than meets the eye. 25, 81

Try to catch his eye. 25

We didn't see eye to eye on it. 15, 72

You need eyes in the back of your head. 25

eye-opener

It was a real eye-opener. 81

eyebrows

That raised a few eyebrows. 25

eyelid

I didn't bat an eyelid. 25

eyes

He couldn't keep his eyes open. 76

He tried to pull the wool over my eyes. 25, 54

I could do it with my eyes closed. 55

I couldn't believe my eyes. 81

I'm up to my eyes in work. 25

Keep your eyes peeled. 25

They're getting married with their eyes wide open. 3

Try to see the situation through my eyes. 3

It was a real eye-opener. 3

face

Don't take it at face value. 26

Face the fact that it's over. 26

He fell flat on his face. 26, 62

He lost face. 26

He's so two-faced. 54

I can't face meeting her again. 16

I couldn't keep a straight face. 26

I couldn't say it to his face. 26

I'll have to face the consequences. 26

It's written all over your face. 26

It's disappeared off the face of the earth. 26

It's nice to put a face to a name. 26

It's time to face the facts. 70

She put a brave face on it. 16, 26

She'll have to face the music. 26

The answer is staring us in the face. 26

They got egg on their face. 30

They want to save face. 26

We came face to face. 26

You have to face the fact he's gone and won't be coming back. 16

You can ask for it until you're blue in the face. You're not getting it! 22, 26

You're pulling a long face today. 26

fact

It's time to face the facts. 70

You must face the fact that it's over. 26

fair

I did tell you in advance, to be fair. 109

That's fair enough. 48

fall (see pages 198–199)

He fell flat on his face. 26,

My plan fell at the first hurdle. 9, 35

It fell into the wrong hands. 32

The bottom fell out of the market in early December. 110

They fell in love. 73

We're falling behind. 9

false

They got me there under false pretences. 54

family

He knows his family tree. 56

He's the black sheep of the family. 14, 56

Music runs in the family. 56

famous

Famous last words! 113

far

It's a far cry from what I'm used to. 75

fast

He's fast asleep. 76, 111

He's going nowhere fast. 4
This is life in the fast lane. 23
fat
It's not over till the fat lady sings. 78
fate
It's a fate worse than death. 37
father
He's following in his father's footsteps. 56, 75
Like father, like son. 56
feather
Birds of a feather flock together. 15
He was feathering his own nest. 15
I was so shocked, you could have knocked me
down with a feather. 17, 81
feel
He feels very much at home over here. 80
I felt like a fish out of water at the party. 80
I'm feeling under the weather. 58
We felt completely out of place. 80
feet
I get itchy feet. 31
I got cold feet. 43
I very much wanted to come to the party, but I
got cold feet. 31
I was dead on my feet. 31, 76
I've been on my feet all day. 83
Put your feet up. 31
She's landed on her feet, hasn't she! 31
Stop dragging your feet. 77
They pulled the rug from under my feet. 81
They're dragging their feet. 31
We were rushed off our feet. 31
We've been rushed off our feet. 83
You have to stand on your own two feet. 31
You have to think on your feet. 31
You must keep your feet on the ground. 31
You'll find your feet soon. 16, 31, 84
You'll soon be back on your feet. 58
fell
It all happened in one fell swoop. 15
fence
You can't sit on the fence. 74
few
I told him a few home truths. 36
I'll see if I can pull a few strings for you. 68
fit
I'm fighting fit. 58
fiddle
He's as fit as a fiddle. 58
I think he's on the fiddle. 54
field
We only want a level playing field. 41
fiery
He's got a fiery temper. 28
fight
Never give up without a fight. 2
I'm fighting fit. 58
They fight like cat and dog. 19, 56, 72
fill
I've had my fill. 24
Who could fill her shoes? 20

final
The bill was the final nail in the coffin. 78
find
Can you find a home for this? 36
You'll find your feet soon. 16, 31, 84
fine
Hurry up! You're cutting it a bit fine. 74
finger
Fingers crossed! 50
I'm keeping my fingers crossed. 27
Come on, get your finger out! 27
He never lifts a finger around the house. 27, 83
He pointed the finger at me. 27
He's got his finger on the pulse. 27
I can count the invitations from him on the
fingers of one hand. 27, 32
I can't put my finger on it. 16, 27
I'm all fingers and thumbs. 27
She can twist him around her little finger. 27, 68
We got our fingers badly burnt. 27, 62
She's got green fingers. 27
finishing line
The finishing line is in sight. 9
fire
Careful – you're playing with fire. 28
It fired my imagination. 28
It was a baptism of fire. 28, 55
She hardly set the world on fire. 28
That added more fuel to the fire. 28
There's no smoke without fire. 28
They're getting on like a house on fire. 28, 36, 72
first
First come, first served. 40
I don't know the first thing about it. 60
It fell at the first hurdle. 9, 35
That was the first I'd heard of it. 60
fish
He's a big fish in a small pond. 29
He's a cold fish. 29
I was so uncomfortable. I felt like a fish out of
water at the party. 14, 45, 80
She's fishing for compliments. 29
That's a different kettle of fish. 75
There are plenty more fish in the sea. 14, 29, 50
fishy
There's something fishy here. 29
fist
He rules with an iron fist. 38
fit
He's as fit as a fiddle. 58
I could fit you in after lunch. 83
I don't think that will fit the bill. 80
It fits like a glove. 20, 80
flak
We've taken a lot of flak. 2
flame
He's an old flame of mine. 28
He shot me down in flames. 28
My plans went up in flames. 28
flap
I was in a flap. 15

flash

I'd say yes in a flash. 77

flat

He fell flat on his face. 26, 62

flesh

It's very different when it's your own flesh and blood. 56

float

I first floated the idea last year. 45

They appeal to the floating voters. 45

flock

Birds of a feather flock together. 15

flog

You're flogging a dead horse. 35

flood

There was a flood of people. 12

floodgates

We don't want to open the floodgates. 78

flounder

They're floundering about. 29

flourish

Business is flourishing. 11

flow

Go with the flow. 12

We'll have to go with the flow. 70

fly

He flew off the handle. 66

I was flying by the seat of my pants. 74

It's not far as the crow flies. 15

Pigs might fly! 51

She's a high flier. 79

The fur is really flying. 19

The sparks fly when they argue. 28

The team got off to a flying start. 77

flying

She passed with flying colours. 47

We got off to a flying start. 9

follow

He's following in his father's footsteps. 4, 56, 75

food

That's food for thought. 30

foot

He's shot himself in the foot. 62

I hope I haven't put my foot in it. 62

I need to get a foot in the door. 18

I never set foot in there. 31

I put my foot down at that. 31

I really put my foot in it. 16, 31

I'm not going to wait on you hand and foot! 31

We got off on the wrong foot. 31. 69, 72

Who's going to foot the bill? 16, 31

footsteps

He's following in his father's footsteps. 4, 56, 75

forces

We've joined forces with another company. 2

foregone

It's a foregone conclusion. 51

fort

Please hold the fort while I'm out. 8, 68

fortune

She must be worth a fortune. 65

forty

I've just had forty winks. 76

foundations

We've laid the foundations. 18

fragile

I'm feeling fragile. 17

free-fall

The market's in free-fall. 10

fresh

He's like a breath of fresh air at work. 52

friend

A friend in need is a friend indeed. 72

We're close friends. 72

frighten

You frightened the life out of me. 37

frosty

She gave me a frosty reception. 7, 43

fruit

It bore fruit at last. 11

fuel

That added more fuel to the fire. 28

full

She's got her hands full with the kids. 83

fur

The fur is really flying. 19

gab

She's got the gift of the gab. 53

gain

We're gaining ground on our competitors. 2

gamble

It's a bit of a gamble. 5

game

It's a whole new ball game. 41, 75

garden

They're leading you up the garden path. 54

gear

They went up a gear. 23

get off

It didn't get off the ground. 10

get

Don't get your knickers in a twist. 20

Don't let it get you down. 47

Get it off your chest. 16

He gets on my nerves. 16, 49

He got on his high horse. 35

He promised he'd get to the bottom of the mystery. 110

He really got my back up. 16

I couldn't get into it. 71

I get the picture. 3

I got in through the back door. 19

I got my fingers badly burned. 27

I don't have enough to get by on. 65

I intend to get to the bottom of it. 70

I want something to get my teeth into. 24

I want to get away from it all. 59

There's something I want to get off my chest. 53

I'll get straight to the point. 53

It took a while to get going. 71

She's got her hands full with the kids. 83

That's what got up my nose. 49

The team got off to a flying start. 77

He's got it in for me. 73
He's got something up his sleeve. 20
We got our wires crossed. 63
They got left behind. 79
They're getting on like a house on fire. 28, 36, 72
Things got out of hand. 32
Wait till I get my hands on him. 32
We got down to brass tacks. 38
We got off on the wrong foot. 31, 69, 72
We have to get cracking now. 78
You can't get a word in edgeways when she starts! 113
You should get a life! 37
You'll soon get the hang of it. 60

gift
She's got the gift of the gab. 53

give
Can I give you a hand? 32
Never give up without a fight. 2
He'd give you the shirt off his back. 20
I gave him a piece of my mind. 39, 66
I gave him the benefit of the doubt. 51, 70
I'd give my right arm for that. 16

glass
People who live in glasshouses shouldn't throw stones. 11

gloomy
Why are you so gloomy? 7

glove
It fits like a glove. 20, 80
You have to handle him with kid gloves. 17

go
Everything went like a dream. 76
Everything went pear-shaped. 30
Go for it. 47
He went over my head and saw the boss. 84
He went right off the rails. 69
He went to pieces. 17, 70
He's going up in the world. 79
I don't know if I'm coming or going. 4
We went our separate ways. 4
He's going nowhere fast. 4
I knew he was going to be difficult from the word go. 113
I was going spare. 49
I went on a spending spree. 64
I went out like a light last night. 76
I went out of my way to be nice to them. 112
I went as red as a beetroot. 22
I think I'm going down with something. 58
It all went out of the window. 18
It didn't go down very well. 24
It took a while to get going. 71
It went over my head. 63
It's been all go in the office today. 86
It's gone downhill. 57
It's touch and go. 51
Let's go halves. 64
My mind went blank. 61
My plans went up in flames. 28
Power can go to your head. 33
Shares have gone through the roof. 18

She's on the go all day. 83
The company went from strength to strength. 52
The joke went down like a lead balloon. 38
The power went to my head. 16
They went under in the recession. 42
They've gone their separate ways. 73
We sat there watching the world go by. 59
We went back to square one. 78
We'll have to go with the flow. 70
We're going round in circles. 23
We're in the slow lane going nowhere. 23
You can go off people, you know. 72

goalposts
They moved the goalposts. 41

gold
It's worth its weight in gold. 57
She's worth her weight in gold. 38
She's got a heart of gold. 34
They were as good as gold. 38
Tickets for the concert are like gold dust. 38
We struck gold there. 38

golden
He was the golden boy. 38
It's a golden opportunity. 38
That's the golden rule. 38
The golden age of drama. 38
They gave him a golden handshake. 38

good
A change is as good as a rest. 59
Did you know there's free beer all night? We're onto a good thing here. 108
He did me a good turn. 72
He makes a good living. 65
I'll put in a good word for you. 53, 68
I've got a good mind to tell him. 39
No news is good news. 50
She's got a good head for numbers. 16
The children were as good as gold. 38
This is a good read. 71
Try to stay in my good books! 72
We made very good time. 77
Your guess is as good as mine. 51

goose
She wouldn't say boo to a goose. 15
They sent me on a wild goose chase. 14, 62

got to
You've got to hand it to him. 32

granted
Don't take anything for granted. 47

grapevine
I heard it on the grapevine. 53

grass
He's a snake in the grass. 54

Greek
It's all Greek to me. 63

green
She's got green fingers. 27
They gave us the green light. 23, 78

grip
It's a gripping read. 71

ground (see pages 202–203)
It failed to get off the ground. 10
It suited me down to the ground. 80
We're gaining ground on our competitors. 2
You must keep your feet on the ground. 31

guess
It's anyone's guess. 51
Your guess is as good as mine. 51

gunning
He's gunning for me. 8

guns
Stick to your guns. 8
It's going great guns. 8

guts
They hate each other's guts. 73

hair
I was tearing my hair out. 49
It's good to let your hair down on holiday. 59

half (see pages 204–205)
I'll meet you halfway – let's say £50? 112
I don't know which one to choose. It's six of one and half a dozen of the other. 40, 75
Sorry, I was half asleep. 76

halves
Let's go halves. 64

hand
Can I give you a hand? 32
He can turn his hand to anything. 32, 60
He handed me the baton. 9
He's an old hand at this. 16, 60
He's been dealt a lousy hand. 5
Never show your hand too early. 5
I can count the invitations from him on the fingers of one hand. 27, 32
I caught him red-handed. 22
I know London like the back of my hand. 60
I like to keep my hand in. 32
I'm not going to wait on you hand and foot! 31
When I retire, I'll hand the reins of the business over to my son. 35
At last! I've got him eating out of the palm of my hand. 68
She's got her hands full with the kids. 83
The right hand doesn't know what the left hand is doing. 32
They had a big hand in it. 32
Things got out of hand. 32
We got the upper hand in the end. 68
We rejected it out of hand. 32
We're living from hand to mouth. 32, 65
You've got to hand it to him. 16, 32

handle
He flew off the handle. 66
You have to handle him with kid gloves. 17

handling
He needs careful handling. 17

hands
It fell into the wrong hands. 32
It's all hands on deck. 6
My hands are tied. 16
The restaurant changed hands last year. 32, 52
They've got time on their hands. 32

Wait till I get my hands on him. 32
You can't take the law into your own hands. 32

handshake
They gave him a golden handshake. 38

hang
You'll soon get the hang of it. 60

hard
I'm a bit hard up at the moment. 65
It was harder than I had bargained for. 81
The ground was rock hard. 111
We learned the hard way. 55

hat
He's talking through his hat. 20
I take my hat off to him. 20
I'd go there at the drop of a hat. 20, 77
Keep it under your hat. 20
That's old hat! 20
We need to pull something out of the hat now. 20

hatch
Don't count your chickens before they're hatched. 47

hatchet
They buried the hatchet. 73

hate
They hate each other's guts. 73

have
He wants to have his cake and eat it. 24
I didn't have the heart to refuse. 34
I had a quick word with him after lunch. 113
I've had my fill. 24
You can't have it both ways. 112

hawk
He watched me like a hawk. 15

haystack
It's like looking for a needle in a haystack. 55

hazy
I'm a bit hazy about it. 7

head
Don't bury your head in the sand. 16, 33
He bit my head off. 24
He went over my head and saw the boss. 84
He's got his head in the clouds. 33
He's got his head screwed on. 33, 60
I'm afraid I can't give you an answer off the top of my head. 33, 110
I can't make head nor tail of it. 33, 63
I could do it standing on my head. 33
I put my head on the block for you. 33, 74
It went over my head. 33, 63
Keep your head down. 2, 8
Power can go to your head. 33
She's got a good head for numbers. 16
She's head and shoulders above the rest. 33, 57
The power went to my head. 16
Things came to a head. 16
We laughed our heads off. 33
We're head over heels in love. 73
You mustn't bury your head in the sand. 70
You need eyes in the back of your head. 25
You need your head examined. 33
You're banging your head against a brick wall. 49
You've hit the nail on the head. 48

headache

I had a splitting headache. 58

heads

Heads will roll. 33

Two heads are better than one. 33, 40

We just kept our heads above water. 33, 42, 45

We should put our heads together. 33

health

She's the picture of health. 58

The doctor gave me a clean bill of health. 58

hear

I heard it on the grapevine. 53

That was the first I'd heard of it. 60

heart

Don't lose heart. 34

He had a change of heart. 52

He's a man after my own heart. 34

Her heart's in the right place. 34

I didn't have the heart to refuse. 34

I learned the poem by heart. 34, 61

I realised in my heart of hearts. 34

I've got your best interests at heart. 34

It broke her heart. 17, 34

It's a subject close to my heart. 34

My heart sank when I saw it. 34, 45

My heart wasn't in it. 16, 34

She set her heart on a new BMW. 34, 79

She's got a heart of gold. 34

Take heart from the news. 34

We had a change of heart. 34

We had a heart-to-heart. 34

heat

I said yes in the heat of the moment. 43

heated

We had a heated discussion. 28, 43

heaven

I moved heaven and earth to help him. 79

I was in seventh heaven. 40

heavy

I found her latest novel very heavy-going in places. 55, 71

I'm a heavy sleeper. 76

heavyweight

The heavyweight politicians are against it. 41

heel

We're head over heels in love. 73

hell

He went off like a bat out of hell. 77

I'm going on the trip, come hell or high water. 45

There isn't a cat in hell's chance. 19

herring

It was a red herring. 22, 29

high

He got on his high horse. 35

He left me high and dry. 45

I'm going on the trip, come hell or high water. 45

It's very high-brow reading. 71

She's a high flier. 79

They're in high spirits. 66

They've got friends in high places. 68

hill

He's over the hill now. 57

hind

He can talk the hind legs off a donkey. 53

hindsight

It's easy to say that with hindsight. 3

history

That's ancient history now. 61

hit

He hit the jackpot. 5

I hit it off with him at once. 72

I hit rock bottom when I lost my job. 110

It hit home later. 36

She nearly hit the roof. 19

Time to hit the road. 23

We hit the buffers. 44

You've just hit the nail on the head. 48

hold

He can never hold a job down for long. 84

His story just doesn't hold water. 45

Hold your horses! 35

Please hold the fort while I'm out. 8, 68

The plan's been put on hold for the moment. 78

hole

He's a square peg in a round hole. 80

home

Can you find a home for this kitten? 36

He comes from a broken home. 17, 56

He could talk until the cows come home. 14, 36

He feels very much at home over here. 80

He's nothing to write home about. 36, 57, 109

I told him a few home truths. 36

It hit home later. 36

It's a home from home for us. 36, 59

Make yourself at home. 36

That really brought it home to me. 36

The lights are on, but there's nobody at home. 36

There's no place like home. 59

They ate us out of house and home. 36

We're home and dry. 36

We're on the home straight now. 9, 36

honest

To be honest, I didn't really like the way they had decorated the place. 109

hoof

I'll eat something on the hoof. 35

hook

He swallowed it hook, line and sinker. 29

I'll let you off the hook this time. 29

I'm hooked on them. 29

hop

We caught them on the hop. 69

horizon

There are problems on the horizon. 52

horns

You'll have to take the bull by the horns. 14, 47, 70

horse

Don't put the cart before the horse. 35

He backed the wrong horse. 41

He got on his high horse. 35

He's a dark horse. 35

Hold your horses. 35

I could eat a horse. 24, 35

I got it straight from the horse's mouth. 14, 35, 53

It's a one-horse race. 35

It's horses for courses. 35, 41

We're just horsing around. 35

You backed the wrong horse. 35

You're flogging a dead horse. 35

Wild horses couldn't drag me in there. 35

hot

Don't get so hot under the collar. 43, 66

Here's the news – hot off the press. 43

That joke landed him in hot water. 45

The question of refugees is a hot potato. 43

They're selling like hot cakes. 30, 43

You'll get into hot water. 43, 69

You're in the hot seat now. 43

You're like a cat on hot bricks. 19

It's a hot-bed of unrest. 43

hour

They agreed at the eleventh hour. 40, 82

They partied into the small hours. 82

house

It brought the house down. 36

People who live in glasshouses shouldn't throw stones. 11

They ate us out of house and home. 36

They should put their own house in order. 36

They're getting on like a house on fire. 28, 36, 72

We did it in-house. 36

Your money's as safe as houses. 36, 74

hungry

They are hungry for success. 79

hurdle

It fell at the first hurdle. 9, 35

It's a major hurdle. 9

ice

We had a drink to break the ice. 78

You're skating on thin ice. 74

iceberg

That's just the tip of the iceberg. 69

icing

That's the icing on the cake. 30

idea

I first floated the idea last year. 45

image

She's the spitting image of her mother. 56, 75

imagination

The film really fired my imagination. 28

in

We had to throw in the towel. 78

inch

I wouldn't trust him an inch. 54

indeed

A friend in need is a friend indeed. 72

injury

To add insult to injury, they didn't even say thank you. 49, 109

insult

To add insult to injury, they didn't even say thank you. 49, 109

interests

I've got your best interests at heart. 34

iron

He ruled with an iron fist. 38

They all pumped iron. 38

They ruled with a rod of iron. 38

It's

It's touch and go. 51

It's on the cards. 51

It's in the bag. 51

It's anyone's guess. 51

It's all up in the air. 51

It's a foregone conclusion. 51

itchy

I get itchy feet. 31

jackpot

He hit the jackpot. 5

jam

He's in a bit of a jam. 23, 69

job

He's in a dead-end job. 4

I'm looking for a steady job. 84

She landed a great job. 84

jog

Let's see if I can jog your memory. 61

join

Join the club! 75

We've joined forces with another company. 2

joke

You must be joking! 48

judge

You shouldn't judge a book by its cover. 71

juice

We left him to stew in his own juice. 30

just

If you want me to drive you, just say the word. 113

keep

He couldn't keep his eyes open. 76

I couldn't keep a straight face. 26

I like to keep my hand in. 32

I'll keep a low profile for a while. 47

I'm keeping my fingers crossed. 27

Keep an eye on things. 25

Keep cool – don't lose your temper. 43

Keep it under your hat. 20

Keep your eyes peeled. 25

Keep your head down. 2, 8

Please keep me posted if you hear anything. 53

She's in a bad mood, so keep out of her way. 112

We just kept our heads above water. 33, 42, 45

We need to keep them onside. 41

We'll have to keep a tight rein on him. 35

You must keep an open mind. 39

You must keep your feet on the ground. 31

You'd better keep a low profile. 70

You've got to keep your wits about you. 47

kettle

That's a different kettle of fish. 75

kick

I could have kicked myself. 49

kid

You have to handle him with kid gloves. 17

kill

Curiosity killed the cat. 19

My feet are killing me. 58

We killed two birds with one stone. 15, 40

kind

She's one of a kind. 75

kiss

It's the kiss of death. 37

kitchen

We took everything except the kitchen sink. 59

knickers

Don't get your knickers in a twist! 20

knock

I can knock £5 off for you. 64

You could have knocked me down with a feather. 17, 81

You could have knocked me for six. 40, 81

knot

They finally tied the knot on Sunday. 56

They're tying the knot. 73

know (see pages 206–207)

He knows the ropes. 6

Polite? He doesn't know the meaning of the word! 113

I don't know one end of a car from the other. 60

I don't know the first thing about it. 60

I know London like the back of my hand. 60

I know what's what. 60

She knows a thing or two about cars. 60

The right hand doesn't know what the left hand is doing. 32

You never know. 50

ladder

He's climbing the career ladder. 84

lady

It's not over till the fat lady sings. 78

land

She landed a great job. 84

She landed on her feet. 31

That joke landed him in hot water. 45

We landed a great contract. 29

lane

This is life in the fast lane. 23

We're in the slow lane going nowhere. 23

lap

He lives in the lap of luxury. 65

We're on the last lap. 9

larger

He's larger than life. 37

last

Famous last words! 113

I book my holidays at the last minute. 82

It's on its last legs. 16, 57

That was the last straw. 49, 66

We're on the last lap. 9

late

He'll tell us sooner or later. 82

laugh

We laughed our heads off. 33

law

I had to lay down the law. 68

You can't take the law into your own hands. 32

lay

I had to lay down the law. 68

We've laid the foundations. 18

lead (adjective)

The joke went down like a lead balloon. 38

lead (verb)

They're leading you up the garden path. 54

leaf

He's turned over a new leaf. 52, 71

league

He's in a league of his own. 57

leap

It was a leap in the dark for us. 74

learn

I learned the poem by heart. 34, 61

I'm learning the ropes. 60

We learned the hard way. 55

lease

I've got a new lease of life. 37, 58, 78

least

It was disappointing, to say the least. 109

leave

He left me high and dry. 45

Your work leaves a lot to be desired. 57, 109

It left a bad taste in my mouth. 24

It left me cold. 43

They got left behind. 79

They left me out in the cold. 43

They'll leave no stone unturned to find him. 79

left

The right hand doesn't know what the left hand is doing. 32

leg

He can talk the hind legs off a donkey. 53

I'm only pulling your leg. 16

Private education costs an arm and a leg. 16, 64

Our TV is on its last legs. 16, 57

lend

The system lends itself to abuse. 80

let

Don't let it get you down. 47

I'll let you off the hook this time. 29

It's good to let your hair down on holiday. 59

Sport is one way of letting off steam. 44

letter

Yesterday was a red-letter day. 22

level

We only want a level playing field. 41

lie (noun)

I told him a little white lie. 21, 54

lie (verb)

I'm going to lie in tomorrow. 76

They're lying through their teeth. 54

life (see pages 208–209)

He'll do anything for a quiet life. 70

He's larger than life. 37

I can't dance to save my life. 37

I can't remember his name for the life of me. 37

I got the shock of my life when I opened the door. 81

I need to put my life back together. 17

It's given me a new lease of life. 37, 58, 78

She made my life a misery. 37
She's the life and soul of the party. 37, 67
That's life! 50
Variety is the spice of life. 30
You frightened the life out of me. 37
Get a life! 37

lifeline
They had to throw us a lifeline. 42

lifetime
It only happens once in a lifetime. 40

lift
He never lifts a finger around the house. 27, 83
We thumbed a lift. 27

light
I went out like a light last night. 76
I'm a light sleeper. 76
It looked different in the cold light of day. 43
It's good to travel light. 59
It's nice light reading. 71
There's light at the end of the tunnel. 4, 44, 50
They gave us the green light. 78
They saw the light. 3
We got the green light. 23
The lights are on, but there's nobody at home. 36

like (see pages 212–213)
Everything went like a dream. 76
He's like a dog with two tails. 66
I felt like a fish out of water at the party. 45, 80
I know London like the back of my hand. 60
I went out like a light last night. 76
I wouldn't like to be in your shoes. 20
It's like getting blood out of a stone. 55
It's like looking for a needle in a haystack. 55
It's like talking to a brick wall. 49
It's like water off a duck's back. 45
She's got a memory like a sieve. 61
The joke went down like a lead balloon. 38
The news spread like wildfire. 77
There's no place like home. 59
They fight like cat and dog. 72
They fit like a glove. 80
They're getting on like a house on fire. 28, 36
They're like two peas in a pod. 56
Tickets are like gold dust. 38
We used to fight like cat and dog. 56
We're like chalk and cheese. 56
You look like death warmed up. 37
You'll stick out like a sore thumb. 27

limbo
We're in limbo at the moment. 69

limit
The sky's the limit. 79

line (see pages 214–215)
He swallowed it hook, line and sinker. 29
There'll be problems one year down the line. 44
It got lost somewhere along the line. 44
It's been difficult all along the line. 44
Try not to step out of line. 8
That was the end of the line for him. 44
The bottom line is, if you're not making money,
you're not doing your job. 110
Thousands live on the breadline. 65

We take a tough line on punctuality. 68
You have to read between the lines. 71

lining
Every cloud has a silver lining. 38

list
I want to do many things – top of the list is travel
to the United States. 110

little
A little bird told me. 15
She can twist him around her little finger. 27, 68
There's little to choose between them. 75
You sometimes have to tell a little white lie. 21,
54

live
I enjoy living dangerously. 74
We were living from hand to mouth. 32
Thousands live on the breadline. 65
We had the time of our lives. 59

living
He makes a good living. 65
It's the worst winter in living memory. 61

load
That's a load of tripe. 71

loaded
They're loaded. 65

log
I slept like a log. 76

long
Long time no see. 82
She's my long-lost cousin. 56
To cut a long story short, we decided to move
house. 109
When I refused to let her leave, she just pulled a
long face. 26
You've come a long way since you started the
course. 112

look
He gave me a black look. 21
It's like looking for a needle in a haystack. 55
Look on the bright side. 50

loose
He's a loose cannon. 67
I'm at a loose end. 83

lose (see pages 216–217)
Don't lose any sleep over it. 47, 76
Don't lose heart. 34
Don't lose sight of our aims. 3
You win some, you lose some. 5, 50
He lost face. 26
I'm afraid you've lost me. 63
I'm lost for words. 113
There's no love lost between them. 72, 73
Why not? You've got nothing to lose. 50, 74

loss
I'm at a loss to explain what happened. 69

lost
She's my long-lost cousin. 56
There's no love lost between them. 72

lot
He's got a lot on his plate at the moment. 83
There's a lot to be said for working from home.
109

Your work leaves a lot to be desired. 57, 109
loud
Actions speak louder than words. 113
lousy
He's been dealt a lousy hand. 5
love
There's no love lost between them. 72, 73
They fell in love. 73
low
You'd better keep a low profile. 47, 70
luck
That's the luck of the draw. 5
lucky
I was dead lucky to be there. 111
Third time lucky. 40, 50
luxury
He lives in the lap of luxury. 65
mad
He drives me mad. 23
major
He's a major player in the business. 41
make
He made a real mess of the job. 62
He makes a good living. 65
He's making waves. 45
His book really made a splash. 42
I can make time for you. 1
Have I made myself perfectly clear? 3
I can't make head nor tail of it. 33, 63, 71
I can't make up my mind. 39
I want to make a clean break. 52
I'll make him eat his words. 113
It made a nice change. 59
Make yourself at home. 36
She made my life a misery. 37
She's making a name for herself in the Law. 84
Things like that make my blood boil. 66
To make matters worse, it started to rain. 109
We just can't make ends meet. 65
We made a meal of it. 24
We made a real pig's ear of it. 62
We made very good time. 77
You've only got a day so make the most of it. 47
man
You can trust him, he's a man of his word. 113
marathon
It's turning into a marathon. 9
marching
He got his marching orders. 2, 8
market
The bottom fell out of the market in December. 110
matter
It's a question of mind over matter. 39
It's only a matter of time. 82
matters
To make matters worse, it started to rain. 109
me
Just between you and me, she's pregnant. 53
You're telling me. 48
meal
We made a meal of it. 24

mean
I see what you mean. 3
meaning
He's not polite. He doesn't know the meaning of the word. 113
means
By all means, help yourself. 86
medal
You deserve a medal. 9
meet
I'll meet you halfway – let's say £50? 112
There's more to him than meets the eye. 25, 81
We just can't make ends meet. 65
memory
I've got a terrible memory for faces. 61
It's the worst winter in living memory. 61
Let me refresh your memory. 61
Let's see if I can jog your memory. 61
She's got a memory like a sieve. 61
She's got a photographic memory. 61
men
That should sort out the men from the boys. 55
mend
We tried to mend the relationship. 17
mention
I don't like the style, not to mention the colour. 109
mess
He made a real mess of the job. 62
message
I get the message. 53
mice
When the cat's away, the mice will play. 19
middle
It's in the middle of nowhere. 59
mildly
I was surprised, to put it mildly. 109
miles
This is miles better. 57
million
Not in a million years. 40
She's one in a million. 40
mind
At the back of my mind I know there's something I should do. 61
He's got a one-track mind. 44
He's got something on his mind. 39
I can't make up my mind. 39
I changed my mind. 52
I gave him a piece of my mind. 39
I was bored out of my mind. 39
I'll bear that in mind. 39, 61
I'm in two minds about it. 29, 40
I've got a good mind to tell him. 39
It gave me peace of mind. 39
It slipped my mind. 39, 61
It's a question of mind over matter. 39
It's all in your mind. 39
Mind your own business. 39
My mind went blank. 61
Never mind. 39
Nobody in their right mind would do it. 39

Nothing springs to mind. 39
Put your mind at rest. 39
That'll take your mind off things. 39
That's a weight off my mind. 39
The thought never crossed my mind. 39
You can do it if you put your mind to it. 39
You must keep an open mind. 39
You should speak your mind. 47
You're out of your mind. 39

minefield
Exporting can be a minefield. 2

minnow
He's a minnow. 29

mint
The car's in mint condition. 57

minute
I book my holidays at the last minute. 82
There you are – and not a minute too soon. 82

misery
She made my life a misery. 37

miss
He's missing the point. 63
I'm afraid you've missed the boat. 62

moment
I said yes in the heat of the moment. 43
We decided on the spur of the moment. 82

money
He's got money to burn. 65
I wouldn't put money on it. 5
She spends money like water. 45

monkey
If you pay peanuts, you get monkeys. 83
Stop monkeying around. 14

month
Not in a month of Sundays. 82

moon
I see him once in a blue moon. 22, 40, 82
We're over the moon. 66

more
He's bitten off more than he can chew. 24, 55, 62
There's more to her than meets the eye. 25, 81
There's plenty more fish in the sea. 29

most
You've only got a day so make the most of it. 47

mouth
Don't put words into my mouth. 63
He was born with a silver spoon in his mouth. 38
I got it straight from the horse's mouth. 14, 35, 53
It left a bad taste in my mouth. 24
They lived from hand to mouth. 32, 65
We found out about the hotel by word of mouth. 113
You took the words right out of my mouth. 48, 113

move
I moved heaven and earth to help him. 79
They keep moving the goalposts. 41

mover
He's one of the movers and shakers. 68

movie
It's a blue movie. 22

mud
It's as clear as mud. 3

murder
She screamed blue murder. 22

music
She'll have to face the music. 26

must
It's a must. 71

mutiny
There's going to be a mutiny. 6

nail
The bill was the final nail in the coffin. 78
You've hit the nail on the head. 48

naked
He was standing in the road stark naked. 111

name
I was left without a penny to my name. 65
It's nice to put a face to a name. 26
She's making a name for herself in the Law. 84

nature
It's second nature to me now. 60

neck
He had the brass neck to say so. 38
He's a real pain in the neck. 67, 16
I don't want to stick my neck out. 74
Parking round here is a pain in the neck. 16
They're breathing down my neck. 84
They're neck and neck. 41

need
A friend in need is a friend indeed. 72
You need your head examined. 33

needle
It's like looking for a needle in a haystack. 55

needs
They'll tailor your holiday to your needs. 80

nerves
He gets on my nerves. 16, 49
He's got nerves of steel. 38

nest
He was feathering his own nest. 15
I've got a nice nest egg. 15
They've flown the nest. 15

net
They slipped through the net. 29
We'll have to cast our net wider. 29

never
Never mind. 39
The thought never crossed my mind. 39
You never know. 50

new
He's turned over a new leaf. 52, 71
I bought a brand new camera. 111
It gave me a new lease of life. 37, 58, 78
It's a whole new ball game. 41, 75

news
No news is good news. 50

nick
The police arrived in the nick of time. 82

night
It'll be all right on the night. 50
We had a night on the tiles. 18

nightmare

The party was a nightmare. 76

nine

I'm on cloud nine at the moment. 40, 66

nineteen

She talks nineteen to the dozen. 53

nip

You should nip the problem in the bud. 70, 78

no (see pages 218–219)

He spends money as if there was no tomorrow. 77

Long time no see. 82

No news is good news. 50

No sooner said than done. 77

There's no love lost between them. 72, 73

There's no time like the present. 82

They'll leave no stone unturned to find him. 79

We'll be there in no time at all. 77, 82

nobody

The lights are on, but there's nobody at home. 36

Nobody in their right mind would do it. 39

nod

He nodded off in front of the TV. 76

non-stop

He drove for 10 hours non-stop. 82

none

It's second to none. 40

nose

He can't see past the end of his nose. 3

That's what got up my nose. 49

You have to pay through the nose there. 64

nosedive

Prices nosedived. 10

nosey

Don't be so nosey. 16

She's such a nosey parker. 67

not

Not at all. 86

Not in a month of Sundays. 82

nothing

He'll stop at nothing to get there. 79

He's nothing to write home about. 36, 57, 109

The party was a disaster – the noise, the complaints, to say nothing of the mess afterwards. 109

There were no problems, at least, nothing to speak of. 109

There's nothing to it. 55

Why not? You've got nothing to lose. 50, 74

now

We meet up now and again. 82

nowhere

He's going nowhere fast. 4

It's in the middle of nowhere. 59

We're in the slow lane going nowhere. 23

nut

It's a tough nut to crack. 55

nutshell

To put it in a nutshell, his work is just not good enough. 109

ocean

£1000 is a drop in the ocean. 45

odd

He's the odd one out. 75

odds

He survived against all the odds. 5

off

Don't take your eye off the ball. 62

He'll sleep it off. 76

He's bitten off more than he can chew. 62

I can't answer off the top of my head. 33

I like places off the beaten track. 59

I was way off course with my guess. 112

I'll let you off the hook this time. 29

I'm a bit off-colour today. 58

That'll take your mind off things. 39

They're well off. 65

We laughed our heads off. 33

off-shoot

It's an off-shoot of the main company. 11

often

I go out every so often. 82

old

He's a bit of an old woman. 67

He's an old flame of mine. 28

He's an old hand at this. 16, 60

That's old hat. 20

once

Once or twice. 40

I'll tell you once and for all. 40

Once bitten, twice shy. 40

Once in a blue moon. 22, 40, 82

Once in a lifetime. 40

Once in a while. 40

Once is enough. 40

one

Don't put all your eggs in one basket. 30

He's got a one-track mind. 40, 44

He's the odd one out. 75

I can count them on the fingers of one hand. 27

I don't know one end of a car from the other. 60

It's a one-horse race. 35

It's back to square one. 40, 78

It's been one thing after another. 83

It's six of one and half a dozen of the other. 75

She's one in a million. 40

She's one of a kind. 75

There's more than one way to skin a cat. 19

Two heads are better than one. 40

We killed two birds with one stone. 40

only

Things can only get better. 50

onside

We need to keep them onside. 41

open

You must keep an open mind. 39

He couldn't keep his eyes open. 76

You're leaving yourself wide open to criticism. 111

She's an open book. 71

They're going into marriage with their eyes wide open. 3

It's time you opened your eyes. 3

We don't want to open the floodgates. 78

opportunity
It's a golden opportunity. 38
order
It's just what the doctor ordered. 59, 80
They should put their house in order. 36
orders
You'll soon get your marching orders. 2, 8
organise
He couldn't organise a piss-up in a brewery. 60
other
I didn't complain about him, it was the other way round. 112
I don't know one end of a car from the other. 60
In other words, it's a waste of time. 113
They're at each other's throats. 72
out
He arrived out of the blue. 22
He's the odd one out. 75
I don't want to stick my neck out. 74
I went out like a light last night. 76
Look at all the down-and-outs. 67
They ate us out of house and home. 36
They pulled out all the stops to finish on time. 79
You'll stick out like a sore thumb. 27, 80
You're out of your mind. 39
over
It's all over now, so go home. 86
It's all over your face. 26
It's not over till the fat lady sings. 78
Over my dead body. 48
The way she dresses is over the top. 110
We're over the moon. 66
overdo
Don't overdo it. 47
overflow
The pub was overflowing. 12
overtake
We've overtaken France now. 23
own
He's a man after my own heart. 34
He's in a league of his own. 57
I'll get there under my own steam. 44
Mind your own business. 39
You can do your own thing. 108
You can't take the law into your own hands. 32
You have to stand on your own two feet. 31
oyster
The world's your oyster. 79
pace
Get another job if you can't stand the pace. 84
He put us through our paces. 35
We drove at a snail's pace. 77
We're working at a steady pace. 9
pain
He's a real pain in the neck. 67
Parking around here is a pain in the neck. 16
paint
Let's paint the town red. 22
palm
I've got him eating out of the palm of my hand. 68

pants
He's got ants in his pants. 14
I was flying by the seat of my pants. 74
paper
The walls are paper thin. 111
They're just papering over the cracks. 70
par
Your work is below par. 57
The exam results are on a par with last year's. 75
Late again! That's par for the course. 41
parker
She's such a nosey parker. 67
parrot
I was as sick as a parrot. 15
parrot
We learnt French parrot fashion. 15
party
She's the life and soul of the party. 37, 67
pass
Don't try to pass the buck. 68, 70
patch
They patched up their differences. 73
path
They're leading you up the garden path. 54
pave
The meeting paved the way for future investments. 112
pay
If you pay peanuts, you get monkeys. 83
You have to pay through the nose there. 64
pea
They're like two peas in a pod. 56
peace
It gave me peace of mind. 39
peanuts
If you pay peanuts, you get monkeys. 83
pear
Everything went pear-shaped. 30
pecking order
He's way down the pecking order. 15
peeled
Keep your eyes peeled. 25
peg
He's a square peg in a round hole. 80
penny
I was left without a penny to my name. 65
The penny finally dropped. 63
They're ten a penny. 40
perennial
It's a perennial problem. 11
photographic
She's got a photographic memory. 61
pick
I need to pick your brains. 60
I picked up a bargain yesterday. 64
Someone has to pick up the pieces. 17
You can pick your friends, but not your relations. 72
pickle
I'm in a pickle. 30
picture
I get the picture. 3

It's a black picture. 21
She's the picture of health. 58

piece
He went to pieces. 17, 70
I gave him a piece of my mind. 39, 66
It's a piece of cake. 30, 55
Someone has to pick up the pieces. 17

pig
This place is a pig-sty. 14
We made a real pig's ear of it. 62
Pigs might fly. 51

pigeons
That put the cat among the pigeons. 19, 69

pinch
I'd take that with a pinch of salt. 30

pipeline
We've got some big projects in the pipeline. 84

piss-up
He couldn't organise a piss-up in a brewery. 60

pitch
It's pitch black with the light off. 111

place
Her heart's in the right place. 34
I wouldn't change places with him. 52
There's no place like home. 59
They've got friends in high places. 68
We felt completely out of place. 80

plain
It was plain sailing after that. 55

plate
He's got a lot on his plate at the moment. 83

play
Careful – you're playing with fire. 28
I advise you to play safe. 74
If you play your cards right, you'll do well. 5
It's child's play. 55
They won't play ball. 41
We only want a level playing field. 41
When the cat's away, the mice will play. 19

player
He's a major player in the business. 41

please
You must be as pleased as punch. 66

plenty
There's plenty more fish in the sea. 29, 50
There's plenty of time. 1

plough
They ploughed a lot of money into it. 11

plug
They pulled the plug on the project. 78

plummet
Share prices plummeted overnight. 10

plunge
He took the plunge at long last and asked her to marry him. 73
House prices plunged in the 70's. 10

pod
They're like two peas in a pod. 56

point (see pages 224–225)
You can't point the finger at me. 27
He's missing the point. 63
I can't see the point. 3

He won't listen to my point of view. 3
I'll get straight to the point. 53
Point taken! 48

poles
Their ideas are poles apart. 75

pond
He's a big fish in a small pond. 29

pool
We use a pool of secretaries. 12

post
Back to your posts, everyone. 8
Please keep me posted if you hear anything. 53

potato
He's a couch potato. 30
The question of refugees is a hot potato. 43

pour
People poured in. 12
They poured cold water on my plans. 43

power
People in the corridors of power should remember who elected them. 18

precious
My time is precious. 1

present
There's no time like the present. 82

press
Here's the news – hot off the press. 43

pretences
They got me there under false pretences. 54

pride
You'll have to swallow your pride. 24

print
Make sure you read the small print. 71

profile
You'd better keep a low profile. 47, 70

public
It's a job in the public eye. 25

pull
He tried to pull the wool over my eyes. 25, 54
I'll see if I can pull a few strings for you. 68
I'm not pulling my punches. 41
I'm only pulling your leg! 16
Pull your socks up. 20, 79
They pulled out all the stops to finish on time. 79
They pulled the plug on the project. 78
They pulled the rug from under my feet. 81
We need to pull something out of the hat now. 20
We ought to pull together. 6
Why are you pulling such a long face? 26

pulse
He's got his finger on the pulse of the business. 27

pump
I'm going to the gym to pump some iron. 38

punch
I'm not pulling my punches. 41
You must be as pleased as punch. 66

purpose
We were talking at cross purposes. 63

pussyfoot

Stop pussyfooting around. 19

put

Don't put all your eggs in one basket. 30, 74

Don't put the cart before the horse. 35

He put on a brave face. 16

He put the brakes on spending. 77

He put us through our paces. 35

I can't put my finger on it. 16, 27

I couldn't put the book down. 71

I need to put my life back together. 17

I'm going to put my foot down. 31

I put my head on the block for you. 74

I put two and two together. 40

I really put my foot in it. 16, 31, 62

I try to put a bit of money aside each month. 64

I was surprised, to put it mildly. 109

I wouldn't put money on it. 5

I'll put in a good word for you. 68

It's nice to put a face to a name. 26

Go home and put your feet up. 31

Ring home. It'll put your mind at rest. 39

She put a brave face on it. 26

They should put their house in order. 36

To put it in a nutshell, his work is just not good enough. 109

We had to put the dog to sleep. 76

We should put our heads together. 33

You can do it if you put your mind to it. 39

quantity

She's a bit of an unknown quantity. 67

question

It's out of the question. 48

It's the sixty-four thousand dollar question. 40

quick

He wants a quick word with you. 53, 113

quiet

He'll do anything for a quiet life. 70

race

It's a one-horse race. 35

It's a race against time. 9

rack

I've been racking my brains. 61

rag

It's like a red rag to a bull. 22, 66

rails

He went right off the rails. 4, 44, 69

rain

I'm as right as rain now. 58

rainy

I'm saving for a rainy day. 64

raise

That raised a few eyebrows. 25

range

They only buy top-of-the-range products. 110

ranks

They've broken ranks. 8

rat

I smell a rat. 14

It was like rats leaving a sinking ship. 6

razor

He's got a razor-sharp mind. 111

read

Don't read too much into it. 71

Make sure you read the small print. 71

She's very well read. 71

This is a good read. 71

You have to read between the lines. 71

real

He's in a real state. 69

It was a real eye-opener. 81

That's a real turn-up for the books. 81

reception

She gave me a frosty reception. 7, 43

recharge

I needed to recharge my batteries. 59

recognition

The place has changed out of all recognition. 52

record

I just want a chance to set the record straight. 109

We did it in record time. 9

recovery

She's well on the way to recovery. 58

red

I caught him red-handed. 22

I saw red. 22

I went as red as a beetroot. 22

I'm in the red. 22, 65

It was a complete red herring. 22

It's like a red rag to a bull. 22, 66

Let's paint the town red. 22

There's so much red tape. 22

They gave me the red carpet treatment. 22

Yesterday was a red-letter day for me. 22

refresh

Let me refresh your memory. 61

rein

We'll have to keep a tight rein on him. 35

I'll hand the reins of the business over to my son. 35

reinforce

We need to reinforce our position. 2

reject

We rejected it out of hand. 32

rest

A change is as good as a rest. 59

Put your mind at rest. 39

She's head and shoulders above the rest. 33, 57

rich

They're stinking rich. 65

ride

They're taking you for a ride. 54

right

He went right off the rails. 44

Her heart's in the right place. 34

I think we're on the right track now. 44

I'd give my right arm for that. 16

I'm as right as rain now. 58

If you play your cards right, you'll do well. 5

Nobody in their right mind would do it. 39

That should be right up your street. 80

The right hand doesn't know what the left hand is doing. 32

You took the words right out of my mouth. 48

ring

His name rings a bell. 61

rip

We were ripped off. 64

ripple

There was a ripple of laughter. 12

rise

He's one of the rising stars of the team. 79

I won't rise to the bait. 29

rivet

The story's absolutely riveting. 71

road

I spent a lot of time on the road. 23

I'm well on the road to recovery. 4

It's time to hit the road. 23

What'll happen a year down the road? 23

robbery

£50 – that's daylight robbery! 54

rock

Don't rock the boat. 6, 84

I hit rock bottom when I lost my job. 110

Prices have hit rock bottom. 111

The ground was rock hard. 111

rocks

Their marriage is on the rocks. 6, 73

rod

They ruled with a rod of iron. 38

roll

He's rolling in it. 65

If this goes wrong, heads will roll. 33

I want to start the ball rolling. 78

You'll just have to roll up your sleeves. 20

roof

Prices went through the roof. 10, 19

She nearly hit the roof. 19

room

There isn't enough room to swing a cat. 14, 19

ropes

I'll show you the ropes. 6, 84

I'm learning the ropes. 60

We're on the ropes. 41

rose

Life's not a bed of roses. 55

round

He drives me round the bend. 23

He's a square peg in a round hole. 80

I didn't complain about him, it was the other way round. 112

It's open all year round. 86

We're going round in circles. 23

row

We had a blazing row. 28

rub

Don't rub him up the wrong way. 19

rug

They pulled the rug from under my feet. 81

rule

As a rule of thumb, check everything twice. 27

He ruled with an iron fist. 38

That's the golden rule. 38

They ruled with a rod of iron. 38

run

He ran his eye over it. 25

I'm feeling run down. 58

Music runs in the family. 56

She ran out of patience. 49

She runs a tight ship. 6

They won't run with the ball. 41

He's running out of money. 1, 4, 44

rush

We were rushed off our feet. 31, 83

rusty

My French is a bit rusty. 60

rut

I'm in a rut. 4

saddle

I got saddled with it. 35

safe

Buy two to be on the safe side. 51, 74

I advise you to play safe. 74

Your money's as safe as houses. 36, 74

sailing

We're sailing close to the wind. 74

It was plain sailing after that. 55

salt

I'd take that with a pinch of salt. 30

She's the salt of the earth. 30, 67

same

I won't, if it's all the same to you. 86

We're all in the same boat. 6, 69, 75

We're not on the same wavelength. 53, 72, 63

sand

Don't bury your head in the sand. 16, 33, 70

save

I can't dance to save my life. 37

I'm saving for a rainy day. 64

It'll save 20 minutes. 1

Saved by the bell. 41

They want to save face. 26

savings

We had to dip into our savings. 64

say

You must be tired. If you want me to drive, just say the word. 113

The Prime Minister's speech was disappointing, to say the least. 109

It's easier said than done. 55

No sooner said than done. 77

She wouldn't say boo to a goose. 15

The party was a disaster – the noise, the complaints, to say nothing of the mess afterwards. 109

There's a lot to be said for working from home. 109

When all's said and done. 86

You can say that again. 48

schedule

Everything is on schedule. 10

score

What's the score? 41

scrape

You're scraping the bottom of the barrel. 57

scratch

I'm afraid your performance wasn't up to scratch. 57

She had to start from scratch. 78

scream

She screamed blue murder. 22

screen

I'm a fan of the silver screen. 38

screw

She's got her head screwed on. 33, 60

sea

I'm all at sea without her. 45

There are plenty more fish in the sea. 14, 29, 50

There's been a sea change lately. 45

We saw a sea of faces. 12

seat

I was flying by the seat of my pants. 74

You're in the hot seat now. 43

second

For a split second I thought you were serious. 77

I'm having second thoughts. 40

It's second nature to me now. 60

It's second to none. 40

You're lucky to get a second bite at the cherry. 24

see

He can't see past the end of his nose. 3

They saw the light. 3

I saw through him. 3

He finally saw reason. 3

I can't see the point. 3

I see what you mean. 3

I must be seeing things. 108

I saw red. 22

My car has seen better days. 57

Long time no see. 82

We don't see eye to eye. 15, 72

sell

He could buy and sell people like you and me. 65

They're selling like hot cakes. 30

sense

It's common sense. 60

separate

They've gone their separate ways. 73

serve

First come, first served. 40

set

He's very set in his ways. 112

I expect that set you back a bit. 64

I just want a chance to set the record straight. 109

I never set foot in there. 31

She hardly set the world on fire. 28

She's set her heart on a new BMW. 79

We have set our sights on a 10% increase. 2, 8, 79

seven

I'm all at sixes and sevens. 40

I was in seventh heaven. 40

shadow

It was her, without a shadow of a doubt. 51

shaker

He's one of the movers and shakers. 68

shape

Everything went pear-shaped. 30

Our plans are taking shape. 52

shark

They're just sharks. 29

sharp

Be here at eleven o'clock sharp. 82

He's got a razor-sharp mind. 111

shatter

It shattered my confidence. 17

sheep

I'm the black sheep of the family. 14, 21, 56

sheet

You look as white as a sheet. 21

ship

It was like rats leaving a sinking ship. 6

ship

She runs a tight ship. 6

shirt

He'd give you the shirt off his back. 20

shirty

Don't get shirty with me. 20

shock

I got the shock of my life when I saw her. 81

shoes

I wouldn't like to be in your shoes. 20

Who could fill her shoes? 20

shoestring

We did it on a shoestring. 20

shoot

He shot me down in flames. 28

He's shot himself in the foot. 62

Have a shot at it. 8

He was out of the room like a shot. 77

I call the shots here. 8, 68

short

He's on a short-list of three. 84

She's not short of a bob or two. 65

To cut a long story short, we decided to move house. 109

We're short of time. 1

short-cut

There's no short-cut to success. 4

short-sighted

That's a very short-sighted view. 3

shoulder

He's got a chip on his shoulder. 17

I need a shoulder to cry on. 72

She has to shoulder a lot of responsibility. 16

She's head and shoulders above the rest. 33, 57

show

Children are often show-offs. 67

I'll show you the ropes. 84

shower

They are a shower. 7

shy

Once bitten, twice shy. 40

sick

I was as sick as a parrot. 15

I'm sick to death of him. 37

side (see pages 226–227)

Buy two to be on the safe side. 74

I wouldn't like to get on the wrong side of him. 62

Just to be on the safe side. 51

Look on the bright side. 50

He's my cousin on my mother's side. 56

side-tracked

I got side-tracked. 4

sieve

She's got a memory like a sieve. 61

sight

At last – the end's in sight. 78

Don't lose sight of our aims. 3

I've set my sights on that job. 2, 8, 79

silly

Don't be silly! 47

silver

Every cloud has a silver lining. 38

He was born with a silver spoon in his mouth. 38

Who are the stars of the silver screen? 38

sing

It's not over till the fat lady sings. 78

sink (verb)

It's sink or swim now. 42, 45

It was like rats leaving a sinking ship. 6

My heart sank when I saw the price. 34, 45

sink (noun)

We took everything except the kitchen sink. 59

sinker

He swallowed it hook, line and sinker. 29

sit

I'm just going to sit tight until he comes. 47

You can't sit on the fence. 74

six

It knocked me for six. 40, 81

It's six of one and half a dozen of the other. 40, 75

I'm all at sixes and sevens. 40

skate

Get your skates on, we're late. 77

You're skating on thin ice. 74

skin

There's more than one way to skin a cat. 19

sky

The sky's the limit. 79

sleep

Don't lose any sleep over it. 47, 76

He'll sleep it off. 76

I couldn't sleep a wink. 76

I slept like a log. 76

Let's sleep on it. 70, 76

We had to put the dog to sleep. 76

sleeper

I'm a heavy sleeper. 76

I'm a light sleeper. 76

sleeve

He's got something up his sleeve. 5, 20, 81

Roll up your sleeves. 20

sliced

They think he's the best thing since sliced bread. 30

slip

It was a slip of the tongue. 62

Sorry, it slipped my mind. 39, 61

They slipped through the net. 29

slow

We're in the slow lane going nowhere. 23

slowcoach

Hurry up, you slowcoach. 67

small

He's a big fish in a small pond. 29

Make sure you read the small print. 71

They partied into the small hours. 82

smashing

She's a smashing person. 17

smell

I smell a rat. 14

smoke

She smokes like a chimney. 19

There's no smoke without fire. 28

snail

We drove at a snail's pace. 77

snake

He's a snake in the grass. 54

snap

She snapped at me. 17

sniff

£3,000 is not to be sniffed at. 109

soar

Prices soared during August. 10

sock

Pull your socks up. 20, 79

soft

The economy made a soft landing. 10

I've got a soft spot for her. 72

some

You win some, you lose some. 50

something (see pages 228–229)

He's got something on his mind. 39

He's got something up his sleeve. 5, 20, 81

I want something to get my teeth into. 24

We need to pull something out of the hat now. 20

somewhere

It got lost somewhere along the line. 44

son

Like father, like son. 56

soon

He'll tell us sooner or later. 82

No sooner said than done. 77

There you are – and not a minute too soon. 82

sore

You'll stick out like a sore thumb. 27, 75, 80

sorrows

He's drowning his sorrows. 42

sort

That should sort out the men from the boys. 55

sorts

I'm feeling a bit out of sorts. 58

soul

She's the life and soul of the party. 37, 67

sound

The baby's sound asleep. 111

sour

Their relationship turned sour. 72

spadework

They did all the spadework. 11

spanner

That threw a spanner in the works. 69

spare

Could you spare five minutes? 1

I was going spare. 49

sparks

The sparks fly when they argue. 28

sparrow

She eats like a sparrow. 15

spawn

They spawned several new companies. 29

speak

Actions speak louder than words. 113

Just speak off the cuff. 20

There were no problems, at least, nothing to speak of. 109

You should speak your mind. 47

spend

I went on a spending spree. 64

It's worth spending at least two days there. 1

spice

Variety is the spice of life. 30

spiral

Prices are in a downward spiral. 10

spirits

They're in high spirits. 66

spit

I was spitting blood. 66

She's the spitting image of her mother. 56, 75

splash

His book really made a splash. 12, 42

We splashed out on a bottle of champagne. 64

split

For a split second I thought you were serious. 77

I had a splitting headache. 58

spoon

He was born with a silver spoon in his mouth. 38

spot

I've got a soft spot for her. 72

It's an accident black spot. 21

spread

The news spread like wildfire. 77

spree

I went on a spending spree. 64

spring

Nothing springs to mind. 39

She's no spring chicken. 15

spur

We decided on the spur of the moment. 82

square

He's a square peg in a round hole. 80

It's back to square one, I'm afraid. 40, 78

suit

It suited me down to the ground. 80

stab

You stabbed me in the back. 8, 54

stabilise

The situation stabilised eventually. 10

stake

There's a lot at stake. 5, 74

stand

Get another job if you can't stand the pace. 84

I can't stand her. 73

I could do it standing on my head. 33

I'm standing in for Mr Smith. 84

If you want to do it, I'm not going to stand in your way. 112

You have to stand on your own two feet. 31

standstill

Everything is at a standstill. 69

star

He is one of the rising stars of the team. 79

stare

The answer is staring us in the face. 26

stark

He was standing in the road stark naked. 111

start

I want to start the ball rolling. 78

She had to start from scratch. 78

The team got off to a flying start. 77

starting blocks

We're still on the starting blocks. 9

state

He's in a real state. 69

steady

I'm looking for a steady job. 84

We're working at a steady pace. 9

steam

He's running out of steam. 4, 44

I'll get there under my own steam. 44

Sport is one way of letting off steam. 44

steel

He's got nerves of steel. 38

steer

I'd steer clear of her. 23

We will try to steer clear of the problems. 10

stem

Problems stem from lack of communication. 11

step

Step on it. We're late. 23

stew

We left him to stew in his own juice. 30

stick

I don't want to stick my neck out. 74

Stick to your guns. 8

You'll stick out like a sore thumb. 27, 75, 80

You've got the wrong end of the stick. 62, 63

sticky

We're on a sticky wicket. 41

still

Don't worry, it's still early days. 78

stink

They're stinking rich. 65

stone

He can't hear anything – he's stone deaf. 111

It's like getting blood out of a stone. 55

They'll leave no stone unturned to find him. 79

You can kill two birds with one stone. 15, 40

stop

He'll stop at nothing to get there. 79

stops (noun)
They pulled out all the stops to finish on time. 79
storm
He came storming into the room. 7
We'll weather the storm. 6
We're waiting for the storm to pass. 6
story
To cut a long story short, we decided to move house. 109
straight
I couldn't keep a straight face. 26
I got it straight from the horse's mouth. 35, 53
Can I just set the record straight? 109
I'll get straight to the point. 53
We're on the home straight now. 9, 36
straw
It's the straw that broke the camel's back. 14
That's the last straw. 49, 66
stream
There was a stream of people coming in. 12
street
That should be right up your street. 80
strength
The company went from strength to strength. 52
stress
I was really stressed out. 58
stride
He took it in his stride. 55
strike
We struck gold there. 38
strings
I'll see if I can pull a few strings for you. 68
struggle
It's an uphill struggle. 55
subject
Let's change the subject. 52
sudden
They stopped all of a sudden. 86
sum
It has been, to sum up, a wonderful year. 109
Sunday
Not in a month of Sundays. 82
surge
The crowd surged forward. 12
surprise
It took me by surprise. 81
surrounded
They were surrounded by rival companies. 2
swallow
You'll have to swallow your pride. 24
He swallowed it hook, line and sinker. 29
swamp
We were swamped by refugees. 12
swan
He's swanning around in his Mercedes. 15
sweep
They wanted to sweep it under the carpet. 70
sweet
He's got a sweet tooth. 24
swim
He's swimming against the tide. 42
It's sink or swim now. 45, 42

swing
There isn't enough room to swing a cat. 14, 19
swoop
His reputation was destroyed in one fell swoop. 15
tacks
Let's get down to brass tacks. 38
tail
He's like a dog with two tails. 66
I can't make head nor tail of it. 33, 63, 71
tailor
They'll tailor your holiday to your needs. 80
take off
The plan never took off. 10
take
Don't take anything for granted. 47
Don't take it at face value. 26
He couldn't take his eyes off her. 25
He said I could stay in his flat and I took him at his word. 113
He took it in his stride. 55
He took the plunge at last and asked her to marry him. 73
He took to the job like a duck to water. 80
He's taking one day at a time. 47
He's trying to take advantage of you. 54, 68
Her career has taken off. 4
I take after my father. 75
I take my hat off to him. 20
I'd take that with a pinch of salt. 30
I'll take my chances. 5
I'll take your word for it. 113
I'm taking a backseat now. 23
It takes two to tango. 40
It took a while to get going. 71
It took me by surprise. 81
No hurry – take your time. 77
Our plans are taking shape. 52
She took me under her wing. 15
You can take heart from the fact that everyone is on your side. 34
That'll take your mind off things. 39
They're taking you for a ride. 54
We take a tough line on punctuality. 68
We're taking on new staff. 84
We've taken a lot of flak. 2
Some people think they can take the law into their own hands. 32
You took the words right out of my mouth. 113
You'll have to take the bull by the horns. 47, 70
talk
He's talking through his hat. 20
It's like talking to a brick wall. 18, 49
Now you're talking! 48
She talks nineteen to the dozen. 53
We were talking at cross purposes. 63
tango
It takes two to tango. 40
tape
There's so much red tape. 22
target
You should set some targets. 2

taste

It left a bad taste in my mouth. 24

It's not my taste. 24

tea

It's not my cup of tea. 30, 80

tear

I was tearing my hair out. 49

teem

The square was teeming with people. 12

teeth

I want something to get my teeth into. 24

They're lying through their teeth. 54

We've got the bit between our teeth. 35

tell

I can't tell the difference between them. 75

I told him a few home truths. 36

Tell me about it! 48

There were five of us all told. 86

To tell you the truth, I'd rather not go. 109

You're telling me! 48

temper

He's got a fiery temper. 28

ten

They're ten a penny. 40

territory

It's uncharted territory for us. 6

test

Test the waters before deciding. 42

tether

I'm at the end of my tether. 49, 66

thereabouts

It starts at three or thereabouts. 82

thick

Blood is thicker than water. 56

They stayed together through thick and thin. 72

thin

He's a bit thin on top. 110

The walls are paper thin. 111

They stayed together through thick and thin. 72

You're skating on thin ice. 74

thing (see pages 230–231)

I don't know the first thing about it. 60

It's been one thing after another. 83

She knows a thing or two about cars. 60

It's the best thing since sliced bread. 30

think

He thinks the world of her. 73

To my way of thinking, every mistake is an opportunity for improvement. 112

You have to think on your feet. 31

You've got another think coming. 81

thinking (adjective)

Get your thinking cap on. 20

third

Third time lucky! 40, 50

thought

I'm having second thoughts. 40

That's food for thought. 30

The thought never crossed my mind. 39

thousand

It's the sixty-four thousand dollar question. 40

three

Two's company, three's a crowd. 40

thrill

You must be thrilled to bits. 66

throat

They're at each other's throats. 72

throw

Keep the good ideas. Don't throw the baby out with the bath water. 47

He's always throwing his weight around. 68

I was thrown in at the deep end. 42, 55

I wouldn't trust him as far as I can throw him. 54

That threw a spanner in the works. 69

They had to throw us a lifeline. 42

We had to throw in the towel. 41, 78

thumb

As a rule of thumb. 27

He's under her thumb. 27

I'm all fingers and thumbs. 27

It got the thumbs down. 27

We sat there twiddling our thumbs. 27, 83

We thumbed a lift. 27

You'll stick out like a sore thumb. 27, 75, 80

tide

A tide of refugees poured in. 12

He's swimming against the tide. 42

The tide is turning in our favour. 45

tie

I'm tied up till after lunch. 83

My hands are tied. 16

They finally tied the knot on Sunday. 56, 73

tight

I'm just going to sit tight until he comes. 47

We'll have to keep a tight rein on him. 35

We're in a tight corner. 69

tighten

We'll have to tighten our belts. 20, 64

tiles

We had a night on the tiles. 18

time

He's living on borrowed time. 58

He's taking one day at a time. 47

I go there from time to time. 82

It's a race against time. 9

It's cold for this time of year. 82

It's only a matter of time. 82

Long time no see. 82

No hurry – take your time. 77

The police arrived in the nick of time. 82

There's no time like the present. 82

They've got time on their hands. 32

Third time lucky! 40, 50

We had a whale of a time. 29, 59

We had the time of our lives. 59

We made very good time. 77

We'll be there in no time at all. 77, 82

We've run out of time. 1

I can make time for you. 1

I value my free time. 1

My time is precious. 1

We're short of time. 1

There's plenty of time. 1

You arrived just in time. 81
I'm just biding my time. 47

tip
It's on the tip of my tongue. 61
That's just the tip of the iceberg. 69

tit-bit
There are some interesting tit-bits in it. 71

toes
We dipped our toes in the water. 16

together
I need to put my life back together. 17
I put two and two together. 40

tomorrow
He spends money as if there was no tomorrow. 77
Tomorrow is another day. 50, 82

ton
She came down on me like a ton of bricks. 18

tongue
It was a slip of the tongue. 62
It's on the tip of my tongue. 61

too
There you are – and not a minute too soon. 82

tooth
He's got a sweet tooth. 24

top
He blew his top when he saw the damage. 110
He's a bit thin on top. 110
He's only 23 and he's at the top of the tree in his profession. 84
I can't give you an answer off the top of my head. 33, 110
I feel like everything's getting on top of me. 110
I really blew my top. 66
I want to do many things – top of the list is travel to the United States. 110
I'm feeling on top of the world. 110
It cost a bit over the top. 64
She was very late and on top of that she was extremely rude. 110
She worked her way to the top of her profession. 112
The company's got to change from top to bottom. 110
The way she dresses is over the top. 110
There's no space, we're living on top of each other the whole time. 110
They only buy top-of-the-range products. 110
They were shouting at the top of their voices. 110

toss
It's a toss-up between France and Italy. 5

touch
We need to touch base for a while. 41
It's touch and go. 51

tough
It's a tough nut to crack. 55
We take a tough line on punctuality. 68

towel
We had to throw in the towel. 41, 78

town
Let's paint the town red. 22

track
He's got a one-track mind. 40, 44
I like places off the beaten track. 59
I think we're on the right track now. 44
We're back on track now. 44

train
He's like an express train. 44

travel
It's good to travel light. 59

trawl
We trawled through the papers. 29

tread
I'm just treading water in this job. 42
It's a delicate area so tread carefully. 47
Tread carefully with him. 74

treatment
They gave me the red carpet treatment. 22

tree
He knows his family tree. 56
He's only 23 and he's at the top of the tree in his profession. 84
You're barking up the wrong tree. 62

trick
A glass of water should do the trick. 80

trickle
We had a trickle of customers. 12

tripe
That's a load of tripe! 71

trouble
He's just a trouble-maker. 67

trousers
She wears the trousers in that house. 20, 68

true
It's a dream come true. 76

trust
I wouldn't trust him an inch. 54
I wouldn't trust him as far as I can throw him. 54

truth
He was economical with the truth. 54
To tell you the truth, I didn't want to go anyway. 109

truths
I told him a few home truths. 36

tunnel
There's light at the end of the tunnel. 4, 50, 44

turbulence
There is a lot of turbulence in the market. 10

turn
He can turn his hand to anything. 32
He did me a good turn. 72
He's turned over a new leaf. 52, 71
The police turned a blind eye to it. 25, 70
The tide is turning in our favour. 45
Their relationship turned sour. 72
There's no turning back. 4
They've turned the corner now. 23

turn-up
It was a real turn-up for the books. 81

twice
Once bitten, twice shy. 40
Once or twice. 40

twiddle

We just sat there twiddling our thumbs. 27, 83

twist

Don't get your knickers in a twist. 20

OK, twist my arm. 68

She can twist him around her little finger. 27, 68

There's a great twist at the end. 71

You're twisting what I said. 63

two

He's so two-faced. 54

I put two and two together. 40

I'm in two minds about it. 29, 40

It takes two to tango. 40

She knows a thing or two about cars. 60

She's not short of a bob or two. 65

They're like two peas in a pod. 56

Two heads are better than one. 33, 40

Two's company, three's a crowd. 40

We killed two birds with one stone. 40

U-turn

They did a U-turn. 23

uncharted

It's uncharted territory for us. 6

under

He's under her thumb. 27

Why are you so hot under the collar? 66

I'm feeling under the weather. 58

They got me there under false pretences. 54

They pulled the rug from under my feet. 81

They went under in the recession. 42

unknown

She's a bit of an unknown quantity. 67

unputdownable

It's an unputdownable thriller. 71

unturned

They'll leave no stone unturned to find him. 79

up

He's going up in the world. 79

I'm a bit hard up at the moment. 65

I'm up to my eyes in work. 83

It's all up in the air. 51

She's an up and coming writer. 79

That should be right up your street. 80

The locals are up in arms about it. 66

We've had our ups and downs. 72

up-root

They can't up-root the entire workforce. 11

uphill

It's an uphill struggle. 55

upper

We got the upper hand in the end. 68

value

Don't take it at face value. 26

I value my free time. 1

voice

They were shouting at the top of their voices. 110

voter

They appeal to the floating voters. 45

wade

I waded through pages of it. 71

wait

I won't wait on you hand and foot. 31

We're waiting for the storm to pass. 6

walk

I felt as if I was walking on air. 66

wall

I'm banging my head against a brick wall. 18, 49

It's driving me up the wall. 49

It's like talking to a brick wall. 18, 49, 53

The writing's on the wall. 51

We've got our backs to the wall. 18

warm

They gave me a warm welcome. 7

I warmed to him straightaway. 7, 43

The party soon warmed up. 7

You look like death warmed up. 37

warpath

Be careful – the boss is on the warpath. 66

waste

What a waste of time. 1

watch

We sat there watching the world go by. 59

water

Blood is thicker than water. 56

Don't throw the baby out with the bath water. 47

He gave me a watered down version. 45

He took to it like a duck to water. 80

His story just doesn't hold water. 45

I shouldn't have gone. I felt like a fish out of water at the party. 14, 45, 80

I'm going on the trip, come hell or high water. 45

I'm just treading water in this job. 42

It's like water off a duck's back. 45

Now we're in deep water. 42

She spends money like water. 45

That joke landed him in hot water. 43, 45, 69

That's water under the bridge now. 45

They poured cold water on my plans. 43

We dipped our toes in the water. 16

We're just keeping our heads above water. 33, 42, 45

waters

Test the waters before deciding. 42

wave

She's on the crest of a wave. 42

There was a wave of protests. 45

He's making waves. 45

wavelength

We're not on the same wavelength. 53, 63, 72

way (see pages 238–239)

By the way, is it all right if I bring my friend? 112

Don't rub him up the wrong way. 19

He's very set in his ways. 112

I didn't complain about him, it was the other way round. 112

I was way off course with my guess. 112

I went out of my way to be nice to them. 112

I'll meet you halfway – £50? 112

If you want to do it, I'm not going to stand in your way. 112

No way! 48

Poets have a way with words. 112

She worked her way to the top of her profession. 112

She's in a bad way. 58
She's not in a good mood today, so keep out of her way. 112
She's well on the way to recovery. 58
Stay the night; that way we can take our time. 112
The course has been difficult but in a way I'll miss it when it's over. 112
The meetings paved the way for future investments. 112
There's more than one way to skin a cat. 19
They've gone their separate ways. 73
They've got a baby on the way. 112
To my way of thinking, every mistake is an opportunity for improvement. 112
We can start late or finish early, it's fine by me either way. 112
We learned the hard way. 55
We went our separate ways. 4
I can bluff my way in any situation. 5
Where there's a will, there's a way. 50
You can't have it both ways. 112
You've come a long way since you started the course. 112

wear
She wears the trousers in that house. 20, 68

weather
I'm feeling under the weather. 7, 58
We'll weather the storm. 6

weed
We need to weed out the poor workers. 11

weight
She's worth her weight in gold. 38, 57
That's a weight off my mind. 39
What he says carries a lot of weight. 68

welcome
They gave me a warm welcome. 7

well
She's very well read. 71
She's well on the way to recovery. 58
They're very well off. 65

wet
Don't be such a wet blanket. 67
He's a bit wet. 7
He's too wet to do it himself. 12

whale
We had a whale of a time. 29, 59**what**
I know what's what. 60

while
It took a while to get going. 71
Once in a while. 40

whisker
They caught the train by a whisker. 19
He thinks he's the cat's whiskers. 19

white
I want it in black and white. 21
It's a white elephant. 21
White collar workers earn more. 21
You look as white as a sheet. 21
You sometimes have to tell a little white lie. 21, 54

whole
It's a whole new ball game. 41, 75

wicket
We're on a sticky wicket. 41

wide
You're leaving yourself wide open to gossip. 111
It's late but I'm wide awake. 111
We'll have to cast our net wider. 29

wild
They sent me on a wild goose chase. 14, 62
Wild horses couldn't drag me in there. 35

wildfire
The news spread like wildfire. 77

will
Where there's a will, there's a way. 50

win
We're winning now. 9
You can't win them all. 50
You win some, you lose some. 5, 50

wind
Let's throw caution to the wind. 7
We're sailing close to the wind. 74

window
My plans all went out of the window. 18

wing
She took me under her wing. 15

wink
I couldn't sleep a wink. 76
I had forty winks. 76

wires
We got our wires crossed. 63

wits
I'm at my wits' end. 49
You've got to keep your wits about you. 47

wolf
That should keep the wolf from the door. 14

woman
He's a bit of an old woman. 67

wood
We must cut out all the dead wood. 11

wool
You can't pull the wool over my eyes. 25, 54

word (see pages 240–241)
Actions speak louder than words. 113
Don't breathe a word of this to anyone. 53
Don't put words into my mouth. 63
Famous last words! 113
He said I could stay in his flat and I took him at his word. 113
He wants a quick word with you. 53
He's not polite. He doesn't know the meaning of the word. 113
I can't tell you – it's too awful for words. 113
You can't believe a word he says. 54
I had a quick word with him after lunch. 113
I knew he was going to be difficult from the word go. 113
I'll put in a good word for you. 53, 68
I'll take your word for it. 113
I'm lost for words. 113
If you want me to drive you, just say the word. 113
In a word, no. 113
In other words, it's a waste of time. 113
It's secret so don't breathe a word to anyone. 113

SECTION 6

Answer Key

Introductory Unit

Task 1: 1 feeling a bit under the weather, 2 in the nick of time, 3 know (London) like the back of my hand, 4 pull a few strings for me, 5 get a word in edgeways, 6 the rat race, 7 follow in his footsteps, 8 cutting it a bit fine, 9 look on the bright side, 10 sweep this under the carpet

Task 2: 1g, 2c, 3d, 4h, 5f, 6b, 7a, 8e

Task 3: 1a literal, 2a non-literal, 3a literal, 4a non-literal, 5a literal, 6a non-literal

Unit 1

Ex 1: 1c, 2f, 3b, 4a, 5h, 6d, 7g, 8e

Ex 2: 1 spend, 2 save, 3 value, 4 waste, 5 ran out of, 6 spare, 7 afford, 8 precious, 9 waste, 10 short of, 11 plenty, 12 make

Ex 3: 1 spend, 2 afford/spare, 3 spare, 4 wasting, 5 save, 6 running out/short

Unit 2

Ex 1: 1 minefields, 2 captures, 3 Battle, 4 march, 5 casualties, 6 targets, targets, 7 flak, 8 bombard, 9 sights, 10 forces, 11 reinforcements, 12 surrounded

Ex 2: 1 gaining ground on, 2 give up without a fight, 3 reinforce, 4 surrounded, 5 joined forces, 6 bombarded

Ex 3: 1e, 2i, 3j, 4d, 5h, 6c, 7a, 8f, 9b, 10g

Ex 4: 1 gain, 2 set, 3 capture, 4 set, 5 give, 6 reinforce, 7 take, 8 join

Unit 3

Ex 1: 1 wide, 2 eye-opener, 3 Hindsight, 4 blinkers, 5 mud, 6 Short-sighted, 7 sight, 8 view

Ex 2: 1h, 2b, 3e, 4g, 5f, 6a, 7c, 8d

Ex 3: 1c, 2a, 3f, 4b, 5d, 6e

Ex 4: 1 as clear as mud, 2 very short-sighted view, 3 lose sight of, 4 from my point of view, 5 seen the light, 6 It's not very clear, 7 I see what you mean

Unit 4

Ex 1: 1 take off, 2 tunnel, 3 ruts, 4 track, 5 crossroads, 6 steam, 7 rails, 8 footsteps, 9 dead-end, 10 short-cut

Ex 2: 1a, 2b, 3e, 4f, 5c, 6g, 7d, 8h

Ex 3: 1c, 2a, 3d, 4f, 5b, 6e, 7h, 8g

Ex 4: 1 going nowhere fast, 2 he'll follow in his father's footsteps, 3 there's no turning back, 4 gone our separate ways, 5 He's well on the road to recovery, 6 light at the end of the tunnel, 7 no short-cut to success, 8 running out of steam, 9 taken off, 10 I'm coming or going

Unit 5

Ex 1: 1 hand, 2 toss, 3 odds, 4 deals, 5 jackpot, 6 stake, 7 bluff, hand, bluff, 8 chips

Ex 2: 1b, 2c, 3a, 4d, 5f, 6e

Ex 3: 1f, 2a, 3b, e, 4d, 5i, 6g, 7h, 8j, 9c

Ex 4: 1 dealt, 2 play, 3 put, 4 got, 5 show, 6 take

Unit 6

Ex 1: 1g, 2c, 3h, 4f, 5b, 6d, 7a, 8e

Ex 2: 1c, 2b, 3a, 4g, 5h, 6e, 7f, 8d

Ex 3: 1d, 2a, 3h, 4g, 5f, 6e, 7b, 8c

Ex 4: 1 all, 2 same, 3 uncharted, 4 pass, 5 rock, 6 ropes, 7 on, 8 bail

Unit 7

Ex 1: 1 breeze, 2 shower, 3 hazy, 4 frosty, 5 gloomy, 6 cloud over, 7 storm, 8 cool

Ex 2: 1 storming, 2 breezed, 3 weather, 4 cooled, 5 warm, 6 frosty, 7 warm, 8 gloomy, 9 wet, 10 shower

Ex 3: 1b, 2e, 3d, 4a, 5c

Ex 4: 1 cloud, 2 warmed up, 3 warmed, 4 hazy, 5 clouded, 6 wind, 7 brighten up

Ex 5: 1d, 2e, 3c, 4a, 5f, 6b

Unit 8

Ex 1: 1 sights, 2 command, 3 shots, 4 line, 5 ranks, 6 march, 7 crossfire, 8 stab
Ex 2: 1 marching, 2 fort, 3 gunning, 4 stick, 5 line, 6 stab, 7 guns, 8 shot/stab
Ex 3: 1 crossfire, 2 sights, 3 command, 4 shots, 5 head, 6 ranks, 7 back, 8 posts
Ex 4: 1 caught, 2 in, 3 gunning, 4 orders, 5 break, 6 set, 7 down, 8 hold, 9 shot/stab, 10 great, 11 stick, 12 call

Unit 9

Ex 1: 1 lap, 2 medal, 3 record, 4 baton, 5 straight, 6 pace, 7 hurdles
Ex 2: 1e, 2f, 3d, 4h, 5g, 6a, 7b, 8c
Ex 3: 1 race, 2 flying, 3 pace, 4 falling, 5 hurdle, 6 finishing, 7 winning, 8 record
Ex 4: 1 We got off to a flying start, 2 We're on the home straight, 3 It's a major hurdle, 4 You deserve a medal, 5 We're still on the starting blocks, 6 We fell at the first hurdle, 7 We're on the last lap
Ex 5: 1 at, 2 at, 3 in, 4 on, 5 up, 6 over, 7 on, 8 on, 9 against, 10 off

Unit 10

Ex 1: 1 nosedives, 2 plummets, 3 collision, 4 course, 5 free-fall, 6 turbulence
Ex 2: 1 soar, 2 collision, 3 course, 4 ground, 5 nosedive
a1, b5, c4, d2, e3
Ex 3: 1b, 2f, 3a, 4e, 5c, 6d
Ex 4: 1: d, b, f, a, c, e 2: g, i, h, j, l, k
Ex 5: 1 going through the roof, 2 going through the roof, 3 plummeting, 4 got off the ground, 5 back on course, 6 out of, 7 out of, 8 on

Unit 11

Ex 1: 1 glasshouse, 2 plough, 3 stem, 4 branches, 5 weeds, 6 crops, 7 dig, 8 dead wood, 9 root out, 10 bear, 11 flourish, 12 perennial
Ex 2: 1 dig, 2 stem, 3 ploughing, 4 weed, 5 cut back, 6 flourish, 7 branch, 8 bear
Ex 3: 1 dead wood, 2 off-shoot, 3 up-rooting, 4 crop, 5 cross-fertilisation, 6 perennial, 7 spadework, 8 glasshouses
Ex 4: 1d, 2f, 3a, 4b, 5g, 6c, 7h, 8e
Ex 5: 1 back, 2 out into, 3 into, 4 from, 5 out, 6 out

Unit 12

Ex 1: 1 pool, splash, 2 teeming, pouring, 3 drip, 4 flood, 5 streams, 6 trickles, 7 overflow, 8 tide, 9 surge, 10 ripples
Ex 2: teeming, overflowing, trickling, stream, floods/pours, sea, pours/floods, surge
Ex 3: 1 ripple, 2 tide, 3 splash, 4 wet, 5 flow, 6 pool, 7 drip, 8 dry up
Ex 4: 1 surge, 2 splash, 3 flow, 4 ripple, 5 stream/tide, 6 sea, 7 tide, 8 pour/flood

Unit 13

Unit 1: 1 wasting, 2 spent, 3 run, 4 spare, 5 save, 6 short
Unit 2: 1 fight, 2 forces, 3 marching, 4 minefield, 5 Keep, 6 flak
Unit 3: 1 see, 2 hindsight, 3 sight, 4 clear, 5 seen, 6 eyes
Unit 4: 1 rut, 2 nowhere, 3 footsteps, 4 taken, 5 back, 6 tunnel
Unit 5: 1 dealt, 2 cards, 3 take, 4 win, lose, 5 hand, 6 toss
Unit 6: 1 boat, 2 boat, 3 deck, 4 uncharted, 5 rats, 6 ropes
Unit 7: 1 warm/cool/frosty, 2 weather, 3 throw, 4 hazy, 5 cloud, 6 stormy
Unit 8: 1 command, 2 orders, 3 down, 4 fort, 5 crossfire, 6 sights
Unit 9: 1 hurdle, 2 record, 3 start, 4 pace, 5 race, 6 line
Unit 10: 1 off, 2 crash, 3 climbing, 4 ground, 5 roof, 6 nosedive
Unit 11: 1 bear, 2 ploughed, 3 cut, 4 weed, 5 dig, 6 root, wood
Unit 12: 1 poured, 2 stem, 3 pool, 4 dried, 5 overflowing, 6 sea

Unit 14

Ex 1: 1 bull, horns, 2 hind, 3 bonnet, 4 pants, 5 chase, 6 bees, 7 Straw, 8 sty, 9 swing
Ex 2: 1 bee, bonnet, 2 fish, sea, 3 cat, bag, 4 fish, water, 5 bull, horns, 6 ants, pants, 7 sheep, family, 8 cows, home
Ex 3: 1a, 2d, 3b, 4c, 5 goose, 6 donkey, 7 chicken, 8 horse, 9 wolf, 10 donkey, 11 camel, 12 donkey, 13 pig, 14 foxed
Ex 4: 1 cat, 2 bull, 3 goose, 4 cat, 5 donkey, 6 bee, 7 rat, 8 fish, 9 donkey, 10 wolf

Unit 15

Ex 1: 1 wings, 2 nest, 3 swoop, 4 peck, 5 flap, 6 Boo
Ex 2: 1e, 2d, 3b, 4a, 5f, 6c
Ex 3: 1 crow, 2 duck, 3 chicken, 4 hawk, 5 goose, 6 sparrow, 7 dodo, 8 parrot
Ex 4: 1d, 2g, 3k, 4f, 5b, 6a, 7h, 8n, 9m, 10i, 11l, 12e, 13j, 14c

Ex 5: 1 duck, 2 birds, 3 hawk, 4 wing,
5 chicken, 6 flap, 7 parrot, 8 goose, 9 crow,
10 swoop, 11 dodo, 12 parrot, 13 nest,
14 swan, 15 pecking, 16 nest

Unit 16

Ex 1: 1d, 2c, 3b, 4a, 5e
Ex 2: 1f, 2i, 3g, 4b, 5d, 6a, 7k, 8e, 9c, 10h,
11j, 12l
Ex 3: 1d, 2e, 3c, 4a, 5b
Ex 4: 1 neck, 2 foot, 3 chest, 4 finger,
5 shoulder, 6 elbow, 7 nosey, 8 cheeky,
9 arm, 10 an arm and a leg, 11 leg, 12 feet
Ex 5: 1 give, 2 put, 3 pulling, 4 put, 5 came,
6 gone, 7 cost, 8 finding, 9 buries, 10 get

Unit 17

Ex 1: 1 shattered, 2 Fragile, 3 smashed,
4 chip, 5 snapped, 6 crack, 7 handle,
8 crushed, 9 mend, 10 kid
Ex 2: 1e, 2c, 3f, 4a, 5b, 6h, 7g, 8d
Ex 3: 1b, 2h, 3e, 4j, 5a, 6f, 7i, 8d, 9g, 10c
Ex 4: 1 broke, 2 chip, 3 shattered,
4 treat, kid, 5 fragile, 6 broken, 7 pieces,
8 broke, 9 crack, 10 pieces

Unit 18

Ex 1: 1 chimney, 2 foundations, 3 roof,
4 ceiling, 5 Bricks, Cement, 6 doorstep,
7 tiles, 8 corridor
Ex 2: 1e, 2d, 3h, 4f, 5b, 6g, 7a, 8c
Ex 3: 1 door, 2 cement, 3 chimney, 4 roof,
5 closed doors, 6 wall, 7 window, 8 corridors,
9 brick wall
Ex 4: 1 foot, door, 2 banging, brick,
3 smokes, chimney, 4 night, tiles, 5 meeting,
closed, 6 talking, brick, 7 door, 8 ton,
9 corridors, 10 doors, 11 door, 12 window,
13 roof, 14 roof, 15 doorstep, 16 cement

Unit 19

Ex 1: 1 pigeon, 2 pussy, 3 claws, 4 fur, fur,
5 rub, fur, rub, 6 curious, 7 Bricks,
8 whiskers
Ex 2: 1a, 2b, 3f, 4g, 5c, 6h, 7e, 8d
Ex 3: 1 whisker, 2 cat, 3 catty, 4 fur,
5 whiskers, 6 claws
Ex 4: 1b, 2d, 3g, 4h, 5a, 6i, 7c, 8f, 9e, 10j
Ex 5: 1 dog, 2 pussyfooting around, 3 hell's,
4 catty, 5 away, the mice will play, 6 among,
7 bag, 8 whiskers

Unit 20

Ex 1: 1 gloves, 2 sleeves, 3 cap, 4 roll up,
5 belt, 6 tighten, 7 twist, 8 knickers
Ex 2: 1e, 2a, 3g, 4c, 5f, 6b, 7d, 8h
Ex 3: 1c, 2f, 3a, 4d, 5b, 6e
Ex 4: 1 coat, 2 belts, 3 sleeves, 4 shoes,
5 shirt, 6 socks, 7 trousers, 8 caps
Ex 5: 1 roll, 2 keep, 3 pull, 4 take, 5 give,
6 pull, 7 tighten, 8 fits, 9 talk, 10 be in

Unit 21

Ex 1: 1d, 2f, 3c, 4h, 5g, 6b, 7a, 8e
Ex 2: 1b, 2a, 3f, 4c, 5d, 6e
Ex 3: 1f, 2b, 3g, 4e, 5c, 6d, 7a, 8i, 9h, 10j
Ex 4: 1 lie, 2 spot, 3 sheep, 4 picture,
5 elephant, 6 market, 7 look, 8 economy

Unit 22

Ex 1: 1 red, 2 In English they are black and
blue. What about your language?
3 red, 4 red, 5 In English they are blue.
6 In English you get a black eye.
Ex 2: 1 blue, 2 blue, 3 red, 4 blue, 5 red,
6 red, 7 red, 8 red, 9 blue, 10 blue
Ex 3: 1 red, 2 blue, 3 blue, 4 red, 5 blue,
6 red, 7 red, 8 red
Ex 4: 1 red, 2 red, 3 blue, 4 red, 5 blue,
6 blue, 7 blue, 8 blue, 9 red, 10 red, 11 blue,
12 red

Unit 23

Ex 1: 1 overtake, 2 steer, 3 dead-end, 4 gear,
5 lanes, 6 collision, 7 crash, 8 backseat,
9 bend, 10 crossroads
Ex 2: 1b, 2g, 3e, 4c, 5j, 6f, 7h, 8a, 9i, 10d
Ex 3: 1h, 2b, 3e, 4j, 5c, 6g, 7f, 8d, 9i, 10a
Ex 4: 1b, 2d, 3c, 4a
Ex 5: 1 drive, 2 drive, 3 give, 4 go, 5 hit,
6 take, 7 go, 8 turn, 9 put, 10 steer

Unit 24

Ex 1: 1b, 2d, 3f, 4c, 5e, 6h, 7a, 8g
Ex 2: 1 I could eat a horse, 2 it's not my
taste, 3 go down well, 4 a sweet tooth, 5 bit
my head off, 6 eat his words, 7 making a
meal of it, 8 had my fill
Ex 3: 1e, 2b, 3a, 4f, 5h, 6c, 7d, 8g
Ex 4: 1 chew, 2 bite, 3 eat, 4 Swallow,
5 teeth, 6 taste, 7 bit, 8 down

Unit 25

Ex 1: 1 bargain, 2 blink, 3 peel, 4 blind,
5 eyebrows, 6 eyelids
Ex 2: 1g, 2d, 3a, 4e, 5b, 6h, 7f, 8c,
9 up to my eyes in work, 10 see eye to eye,

11 pull the wool over my eyes, 12 need eyes in the back of my head
Ex 3: 1h, 2c, 3a, 4i, 5d, 6b, 7g, 8f, 9e
Ex 4: 1 bat, 2 turn, 3 need, 4 run, 5 see, 6 keep, 7 keep, 8 meets, 9 in, 10 up, 11 with, 12 to, 13 to, 14 on

Unit 26

Ex 2: 1 the fact, 2 the music, 3 a full meal, 4 work, 5 the consequences, 6 lose, 7 keep, 8 got, 9 putting, 10 put, 11 save
Ex 3: 1b, 2d, 3h, 4a, 5f, 6e, 7c, 8g
Ex 4: 1h, 2b, 3f, 4a, 5g, 6d, 7c, 8e

Unit 27

Ex 1: 1h, 2e, 3a, 4f, 5g, 6b, 7i, 8c, 9d
Ex 2: 1 finger, 2 thumb, 3 finger, 4 fingers, 5 thumbs, 6 finger, 7 thumb, 8 thumbs, 9 thumb, 10 finger
Ex 3: 1f, 2c, 3d, 4g, 5e, 6a, 7h, 8b
Ex 4: 1 stick, 2 twist, 3 pull, 4 put, 5 count, 6 keep, 7 give, 8 twiddle, 9 thumb, 10 get

Unit 28

Ex 1: 1 fuel, 2 blaze, 3 row, 4 ambition, 5 baptism, 6 temper, 7 sparks, 8 flames
Ex 2: 1 burning, 2 fire, 3 blazing, 4 fiery, 5 heated, 6 fire, 7 fire, 8 smoke, 9 flames, 10 sparks
Ex 3: 1a, 2d, 3e, 4b, 5g, 6f, 7c
Ex 4: 1 set, 2 have, 3 play, 4 get, 5 add, 6 fire, 7 go, 8 burn

Unit 29

Ex 1: fish, fishing line, net, line, hook, bait, cod, haddock, rise to the bait, mackerel, trawl, cast nets, trawlers, fresh-water fishing, angling, rod and line, cast, salmon, up river, down river, spawn, tiddlers
Ex 2: 1h, 2f, 3g, 4b, 5a, 6j, 7d, 8c, 9i, 10e
Ex 3: 1b, 2c, 3e, 4d, 5a, 6f
Ex 4: 1c, 2d, 3b, 4e, 5a
Ex 5: 1 landed, contract, 2 plenty, sea, 3 rise, bait, 4 let, hook, 5 cast, wider, 6 whale, time

Unit 30

Ex 1: 1 couch, 2 sliced, 3 stew, 4 icing, 5 spices, 6 variety, 7 pinch, 8 pickle
Ex 2: 1d, 2b, 3h, 4a, 5j, 6g, 7c, 8i, 9e, 10f
Ex 3: 1e, 2c, 3b, 4f, 5a, 6d
Ex 4: 1d, 2c, 3a, 4b
Ex 5: 1 juice, 2 salt, 3 bread, 4 life, 5 cakes, 6 face, 7 cake, 8 earth, 9 cucumber, 10 tea

Unit 31

Ex 1: 1 feet, 2 feet, 3 feet, 4 feet, 5 foot, 6 foot, 7 foot, 8 foot, 9 feet, 10 foot
Ex 2: 1 think on your feet, 2 dragging their feet, 3 stand on your own two feet, 4 didn't put a foot wrong, 5 put my foot down, 6 foot the bill
Ex 3: 1d, 2b, 3a, 4c, 5g, 6e, 7f, 8h
Ex 4: 1 on, 2 foot, 3 your, 4 dead, 5 off, 6 in, 7 cold, 8 wrong, 9 set, 10 put

Unit 32

Ex 1: 1 changed hands, 2 I've got my hands full, 3 out of hand, 4 things get out of hand, 5 time on my hands, 6 get my hands on, 7 living from hand to mouth, 8 had a big hand
Ex 2: 1 give, 2 count, 3 turn, 4 fell, 5 take, 6 hand, 7 know, 8 keep
Ex 3: 1 hand, 2 hand, 3 hands, 4 hands, 5 hand, 6 hands, 7 hands, 8 hands, 9 hand, 10 hand

Unit 33

Ex 1: 1 examines, 2 block, 3 bury, 4 roll, 5 tail, 6 screw
Ex 2: 1f, 2a, 3h, 4d, 5e, 6g, 7c, 8b
Ex 3: 1 put, 2 keep, 3 bury, 4 examined/examining, 5 goes, 6 laughed, 7 roll, 8 screwed
Ex 4: 1 I could do it standing on my head, 2 He's got his head screwed on, 3 Don't bury your head in the sand, 4 It went right over my head/I couldn't make head nor tail of it, 5 We're keeping our heads above water, 6 You need your head examined/ examining
Ex 5: 1 above, 2 to, 3 of, 4 above, 5 in, 6 over, 7 on, 8 off, 9 off, 10 on

Unit 34

Ex 2: 1 sank, 2 lose, 3 set, 4 take, 5 have, 6 break
Ex 3: 1b, 2g, 3h, 4a, 5c, 6f, 7i, 8d, 9j, 10e
Ex 4: 1 by, 2 in, 3 of, 4 in, 5 after, 6 of, 7 to, 8 in

Unit 35

Ex 1: 1 cart, 2 hooves, 3 reins, 4 bit, 5 hurdles, 6 saddle
Ex 2: 1b, 2c, 3g, 4f, 5a (putting...), 6e, 7d, 8h
Ex 3: 1 one, 2 dead, 3 high, 4 dark, 5 Wild, 6 wrong
Ex 4: 1c, 2d, 3b, 4e, 5a
Ex 5: 1 on, 2 between, 3 for, 4 before, 5 on, 6 from, 7 with, 8 at, 9 through, 10 on

Unit 36

Ex 1: 1b, 2f, 3g, 4d, 5c, 6h, 7e, 8a
Ex 2: 1 home, 2 house, 3 house, 4 home,
5 home, 6 home, 7 home, 8 in-house,
9 house, 10 houses
Ex 3: 1c, 2a, 3f, 4e, 5b, 6h, 7d, 8g
Ex 4: 1 fire, 2 home, 3 truths, 4 order,
5 home, 6 home, 7 down, 8 about, 9 home,
10 straight

Unit 37

Ex 1: 1 kiss, 2 lease, 3 soul, 4 fate, 5 misery,
6 dice, 7 warm up
Ex 2: a death, b life, c life, d life, e death,
f life, g death, h death, i death, j life
1h, 2a, 3c, 4e, 5g, 6d, 7i, 8b, 9j, 10f
Ex 3: 1 death, 2 life, 3 death, 4 life, 5 life,
6 death
Ex 4: 1 You look like death warmed up,
2 You're dicing with death, 3 She can't sing to
save her life, 4 It's given me a new lease of
life
Ex 5: 1 fate, 2 warmed, 3 save, 4 make,
5 soul, 6 door, 7 life, 8 kiss, 9 catch,
10 frightened

Unit 38

Ex 1: 1b, 2i, 3f, 4e, 5g, 6c, 7a, 8d, 9h
Ex 2: 1a, 2b
Ex 3: a iron, b brass, c steel, d iron, e iron,
f lead, g brass, h brass
1c, 2a, 3e, 4b, 5h, 6f, 7g, 8d
Ex 4: 1 gold, 2 golden, 3 silver, 4 golden,
5 rod, 6 iron, 7 brass, 8 brass, 9 steel,
10 golden

Unit 39

Ex 1: 1d, 2b, 3a, 4e, 5g, 6f, 7h, 8c
Ex 2: 1a, 2d, 3b, 4c
Ex 3: 1c, 2g, 3j, 4h, 5a, 6d, 7f, 8b, 9e, 10i
Ex 4: 1 slipped my mind, 2 put your mind to,
3 not in your right mind, 4 make up your
mind, 5 give someone a piece of your mind,
6 have something on your mind, 7 of, 8 off,
9 out, 10 about, 11 at, 12 in, 13 on, 14 of,
15 in, 16 off, 17 to, 18 up

Unit 40

Ex 1: a three's, b one, c one, d two, one,
e two, f two, g two, h first, i six, j twice
1f, 2d, 3a, 4e, 5b, 6h, 7j, 8i, 9c, 10g
Ex 2: 1 million, 2 Thousands, 3 million,
4 thousand
Ex 3: 1f, 2a, 3g, 4b, 5i, 6j, 7e, 8c, 9d, 10h
Ex 4: 1 once in a lifetime, 2 once and for all,
3 once or twice, 4 once is enough, 5 once in a
blue moon, 6 once in a while
Ex 5: 1 one, 2 two, two, 3 Two, three,
4 First, first, 5 Once, twice, 6 sixes, sevens,
7 six, 8 ten, 9 nine, 10 two

Unit 41

Ex 1: 1 belt, 2 punches, 3 ropes, 4 bell,
5 towel
Ex 2: 1b, 2c (backed ...), 3f, 4e, 5h, 6g, 7a,
8i, 9j, 10d
Ex 3: 1e, 2b, 3f, 4a (dropped ...), 5c, 6d
Ex 4: 1 court, 2 goalposts, 3 towel, 4 whole,
5 par, 6 base, 7 neck, 8 horses, 9 pull, 10 bell

Unit 42

Ex 1: 1 sank, 2 tide, 3 deep, depth, 4 crest,
5 tread, drown, 6 sorrows
Ex 2: 1e, 2g, 3a, 4c, 5b, 6d, 7h, 8f
Ex 3: 1 make, 2 drowned out, 3 throw,
4 test, 5 sink, swim, 6 dive, 7 treading
Ex 4: 1 end, 2 water, 3 lifeline, 4 sink, 5 tide,
6 water, 7 depth, 8 drown, 9 make, 10 wave

Unit 43

Ex 1: a feet, b left, c lost, d reception,
e blood, f cucumber, g light, h water, i out,
j cool, 1i, 2g, 3j, 4h, 5e, 6b, 7f, 8d, 9c, 10a
Ex 2: 1b, 2f, 3a, 4i, 5e, 6j, 7g, 8c, 9d, 10h
Ex 3: 1 cool, 2 lukewarm, 3 hot, 4 cold,
5 cold, 6 hot, 7 hot, 8 cold

Unit 44

Ex 1: 1 railway tracks, rails, tunnels,
derailed, off the rails, railway line, station,
buffers, hits the buffers, steam trains, diesel
or electric, express trains
Ex 2: a tunnel, b track, c steam, d buffers,
e steam, f rails, g track, h steam, i track,
j express 1d, 2c, 3i, 4a, 5e, 6f, 7b, 8h, 9g, 10j
Ex 3: 1b, 2c, 3a, 4d
Ex 4: 1 out, 2 off, 3 on, 4 of, 5 at, 6 off,
7 under, 8 along, 9 down, 10 on

Unit 45

Ex 1: 1e, 2g, 3d, 4h, 5a, 6c, 7f, 8b, 9 water
under the bridge, 10 keeping our heads above
water, 11 spend money like water, 12 land
him in hot water, 13 like water off a duck's
back, 14 watered down, 15 doesn't hold
water, 16 like a fish out of water
Ex 2: 1 floated the idea, 2 floating voters,
3 sink or swim, 4 my heart sank
Ex 3: 1g, 2f, 3d, 4h, 5a, 6b, 7e, 8c
Ex 4: 1 in, 2 at, 3 off, 4 in, 5 under, 6 above,
7 out, 8 of

Unit 46

Unit 14: 1 cat, 2 hind, 3 bull, 4 mouth,
5 years, 6 sea

Unit 15: 1 crow, 2 hawk, 3 nest, 4 stone,
5 wing, 6 back

Unit 16: 1 arm, 2 hands, 3 legs, 4 finger,
5 leg, 6 back

Unit 17: 1 pieces, 2 home, 3 up, 4 lives,
5 fragile, 6 mend

Unit 18: 1 back, 2 brick, 3 roof, 4 door,
5 chimney, 6 wall

Unit 19: 1 hell's, 2 Stop, 3 pigeons, 4 wrong,
5 bag, 6 killed

Unit 20: 1 trousers, 2 pull, 3 tighten,
4 shoes, 5 hat, 6 sleeve

Unit 21: 1 market, 2 lie, 3 sheet, 4 eye,
5 black, 6 collar

Unit 22: 1 red, 2 face, 3 blue, 4 bolt, 5 moon,
6 rag

Unit 23: 1 bend, 2 circles, 3 crossroads,
4 brakes, 5 fast, 6 clear

Unit 24: 1 words, 2 sweet, 3 swallow,
4 chew, 5 taste, 6 horse

Unit 25: 1 to, 2 meets, 3 catch, 4 head,
5 turn, 6 keep

Unit 26: 1 brave, 2 to, 3 value, 4 flat,
5 staring, 6 blue

Unit 27: 1 pull, 2 crossed, 3 thumbs, 4 at,
5 lifts, 6 up/down

Unit 28: 1 smoke, 2 baptism, 3 smoke,
4 row, 5 burn, 6 fire

Unit 29: 1 line, 2 job, 3 mind, 4 hook,
5 through, 6 sea

Unit 30: 1 bread, 2 juice, 3 face, 4 spice,
5 salt, 6 cool

Unit 31: 1 put, 2 find, 3 in, 4 two, 5 cold,
6 rushed

Unit 32: 1 out, 2 law, 3 give, 4 out, 5 on,
6 turn

Unit 33: 1 better, 2 top, 3 block, 4 laughed,
5 tail, 6 clouds

Unit 34: 1 right, 2 say, 3 change, 4 hearts,
5 in, 6 sank

Unit 35: 1 straight, 2 cart, 3 tight, 4 saddled,
5 teeth, 6 dead

Unit 36: 1 at, 2 truths, 3 straight, 4 no-one,
5 fire, 6 houses

Unit 37: 1 bored, 2 up, 3 fate, 4 lease,
5 soul, 6 dicing

Unit 38: 1 cloud, 2 heart, 3 weight, 4 steel,
5 handshake, 6 good

Unit 39: 1 two, 2 slipped, 3 piece, 4 on,
5 right, 6 business

Unit 40: 1 sixes, 2 Third, 3 one, 4 two,
5 dozen, 6 mind

Unit 41: 1 goalposts, 2 ball, 3 touch, 4 level,
5 horse, 6 course

Unit 42: 1 deep, 2 above, 3 sink, 4 under,
5 out, 6 water

Unit 43: 1 lost, 2 day, 3 heat, 4 feet, 5 to,
6 collar

Unit 44: 1 tunnel, 2 under, 3 track, 4 rails,
5 steam, 6 ran

Unit 45: 1 like, 2 fish, 3 head, 4 depth,
5 bridge, 6 go

Unit 47

Ex 1: a speak, b make, c keep, d take,
e bide, f sit, g tread, h take, i keep, j go
1b, 2c, 3d, 4f, e, 5j, 6h, 7a, 8g, 9i

Ex 2: 1g, 2e, 3b, 4d, 5h, 6a, 7c, 8f

Ex 3: 1 Take one day at a time, 2 Go for it,
3 Don't overdo it, 4 Take the bull by the
horns, 5 Sit tight, 6 Don't lose any sleep over
it, 7 Don't take anything for granted, 8 Keep
your wits about you

Unit 48

Ex 1: a joking, b contrary, c dead, d No,
e question, f taken
1f, 2d, 3e, 4c, 5b, 6a

Ex 2: a enough, b Tell, c talking, d mouth,
e me, f nail, g again 1c, 2b, f, 3a, 4e, 5g, 6d

Ex 3: 1 over, 2 must, 3 out, 4 way, 5 head,
6 enough, 7 me, 8 that, 9 now, 10 tell

Unit 49

Ex 1: 1 insult, 2 patience, 3 wits, 4 bend,
5 tether, 6 distractions, 7 injury, 8 tear,
9 bang, 10 straw

Ex 2: a end, b wits, c nerves, d nose,
e insult, f straw 1c, 2a, 3e, 4d, 5f, 6b

Ex 3: 1 myself, 2 hair, 3 bend, 4 running,
5 brick, 6 spare, 7 distraction, banging,
8 wall

Ex 4: 1 driving, 2 getting, 3 kicked, 4 driving,
5 banging, 6 going, 7 tearing, 8 talking,
9 gets, 10 running

Unit 50

Ex 1: a bright, b fish, c world, d another,
e win, f better, g light, h life
1b, 2d, 3g, 4 life, all, 5 fish, end, 6 side, only

Ex 2: a You win some, you lose some,
b You've got nothing to lose, c Where there's
a will there's a way, d His bark is worse than
his bite 1b, 2d, 3a, 4c

Ex 3: 1a, 2b, 3d, 4e, 5c

Ex 4: 1 tunnel, 2 world, 3 bright, 4 know,
5 time, 6 crossed, 7 get, 8 win, lose,
9 nothing, 10 bark, bite, 11 No, 12 win

Unit 51

Ex 1: 1c, 2a, 3e, 4f, 5b, 6d
Ex 2: 1c, 2d, 3a, 4b
Ex 3: 1d, 2c, 3b, 4a
Ex 4: 1 Just to be on the safe side, 2 It's anyone's guess, 3 It's all up in the air, 4 Without a shadow of a doubt, 5 Pigs might fly, 6 It's touch and go, 7 I can feel it in my bones, 8 Your guess is as good as mine, 9 The writing's on the wall, 10 I'll give her the benefit of the doubt

Unit 52

Ex 1: 1 horizon, 2 leopard, spots, 3 recognition, 4 leaf, 5 tune, 6 strength
Ex 2: 1 mind, 2 plan, 3 hands, 4 subject, 5 places, 6 ways, 7 tune, 8 heart, 9 direction, 10 recognition
Ex 3: 1e, 2b (going ...), 3c, 4f, 5a (turned ...), 6d
Ex 4: 1 He's turned over a new leaf, 2 She's a breath of fresh air, 3 I want to make a clean break, 4 It's changed out of all recognition, 5 A leopard can't change its spots, 6 Could you change the subject, 7 The newsagent has changed hands, 8 The holiday is taking shape

Unit 53

Ex 1: 1 hind, 2 wavelength, 3 bush, 4 beat, 5 Bricks, 6 dozen, 7 grapevine, 8 gab
Ex 2: 1h, 2f, 3a, 4i, 5b, 6c, 7g, 8d, 9j, 10e
Ex 3: 1a, 2d, 3e, 4b, 5g, 6f, 7h, 8c
Ex 4: 1 She talks nineteen to the dozen, 2 We're on the same wavelength, 3 Get it off your chest, 4 It's like talking to a brick wall, 5 I'll keep you posted, 6 You can't get a word in edgeways, 7 It's just between you and me, 8 I got it from the horse's mouth
Ex 5: 1 bush, 2 edgeways, 3 wall, 4 wavelength, 5 mouth, 6 donkey, 7 chest, 8 gift, 9 me, 10 heard

Unit 54

Ex 1: 1 wool, 2 inch, 3 stab, 4 snake, 5 pretence, 6 robbery, 7 path, 8 fiddle
Ex 2: 1d, 2f, 3a, 4h, 5c, 6b, 7g, 8e
Ex 3: 1e, 2a, 3f, 4b, 5c, 6g, 7h, 8d
Ex 4: 1 through, 2 up, 3 over, 4 under, 5 behind, 6 for, 7 in, 8 of, 9 with, 10 on

Unit 55

Ex 1: 1 stride, 2 nut, 3 tough, chew, 4 baptism, 5 needle, 6 pie, 7 haystacks, 8 bites, 9 crack
Ex 2: 1e, 2c, 3d (in his stride), 4b, 5a, f

Ex 3: a uphill, b said, c heavy, d hard, e boys, f chew, g work, h deep, i needle, j depth, k bed, l blood, m nut, n baptism
1i, 2n, 3m, 4a, c, 5g, 6f
Ex 4: 1 I could do it with my eyes closed, 2 I've bitten off more than I can chew, 3 It's easier said than done, 4 It's plain sailing, 5 She's taken it in her stride, 6 It's like trying to get blood out of a stone, 7 nut, 8 fire, 9 needle, 10 way, 11 end, 12 roses, 13 stride, 14 struggle

Unit 56

Ex 1: 1 blood, 2 pod, 3 chalk, 4 spitting, 5 flesh, 6 knot
Ex 2: 1g, 2a, 3d, 4b, 5h, 6c, 7e, 8f
Ex 3: 1 image, 2 footsteps, 3 homes, 4 side, 5 tree, 6 family, 7 relative, 8 cheese
Ex 4: 1 long-lost relative, 2 black sheep of the family, 3 like two peas in a pod, 4 a broken home, 5 blood is thicker than water, 6 the spitting image of his mother/father
Ex 5: 1 family, 2 family, 3 family, 4 son, 5 blood, 6 dog, 7 pod, 8 water, 9 cheese, 10 footsteps

Unit 57

Ex 1: 1 par, 2 barrel, 3 scratch, 4 miles, 5 scrape
Ex 2: a league, b condition, c head, d days, e home, f miles, g world, h legs, i gold, j par
1h, d, 2c, a (league of his own), 3f, 4j, 5e, 6i (her weight in gold), 7b, g
Ex 3: 1a, 2e, 3d, 4b, 5f, 6c
Ex 4: 1 about, 2 barrel, 3 shoulders, 4 gold, 5 cracked, 6 scratch, 7 own, 8 desired, 9 last, 10 better, 11 This car's in mint condition, 12 It's seen better days, 13 It's miles better, 14 Your work is not up to scratch

Unit 58

Ex 1: 1 complain, 2 recovery, 3 split, 4 fiddle, 5 lease
Ex 2: 1i, g, 2a, 3b, 4h, 5e, 6d, f, c
Ex 3: a sorts, b killing, c splitting, d down, e run, f out, g going, h colour, i bad, j weather
1f, 2i, 3c, 4b, 5g, 6a, h
Ex 4: 1 weather, 2 fiddle, 3 feet, 4 way, 5 down, 6 headache, 7 complain, 8 colour, 9 picture, 10 lease, 11 rain, 12 clean

Unit 59

Ex 1: 1c, 2d, 3b, 4a
Ex 2: 1g, 2a, 3d, 4h, 5f, 6c, 7b, 8e

Ex 3: 1a, 2c, 3h, 4f, 5d, 6e, 7g, 8b
Ex 4: 1 change, rest, 2 away, all, 3 no, home,
4 whale, time, 5 just, doctor, 6 time, lives

Unit 60

Ex 1: 1 nature, 2 clues, 3 ropes, 4 screwed,
5 rusty, 6 pick, pick, 7 brains
Ex 2: 1b, 2c, 3a, 4d, 5e, 6h, 7i, 8f, 9j, 10g
Ex 3: a head, b hand, c what, d clue, e ropes,
f hang, g end, h knowledge
1c, 2b, 3d, 4f, 5e, 6a, 7h, 8g
Ex 4: 1 two, 2 get, 3 hand, 4 about, 5 a,
6 heard, 7 my, 8 ropes, 9 on, 10 second

Unit 61

Ex 1: 1 tip, 2 blank, 3 dim, 4 jog, 5 sieve,
6 slip
Ex 2: 1g, 2b, 3d, 4c, 5f, 6a, 7h, 8e, 9i
Ex 3: 1a, 2c, 3f, 4b, 5h, 6e, 7d, 8g
Ex 4: 1 mind, 2 memory, 3 heart, 4 bell,
5 mind, 6 memory, 7 sieve, 8 brains,
9 tongue, 10 yesterday

Unit 62

Ex 1: 1 slip, 2 goose, 3 chew, 4 barking,
5 tongue
Ex 2: 1c (missed ...), 2g (barking ...), 3d,
4a (got my ...), 5h (taken our ...), 6e (put my
...), 7f (shot myself ...), 8b (fall flat on our
faces)
Ex 3: 1c, 2e, 3d, 4b, 5f, 6a
Ex 4: 1 I've put my foot in it, 2 I've bitten off
more than I can chew, 3 I've been on a wild
goose chase, 4 I got my fingers burnt,
5 miss, 6 get your, 7 bitten, 8 barking, 9 got,
10 fall, 11 make, 12 make, 13 put, 14 take

Unit 63

Ex 1: 1 head or tail, 2 stick, 3 wires,
4 purpose
Ex 2: 1f, 2a, 3d, 4b (twisting what I said),
5e, 6c
Ex 3: 1b, 2a, 3d, 4c (Note that a and b are
very close in meaning.)
Ex 4: 1f, 2d, 3c, 4b, 5a, 6e
Ex 5: 1 wavelength, 2 stick, 3 purposes,
4 head, 5 tail, 6 penny, 7 Greek, 8 wires,
9 depth, 10 point, 11 lost, 12 add

Unit 64

Ex 1: 1 knock off, 2 tighten, 3 splash, 4 rip
off, 5 set back, 6 pick it up
Ex 2: 1 a bit over the top, 2 set him back a
bit, 3 picked up, 4 pay through the nose,
5 dirt cheap, 6 an arm and a leg,

7 ripped off, 8 knocked £45 off
Ex 3: 1 tighten, 2 go, 3 splash out, 4 break,
5 go on, 6 dip into, 7 put, 8 save
Ex 4: 1 go, 2 spree, 3 arm, leg, 4 break,
5 cheap, 6 out, 7 pick, 8 into, 9 rainy,
10 tighten, 11 aside, 12 nose, 13 bit, 14 back

Unit 65

Ex 1: 1 loaded, 2 lap, 3 stinks, 4 fortune
Ex 2: A: a, d, g, h, B: b, c, e, f
1f, 2e, 3b, 4a, 5c, 6g, 7d, 8h
Ex 3: 1a, 2c, 3d, 4j, 5i, 6h, 7g, 8f, 9e, 10b
Ex 4: 1 from, to, 2 without, to, 3 in, of, 4 on,
5 up, 6 by on, 7 off, 8 in, 9 of, 10 in

Unit 66

Ex 1: 1 moon, 2 air, 3 bits, 4 world, 5 tails,
6 spirits, 7 cloud, 8 punch
Ex 2: a blow, b fly, c give, d spit, e make
1a (my top), 2d, 3e, 4b, c (a piece of my mind)
Ex 3: a rag, b straw, c collar, d arms,
e tether, f warpath, 1f, 2a, 3c, 4d, 5b, 6e
Ex 4: 1 at, of, 2 under, 3 on, 4 in, 5 to, 6 off,
7 on, 8 to, 9 over, 10 on, 11 Everyone's up in
arms about it, 12 That's the last straw, 13 It
makes my blood boil, 14 I'm going to give him
a piece of my mind, 15 I'm as pleased as
punch
Ex 5: 1 collar, 2 rag, 3 boil, 4 thrilled,
5 tether, 6 handle

Unit 67

Ex 1: 1 blanket, 2 bachelor, 3 quantity,
4 confirm, 5 coach, 6 cannon, 7 soul,
8 Jekyll and Hyde
Ex 2: 1g, 2b, 3e, 4f, 5a, 6c, 7d, 8h
Ex 3: 1f, 2c, 3g, 4e, 5h, 6d, 7b, 8a
Ex 4: 1 a backseat driver, 2 a wet blanket,
3 a nosey parker, 4 someone who's a bit of an
old woman, 5 a show-off, 6 a confirmed
bachelor, 7 a slowcoach
Ex 5: 1 a show-off, 2 a backseat driver,
3 a nosey parker, 4 a wet blanket, 5 the life
and soul of the party, 6 an unknown
quantity, 7 a loose cannon, 8 a confirmed
bachelor

Unit 68

Ex 2: 1d, 2a, 3c, 4g, 5b, 6h, 7e, 8f
Ex 3: a call, b carry, c pass, d pull, e wear,
f hold, g eat, h take, i twist, j take
1f, 2g (eating ...), 3h (takes ...), 4d, 5e (wears
...), 6i (twist me around her little finger), 7b,
8a, 9c, 10j
Ex 4: 1 arm, 2 upper, 3 word, 4 friends,
5 shots, 6 lay, 7 fort, 8 advantage, 9 beck,

10 trousers, 11 weight, 12 tough, 13 strings,
14 shakers, 15 palm, 16 buck, 17 throw,
18 finger

Unit 69

Ex 1: 1 jam, 2 limbo, 3 spanner, 4 hop,
5 rails, rails, 6 creek, 7 blink
Ex 2: 1T, 2F, 3T, 4T, 5T, 6F, 7F, 8F, 9F, 10T,
11 in the same boat, 12 in a real state,
13 threw a spanner in the works, 14 in a
tight corner, 15 caught on the hop
Ex 3: a at, b up, c in, d in, e out of, f in, g at,
h on   1f, 2g, 3c, 4e, 5h, 6b, 7a, 8d
Ex 4: 1 boat, 2 corner, 3 depth, 4 foot, 5 hop,
6 cloud, 7 standstill, 8 rails, 9 blink,
10 water

Unit 70

Ex 1: 1 bull, 2 carpets, 3 bury, 4 buds,
5 flow, 6 cracks, 7 horns, 8 sweep, 9 doubt,
10 nip
Ex 2: 1f, 2c, 3b, 4d, 5a, 6e
Ex 3: 1c, 2a, 3e, 4d, 5b, 6f, 7j, 8h, 9i, 10g
Ex 4: 1 Sweep it under the carpet, 2 Paper
over the cracks, 3 Cross that bridge when we
come to it, 4 Nip it in the bud, 5 Take the
bull by the horns, 6 Get to the bottom of it,
7 Bury your head in the sand, 8 Turn a blind
eye, 9 pass, 10 nip, 11 get, 12 sweep,
13 face, 14 go, 15 eye, 16 profile, 17 flow,
18 bridge, 19 doubt

Unit 71

Ex 1: 1 leaf, 2 dip, 3 wade, 4 cover, 5 twist,
6 jargon, 7 load, 8 print, 9 tripe, 10 grip
Ex 2: 1c, 2d, 3b, 4a, 5a, 6a, 7c, 8a, 9d, 10d,
11a, 12a, 13a, 14a, 15b, 16a, 17c, 18b
Ex 3: 1f, 2a, 3e, 4b, 5d, 6c
Ex 4: 1 leaf, 2 lines, 3 load, 4 cover, 5 tail,
6 print, 7 while, 8 cover

Unit 72

Ex 2: 1b, 2e, 3g, 4a, 5f, 6d, 7c, 8h
Ex 3: 1 spot, 2 close, 3 hit, 4 house,
5 wavelength, 6 books, 7 turn, 8 foot, 9 need,
10 pick
Ex 4: 1 through thick and thin, 2 don't see
eye to eye, 3 at each other's throats, 4 got off
on the wrong foot, 5 offer/provide a shoulder
to cry on, 6 do a good turn
Ex 5: 1 on, 2 on, 3 through, 4 on, on, 5 on,
6 at, 7 between, 8 in, 9 to, 10 for

Unit 73

Ex 1: 1 rocks, 2 stand, 3 guts, 4 crush,
5 knot, 6 plunge, plunge, plunge

Ex 2: a knot, b crush, c plunge, d love,
e rocks, f heels
1 fallen in love, 2 had a crush, 3 the knot,
the plunge, 4 on the rocks, 5 fall in love
Ex 3: 1b, 2c, 3a, 4d, 5e
Ex 4: 1 ways, 2 love, 3 got, 4 taking, 5 can't,
6 crush, 7 lost, 8 out, 9 tying, 10 over,
11 guts, 12 rocks

Unit 74

Ex 2: 1d, 2e, 3h, 4c, 5a, 6b, 7f, 8g
Ex 3: 1d, 2a, 3h, 4e, 5g, 6f, 7c, 8b
Ex 4: 1 cutting, fine, 2 sailing, wind,
3 careful, skating, 4 put, block, 5 just, safe,
6 stick, neck, 7 leap, dark, 8 eggs, basket

Unit 75

Ex 1: 1g, 2c, 3a, 4j, 5h, 6i, 7d, 8f, 9b, 10e
Ex 2: 1 Join, 2 stick out, 3 tell, 4 follow,
5 take after, 6 choose
Ex 3: 1b, 2a, 3c
Ex 4: 1 poles apart, 2 stick out like a sore
thumb, 3 on a par, 4 six of one and half a
dozen of the other, 5 carbon copy
Ex 5: 1 boat, 2 thumb, 3 fish, 4 cheese,
5 footsteps, 6 copy, 7 out, 8 difference,
9 club, 10 apart

Unit 76

Ex 1: 1 blink, wink, 2 crash, 3 nightmare,
4 nod, 5 log, 6 snore
Ex 2: 1 log, 2 light, 3 wink, 4 light, 5 winks,
6 nodded off, 7 feet, 8 crashed out, 9 open,
10 dead, 11 lie in, 12 fast, 13 sleep,
14 heavy, 15 feet, 16 winks, 17 light, heavy,
18 log, 19 fast, 20 dead
Ex 3: 1e, 2d, 3a, 4f, 5c, 6g, 7b, 8h
Ex 4: 1 slept, 2 sleep, 3 crashed, 4 dream,
5 come, 6 lose, 7 went, 8 went, 9 lie, 10 sleep

Unit 77

Ex 1: 1 drag, 2 brake, 3 blink, 4 skates,
5 split, 6 snail, 7 flash, flash, 8 shot, 9 bats
Ex 2: 1c (has spread ...), 2f, 3a, 4g, 5d, 6b,
7h, 8e
Ex 3: 1d, 2e (dragging his feet), 3a (got off ..),
4c, 5b, 6g, 7h, 8f
Ex 4: 1 drop, 2 bat, 3 like, 4 split, 5 said,
6 in, 7 put, 8 spread, 9 get, 10 take, 11 get,
12 drag

Unit 78

Ex 2: a life, b light, c curtains, d towel,
e plug, f ice, g bud, f coffin
1d, 2f, 3b, 4a, 5e (pulled the plug on), 6c, 7g
(nip it in the bud), 8h

Ex 3: 1c, 2a, 3h, 4f, 5e, 6b, 7d, 8g
Ex 4: 1 break, 2 put, 3 throw, 4 give, 5 get,
6 open, 7 call, 8 nip, 9 pull, 10 start

Unit 79

Ex 2: 1b, 2d, 3f, 4a, 5c, g, 6h, 7e
Ex 3: a move, b pull, c set, d leave, e set,
f pull, g stop, h get, 1a, 2d, 3h, 4e, 5g, 6c, 7b
Ex 4: 1 up, 2 heaven, 3 socks, 4 star,
5 oyster, 6 limit, 7 stone, 8 sights, 9 flier,
10 world, 11 stops, 12 nothing, 13 left,
14 hungry, 15 burning

Unit 80

Ex 2: 1d, 2h (taken to it ...), 3a, 4e (feels ...),
5c, 6g, 7f, 8b (lent itself)
Ex 3: 1c, 2i, 3j, 4h, 5a, 6g, 7f, 8d, 9e, 10b
Ex 4: 1 out, 2 for, 3 out, 4 in, 5 out, 6 like,
7 in his element, 8 square peg in a round
hole, 9 cup of tea, 10 up your street, 11 a
duck to water, 12 sore thumb, 13 down to
the ground, 14 fish out of water

Unit 81

Ex 1: 1 rug, 2 bargain, 3 blessing, 4 bump,
5 disguise, 6 feathers, 7 sleeve
Ex 2: 1e (knocked me down with a feather),
2g (took me completely by surprise), 3f, 4h,
5c (something up my sleeve), 6d (knocked
him for six), 7b, 8a
Ex 3: 1a, 2c, 3e, 4g, 5d, 6b, 7h, 8f
Ex 4: 1 You could have knocked me down
with a feather, 2 I've got something up my
sleeve, 3 That's a turn-up for the books,
4 There's more to her than meets the eye,
5 It was a blessing in disguise, 6 He arrived
out of the blue, 7 eyes, 8 life, 9 feet, 10 six

Unit 82

Ex 1: 1d, 2b, 3e, 4a, 5c
Ex 2: 1f, 2d, 3a, 4b, 5c, 6e, 7 Long time no
see, 8 It's only a matter of time, 9 there's no
time like the present, 10 It's very cold for this
time of year, 11 We decided on the spur of
the moment, 12 Tomorrow is another day
Ex 3: 1d, 2e, 3c, 4i, 5g, 6b, h, 7a, f, 8a, 9g,
10d, 11e, 12b/h, 13i, 14a/f, 15b, 16c
Ex 4: 1 on, 2 in, 3 at, 4 in, 5 for, 6 from, to

Unit 83

Ex 1: 1 thumbs, 2 loose, 3 burn, 4 fit,
5 rush, 6 candles
Ex 2: a finger, b hands, c candle, d feet,
e end, f thumbs, g eyes, h plate
1g, 2f (twiddling my thumbs), 3h, 4c (burning

the candle at both ends), 5d, 6e, 7a (lifts a
finger), 8b
Ex 3: 1e, 2c, 3d, 4a, 5f, 6b
Ex 4: 1 burning the candle at both ends,
2 on my feet all day, 3 one thing after
another, 4 rushed off my feet, 5 dead all
morning
Ex 5: 1 up, 2 after, 3 on, 4 at, 5 till, 6 on,
7 off, 8 on, 9 at, 10 in

Unit 84

Ex 1: 1 steady, 2 pipeline, 3 rock, 4 dead-
end, 5 ropes, 6 ladder
Ex 2: 1c, 2b, 3e, 4f, 5d, 6a
Ex 3: a make, b climb, c take on, d rock,
e show, f stand, g hold, h breathe, i find, j go,
k land, l stand in
1b, 2i, 3c, 4h (breathing down my neck),
5l (standing in for him), 6j (go over his head),
7g, 8k (landed a great job)
Ex 4: 1 ladder, 2 feet, 3 job, 4 pace,
5 pipeline, 6 yourself, 7 neck, 8 staff, 9 head,
10 down

Unit 85

Unit 47: 1 about, 2 sleep, 3 most, 4 get,
5 day, 6 chickens
Unit 48: 1 said, 2 that, 3 telling, 4 words,
5 dead, 6 out
Unit 49: 1 brick, 2 nose, 3 insult, 4 bend,
5 kicked, 6 going
Unit 50: 1 end, 2 light, 3 lose, 4 lucky,
5 side, 6 only
Unit 51: 1 good, 2 guess, 3 air, 4 safe, 5 on,
6 doubt
Unit 52: 1 leaf, 2 recognition, 3 plan, 4 on,
5 taking, 6 clean
Unit 53: 1 same, 2 bush, 3 keep, 4 between,
5 hind, 6 straight
Unit 54: 1 white, 2 wool, 3 inch, 4 teeth,
5 garden, 6 take
Unit 55: 1 struggle, 2 bed, 3 stride, 4 out,
5 plain, 6 men, boys
Unit 56: 1 black, 2 son, 3 tie, 4 water, 5 cat,
6 image
Unit 57: 1 legs, 2 all, 3 nothing, 4 weight,
5 beating, 6 better
Unit 58: 1 bill, 2 out, 3 headache, 4 off,
5 out, 6 fiddle
Unit 59: 1 time, 2 away, 3 rest, 4 whale,
5 travelling, 6 recharge
Unit 60: 1 back, 2 first, 3 get, 4 thing, 5 got,
6 to
Unit 61: 1 sieve, 2 blank, 3 memory,
4 brains, 5 mind, 6 tip
Unit 62: 1 foot, 2 wrong, 3 fingers, 4 wrong,
5 chew, 6 wild

Unit 63: 1 tail, 2 wires, 3 over, 4 point, 5 depth, 6 same

Unit 64: 1 leg, 2 back, 3 dip, 4 on, 5 spree, 6 belts

Unit 65: 1 mouth, 2 lap, 3 in, 4 money, 5 up, 6 by

Unit 66: 1 piece, 2 bits, 3 top, 4 world, 5 moon, 6 high

Unit 67: 1 drivers, 2 soul, 3 pain, 4 dick, 5 earth, 6 unknown

Unit 68: 1 friends, 2 strings, 3 wears, 4 weight, 5 word, 6 fort

Unit 69: 1 wrong, 2 corner, 3 off, 4 same, 5 hop, 6 under

Unit 70: 1 bridge, 2 blind, 3 cracks, 4 bottom, 5 doubt, 6 carpet

Unit 71: 1 to, 2 end, 3 small, 4 leaf, 5 get, 6 book

Unit 72: 1 house, 2 foot, 3 eye, 4 air, 5 good, 6 shoulder

Unit 73: 1 heels, 2 rocks, 3 ways, 4 knot, 5 hate, 6 in

Unit 74: 1 safe, 2 ice, 3 fence, 4 fine, 5 lose, 6 safe

Unit 75: 1 sore, 2 cheese, 3 dozen, 4 world, 5 boat, 6 footsteps

Unit 76: 1 wink, 2 out, 3 light, 4 dream, 5 dream, 6 sleep

Unit 77: 1 said, 2 put, 3 skates, 4 time, 5 like, 6 time

Unit 78: 1 call, 2 one, 3 sight, 4 cracking, 5 towel, 6 on

Unit 79: 1 earth, 2 sights, 3 nothing, 4 heart, 5 limit, 6 hungry

Unit 80: 1 hole, 2 tea, 3 fish, 4 ground, 5 street, 6 out

Unit 81: 1 believe, 2 eye, 3 six, 4 sleeve, 5 blue, 6 surprise

Unit 82: 1 time, 2 spur, 3 minute, 4 end, 5 time, 6 later

Unit 83: 1 up, 2 rushed, 3 in, 4 lifts, 5 plate, 6 go

Unit 84: 1 pipeline, 2 over, 3 feet, 4 ropes, 5 on, 6 boat

Unit 86

Ex 2: 1e, 2c, 3g, 4h, 5d, 6f, 7b, 8a

Ex 3: 1g, 2d, 3a, 4c, 5h, 6e, 7b, 8f

Ex 4: 1h, 2d, 3a, 4f, 5c, 6g, 7b, 8e, 9 round, 10 at, 11 sudden, 12 same, 13 by, 14 said, 15 being, 16 know, 17 along, 18 by

Unit 87

Ex 1: 1 wears, 2 pick, 3 leap, bound, 4 foremost, 5 forth, forth, 6 bred, 7 tear, 8 Sick, sick

Ex 2: 1c, 2h, 3a, 4g, 5f, 6i, 7j, 8e, 9d, 10b

Ex 3: 1e, 2a, 3f, 4i, 5c, 6g, 7b, 8d, 9j, 10h

Ex 4: 1 quiet, 2 take, 3 downs, 4 go, 5 bred, 6 early, 7 again, 8 off, 9 choose, 10 ends, 11 about, 12 see, 13 tear, 14 foremost, 15 tired, 16 round, 17 large, 18 about, 19 bounds, 20 outs

Unit 88

Ex 1: 1 dried, 2 let live, 3 kicking, 4 white, 5 tested, 6 far, 7 forget, 8 cons, 9 again, 10 sound, 11 sweet, 12 cheese, 13 eggs, 14 age, 15 error, 16 hard, 17 dry, 18 low, 19 dry, 20 Q's

Ex 2: 1g, 2d, 3f, 4h, 5c, 6i, 7b, 8e, 9j, 10a

Ex 3: 1b, 2a, 3g, 4c, 5h, 6d, 7f, 8e

Ex 4: 1c, 2d, 3b, 4g, 5f, 6e, 7a

Unit 89

Ex 2: 1h, 2a, 3i, 4c, 5b (turned my back), 6d, 7f, 8e, 9g (get my back up)

Ex 3: 1c, 2h, 3g, 4e, 5a, 6f, 7d, 8b (get his own back)

Ex 4: 1 like water off a duck's back, 2 fell off the back of a lorry, 3 you scratch my back, I'll scratch yours, 4 deserve a pat on the back, 5 like the back of my hand, 6 take a back seat, 7 get your own back, 8 put your back into it, 9 in the back of beyond, 10 got our backs to the wall

Unit 90

Ex 2: 1d, 2h (cut me dead), 3c, 4a, 5g, 6e (cut our losses), 7b, 8f

Ex 3: 1d, 2b, 3e, 4h, 5a, 6c, 7g, 8f

Ex 4: 1 ways, 2 above, 3 knife, 4 out, 5 size, 6 ice, 7 remark, 8 about, 9 short, 10 fine

Unit 91

Ex 1: 1 deep, 2 bitter, 3 candles, 4 loose, 5 burn, 6 stick

Ex 2: 1h, 2b, 3e, 4f, 5d, 6c, 7a, 8g

Ex 3: 1f, 2e (burning the candle at both ends), 3a, 4c, 5g, 6d, 7h, 8b

Ex 4: 1 world, 2 days/months, 3 deep, 4 trouble, 5 loose, 6 things, 7 sight, 8 story, 9 receiving, 10 day

Unit 92

Ex 1: 1 deaf, 2 trap, 3 nets, 4 lap, 5 grace, 6 heel, 7 seam, 8 wayside

Ex 2: 1e, 2d (falls ...), 3c (falling ...), 4i (fell ...), 5a (fallen ...), 6g (fell ...), 7b (fell ...), 8h, 9f (fell ...), 10j (falling ...)

Ex 3: 1c, 2f (fallen on her feet), 3g, 4b (fell to me), 5h (fell ...), 6a (fallen ...), 7d, 8e

Ex 4: 1 laughing, 2 hands, 3 love, 4 times, 5 lap, 6 wayside, 7 net, 8 ears, 9 seams, 10 place, 11 grace, 12 trap

Unit 93

Ex 1: 1a, 2f, 3c, 4j, 5e, 6g, 7d, 8b, 9i, 10h
Ex 2: 1e, 2a, 3d, 4f, 5b, 6c
Ex 3: 1h, 2f, 3a, 4c, 5g, 6d, 7e (brought out the best in her), 8b
Ex 4: 1 bring, 2 make, 3 seen, 4 paid, 5 do, 6 feeling, 7 take, 8 throwing

Unit 94

Ex 2: a suit, b get off, c keep, d stand, e keep, f cover, g prepare, h cut, i hit, j break, 1a (suit him down to the ground), 2f (cover, ground), 3g (prepare the ground), 4b (get off the ground), 5c (keep your ear to the ground), 6h (cut the ground from under my feet), 7d (stood my ground), 8i (hit the ground running), 9e (keep my feet on the ground), 10j (break new ground)
Ex 3: 1e, 2c, 3f, 4d, 5a, 6h, 7g, 8b
Ex 4: 1 into, 2 down, 3 to, 4 under, 5 on, 6 off, 7 in, 8 down

Unit 95

Ex 1: 1f, 2d, 3a, 4b, 5e, 6c
Ex 2: 1e, 2a, 3b, 4f, 5c, 6d
Ex 3: 1b, 2a, 3f, 4c, 5g, 6e, 7h, 8d
Ex 4: 1e, 2f, 3a, 4h, 5b, 6d, 7c, 8g, 9 –, 10 a, 11 the, 12 a, 13 the, 14 the, 15 a, 16 a, 17 the, 18 –

Unit 96

Ex 2: 1c, 2g, 3j, 4b, 5f, 6i, 7a, 8d, 9h, 10e
Ex 3: a far, b thing, c of, d all, e hand, f never, g let, h out, 1 never know, 2 for all I know, 3 I'll let you know, 4 know it inside out, 5 as far as I know, 6 know of him, 7 knows a thing or two about, 8 The right hand doesn't know what the left is doing
Ex 4: 1 first, 2 sight, 3 inside, 4 two, 5 back, 6 meaning, 7 never, 8 far, 9 all, 10 that, 11 best, 12 let

Unit 97

Ex 1: When I was young, my parents gave me an excellent <u>start in life</u> and I always played a full part in <u>the life of</u> my school. Later, I enjoyed <u>student life.</u> I have been in interested in politics for all of <u>my adult life</u>, and I've always been <u>active in public life.</u> <u>Family life</u> is very important to me and when my son was <u>fighting for his life</u> after his accident, I gave up all political activity for a while. Later, when the scandal hit me, I <u>fought</u> – unsuccessfully – <u>for my political life,</u> so I had to give up for good. If only my <u>private life</u> had stayed private!

Ex 2: 1 double life, 2 working life, 3 everyday life, 4 shelf life, 5 public life
Ex 3: 1g, 2h, 3c, 4b, 5f, 6e, 7d, 8a
Ex 4: 1a, 2d, 3f, 4b, 5e, 6c
Ex 5: 1 walks, 2 public, 3 kiss, 4 double, 5 loss, 6 time, 7 spice, 8 on, 9 facts/meaning 10 get

Unit 98

Ex 1: 1e, 2d, 3c, 4a, 5b
Ex 2: a a light snack, b light relief, c light or heavy industry, d heavy going, e a light or heavy lunch, f a light day, or more commonly, a heavy day, g light or heavy casualties, h light or heavy traffic, i light or heavy work, j light or heavy rain, k heavy fighting, l heavy losses, m a light or heavy shower, n light reading, o a heavy cold, p a heavy heart, q a light or heavy sleeper, r light entertainment, s a light aircraft, t a light or a heavy meal
Ex 3: 1 heavy meal, 2 heavy industry, 3 light, 4 heavy cold, 5 light sleeper, 6 heavy casualties, 7 light entertainment, 8 light relief, 9 heavy going, 10 heavy shower, 11 heavy losses, 12 heavy day, 13 light work, 14 light snack, 15 heavy heart, 16 light lunch, 17 light aircraft, 18 light reading, 19 heavy rain, 20 Heavy fighting
Ex 4: 1a, 2a/b, 3a/b, 4a, 5a, 6a/b

Unit 99

Ex 1: 1 sieve, 2 logs, 3 plague, 4 clockwork, 5 dirt, 6 bricks, 7 maniac, 8 ton
Ex 2: 1h, 2e, 3a, 4f, 5g, 6c, 7d, 8b 9 You look like death warmed up, 10 He treats her like dirt, 11 It's like water off a duck's back, 12 He eats like a horse, 13 She's taken to it like a duck to water, 14 He drinks like a fish, 15 I've got a memory like a sieve, 16 He smokes like a chimney
Ex 3: 1d, 2a, 3f, 4e, 5b, 6h, 7c, 8g, 9 I slept like a log, 10 She spends money like there's no tomorrow, 11 He speaks it like a native, 12 Everything went like clockwork, 13 He drives like a maniac, 14 came down on me like a ton of bricks, 15 I felt like a fish out of water, 16 Avoid it like the plague
Ex 4: 1 She speaks English like a native, 2 He drives like a maniac, 3 Everything went like clockwork, 4 I've got a memory like a sieve, 5 I felt like a fish out of water at the meeting, 6 You look like death warmed up, 7 It's like water off a duck's back, 8 She eats

like a horse, 9 smoke, 10 come, 11 take,
12 avoid, 13 drink, 14 look, 15 treat, 16 sleep

Unit 100

Ex 2: 1b, 2d, 3a, 4c, 5f, 6e
Ex 3: 1c, 2d, 3g, 4b, 5e, 6a, 7h, 8f
Ex 4: 1 hold, 2 drop, 3 is, 4 draw, 5 bring,
6 think, 7 read, 8 sign

Unit 101

Ex 1: 1c, 2e, 3a, 4f, 5b, 6d
Ex 2: 1i, 2g, 3b, 4h, 5a, 6f, 7d, 8c, 9j, 10e
Ex 3: 1i, 2c, 3f, 4a, 5d, 6h, 7g, 8e, 9b
Ex 4: 1 I'm lost for words, 2 Don't lose any
sleep over it, 3 I lost track of time, 4 I need to
lose some weight, 5 Don't lose heart, 6 I'm
making up for lost time, 7 I've lost my
bearings, 8 I've lost count of the number of
times I've been there

Unit 102

Ex 1: 1e, 2a, 3h, 4j, 5i, 6b, 7g, 8d, 9f, 10c
Ex 2: 1b, 2c, 3a, 4d
Ex 3: 1c, 2e, 3a, 4b, 5d
Ex 4: 1d, 2e, 3a, 4c, 5f, 6b
Ex 5: 1 Parts of Belfast were no-go areas,
2 There's no smoke without fire, 3 I'll be with
you in no time, 4 There's no going back,
5 It's no joke bringing up children as a single
parent, 6 There's no place like home, 7 It's a
real no-no, 8 No news is good news

Unit 103

Ex 1: 1g, 2f, 3a, 4b, 5h, 6c, 7e, 8d, 9 a flood
of enquiries, 10 a string of excuses, 11 a
word of advice, 12 a spot of bother, 13 a
whole host of reasons, 14 in the nick of time,
15 piles of money, 16 a mountain of work
Ex 2: a time, b visitors, c garlic, d advice,
e tears, f luck, 1f, 2b, 3e, 4d, 5c, 6a
Ex 3: a criticism, b paint, c lies, d doubt,
e soda, f warning, 1c, 2b, 3e, 4f, 5a, 6d
Ex 4: 1 electricity, 2 respect, 3 ideas, 4 fault,
5 questions, 6 disaster

Unit 104

Ex 1: 1h, 2b, 3c, 4i, 5j, 6g, 7a, 8e, 9f, 10d
Ex 3: 1b, 2f, 3c, 4h, 5a, 6e, 7g, 8d
Ex 4: 1 give, 2 believe, 3 laugh, 4 sink

Unit 105

Ex 1: 1e, 2f, 3a, 4h, 5g, 6c, 7b, 8i, 9d, 10j
Ex 2: 1h, 2e, 3a, 4g, 5b, 6f, 7c, 8d
Ex 3: 1 high point, 2 whole point, 3 strong
points, 4 talking point, 5 sore point, 6 low
point, 7 vantage point, 8 turning point

Ex 4: 1 beside, 2 point, 3 finger, 4 to,
5 score, 6 got, 7 case, 8 see, 9 get, 10 strong

Unit 106

Ex 1: 1 coins, 2 Grass, 3 luck
Ex 2: a get, b let, c look, d hear, e take,
f side
1c, 2d (heard ...), 3b, 4a (get on the wrong
side of her), 5e, 6f (siding ...)
Ex 3: 1e, 2d, 3a, 4c, 5b
Ex 4: 1c, 2b, 3f, 4h, 5d, 6a, 7e (which side
her bread is buttered, 8g
Ex 5: 1 I can see both sides of the coin,
2 Time is not on our side, 3 He's on the
wrong side of 60, 4 You got out of bed on the
wrong side, 5 Look on the bright side,
6 I know which side my bread is buttered,
7 This side of December, 8 Let's put this to
one side

Unit 107

Ex 1: 1 something, 2 nothing, 3 nothing,
4 something, 5 nothing, 6 nothing,
7 something, 8 nothing, 9 nothing,
10 something, 11 anything, 12 anything,
13 something, 14 nothing, 15 nothing
Ex 2: 1d, 2b, 3c, 4a
Ex 3: 1a, 2d, 3c, 4b, 5e, 6f
Ex 4: 1 write, 2 came, 3 cost, 4 short, 5 sort,
6 choose, 7 for, 8 trouble, 9 There's

Unit 108

Ex 1: 1a, 2b, 3d, 4g, 5e, 6f, 7h (knows ...), 8c
Ex 2: 1a, 2c, 3d, 4b
Ex 3: 1c, 2e, 3d, 4a, 5b (making ...), 6g (do
my own thing), 7h, 8f
Ex 4: 1 first, 2 another, 3 good, 4 morning,
5 own, 6 considered, 7 near, 8 those,
9 past, 10 done

Unit 109

Ex 1: 1g, 2d, 3f, 4b, 5a, 6h, 7e, 8c, 9g, 10d,
11a, 12e, 13h, 14c, 15f, 16b
Ex 2: 1b, 2a, 3d, 4c
Ex 3: 1b, 2c, 3f, 4a, 5g, 6e, 7h, 8d
Ex 4: 1 all, 2 short, 3 straight, 4 desired,
5 injury, 6 worse, 7 about, 8 seen, 9 for,
10 nutshell
Ex 5: 1 injury, 2 add, 3 straight, 4 insult,
5 mild, 6 sniff

Unit 110

Ex 1: 1 list, 2 bet, 3 rock, 4 blew, 5 voice,
6 pit
Ex 2: 1 top, 2 bottom, 3 bottom, 4 top,
5 bottom, 6 top, 7 bottom, 8 bottom

Ex 3: 1g, 2f, 3h, 4a, 5c, 6b, 7d, 8e
Ex 4: 1 you can bet your bottom dollar, 2 off the top of my head, 3 get to the bottom of this, 4 I've searched from top to bottom, 5 over the top, 6 top of the list, 7 hit rock bottom, 8 thin on top

Unit 111

Ex 2: 1c, 2d, 3a, 4e, 5f, 6b, 7h, 8g
Ex 3: 1f, 2c, 3i, 4a, 5j, 6b, 7h, 8e, 9g, 10d
The more metaphorical expressions are:
1 crystal clear, 2 razor sharp, 3 wide open
Ex 4: 1 wide, 2 dirt, 3 blind, 4 bitter, 5 broad, 6 pitch, 7 stone, 8 razor, 9 bone, 10 crystal, 11 wide, 12 fast, 13 rock, 14 dead, 15 stark, 16 paper, 17 brand, 18 rock

Unit 112

Ex 2: 1f, 2g (set in his ways), 3a (worked my way ...), 4e, 5b (has ...), 6i (stand in your way), 7j, 8c (went out of my way), 9d, 10h (keep out of his way)
Ex 3: 1c, 2e, 3a, 4d, 5b, 6h, 7f, 8g
Ex 4: 1 worked my way to the top, 2 won't stand in your way, 3 way with words, 4 set in her ways, 5 have it both ways, 6 went out of my way, 7 come a long way in the last two years, 8 either way

Unit 113

Ex 1: 1c, 2a, 3f, 4d, 5b, 6e
Ex 2: 1c, 2e, 3a, 4b, 5d
Ex 3: a take, b get, c know, d have, e say, f breathe, g take, h eat
1f, 2e, 3c, 4d, 5g (took her at her word), 6h (eat my words), 7b, 8a (take your word for it)
Ex 4: 1 for, 2 by, 3 in, 4 in, 5 in, 6 from, 7 for, 8 of, 9 for, 10 in

Unit 114

Unit 86: 1 done, 2 being, 3 told, 4 along, 5 over, 6 go
Unit 87: 1 quiet, 2 tired, 3 see, 4 downs, 5 bred, 6 choose
Unit 88: 1 long, 2 day, 3 high, 4 pros, 5 now, 6 trial
Unit 89: 1 hand, 2 pat, 3 scratch, scratch, 4 burner, 5 water, 6 behind
Unit 90: 1 knife, 2 out, 3 story, 4 corners, 5 dead, 6 fine
Unit 91: 1 road, 2 no, 3 bitter, 4 loose, 5 stick, 6 story
Unit 92: 1 about, 2 deaf, 3 seams, 4 lap, 5 feet, 6 place
Unit 93: 1 knowledge, 2 sorry, 3 world, 4 days, 5 money, 6 better
Unit 94: 1 gaining, 2 thin, 3 cover, 4 down, 5 into, 6 grounding
Unit 95: 1 mind, 2 chance, 3 go, 4 trouble, 5 time, 6 through
Unit 96: 1 about, 2 thing, 3 let, 4 out, 5 going, 6 How
Unit 97: 1 life, 2 loss, 3 walks, 4 Variety, 5 public, 6 kiss
Unit 98: 1 snack, 2 sleeper, 3 day, 4 traffic, 5 rain, 6 cold
Unit 99: 1 sieve, 2 tomorrow, 3 water, 4 warmed, 5 ton, 6 back
Unit 100: 1 along, 2 between, 3 signed, 4 draw, 5 Hold, 6 toe
Unit 101: 1 nothing, 2 sleep, 3 love, 4 time, 5 words, 6 weight
Unit 102: 1 home, 2 luck, 3 end, 4 present, 5 point, 6 wonder
Unit 103: 1 flood, 2 pack, 3 excuses, 4 coat, 5 word, 6 dash
Unit 104: 1 not, 2 like, 3 cry, 4 later, 5 swim, 6 take
Unit 105: 1 strong, 2 blank, 3 sore, 4 to, 5 up, 6 beside
Unit 106: 1 bed, 2 other, 3 wrong, 4 Time, 5 bright, 6 story
Unit 107: 1 nothing, 2 something, 3 something, 4 nothing, 5 nothing, 6 anything
Unit 108: 1 first, 2 first, 3 one, 4 being, 5 past, 6 those
Unit 109: 1 truth, 2 short, 3 put, 4 desired, 5 nutshell, 6 at
Unit 110: 1 head, 2 of, 3 world, 4 thin, 5 line, 6 voice
Unit 111: 1 cheap, 2 open, 3 sharp, 4 awake, 5 black, 6 hard
Unit 112: 1 set, 2 thinking, 3 out, 4 with, 5 long, 6 both
Unit 113: 1 mouth, 2 good, 3 have, 4 his, 5 breathe, 6 say

ADD YOUR OWN IDIOMS

ADD YOUR OWN IDIOMS

ADD YOUR OWN IDIOMS

ADD YOUR OWN IDIOMS